The
Human
Animal
Earthling
Identity

The Human Animal Earthling Identity

Shared Values Unifying
Human Rights, Animal Rights,
and Environmental Movements

CARRIE P. FREEMAN

The University of Georgia Press
ATHENS

Chapter 2 appeared, in a different form, under the title "Embracing Humanimality: Deconstructing the Human/Animal Dichotomy," in *Arguments about Animal Ethics*, edited by Greg Goodale and Jason Edward Black (Lanham, Md.: Lexington Books, 2010), 11–30. Copyright © 2010 by Lexington Books. Reproduced with permission of the Licensor through PLSclear. Chapter 3 appeared, in a different form, under the title "Perceiving Ecocultural Identities as Human Animal Earthlings," in *Routledge Handbook of Ecocultural Identity*, edited by Tema Milstein and José Castro-Stotomayor (New York: Routledge, 2020), 431–444. Reproduced with the permission of the Taylor & Francis Group.

Published by the University of Georgia Press
Athens, Georgia 30602
www.ugapress.org
© 2020 by Carrie P. Freeman
All rights reserved
Designed by Kaelin Chappell Broaddus
Set in 9.5/12.5 Quadraat OT Regular by Kaelin Chappell Broaddus

Most University of Georgia Press titles are
available from popular e-book vendors.

Printed digitally

The author will donate a portion of the annual royalties
to the Environmental Paper Network.

Library of Congress Cataloging-in-Publication Data

Names: Freeman, Carrie P., author.
Title: The human animal earthling identity : shared values unifying human
    rights, animal rights, and environmental movements / Carrie P. Freeman.
Description: Athens : The University of Georgia Press, [2020] |
    Includes bibliographical references and index.
Identifiers: LCCN 2020024973 | ISBN 9780820358208 (hardback) |
    ISBN 9780820358192 (paperback) | ISBN 9780820358215 (ebook)
Subjects: LCSH: Social movements--Moral and ethical aspects. | Values.
Classification: LCC HM881 .F693 2020 | DDC 303.48/4—dc23
LC record available at https://lccn.loc.gov/2020024973

To all the species and cultures we have lost to extinction, and to those people who are trying to save the rest of us and create a healthy planetary home where we treat fellow living beings with respect. In solidarity.

CONTENTS

Photographs appear after page 132.

FIGURES AND TABLES

Figure

Tables

ACKNOWLEDGMENTS

I am most grateful to the activists who participated in interviews for this book to share their insights on social change as well as the sixteen social movement organizations I studied that are working so hard to fight injustice and protect living beings. In the years I was working on this book, I was fortunate to have the help of doctoral student assistants at Georgia State University: Angie McAdam, who helped identify scholarly literature; Megan Mapes, who helped with copyediting and bibliography formatting; Alan Campfield, who organized research data to identify overlapping values; and Allen Zimmerman, who helped me with the index. I'm grateful to the Culture & Animals Foundation for awarding me a grant to start the book, and to Georgia State University's College of Arts & Sciences for awarding me a Research Initiation Grant to finish the book. Finally, I'd like to thank the peer reviewers and the UGA Press staff, especially Bethany Snead for being a supportive editor throughout the process.

The
Human
Animal
Earthling
Identity

INTRODUCTION

     This is no ordinary time. Our planet is suffering through a mass extinction of species caused largely by one species—ours. The health, well-being, and very existence of all living beings, including us, is threatened by global climate crisis, war and militarization, corporate exploitation, industrial extraction and inequitable distribution of shared planetary resources, mass killing of domestic and wild animals by industrial agriculture and fishing, global pandemics from the meat and wildlife trades, unsustainable consumption and mass pollution, and growing economic and social inequality and poverty. Given the magnitude and urgency of these problems, it is vital for social movement organizations (SMOs) to work together to more powerfully remedy these crises. This solidarity should strengthen social movement efforts to protect living beings, our ecologically interdependent home habitats (both 'wild' and urban), and the natural resources on which all life depends. Therefore, through this project I embrace the broader goal of merging social movement campaigns (on behalf of human and nonhuman causes) to create more empowered alliances that can advocate against exploitation of life on an international level and for equitable, compassionate, and sustainable practices. To contribute a key piece to that larger goal, I concentrate in this book on the opportunity for all social movement advocacy campaigns to embody values that predispose people toward socially responsible and altruistic dispositions. I advocate for movements to coordinate communication efforts to foster a cultural shift in human identity away from an egoistic anthropocentrism (narrow self-focus) toward a humbler universal benevolence where people begin to see themselves, not just as a certain type of individual human, but more collectively as what I call a "human animal earthling."

     In this book I address not only what we value but *whom*. My specific goals are to (1) identify core values among various social movements to protect the rights, freedoms, and interests of humans, nonhuman animals, nature, and ecosystems; (2) suggest mutual values on which all social movements can collectively frame campaigns influencing human identity and worldviews (whether working independently as allies or collectively as global coalitions); and (3) reframe these values to be less anthropocentric (human centered) and more biocentric (inclusive of all life on earth).

The three broad-based international movements I am interested in unifying are as follows:

1. human rights (e.g., Amnesty International, CARE, Human Rights Watch, Minority Rights Group International, and Anti-Slavery International);
2. animal protection (e.g., People for the Ethical Treatment of Animals, World Wildlife Fund, Animal Equality International, International Fund for Animal Welfare, and Sea Shepherd Conservation Society); and
3. environmentalism (e.g., Greenpeace, the Nature Conservancy, Friends of the Earth International, Rainforest Action Network, Oceana, and 350.org).

To clarify terms, *human rights* includes anti-exploitation movements (such as fair labor and antislavery causes) and, more broadly, civil rights movements (equality and social justice causes protecting and politically enfranchising all humans but especially groups marginalized based on gender, sexual orientation, race and ethnicity, ability, class, and political or religious beliefs). By *animal protection* I mean to include a spectrum of rights and welfare groups protecting individual nonhuman animals of all species (both domesticated and wild/free). This can include 'animal welfare' causes to reduce animal suffering and take care of orphaned or injured wild animals or homeless domesticated animals. Animal protection also includes 'animal rights' or 'animal liberation' causes that advocate for the freedom of nonhuman animals from human use, control, killing, and exploitation (such as in agribusiness and the food and fishing industries, research laboratories, the pet trade, the fashion industry, the hunting industry, zoos and aquaria, and other entertainment industries). This includes supporting veganism (a boycott of any products taken from animals). By *environmentalism* I mean to include a broad array of groups that protect all living beings and species (in air, land, and sea) and the ecosystems and ecological processes that support life on earth. Environmental groups often work to conserve freshwater and other natural resources that species (especially humans) depend on for survival; protect and restore the health and well-being of ecosystems, wilderness habitats, urban environments, and all their inhabitants, especially vulnerable populations such as indigenous or disadvantaged minority human groups or endangered wild species; stem the tide of mass extinction of species and support biodiversity; and advocate against pollution, including greenhouse gas emissions, and the inequitable burdens that dirty industries often place on the poor and people of color.

To find common ground among this wide variety of causes, I explore their campaign messages and the general discourse on their websites as well as interview their leaders so that they can clarify their goals and values in relation to other causes and explain their advocacy strategies for educating and mobilizing the public, based on what SMOs want us to care about and what kind of person they want us to be. The following research questions guide my inquiry and structure the book:

1. Who matters most in social movement messages?
2. What is valued as good/right/ideal? What kind of values are the social movement messages appealing to or seem to be assumed in the identity of the audience members?
3. Which of these values overlap between movements and are, thus, more universal?
4. In what ways do these universal values need reframing to be less anthropocentric (or more biocentric or sentience focused) in their application and scope?
5. Which values are most applicable to a human animal earthling's identity?

The goal of my project is to identify and promote the values that are foundational to fostering and framing a more inclusive, biocentric worldview and human identity as 'human animal earthlings' in the hope that this expanded sense of self on an individual level will foster human cultures on the societal level that are inherently more sustainable and just toward all living beings.

Significance and Justification of an Identity-Focused Social Change Project

To establish significance, this section summarizes some of the grave problems affecting planetary life, especially environmental issues that threaten current and future generations' ability to survive, and how the solutions are not just reliant on technologies, policies, economics, behaviors, or information. Scholars in this section explain how solutions must address *ideologies* at the heart of the problems, using *morally motivated* arguments to inspire action, by priming *altruistic values* such as caring about others and *identifying* with them as members of our community.

DEFINING CORE PROBLEMS AND SOLUTIONS

Some scientists renamed our current geological epoch the "Anthropocene" to represent the profound and unprecedented destructive impact that the human species is having on the earth's biological systems, not only throughout the tens of thousands of years of evolution and migration of our species across continents but especially intensified by many cultures since the industrial revolution (Harari 2015; Steffen, Crutzen, and McNeill 2007; Wilson 2016).[1] The impetus falls on humans, as "devolutionizers" (Callicott 1993), to solve the environmental problems many human societies throughout history have created for fellow earthlings, as most other species generally live in greater harmony with the needs of their ecosystem and tend to be less excessive and more sustainable.[2] But critical theorist and activist Steven Best (2014, 162) echoes a concern many activists have, wondering if humanity will find the motivation to tackle this immense ecological challenge: "Will people remain inert, apathetic, delusional, and fail to mount global and united resistance movements adequate to stop the aggression, nihilism, and death drive of an omnicidal system?" Alluding to this uphill battle for material and ideological transformation, Best asks: "Can humanity dramatically change its entire mode of existence—from moral and psychological outlooks to their economic and political institutions—in order to forestall planetary catastrophe?" (162).

When answering this question, scientist Jared Diamond (1992, 8) refers to humans as "the third chimpanzee," yet he cautions that we are a much more destructive primate, or indeed animal, than any other: "Predation on us is now negligible, no habitat is beyond our influence, and our power to kill individual animals and destroy habitats is unprecedented." So how can we urge our 'dangerous' human species to view ourselves more humbly in relation to other species and to willingly take a drastically different, more harmonious path in concert with other earthlings? Diamond (2005) answers this question at the end of his book *Collapse* (about the extinction of certain past human cultures) in his final advice on how we can avoid causing our own society to go extinct—by calling for humans to reprioritize our *values and long-term planning* and to utilize media technology to communicate these values and goals globally so that we can work together to achieve sustainability.

But the vast and varied environmental movement does not have one overarching value that articulates its common goal, unlike social justice movements' clear goals of justice, freedom, and equality, laments Canadian environmentalist Graham Saul (2018). While Saul's interviews with over one hundred Canadian activists did not yield a clear answer to the question of what environmentalists were fighting for, I would argue that, combining some of the popular values interviewees mentioned— survival, sustainability, and protection—the common value seems to be *life*. I support Saul's (2018) plea for environmentalists to create more unity around a shared *moral* message to inspire humanity to transform our relationship with the natural world.

As a communication scholar, activist, and vegan, I wrote this book because I agree that a foundational solution to our ecological crisis (and a crisis of mass injustice) involves promoting a discourse that reconceives our own moral values and identity to be less self-centered (and indeed less human centered), which should then influence us to adapt our lifestyles and public policies to fit new, more biocentric values. Understandably, environmentalists might be tempted to focus on a more expedient approach to change by creating messages primarily encouraging *ecofriendly policies and individual behaviors* (sometimes based on self-centered or extrinsic motivations); however, my viewpoint in this book is influenced by Crompton and Kasser's (2009) more ideological strategic approach to environmental advocacy that suggests environmental messages should foster *altruistic and less anthropocentric values* based on deeper intrinsic motivations formational to our identities and worldviews.

WHY IDENTITY AND VALUES ARE
FOUNDATIONAL TO SOCIAL CHANGE

When I interviewed activists for my first book, Alex Hershaft, founder of the Farm Animal Rights Movement, made it clear that animal rights are not about animals but about us (Freeman 2014). He did not mean this in a self-centered way. While some may look at animal protection and environmental movements, or even human rights movements on behalf of minority groups, as being about 'the other,' ultimately the movements are asking 'us' (the dominant group) to act—to embrace 'them' into our collective sphere of moral concern. As the Black Lives Matter title infers, those whose worth has been discounted deserve to matter too. And this means that we (if we are in the dominant or privileged group) may have to rethink not just who they are to us but *who we are* as well. For example, in considering what the animal rights cause is about, attorney Lee Hall (2010) describes it as ending our sense of human entitlement to exploit and control nonhuman animals. But she notes the cause also takes an affirmative stance, focused on identity: "What's essential is what and who they [nonhuman animals] are, and how we come to grips with that. This all depends on what and who *we* strive to become" (93).

The struggle for social change is at heart a struggle over ideas. We often do not see the intentional ideological work done to construct and continually maintain the status quo power structure meant to make current inequalities seem natural, normal, and taken for granted (S. Hall 1997). In his work advocating for total liberation for all species, sociologist David Pellow (2014, 10) emphasizes the importance of ideas: "I find that the ideas that legitimate and support inequality are just as consequential, if not more so, as material inequality itself. Those *ideas* are ultimately what these social movements are combating." Foundational to my belief in the power of communication and ideologies to influence material inequalities is philosopher Michel Foucault's (1990, 1155) claim: "Discourse is the thing for which and by which there is struggle. Discourse is the power which is to be seized."

These influential ideas include our self-perceptions about who we are in comparison to 'others.' Semiotics scholar Dario Martinelli (2008) asks us to critically examine the common Western ideology of anthropocentrism and how it functions to construct a privileged view of the human species (especially white males) and our exalted importance in the natural world: "Anthropocentrism interprets nature as (a) an entity existing apart *from* and *for the benefit of* humans; so that (b) nothing in nature can be considered in itself, autonomously from humans; and (c) it is ethically acceptable for humans and non-humans to be treated in different ways" (79). Best (2014, 134) recognizes the core need to deconstruct and replace the self-narratives of superiority that we have used to define ourselves in many Western cultures: "Once we see what flimsy, fallacious, and corrupt constructs anthropocentrism and speciesism are, and how deeply embedded they are in the philosophies, values, and narratives of 'civilization,' we can begin to grasp their catastrophic effects and implications." He claims we cannot "avert social and ecological catastrophe" unless we employ a "parallel conceptual revolution that involves the construction of new values, worldviews, narratives, and species identities."

In further support of the vital role that values play in social change, renowned biologist Edward O. Wilson (2016), in his book *Half-Earth: Our Planet's Fight for Life*, often refers to the need for a *moral shift* when discussing how to stop biodiversity loss in this planet's sixth mass extinction. He claims a renewed emphasis on humanity's moral obligations to others is necessary in order to create the political willpower to greatly expand wildlife habitat protection: "Only a major shift in moral reasoning, with greater commitment given to the rest of life, can meet this greatest challenge of the century" (211). According to Wilson, the most dangerous worldview is a new kind of extreme Anthropocene view (which could really be called an anthropocentric view) that now sees conservation as an effort primarily to make what is left of nature (which is perceived as already domesticated) work for humanity and our economy. He critiques this instrumental 'conservation' view as being a far cry from the deep ecology view of nature as intrinsically valuable, in which humans should make sacrifices to reduce our harm. He states that the living world will not be saved by human-centric views that rely on economic measures or god's will. Wilson's chapter on solutions focuses on the values of altruism and biophilia (love of nature): "I believe we've learned enough to adopt a transcendent moral precept concerning the rest of life. It is simple and easy to say: Do no further harm to the biosphere" (212). He laments our current misguided focus on economics and self-interest: "We thrash about, appallingly led, with no particular goal in mind other than economic growth, unfettered consumption, good health, and personal happiness" (2).

To create a moral shift, we should no longer see ourselves as demigods and other species as lower life-forms.[3] Instead, Wilson (2016, 50–51) warns we must urgently cultivate a new self-identity recognizing that we are part of the natural world:

> In order to settle down before we wreck the planet, we should at the very least learn to think about where our species really came from and what we are today. . . . There is an unbreakable chain in self-understanding that thinking people largely neglect. One of the lessons is that we are not as gods. We're not yet sentient or intelligent enough to be much of anything. And we're not going to have a secure future if we continue to play the kind of false god who whimsically destroys Earth's living environment.

Wilson describes the human species as "magnificent in imaginative power and exploratory drive, yet yearning to be more master than steward of a declining planet. . . . Yet arrogant, reckless, lethally predisposed to favor self, tribe, and short-term futures" (1). The solution for preservation of the biosphere is for humans to let go of our self-centeredness and superior self-identity and emphasize our historical kinship with other species and nature: "The millions of species we have allowed to survive there [nature], but continue to threaten, are our phylogenetic kin. Their long-term history is our long-term history. Despite all of our pretenses and fantasies, we always have been and will remain a biological species tied to this particular biological world" (211). In this quote, Wilson foregrounds the earthling component of what I am referring to as a 'human animal earthling' identity.

Similarly, in her book *EcoMind*, environmentalist Frances Moore Lappé (2011, 16) also encourages a human identity where we see ourselves as connected with fellow earthlings and nature rather than following the predominant way of seeing 'the environment' as something separate from us or below us: "As we rethink the premises underlying this worldview, we move to a different place altogether—a place where we experience ourselves and our species embedded in nature." She is optimistic that our human nature is not flawed and selfish; it has many good traits that will contribute toward ecological solutions, including cooperation, empathy, fairness, efficacy (problem-solving), meaning, imagination, and creativity. In support of the priming power of identity, she says "how we think about who we are has tremendous power over how we act" (90), as negative core assumptions can limit our potential to solve environmental problems. She promotes a democratic way of living that follows a system of values that will bring out the best in us—inclusion, fairness, and mutual accountability. Psychologist and animal activist Melanie Joy (2014, 89) also emphasizes the need for a values-based change of heart, not just a change in policies: "Genuine and lasting change requires a paradigm shift, a transformation of the mentality that propped up the old order. We must knock out the foundations of oppression and cultivate the values that form the foundation of justice, values such as compassion, integrity, and reciprocity."

To facilitate the values that foster peace, justice, and sustainability, Zoe Weil (2014) finds that humane education in schools is a primary solution to creating broad-based systemic change.[4] Her view of humane education is not limited to just discussing kind treatment of companion animals but rather "providing accurate information about the interrelated challenges of our time by drawing connections between human rights, environmental preservation, and animal protection" (299), including animal rights. In her work in schools and communities, she promotes such values as curiosity, creativity, critical thinking, reverence, respect, responsibility, inquiry, introspection, and integrity.

A concern about values, ideologies, and worldviews is also expressed by Naomi Klein (2014) in her popular climate crisis book *This Changes Everything*. She concludes that we need a shift in the cultural context to "think big, go deep, and move the ideological pole far away from the stifling market fundamentalism that has become the greatest enemy to planetary health" (26). An ideological shift is challenging to accomplish within a neoliberal culture where we have been cultivated to depend on fossil fuels, since "we are still living inside the story written in coal" (177).

She advocates for changing the story of humanity so that we identify ourselves as a regenerative rather than extractive species. Best (2014) also points to global capitalism as the exploitative force largely responsible for thwarting the efforts of social movements: "In the last three decades, neoliberalism and global capitalism have destroyed social democracies, widened gaps between rich and poor, dispossessed farmers, assaulted indigenous peoples, and marketized the entire world, all the while escalating the war on animals and intensifying the assault on every ecosystem and on the earth" (160).

As a solution with the potential to join all social movements together in a common cause, Klein (2014) argues that climate change can be the central global issue of our time to rally around. The climate crisis battle in particular must be seen as a larger battle of worldviews, "a process of rebuilding and reinventing the very idea of the collective, the communal, the commons, the civil, and the civic after so many decades of attack and neglect" (460). To change a worldview requires game-changing strategies—ones that "don't merely aim to change laws but change patterns of thought" (460). Thus we not only need carbon-oriented laws but ones for economic justice that change values and help us debate what we owe one another in a shared humanity—helping us recognize who we are and what we really care about (more than economic growth and profits). In this era of anthropogenic global warming, philosopher Ronald Sandler (2012) proposes some values humans must embrace: flexibility and openness to change, tolerance of uncertainty, restraint, patience, and responsibility.

Animal ethics scholars Núria Almiron, Marta Tafalla, and Catia Faria contend that since the cause of climate inaction is largely ideological, the best way to inspire the needed revolutionary actions is not just for communicators to appeal to environmental statistics but also to ethical concerns for the unfair, catastrophic impacts free-living animals suffer from human actions; this fosters an egalitarian, nonspeciesist ethic of care for fellow animals that transcends the anthropocentric rationales for social change, since an identity that privileges human interests above all others is why our species has justified such environmental degradation in the first place (Almiron and Faria 2019; Almiron and Tafalla 2019). This mirrors suggestions that sustainability/environmental education can be more effective if it moves beyond an anthropocentric orientation (based on instrumental views of nature) and incorporates an inherent respect for nonhuman beings that draws on animal welfare, animal rights, and deep ecology principles and ignites the "human capacity for empathy and compassion" (Kopnina and Cherniak 2015, 374).

In support of Lappé's sentiments about the goodness of human nature, Klein (2014) contends that we must believe humanity is not selfish and greedy. Our policies must be part of a larger story of seeing ourselves more interdependently than individually. Transformative social movements can show humanity "a better version of itself" (460).

The Logic and Benefits of Social Movement Collaboration

So who is best positioned to champion a values- and identity-based social change effort? I argue in this section that it is social movement organizations—or, at least, that is the best place to start based on the sociopolitical role of social movements as moral entrepreneurs. But I hope to establish that the global issues impacting all life cannot be solved by piecemeal, individual efforts of separate social movements with their big hearts and small pocketbooks, especially when they face the most well-funded, powerful oppositional forces. And those opponents and oppressive systems are often the same (whether you are advocating for humans, other animals, or nature) and therefore strategically require a more collective, integrated communication effort across all social movements to use values-based campaigns that sound the alarm, identify culprits, outline solutions, change laws and practices, and transform power relationships.

THE ROLE OF SOCIAL MOVEMENTS

Social movement organizations (SMOs) will likely be the key entities initially working to drive needed changes to cultural identity, values, lifestyle, and policies, by strategically communicating to mobilize resources and influence target publics (government, media, industry, consumers/citizens, interest groups, etc.) (McAdam, McCarthy, and Zald 1996). In some cases, SMOs and nongovernmental organizations (NGOs) are the primary groups advocating for needed action on issues such as animal rights or climate crisis, especially less politically and economically popular solutions such as reducing or eliminating meat consumption (Laestadius et al. 2013).

Geophysicist Brad Werner argues that the only way the earth could be saved is if a mass social movement formed to provide resistance *outside of the capitalist culture* that has made depletion of resources barrier-free (in Klein 2014). Yet Klein (2014) observes that many environmental organizations work too comfortably with corporations, asking for too little change.[5] She prefers the stronger corporate divestment and climate action campaigns of 350.org, Food and Water Watch, Rainforest Action Network, Friends of the Earth, and Greenpeace (many of which I will be studying in this book).

A Green Alliance UK study on how to create a high level of public mobilization on the climate crisis concludes that change will be driven by a "third sector" of diverse community groups and social networks rather than by governments, businesses, or individual consumers, as the latter trio of groups are at an impasse based on democratic- and market-based constraints that produce fear over the financial costs and potential overreach of government regulations that could result (Hale 2010). The study suggests the environmental movement can continue to be a leader if it starts to "employ new arguments that emphasise the breadth of issues impacted by climate change and build much broader coalitions of support" (264) that show how environmental issues like climate change are also multifaceted, diverse issues of health, housing, poverty, security, justice, and human rights that different interest groups can address in multiple ways (rather than in one overarching global environmental campaign). Additionally, environmental SMOs should create multiple alliances across local and international communities to foster deeper commitments and stronger social foundations that make policy changes more politically viable (Hale 2010).

WHY MOVEMENTS SHOULD COLLABORATE

In writing books supporting an alliance between environmental and animal activists, Lisa Kemmerer (2015a) and Amy Fitzgerald (2018) highlight the two movements' similarities (e.g., they both challenge anthropocentrism, support wilderness, and target common opponents) and the strategic benefits of joining forces to increase membership, financial resources, and lobbying power. Similarly, sociologist Carol Glasser (2015, 46) explains that "coalition building expands and sustains the momentum that is necessary to combat the institutionalized economic and political structures that are destroying both animals and the Earth." Coalition building creates "formidable opposition to dominating forces" (46) by connecting minority groups and generating a wider base of support, encouraging all justice movements to recognize each other as allies, not competitors. In her scholarship on the intersectional nature of power structures (i.e., considering how race, class, gender, and species operate in concert), Claire Jean Kim (2015) advocates for social movements working in solidarity to dismantle the "synergistic relations" (18) between various forms of capitalist domination: "The American left is thoroughly segmented. Each cause has its cluster of advocacy organizations and corresponding academic field(s). Each engages the enemy from a separate bunker. Each resists coercive universalisms and coalitional possibilities, except momentarily. In the meantime, the forces of neoliberal capitalism face few obstacles as they transform racialized others, nonhuman animals, and the earth into 'resources' in the game of perpetual capital accumulation" (287).

Social movements often work separately on their own causes and can be in competition with one another, whether competing for limited human and financial resources or competing ideologically over what the most pressing problems are and who merits or needs protection most (McAdam, McCarthy, and Zald 1996). As an example regarding what and whose protection is most 'important' (or we could say foundational), I recognize that, if I must prioritize the most critical issue facing the world today, it is the mass extinction of species caused by humans' exponentially increasing degradation of our environmental life-support systems (related to climate crisis and industrial agribusiness) (Kolbert 2014).[6] Recognizing this wildlife conservation issue as a priority helps exemplify how environmentalism connects all social movements by protecting the biodiversity of life worldwide.

While the goal of environmentalism—to preserve life-support systems—may make it obvious why movements on behalf of human and nonhuman animals should be concerned about protecting the environment, it may not be as obvious why environmentalism needs other movements. Environmentalists themselves are human, as are the target audiences of their campaigns, so their campaigns must keep human interests in mind to some extent. But if environmentalism protects the rights of the human animal, then for moral consistency, environmentalists should also explicitly embrace the rights of nonhuman animals (Freeman 2015). Mainstream environmental activism already indicates an implicit belief in animal rights, since environmentalists favor some individual sentient beings, primarily endangered species and humans; however, environmentalists do not provide a sound justification for limiting those privileges to the human animal (even when we may be the most destructive species) while at the same time using lethal or violent methods of dealing with some other animals deemed problematic. But a justification can be provided by enacting the animal rights philosophy of respecting *individual, sentient* living subjects (Freeman 2015). In their book *Zoopolis*, Donaldson and Kymlicka (2011, 36) lament how both humanists and ecologists overlook nonhuman animal sentience and subjectivity: "Both tend to collapse the question of animals into the question of nature writ large, denying that animals, as subjects, need to be protected the way human subjects are, and not simply as components of nature."

Conversely, human rights advocates should also embrace animal rights as a morally consistent way to protect the interests of the human animal too, as certain humans may otherwise face severe disadvantages if we decided to 'manage' our species in the way other invasive or destructive animal species are managed under environmental policies, which often includes culling (Freeman 2015). The rights of some humans are most at risk by the exception of being reclassified as 'animals' (nonhumans) in need of taming; therefore, Vasile Stanescu (2012) calls for animal rights as a minimum protection for all animals (humans included) against basic abuses and imprisonment. It is also in humanity's own mental health interests to avoid dissonance and be morally consistent in the way we treat other sentient beings and dispense justice, thus improving our own self-image as a compassionate and fair species. For now, many in Western culture live with the shame, mostly subconsciously but some consciously, of our (ab)use of fellow animals and the natural world for our gratification (Derrida and Roudinesco 2004; Joy 2010). Admittedly, arguing for animal rights based on the appeal to our own (human) rights and health is an instrumental rationale, and there are more magnanimous reasons for humans to be motivated to extend rights or freedoms to fellow animals. These reasons rely on notions of kinship and empathy for the feelings of fellow sentient earthlings and their mutual desires to be free of suffering and domination; this understanding fosters an acknowledgment of the lack of sound reasons to discriminate against someone purely on the basis that she or he is not human (Donovan and Adams 2007; Regan 1983; Singer 1990; Steiner 2008).

The human rights and environmental movements are useful to the animal protection movement, since it interacts so closely with human culture and nature by protecting both domesticated animals as well as wild/free animals from human (ab)use. The focus of animal rights philosophy on privileging sentient living subjects relies on the expansion of some of the rights that already exist for human subjects, thanks to social justice movement efforts.[7] And the animal protection movement also relies on the work of environmentalists to raise the status of nonhuman life in human culture and to protect wildlife and their habitats from destruction.

Another unifying factor is that all these movements are often targeting similar opponents, typically governments (with laws that are either too oppressive or too lenient) or businesses (often powerful transnational corporations) that are exploiting living beings and resources in a profit-seeking race to the bottom in a competitive global market—often a 'free market,' meaning free of ethical standards to protect the vulnerable (Freeman 2015). In her work in environmental and social justice activism, Debra Erenberg (2015) observes that some corporations will exploit anyone vulnerable (human or nonhuman). It was this same observation, specifically of the way the agribusiness industry exploits workers (including children), nonhuman animals, and nature, that led vegan activist [L]auren Ornelas (2014) to start the Food Empowerment Project to promote food justice for both human and nonhuman animals.

Whether it is agribusiness, fossil fuel companies, the biotech industry, the banking sector, real estate developers, or manufacturers, certain wealthy and powerful industries serve as daunting opponents for hundreds of individual, small, nonprofit SMOs. So social movements naturally try to garner public support to get numbers on their side for leverage, even though many in the public may be culturally, ideologically, or materially allied with the common exploitative system. Media systems often help manufacture consent toward status quo power systems or distract people from social issues by promoting self-interest and the materialistic individualism of consumer culture (Brockhoff 2010; Herman and Chomsky 1988; Shanahan and McComas 1999). Institutions such as education, religion, or government may also contribute to supporting dominant viewpoints, which is especially true where corporations have undue influence over public policy and laws. But despite these obstacles, the primary fair method for social movements to garner more power is to join forces in solidarity and find a way to engage with the public in that union. As an allied force, SMOs are more likely to democratically influence governmental, institutional, and corporate practices in a significant way. This requires teamwork and people who strongly identify themselves as loyal members of that team.

The next section largely draws from ecofeminism and critical animal studies to add some additional points in favor of why an intersectional approach to social and ecological justice is necessary and inevitable.[8]

THE NEED FOR AN INCLUSIVE, INTERSECTIONAL APPROACH

Sociologist Patricia Hill Collins (2000, 18) uses the term "matrix of domination" to highlight the overarching system of oppression that connects all types of exploitation. Glasser (2015, 45) contends that championing total liberation for all beings begins with "an ethic of intersectionality" that acknowledges all causes must support one another: "Individuals may be affected by multiple oppressions at once; experiences of oppression differ within any oppressed group; all social justice causes are fighting the same oppressive structures; any organization that supports any part of this oppressive structure will ultimately strengthen forces of oppression and delay liberation." As a subdiscipline, ecofeminism exposes how dualisms, hierarchies, and logics of domination maintain inequalities (Glasser). "This logic of domination justifies and institutionalizes up-down and either-or ways of thinking" that are based on creating hierarchies of superior versus inferior beings (44).

Critical animal studies scholars acknowledge how oppression of humans, other animals, and nature is interconnected and should be tackled cooperatively between movements rather than being viewed competitively (i.e., one versus the other or viewing some victims as more worthy). To avoid visualizing different beings and causes stacked in order of importance on a ladder, I like the circular wheel metaphor that Joy (2014, 89) employs: "the oppressive-powers-that-be depend on a divide-and-conquer mentality that pits oppressed groups against one another, as though oppressions were rungs on a hierarchical ladder rather than spokes on a wheel." Intersectional activist Christopher-Sebastian McJetters (2014, 131) acknowledges the futility of activists "tallying up who has suffered the greater injustice" and, instead, suggests that all social movements defeat tyranny through solidarity, by choosing to "seek freedom for everyone." Similarly, Kim (2015, 15) takes the theoretical premise that it is not an either/or option, in particular between focusing on race versus focusing on species: "My argument is that our interpretive success depends on our ability and willingness to engage with these two taxonomies of power, race and species, at once—and to understand their connectedness." To expand on this point, Sarat Colling, Sean Parson, and Alessandro Arrigoni (2014) contend that true total liberation must incorporate a "groundless solidarity" (64)—which is a conceptual basis for organizing a 'movement of movements' (in anarchist fashion) that does not seek to prioritize one resistance struggle as having primacy over others. Groundless solidarity recognizes that dismantling political oppression must occur across all fronts for mutual benefit to all social movements (Day 2005).

Pellow (2014, 6) laments that intersectional analysis in academia has often been limited to human categories (race, class, gender, etc.), ignoring differences based on species: "By focusing primarily on human inequality, we miss a great deal with regard to how far and wide inequalities actually extend." He champions what he calls the study of "socioecological inequality" that focuses on "hierarchical relationships among humans, ecosystems, and nonhuman animals that produce harms across each sphere" (7). It "underscores that humans, ecosystems, and nonhumans are intertwined in the production of inequality and violence and that relationships that might privilege humans in the short run may also place them in jeopardy in the long term" (7). In fact, Pellow identifies humanism itself as a threat to human rights, as it causes us to live within a narrow mind-set of domination that leads to injustice and environmental destruction: "Human liberation must involve emancipation from the long list of oppressions that exist in society, including the shackles of humanism itself, which constrains us to live in ways that are ecologically unsustainable, dominionist with respect to nonhuman natures, and socially unjust" (15).

With a similar indictment of humanism, this time focused on radical social movements and leftist politics, Steven Best (2014, 109) argues that they "uncritically reproduced the pathologies of Western anthropocentrism" and thus failed to "break with the repressive mindsets and institutions" that foster oppression and domination. He calls the political left "fragmentary, weak, noninclusive, and regressive in their views toward nonhuman animals" (xi), even "unenlightened and pre-scientific" (109), which undermines their claims to be "avant-garde" thinkers. Even when initial alliances did form between social justice and environmental causes, acknowledging some mutual oppression (such as in agribusiness), Best laments that they neglect to include animal liberation and veganism. Yet he optimistically notes that if social justice, environmentalism, and animal liberation joined forces for "total liberation," it would "overflow with potential for advancing progressive values (such as rights, liberty, justice, equality, community, and peace), for creating ecological societies, and for overcoming human alienation from other animal species and the earth as a whole" (Best 2014, xi).

Ecofeminist scholars have always included nonhuman species as part of intersectional analyses of injustices: "Ecofeminists exposed various connections between different forms of oppression, more precisely between sexism and environmental degradation. . . . Indeed, these thinkers and writers have demonstrated that we must simultaneously work against poverty, racism, environmental degradation, sexism, speciesism, and homophobia, because all are connected. . . . Social justice requires that we dismantle *systems of oppression* undergirding a plethora of 'isms'" (Kemmerer 2015a, 1). She notes that Western activists can also learn from Eastern philosophies that emphasize interdependence and oneness, as Westerners may have the tendency to separate their cause from others and privilege it as more important (Kemmerer 2015a). Ecofeminist and vegan scholar Carol Adams (1990) has long promoted an intersectional approach to activism, particularly acknowledging the interconnections between discrimination based on gender, race, and species, especially critiquing the patriarchal consumption of women and nonhuman animals as objects of pleasure. She explains: "Analyzing mutually reinforcing logics of domination, and drawing connections among practical implications of power relations, has been a core project of ecofeminism" (Adams 2014, 10).

Adams (2014) claims that it is not helpful for animal activists to see their struggle as a historical extension and progression of a human rights struggle, as it implies that the latter is largely resolved and now we can move down the hierarchy to help nonhumans, which obscures how all the injustices are interconnected and mutually reinforcing. Conversely, this can parallel with humanist arguments from some human social justice movements that we should wait and deal with 'animals' later once we have resolved human welfare issues, as humans are more important. Accordingly, Kim (2015) contends that it does not make sense to work in a piecemeal fashion against neoliberalism and merely end one form of supremacy (like racism) while leaving other supremacies (like speciesism) intact. Instead, she suggests that activists work holistically to deploy "critical and transformational politics to radically restructure our relationship with each other, animals, and the earth outside of domination" (21).

Yet working together on transformational politics does not mean that each SMO must lose its independence nor its focus on certain issues of importance to its members. Glasser (2015, 45) explains: "It is possible to have single-issue campaigns that are pragmatically focused on one type of exploitation, rooted within a specific sociocultural context, but that still need to ideologically embrace an ethic of intersectionality, embracing the mutually reinforcing nature of oppression, thereby avoiding the exploitation of others." Glasser's quote gets to the heart of my book's mission to have all social movement campaigns support each other on a fundamental level as allies, based on encouraging similar values and identities as human animal earthlings. Even if all SMO campaigns are not coalition based and broadly focused, a goal here is not to undermine anyone else's cause in the process of promoting one's own.

Author Perspective

I'd like to share my perspective and background to provide context for the ways in which my life experiences and worldviews influence this book's insights (in ways that help and hinder). I am a middle-class, middle-aged, able-bodied, white, progressive, atheist (but raised Christian), cisgender female human, born, raised, and educated in the United States as a native English speaker (with ancestors who primarily were European settler colonists in the eighteenth and nineteenth centuries, including Irish 'potato famine' immigrants). To help overcome some of my ethnocentrism, I'm fortunate to frequently travel to many countries and bioregions, thanks to academic conferences and because my late husband was South African.

I became a grassroots activist as an undergraduate at the University of Florida in 1989, went vegetarian upon graduation, then vegan in the mid-1990s, and have founded, led, and participated in several grassroots animal rights and vegetarian groups in the various cities where I have lived (in addition to working my day jobs in corporations, nonprofits, and universities). I now live in the piedmont region of the southeastern USA, the foothills of the Appalachian Mountain range, in the city of Atlanta, with my dog Elliott and near my family (also near lots of trees, bees, mosquitos, birds, squirrels, chipmunks, and apparently coyotes, although I never see them). I work just a few miles from home, at Georgia State University downtown, where I serve as the faculty adviser to the student animal rights club, People for the End of Animal Cruelty and Exploitation (PEACE), and work on campus sustainability committees. As a tenured associate professor of communication, I teach a diverse group of future media-makers on topics such as ethics, strategic communication, and environmental advocacy. I also research and publish on these topics, including coauthoring (with my former dissertation adviser, Dr. Debra Merskin) guidelines for animal- and ecofriendly media at animalsandmedia.org.

To maintain my sanity amidst a chaotic world, I watch comedy programs, and I also produce media programs. I have been cohosting at least two eco and animal radio shows a month on Radio Free Georgia for almost a decade (with Melody Paris and Sonia Swartz); the shows amplify the voices of authors and activists and provide a 'human animal earthling' perspective on progressive issues.

Summary of the Book's Chapters

Building on many of the points I introduced in this chapter, the next chapter includes a lengthy review of scholarly studies and theories that establish cross-cultural universal values and their connection to identity, and how both are influential in social change efforts. I review examples of how social causes (social justice, animal protection, and environmentalism) have worked together in the past, and the ideological basis for what they have in common that enables them to be more supportive of each other's efforts. This includes a discussion of some of the legitimate tensions that separate them, including hunting, nonnative species, farming and fishing of animals, and human minority-group cultural practices using animals. Because most of these issues deal with animals and debates about human entitlement and our self-perception in relation to 'animals,' chapter 2 addresses the benefits of deconstructing the human/animal binary and interrogating the relevance of species boundaries and the 'humane-ness' of humanity. It concludes with my recommendation that animal advocates emphasize both our kinship with animals as sentient beings but also the benefits of appreciating diversity among species.

Chapters 3 through 8 comprise various empirical studies of rights movements and activism to answer my research questions about who and what matters to each social movement. To begin, chapter 3 is a pilot study comparing six global rights declarations/charters on behalf of humans, nature, and animals, which establishes the four organizational categories I use throughout the book—life-supporting values, fairness values, responsibility values, and unity values. Chapters 4, 5, and 6 explain the findings of my examination of sixteen global SMO campaign messages separated into human rights, animal protection, and environmental SMOs, to identify for whom each cause advocates, what values they promote as good versus bad, and where they place blame for problems. Then in chapter 7, I create tables identifying common ground between the three social movement causes, in terms of where their values, virtues, constituents, and targeted opposition groups overlap and are, thus, universal to all movements. In chapter 8, I synthesize interviews with nineteen activists, drawing on the wisdom and experiences of activists (either presidents or communication specialists) in many of the SMOs I studied as well as reaching out to some prominent activists who already lead the charge in intersectional activism on behalf of humans and nonhumans. That chapter discusses these activists' views on how, when, and why to collaborate across causes; how all the struggles are interrelated; sources of our social problems; ways each movement could be more supportive allies for other movements; values that SMOs currently appeal to in campaigns; and values they think society needs to prioritize.

All these studies culminate in the final recommendations chapter, which answers my prescriptive research questions about what shared values and virtues comprise an inclusive 'human animal earthling' identity, and how SMOs across causes can frame those key values in ways that are biocentric (not just anthropocentric) and incorporate an appreciation for animal sentience; in this way we broaden the notion of which beings deserve the benefits of these values supporting life, fair treatment, responsibility, and unity. This chapter includes many illustrative examples of how SMO campaigns are and could be more supportive allies to other causes, so you can see how my recommendations could be enacted in practice. I end by offering thirteen 'human animal earthling' project areas that are ripe for collaboration between causes, with ideas for overcoming some of the differences that have traditionally divided causes.

Focus, Limitations, and Further Research

I have asked, as you might: Is this primarily a book about human rights, animal rights, or environmentalism? If I had to pick, I would categorize it broadly as an *environmental* book because that is the most inclusive and foundational issue affecting all living beings, so I believe environmentalism embeds all other movements within it, just as nature incorporates all species. But I think readers will notice that I center *animals* at the heart of the book, nonhuman animals in particular. While some readers may wish I had privileged human issues further, as anthropocentrism is the most common lens through which we see the world, I think it is vital to decenter our own species in order to expand our identity to include the animal kingdom and all species on earth. We must question the very entitlement that leads us to profoundly and catastrophically exploit the more-than-human world, and each other, in the first place. So I believe that my 'bias' as a critical animal studies scholar and animal advocate is an asset in writing this particular book, and I ask that you be open to seeing the value of the animal rights movement as an ethical force with the potential to logically connect the rights of the human animal with the rights of the broader natural world. Animal rights tends to be the missing link in most analyses of injustice or exploitation, and the interests of nonendangered wildlife or domesticated animals get unapologetically overlooked as unimportant in comparison to humans, endangered species, or ecosystems. But equitably applying an ethic of care and principles of justice leads to the conclusion that other sentient animals, besides humans, deserve to have their interests respected if anyone's interests are to be respected at all.

Admittedly, this book's topic is so broad and interdisciplinary, and indeed global, that it won't be able to do justice to deeply analyzing and connecting all the scholarly disciplines, perspectives, geographic regions, cultures, and issues it raises. But as a starting point, it does serve as a committed and detailed inquiry toward the goal of identifying ways to strategically align varied social movement campaigns for needed solidarity in addressing globally interconnected problems of the twenty-first century; and I think the empirical study of global rights charters, major social movement campaigns, and activist insights, put in scholarly context, provides a rigorous grounding for my recommendations in the last chapter. And I intend to build on these initial findings in future research (and hope others will too), by investigating how the values and virtues of a 'human animal earthling' identity can also be fostered by other social forces, such as the media, educational institutions, government agencies, religious groups, and artists. This needs to be a team effort.

CHAPTER ONE

Literature and Thoughts on Identifying Common Values between Different Social Movements

The goals of my analysis in this book will be to (1) identify core values and areas of ideological overlap between ethical philosophies supporting the welfare and rights of humanity, other animals, and the environment; (2) suggest mutual values upon which all social justice movements can collectively frame campaigns influencing human identity (whether working independently or as global coalitions between human rights, animal rights, and environmentalists); and (3) reframe these values to be less anthropocentric and more biocentric (inclusive of all life on earth).

In this chapter I provide the background and context needed to better engage with these goals and set the stage for my empirical analysis of social movements later in the book. First, I review literature on values and identity from psychology and communication scholars who discuss how they can be used in advocacy campaigns. They recommend that social movements, particularly environmentalists, promote self-transcendent values (biospheric and altruistic) to cultivate an environmental identity apt to produce needed attitude and behavior changes toward nonhuman life. Next, I summarize the literature and my own insights showing the benefits of ideological unification of human and nonhuman causes and how the rights of animals are a logical bridge connecting the nature/culture divide. To put this in context for cultivating a human animal earthling identity, I examine historical alliances as well as the ideological overlap and divergences in the ethical philosophies foundational to human rights, animal rights, and environmentalism. I explore studies acknowledging the challenges posed by taking an intersectional approach to addressing human and nonhuman issues collectively and how the biases, tensions, and philosophical differences of the various social movements may be overcome, in part to find some common ideological ground for creating a just and sustainable humanimality.

Values and Identity-Based Campaigning

My values-based advocacy strategy in this book is influenced by linguistic strategist George Lakoff, psychologist Tim Kasser, and a former change strategist for the World Wildlife Fund, Tom Crompton. For campaigns to resonate, Lakoff (2004, 74) suggests that advocacy organizations, rather than speaking primarily in factual terms, should talk in terms of a clear set of simple *values* that accurately reflect what the organization stands for and truly express its "moral vision." While campaigns surely must include rational arguments and facts, these should be embedded within a moral message that helps shape our cultural identity and values (Lakoff).

Crompton and Kasser (2009) conclude that the environmental movement's current approach of campaigning for organizational policy changes and consumer behavioral changes has been inadequate to solve the environmental crisis. They call instead for more identity-based campaigns to cultivate benevolent intrinsic values in the public. Even if advocacy organizations within a coalition do not seek the same specific policy change, they should focus on *cognitive* impacts by agreeing to frame their various campaigns around the same set of specific, deep, intrinsic values. In this way, even if identity campaigns 'fail' to change practices in the short term, they may succeed in the long-term goal of mutually promoting a needed cultural values and identity shift (Crompton and Kasser 2009).[1]

IDENTITY

The concept of identity is unique in its ability to allow us to broach major sociopolitical questions such as "how to bring public issues and personal troubles into the same frame" (Jenkins 2004, 24). Various scholars have defined identity, noting that identity is multifaceted and constituted by both personal and social factors. In his book *Social Identity*, Richard Jenkins (4) describes identity as a reflexive process "to associate oneself with, or attach oneself to something or someone else (such as a friend, a sports team, or an ideology)," showing how our beliefs shape our sense of belonging to certain groups. It is through identity that we are able to establish what our purpose is and where we belong in this world: "Identity is our understanding of who we are and of who other people are and, reciprocally, other people's understanding of themselves and of others (which includes us)" (5). But Jenkins acknowledges that our identities are negotiable and evolving, not fixed.

A similar dynamic and reflective element to identity is found in Anthony Giddens's (1991, 53) definition of self-identity: "It is the self as reflexively understood by the person in terms of her or his biography." Giddens emphasizes the narrative element—the trajectory in one's idea of one's own personhood. In the age of high modernity, one makes and remakes one's identity in large part through a choice of lifestyle, something Giddens sees as going beyond shallow consumerism: "A lifestyle can be defined as a more or less integrated set of practices which an individual embraces, not only because such practices fulfill utilitarian needs, but because they give material form to a particular narrative of self-identity" (81). The habitual practices of a lifestyle provide order and unity, giving one a sense of "ontological security" and helping them clarify what behaviors would be "out of character" (82).

Identities function both to set us apart and to unite us. They establish "relationships of similarity and difference" between individuals and/or collectivities (Jenkins 2004, 5). Jenkins acknowledges how one's idea of selfhood is often based on a *collective identity*—a symbolically constructed idea of similarity with a group: "But in the shade of that image a range of diversity and heterogeneity exists with respect to what people do: collective identity emphasizes similarity, but not at the expense of difference" (133). This recognizes that even a collective identity is not so fixed and homogeneous that it precludes some natural level of diversity among members. Additionally, identifying with a group can have different meanings for different individuals. Jenkins explains that "it is possible for individuals to share the same nominal identity and for that to mean very different things to them in practice, to have different consequences for their lives, or for them to 'do' or 'be' it differently" (22).

Identity helps us explain ourselves in a meaningful way based on who we are and are not. In their book *Identity Theory*, Burke and Stets (2009, 3) provide this definition: "An identity is the set of meanings that define who one is when one is an occupant of a particular role in society, a member of a particular group, or claims particular characteristics that identify him or her as a unique person." This emphasizes that one's identity functions in relation to others and society; it is affected by and affects culture: "There is, thus, an elaborate system of mutual influences between characteristics of the individual and characteristics of society" (4). In support of my thesis that identity is key to social change, Burke and Stets state: "Change the nature of the individuals and the nature of society changes" (4).

VALUES

Part of what determines our identity and character is our values. Values researcher and psychologist Shalom Schwartz (1994) defines values as "desirable trans-situational goals, varying in importance, that serve as guiding principles in the life of a person or other social entity. Implicit in this definition of values as goals is that they: (1) serve the interests of some social entity, (2) motivate action—giving it direction and emotional intensity, (3) function as standards for judging and justifying action, and (4) are acquired both through socialization to dominant group values and through the unique learning experiences of individuals" (21). Values are "enduring beliefs" about the conduct and states of existence one prefers (Rokeach 1973, 5). Values represent "ideals" (Hitlin and Piliavin 2004, 361) and shape, and are shaped by, ideology (Maio et al. 2003).

Values influence both attitudes and behaviors to varying degrees. Central to our sense of "personhood," values are more "durable" and positive than attitudes; attitudes are evaluations of something or someone as positive or negative (Hitlin and Piliavin 2004, 361). Bardi and Schwartz (2003, 1207) find that "values motivate behavior, but the relation between values and behaviors is partly obscured by norms," as social pressures and other factors may inhibit value-congruent behaviors. If campaign messages showcase how a particular value relates to a certain issue, then it is more likely to activate that value's influence on the audience's behavior. Verplanken and Holland (2002, 434) conclude that values give "meaning to, energize, and regulate value-congruent behavior, but only if values were cognitively activated and central to the self."

Schwartz (1994) has identified values that are universal to all humans on some level. After extensive empirical cross-cultural testing, Schwartz (2012) and his colleagues refined these universal values into these nineteen areas: self-direction of thought, self-direction of actions, stimulation (excitement), hedonism, achievement, power over others, power to control resources, saving face over one's image, personal security, societal security, tradition, conformity to social rules, interpersonal conformity to avoid upsetting others, humility, benevolence by being dependable and trustworthy, benevolence by caring for others in one's group, universalism to show concern for protection and justice for all people, universalism to show concern for preservation of nature, and universalism to show tolerance for difference.

These nineteen values relate to one another on a motivational continuum, which Schwartz et al. (2012) chart on a circle, arranged around the extent to which the values represent a social orientation (versus self-interest) and an openness to change (versus resistance to change). On the circle, self-transcendent/social values (like benevolence and universalism) are opposite of self-enhancement/individualistic values (like power and achievement); values representing openness to change/growth (like self-direction and stimulation) are opposite of more preservational/conservational values (like conformity, tradition, and security). Although people will rank value priorities differently depending on the situation and pressures they face, in general, Bardi and Schwartz (2003) find that people across all cultures rank benevolence,[2] self-direction, and universalism the highest and rank power and tradition as the lowest, which implies a respect for self-transcendence and openness.

In addition to these findings in social psychology, ethicists also research values. Communitarian ethicist Clifford Christians (2008) proposes that ethical protonorms in all human cultures are based on the sacredness of human life, human dignity, nonviolence, and truthfulness. In a search for cross-cultural common values that can guide the world through crisis, Rushworth Kidder (1994) interviewed several dozen moral leaders and activists from a variety of cultures. In summarizing their ideas on creating positive social change, he devised this list of eight universal values: love (compassion), truthfulness (trust), fairness (equity), freedom (democracy), unity (cooperation and community), tolerance (respect for diversity), responsibility (taking care of yourself and others), and respect for life (nonviolence).

Social Justice Values. Studies employing Schwartz's universal values categories reveal that people who identify with universalist values are more likely to view minority groups positively, while conversely, those who identify more with preservational/conservational values (like security, tradition, and conformity) are more likely to devalue a variety of racial, ethnic, and gender minority groups and express "group-focused enmity" and prejudice toward them as out-groups (Beierlein, Kuntz, and Davidov 2016, 77). Universal values are also associated with prosocial concerns such as ending poverty and hunger, in addition to reducing prejudice (Schwartz 2010). To increase interest in antiracism and social justice activism among whites, it helps to enhance their awareness of white privilege (Stewart et al. 2012). Although many Christian conservatives do work for charitable and social justice causes, white Christians who are more conservative (rather than liberal) are less likely to be aware of white privilege and engage in social justice activism (Todd, McConnell, and Suffrin 2014). While it is known that people who identify with right-wing authoritarianism and social dominance are more likely to express prejudice, studies indicate that prejudice may be mitigated in those who increase their capacity to feel empathy and apply moral reasoning to decision-making (MacFarland 2010).

An antisocial practice that increases prejudice is dehumanization—a process that exposes a group of humans to increased discrimination and even violence, based on categorizing them as less humanlike and more animalistic, perceiving them as an out-group (Haslam 2006). Costello and Hodson (2010) find that one of the factors that predicts out-group prejudices toward certain humans is if someone believes that humans are distinctly different from and superior to animals. According to this "interspecies model of prejudice," an ideology that supports domination and exploitation of *nonhuman animals* also leads to support for similar inferior treatment of human groups (such as other races or immigrants) who are perceived to be more like nonhuman animals.

This dehumanization prejudice is also found in children and often also in their parents; white children who believed in the human/animal divide were more likely to see black children as having less humanlike traits and emotions (Costello and Hodson 2014). But researchers have evidence to suggest that dehumanizing racial prejudices could be unlearned in children if they spent more time with nonhuman animals and were exposed to information about how animals are similar to humans. Notably, the direction of the framing matters, and it is more likely to improve the moral concern for racial out-groups if you show how animals are like humans rather than showing how humans are like animals (Costello and Hodson 2010).

Values regarding Animals. Animals seem to mean a lot to humans, and nonhuman animals are often represented in popular culture, but sometimes dismissively, as ways to symbolically explore our own lives (Corbett 2006; Merskin 2018). Stephen Kellert (1983), a prolific researcher on attitudes toward animals, contends that since nonhuman animals are the most sentient characters of the natural world, people's views on animals can serve as a barometer for their fundamental views of nature.

Kellert (1983) identifies eight value-orientation categories to describe people's views of nonhuman animals: humanistic (loving individual pets), neutralistic/negativist, moralistic (opposing cruelty), utilitarian (using animals), naturalistic (valuing wildlife and nature), ecologistic (appreciating ecosystems and habitats), dominionistic (controlling), and scientistic (biological). The latter two were found to be the least common, and the first four were the most common views in the United States in the late 1970s study. Higher levels of education were associated with more knowledge of and affinity for animals. Americans who farmed, hunted, or fished tended to value animals in utilitarian and dominionistic ways (Kellert).

Humans display strong and varying preferences about animals based on species. The animal species most disliked by U.S. Americans in the late 1970s include 'pests' (insects) and animals associated with danger or disease (rats and snakes), while people most liked companion mammals (dogs and horses) and certain wild mammals, birds, fishes, and attractive insects (butterflies, ladybugs, robins, eagles, elephants, salmon, and trout) (Kellert 1989). A 2014 update to this study revealed that Americans' views on some land predator species had become slightly more favorable, namely wolves, coyotes, and cougars (George et al. 2016). This may be attributed to a trend in modernization away from Americans viewing wildlife in terms of domination and toward viewing them in mutualistic terms, as extended kin deserving of care (Manfredo, Teel, and Henry 2009).

Kellert's (1995) research on children's attitudes shows younger kids are typically not sympathetic toward animals or at least always put humans first. So he recommends humane education programs in elementary school. Zoe Weil (2004) describes the humane education process as empowering children to critically analyze problems such as injustice and suffering facing humans, other animals, and nature; children identify solutions applying an empathetic moral lens of reverence, respect, and responsibility toward all living beings.

In general, caring for animals is associated with being idealistic (and following universal moral principles) rather than relativistic in one's ethical philosophy (Su and Martens 2018). And to dispel the myth that animal lovers are misanthropic, studies reveal that they care greatly about human welfare. Those who work for animal protection have been found not only to be more empathetic to nonhuman animals than the general population (in an Australian study) but also to score higher on empathy directed toward humans (Signal and Taylor 2007). And people who are more concerned about the welfare of farmed animals are also more concerned about human farmworkers and tend to have political orientations favoring economic equality and tolerance of out-groups (Deemer and Lobao 2011). This relates to Costello and Hodson's (2010) findings that those who believe in the rights of nonhuman animals (eschewing speciesism) are more likely to believe in the rights and welfare of all human groups too (eschewing racism and dehumanization).

Communication scholars Debra Merskin (2018) and Julia Corbett (2006) remind us that we need animals and should show care and respect in the values we convey about them in our cultural messages. "We share a common environment and are both subject to the effects of its degradation," Corbett explains. "The destiny of many animals, therefore, depends not just on our actions, but on the subjective feelings that we communicate about them" (212).

Environmental Values. To apply values to environmental campaign-messaging strategies, Jamieson (2007, 481) recommends that environmentalists frame climate change as a *moral* issue, appealing to such values as care, empathy, and responsibility in calling for "long-term sustainable changes in the way we live." Jamieson's moral frame is reminiscent of biologist E. O. Wilson's (2016) suggestion that getting society to conserve half the planet for wildlife habitat will require a *moral shift*. Crompton (2008) also calls for *values-based* environmental campaigns, saying environmentalists should not continue to rely on pragmatic green consumerism messages nor expedient appeals to consumers' financial self-interest. He argues that the severity of environmental crisis requires drastic changes (not "simple and painless" small steps) that necessitate a reevaluation of our identity and self-centered values. This seems to suggest that what environmental communication scholar Robert Cox (2006) refers to as "critical rhetoric" (an ideological critique of the status quo) should more directly influence "campaign rhetoric" (goal-oriented appeals) so that activist campaigns are not too pragmatically restrained to ask for major needed change.

Crompton's studies on human identity with psychologist Tim Kasser find that promoting and activating intrinsic values (inherently rewarding pursuits) in the broader culture is vital to inspiring major lifestyle changes to solve 'bigger than self' problems like climate change (Crompton and Kasser 2009). Intrinsic values include community and friendship, self-respect, creativity, social justice, and benevolence, in opposition to extrinsic values focused on external rewards such as social status and prestige, popularity, power, or money. Drawing on Schwartz (1994), Crompton and Kasser (2009) align intrinsic with self-transcendent values in opposition to extrinsic or self-enhancing values. Therefore, they recommend that all social movement campaigns encourage such intrinsic values as community (make the world a better place), affiliation (healthy interpersonal relationships), and self-acceptance (trying to grow as a person) along with such self-transcendent values as benevolence (honesty, loyalty, and helpfulness), universalism (caring about the environment, social justice, and peace), and self-direction (freedom to pursue one's own goals).

Crompton and Kasser (2009) discourage environmental campaigners from instrumentally using appeals to extrinsic values, which can inadvertently exacerbate the underlying cause of environmental problems. As proof, the authors cite a variety of studies showing that people who endorse self-enhancing and materialistic values are less likely to engage in pro-environmental behaviors, and they express more negative attitudes toward nature and exhibit lower levels of biophilia (affiliation with living beings), as they generally see themselves as consumers of nature and focus on how things affect them directly (Crompton and Kasser). Similarly, based on a review of environmental value studies, Steg and De Groot (2012) conclude that "individuals who strongly endorse self-transcendent values are more likely to have pro-environmental beliefs and norms and to act pro-environmentally, while the opposite is true for those who strongly endorse self-enhancement values" (84).

There is some hope for reducing materialism and selfish motivations promoted in consumer culture: materialistic values can be culturally reshaped since they are more socially influenced than biologically predisposed (J. Giddens, Schermer, and Vernon 2009; Kasser et al. 2004). Another study finds that when extrinsically oriented people were primed to first consider intrinsic values like community, it increased their social and ecological concerns, suggesting that campaign messages appealing to intrinsic values could activate these deeper values even in people who identify as being more extrinsically oriented (Chilton et al. 2012). To increase the likelihood that campaign messages will be salient and lead to congruent action, it is helpful for campaigners to provide cognitive support for a particular value (via rationales to defend the usefulness of the value) (Maio et al. 2001) and to prime and activate the particular self-transcendent value needed, such as biospheric and/or altruistic values (Verplanken and Holland 2002).

The self-transcendent values category can be parsed into distinct subcategories: biospheric (inherent valuing of nonhuman nature) and altruistic (inherent valuing of human welfare).[3] Studies find that biospheric and altruistic values are correlated with pro-environmental and prosocial beliefs and actions, in opposition to egoistic or self-enhancement values. But when conflicts between biospheric and altruistic values arise, predictably, people who identify more strongly with altruism are more likely to side with humanitarian over environmental choices (Steg and De Groot 2012).[4] This implies that cultivating self-transcendent values alone (be they altruism, benevolence, or universalism) may not be sufficient to ensure a needed cultural shift toward valuing nonhuman life if anthropocentric identities continue to prevail, leaving nonhumans at a disadvantage.

Environmental Identity. Values and goals influence one's identity, defined as self-perception or who one thinks of oneself as being (Crompton and Kasser 2009). Certain parts of one's identity may be more flexible and open to choice in response to personal preferences and changes in circumstances (e.g., political, ideological, occupational, geographical, or cultural) (Clayton 2012). Identity helps you locate yourself socially, such as establishing a sense of belonging to in-groups of similar individuals in opposition to out-groups of others perceived as different (Crompton and Kasser 2009). In evaluating the world, people are motivated to seek consistency with their identity, so they often validate their own group to increase their self-esteem. They may do so in part by creating prejudices toward the out-groups.

For example, due to anthropocentric identities, people view nonhuman animals and nature as the "ultimate out-group" (14) and tend to think less of nonhumans' abilities, creating a sense of indifference toward them. Crompton and Kasser (2009) caution against social justice campaigns that increase this prejudice, such as environmental campaigns that fail to account for nonhuman animal suffering in their policies or ignore the interests of nonendangered individual animals. The authors propose an identity-based solution to reducing this nonhuman discrimination (in nonmisanthropic ways) by activating the values of empathy and egalitarianism, while positioning humans as part of nature and the animal kingdom.

This relationship to nature is part of creating an "environmental identity," which psychologist Susan Clayton (2012, 167) defines as "a sense of connection to some part of the nonhuman natural environment that affects the way we perceive and act toward the natural world; a belief that the environment is important to us." This can be nurtured in part by time spent with nonhuman animals and in the outdoors, including gardening. People with higher notions of environmental identity are more likely to support animal rights and believe that other species' interests and future human generations should be considered in decision-making (Clayton 2008). The more people feel related to the natural environment as part of their self, the more it predicts pro-environmental behaviors, according to Schultz's (2001) notion of "inclusion of nature in the self" scale. A feeling of interdependence is a key component to an environmental identity, as Clayton (2012, 172) explains: "This interdependence should imply an increased perception of similarity with, and moral standing accorded to, nonhuman natural entities, and a sense that threats to the natural world are personally relevant."[5]

In his book *The Power of Identity*, Castells (2010) notes that environmentalism is a diverse global movement, lacking a unified identity. He categorizes the following examples of primary identities for various types of environmental organizations: nature lovers (conservationists), local communities (place-based protection of one's home space), the green self (deep ecology and ecofeminist countercultures), internationalist eco-warriors (global sustainable development), and concerned citizens (green politics) (171). But these contain common themes that form a "coherent ecological discourse" (180) that poses a direct challenge to the dominant processes of our modern networked society. These common themes include an ambiguous deep connection with science and technology, control over space and the emphasis on locality and lived experiences, a belief in grassroots democracy, and a revolutionary new temporality via introduction of glacial/evolutionary time (as opposed to anthropocentric and capitalist-based clock-time).

An evolutionary time perspective emphasizes our unity as a biological species rather than seeing ourselves as separate cultural groups or citizens of various nation-states: "Through fundamental struggles over the appropriation of science, space, and time, ecologists induce *the creation of a new identity*, a biological identity, *a culture of the human species as a component of nature*" (Castells 2010, 184). Yet a socio-biological identity by species is broad enough to "be easily superimposed on multifaceted, historical traditions, languages, and cultural symbols. . . . It is the only global identity put forward on behalf of all human beings, regardless of their specific social, historical, or gender attachments, or of their religious faith" (185). But despite its allowance for (or transcendence of) cultural diversity, identification as the same species requires moving beyond a state-nationalist identity, as ecological problems often must be addressed internationally and cannot be solved piecemeal on a nation-to-nation basis (Castells). Similar to the popular eco-bumper sticker, our species must "think globally, act locally."

To encourage humanity to adopt this new identity, environmental discourse must "weave threads of singular cultures into a human hypertext, made out of historical diversity and biological commonality," which Castells (2010) calls "green culture" (185). His notion of green culture draws on Petra Kelly's spiritual view acknowledging humans' interconnectedness in the web of life—necessitating an "inner revolution" (Kelly 1994, 40) that plays into what Joanna Macy (1991) refers to as "the greening of the self."

A challenge may be that our humanness is so engrained in our identity that we hardly acknowledge it as a species-based collective identity—one that affords us a privilege to express our needs and desires based on our sense of self. Consider Jenkins's (2004, 54) commentary: "Human-ness is largely taken for granted, and, once granted, human-ness is for the most of us largely irrelevant thereafter. . . . Human-ness and selfhood, as primary identities, are typically entailed in each other: there seems to be a close connection between the perceptions of one and perceptions of the other." I would add that it is our animality that goes unidentified for most humans; for some, their biological animality may be taken for granted, but for many whose religions separate animals from humans, their humanness defines them in direct opposition to the animal. Yet I contend it is our animality that needs to be foregrounded as part of our identity. Studies have shown that the more strongly we identify with fellow animals, the more likely we are to care about animal rights and act to defend them, so authors recommend campaigns that emphasize "we're all animals" as a way to view nonhuman animals as part of our in-group (Plante et al. 2018, 174).

OUR IDENTITY AS A JUST AND SUSTAINABLE HUMANIMAL

Self-transcendent values of justice and social well-being are often lacking in environmental rhetoric, according to environmental scholar Julian Agyeman (2007). He calls for a merger of social justice (altruistic values) and environmentalism (biospheric values) via a notion of "just sustainability." In this book, I want to build on Agyeman's notion of just sustainability and incorporate a missing animal rights ethic (sentientism) by proposing that we strive for a "just and sustainable humanimality." My incorporation of the neologism *humanimal* situates humans in the context of our place in the animal kingdom and implies that the principle of fairness extends to other animals as well as our own species.[6] This helps mitigate the anthropocentrism connoted by notions of justice and sustainability.

For an anthropocentric movement such as human rights to see the value in collaborating with the animal rights and environmental movements requires cultivating a new, more humble and integrated identity for humans as *human animal earthlings*. Here, humans would begin to identify not just egocentrically with our own species but with the animal kingdom as a whole and the mutual status we share as living beings on planet earth. I believe each component of this multifaceted identity that I am proposing for humanity is important to mutually reinforcing a holistic outlook necessary to heal planetary environmental crisis:

1. The *earthling* component places us into a much larger context of all life on earth (transcending the categorization of species); humans become yet another species interdependent upon thriving ecosystems, part of a much larger and diverse family sharing planet earth amidst a vast universe. No fellow earthling is an 'alien' other.

2. The *animal kingdom* component represents a narrower categorization than earthling but still transcends the species barrier. Reminding humans that they are part of the animal kingdom is a key link bridging human culture with 'nature' (where we tend to situate nonhuman animal cultures), breaking the problematic culture/nature and human/animal dichotomies. We are each asked to identify with being a fellow animal—an individual with some drive to live, some conscious ability to think and problem-solve, and some subjective emotional perspective and feelings about our living situation and treatment. The animal component asks us to recognize kinship and appreciate the sentience and desires of *other* animals besides just the human animal.

3. The *human* component recognizes that there are some unique aspects to being part of a species—aspects that are influenced both by biology and culture. This acknowledges that while animal rights shares some basic similarities with human rights in terms of respecting the life and liberty of sentient individuals, the culture of most human communities is often unique from other animal cultures, which therefore helps determine what constitutes uniquely "human rights" (e.g., voting rights, clothing, privacy, education, freedom of expression and beliefs, gender equality, and health care). Some of the civic engagement aspects of human rights are not applicable to nonhuman animals.

Historical Alliances between Social Causes

For historical context, this section offers some examples of when human rights advocates have partnered with animal advocates or environmental advocates on common issues since the nineteenth century, also including some wildlife conservation alliances between animal and environmental advocates. This demonstrates that social movements can overcome ideological differences to form alliances and exemplify aspects of groundless solidarity. This small sampling often draws on U.S. social movements more familiar to me and fails to do justice to covering the full history of alliances across all global regions, decades, and movements.[7] I start with the humane alliances protecting the defenseless—human children and nonhuman animals.

In the late 1800s (the Gilded Age), children and nonhuman animals came to be viewed paternalistically as innocent and defenseless beings (both animalistic in nature) in need of mercy and protection (Pearson 2011). Many U.S. humane societies, originally founded to arrest individuals who abused nonhuman animals, expanded their law enforcement to arrest child abusers too. This was prompted by the first child abuse case in New York being prosecuted with the help of Henry Bergh's ASPCA in 1874; the ASPCA proved to be the only agency who would remove Mary Ellen Wilson from her abusive home, viewing the child sympathetically as a "little animal" (2). In her book on this alliance, *The Rights of the Defenseless*, Pearson (2011) contends "the linkage of animals with children formed part of an ideology of sentimental liberalism, a rhetoric forged by animal and child protectionists that reconciled dependence with rights and pledged the use of state power to protect the helpless" (3). Sentimentalism draws upon feeling and emotion to motivate virtuous action, and child and animal welfare reformers "generated powerful rhetoric and compelling narratives of sympathy, progress, and freedom" (3).

By the early 1900s (the Progressive Era), some reformers stopped employing Gilded Age liberalistic approaches that viewed cruelty as primarily a moral failing of individuals requiring policing. Cruelty came to be viewed as a systemic problem to be addressed and prevented at the macro scale of government (Pearson 2011). "Reformers realized that the state was the only force powerful enough to control business," Pearson notes. "And they increasingly asked it to regulate the conditions of both production and consumption" (17). For example, more child welfare advocates started to realize that the abuse of children is often due to employers and the challenges of poverty than to cruel parents, so they attempted to reform child labor and aid parents to keep family units together. An example related to Progressive Era animal protection involves the Horse Aid Society of New York, which took a more humanitarian approach to address cruelty than the punitive approach of the ASPCA, as the former worked with horse owners to provide better veterinary care, training, and resources to relieve the suffering of both horses and their drivers. The newer approach was less anticruelty and more prowelfare (Pearson).

Animal protection and child protection are now separate entities, due in part to "a competitive language positioning animals-as-commodities against children-as-investments" (Pearson 2011, 200). Child advocates (then and now) often show some speciesist incredulity and disdain that mere animals received so-called better protections and were presumably more important to the government than children, for whom fewer laws existed for many years (Pearson). However, for perspective, many of those first animal laws in the nineteenth century addressed farmed animals and horses, who were used for profit by industry; the laws provided the most minimal protections, not liberation or rights, and federal laws for farmed animals have not advanced much in the United States over a century later (Beers 2006; Freeman 2014). Given the commodity status of domesticated nonhuman animals as legal property and the legality of killing many wild animals for sport, I have never felt it fair to make blanket social critiques claiming people misguidedly care more about 'animals' than human beings, as that endorses human supremacy logic. But I agree that based on racism, sexism, classism, etc., some people seem to find it easier to sympathize with a suffering nonhuman animal (of a favored species) than they might with a disadvantaged human who is experiencing discrimination or poverty; the former is viewed as innocent (lacking agency, like a child), and the latter is viewed as partially culpable for their own problems (lacking responsibility expected of adult humans).

Pearson (2011) notes some arguments that animal welfare advocates were motivated by racist or classist beliefs to impose middle-class "bourgeois moral sensibility" (7) on the working class and immigrants, a cultural imperialism argument that still exists today (Kim 2015). But Pearson (2011) contends this is reductionist and does not account for the wide variety of animal activism motivations and tactics in the nineteenth and twentieth centuries (Beers 2006). In a discussion about early animal activists in the United States, Diane Beers sees them as humanitarians: "Many of those dedicated to animal issues were also actively involved with more than one human reform initiative, including abolition, women's rights, urban reform, worker reform, and civil rights. Such a wide spectrum of social justice interests effectively smashes the image of the myopic, misanthropic animal lover" (Beers 2006, 9).

UK and U.S. advocates for the abolition of animal enslavement have historically drawn moral comparisons with the movement to abolish human slavery (and many were supportive of both liberation movements in the nineteenth century). But the support was not typically reciprocated, and the two movements do not have an active history of working together (Wrenn 2014); most human slavery abolitionists and civil rights advocates want to steer clear of such comparisons with animals, viewing this as further dehumanizing to people of color (as seen within the hegemony of speciesism and white supremacy) (Kim 2015; Wrenn 2014).

There are some connections between women's rights and animal protection. The mainly white, middle- to upper-class women working in the U.S. humane movement in the Victorian era began to connect female oppression with the oppression of animals, as they also worked on women's rights and other social justice reforms (Beers 2006; Gaarder 2011). For example, Victorian era activists such as Frances Power Cobbe connected the cruelty of vivisection to domestic violence against women—torture of animals and "wife torture" (Gaarder 2011, 7). While these coalitions are not prominent, feminist advocacy efforts continue to problematize male violence against both women and animals, including sheltering both victims (Adams and Donovan 1995; Luke 2007). As in most social movements, sexism has always existed within the animal advocacy movement; consider that prominent Victorian era animal activist and social reformer Caroline Earle White helped found the Pennsylvania SPCA but had to have her husband sit on the board and speak on her behalf since women were not allowed to serve in leadership positions (Beers 2006). Others like Emily Appleton also had to let their husbands take the spotlight, as men controlled the organizations that were largely dependent on the volunteer labor of women (Beers 2006)—sexist divisions of labor that remain a problem in the animal protection movement today, requiring feminists and animal advocates to still work in tandem (Gaarder 2011). Feminists inside and outside the animal movement have also campaigned for advocacy messages to avoid using gender stereotypes and women's bodies as a means to achieve animal protection (Wrenn 2015).

Sexism and speciesism intersect in many other ways, such as when female activists working on animal causes are derided for being overly emotional and sentimental—especially about nonhuman beings not deemed to be worthy enough of such caring—or accused of applying misplaced motherly instincts nursing animals while neglecting their families (Beers 2006). In my experience, I have noted that the environmental movement, perceived as more masculine, is associated with respected concepts of science and rationality, while the animal protection movement, associated more with femininity, is diminished by comparison as sentimental and unrealistic (Donovan and Adams 2007).

The mistreatment of human workers and nonhuman animals by industry, especially the animal agribusiness industry, has offered opportunities for alliances. Upton Sinclair's 1906 book The Jungle offered harsh critiques of the grotesque and unsafe conditions at Chicago's meatpacking plants, with the aim to expose brutal industry treatment of immigrant laborers and animals. Ultimately, the outrage caused by Sinclair's book ended up leading to meat sanitation and public health laws rather than worker safety or animal welfare laws (Lis 2012). Lis notes that U.S. labor unions did successfully advocate for slower kill speeds in slaughterhouses in the mid-twentieth century, which did reduce some worker injuries and brought minor improvements to animals' last moments (fewer of them conscious upon being dismembered). But kill speeds increased again post World War II as the meat industry intensified and expanded to the factory farm system we have today. Opportunities for labor and animal welfare coalitions exist, as slaughterhouses are notoriously dangerous places to work (and obviously fatal for farmed animals) (Pachirat 2011). Lis (2012) also suggests that small farmers and animal welfare advocates should form coalitions to legally combat meatpacking conglomerates based on unfair market conditions (antitrust laws) and animal cruelty. There are also environmental justice coalitions to be formed against industrial animal farms, as poor and rural neighborhoods face pollutants, stench, and lower property values due to the proximity of factory farms (Imhoff 2010).

This shows how industry can be a mutual target of human, animal, and environmental protection movements. Consider Rachel Carson's (1962) groundbreaking environmental book, *Silent Spring*, which warned that the widespread use of industrial chemical pollutants caused health risks to humans, other animals, and nature, sparking many environmental and public health campaigns to ban the use of specific toxins, like DDT (Gaarder 2011). The peace movement and the environmental movement also formed alliances in the late twentieth century, particularly against the nuclear threat (weapons, radiation, and waste), such as campaigns by Greenpeace (Zelko 2013).

Also in the latter part of the twentieth century, an environmental health movement emerged, led by local communities in a human rights context to protest toxic pollutants sickening people in local neighborhoods (Davies 2015). This is especially true for neighborhoods of color, such as black residents of North Carolina lying down in the road in 1982 in an attempt to stop hazardous PCBs from being buried in their neighborhood (Bullard 2005). These grassroots campaigns to fight environmental racism and injustice have finally garnered more support from the mainstream environmental movement in recent years and are aligned with the environmental health movements and climate justice movements (Agyeman 2013; Bullard 2005; Davies 2015; Knox 2018). To demonstrate the value of human rights and environmental legal advocacy groups working together on environmental justice campaigns in the Global South, Sumudu Atapattu (2018) highlights extractive industries' pattern of exploiting both vulnerable humans and nature: "From Shell Oil in Ogoniland, Nigeria to Chevron in Ecuador, and from Bhopal, India to Freeport-McMoRan in Indonesia, the world is replete with examples of corporate excesses and impunity. Time and time again we hear of gross human rights violations and severe environmental degradation associated with multinational corporations operating in developing countries" (231). Atapattu critiques the "power asymmetry" (437) between multinational companies and developing countries and the health problems caused by industrial pollution in poor communities, without compensation, such as the lead poisoning of children living near the mine in La Oroya, Peru (operated by a U.S. company). Rights to informed consent must be enforced, as indigenous communities are often not informed of World Bank–funded 'development' projects "until the bulldozers arrive" (450) and it's too late to stop the displacement. Increasingly, human rights and environmental advocates have won legal protection for the human right to a clean environment and stable climate, strengthening both movements within national laws (Knox 2018), but Atapattu (2018, 448) argues that "the intersections of injustices that compound inequities need attention" to further strengthen environmental rights and human rights in international law. And existing laws need enforcement under an environmental justice platform; for example, racial minority populations in the United States, regardless of income, are exposed to higher levels of pollution and lower levels of federal pollution enforcements (Knox 2018).

Legal protection is also needed because environmental activists worldwide that threaten monied interests face violence and other risks to their own civil rights (Glazebrook and Opoku 2018). The group Global Witness (2017) documents the killings of eco defenders (almost one thousand people reported dead from 2010 to 2016), noting that the majority are in Latin America (such as Nicaragua and Honduras) and almost half of those murdered are indigenous peoples, such as those protesting oil, mining, or logging operations in their communities. Women eco defenders are especially targeted for sexual violence and harassment for additionally challenging patriarchal gender norms (Glazebrook and Opoku 2018). Kenyan activist Phyllis Omodo gained international attention for her fight against a battery smelter in Mombasa that sickened her baby with lead; with support from Human Rights Watch and the Goldman Environmental Foundation, she was able to establish an organization that has closed the plant and fights for health compensation to victims (Knox 2018).

To briefly touch on campaigns where animal protection and environmental protection have historically collaborated, they tend to revolve around wildlife conservation, not domestic animal welfare. In fact, many wildlife conservation organizations, such as the World Wildlife Fund or the Sea Shepherd Conservation Society, can be described both as animal and environmental protection groups. Organizations with wildlife campaigns work to defend endangered species by passing legal protections, conserving habitats, enforcing anti-poaching laws (especially for charismatic megafauna like tigers, elephants, rhinos, and sea turtles), and defending predatory species (like wolves and sharks) from persecution (Fitzgerald 2018; Kemmerer 2015). For a historic example, consider the decimation of birds like the snowy egret to produce feathered hats that were all the rage in female fashion at the turn of the twentieth century in the United States. Several women from Boston's social elite organized the legal fight and a consumer boycott to stop the plumage trade, eventually leading to the Migratory Bird Treaty Act of 1918 and the birth of the Audubon Society, a successful NGO that still advocates for birdlife and their habitats today (Souder 2013). Additionally, protection of marine mammals from hunting has been a coordinated global effort between animal and environmental groups to make trade in marine mammal parts illegal and socially unacceptable in many countries. For example, in the latter half of the twentieth century, activists collectively fought the seal hunt in Canada and the commercial hunting of whales by countries like Norway, Iceland, and Japan (Essmlali and Watson 2013; Zelko 2013). With a preferred emphasis on national or commercial operations, coalitions to stop smaller, traditional hunts of marine mammals by indigenous groups have become less popular, especially with environmental groups in recent decades (Kim 2015).

Ideological Overlap between Human Rights, Animal Rights, and Environmental Ethics

Animal rights and human rights are both anti-instrumental philosophies that problematize exploitation and objectification of anyone (Adams 1990). Animal ethics justifies the rights of nonhuman animals largely based on an extension of human rights to respect the life and liberty of all sentient individuals (Francione 1996; Regan 1983; Singer 1990). Donaldson and Kymlicka (2011, 47) support a view of animal rights that is broad enough to incorporate humans and universal enough to appeal to many human cultures—favoring the "universality of protection of inviolable rights for vulnerable selves." Additionally, attorney Lee Hall's (2010, 26) definition of animal rights could also apply, in large part, to the rights of the *human* animal: "It's the forthright claim that conscious beings should be allowed to live on their own terms, not the terms set down by those who seek to control and exploit." The focus is not on handing out privileges but on guaranteeing autonomy from domination: "The ultimate good is the allowance to continue being free, interacting with other members of one's biocommunity in the way this animal evolved to do, propagating, flourishing" (35). Yet Lee Hall (2010, 93) implies a focus on freedom going beyond being just *anti*-exploitation (freedom from) but also *pro*-individuality (freedom to): "Animal rights is not just an idea of what they will stop being; it affirmatively expects other animals to express their lives as they will, to flourish on their terms."[8]

I argue that the rights of the *human* animal (while distinct in some key ways) are encompassed within the broader category of animal rights. As such, I believe that animal rights are critical as a bridge between human rights and environmentalism, as animal rights explicitly connect the disconnected human animal back with the natural world (the world of the 'animal'). Animal rights principles also better protect humans from the "fascism" (Regan 2002, 107) that could result from applying group-dominant environmental principles to equally govern all species. These environmental principles that privilege the health of the biotic community (the greater good) would, if applied equally, threaten the individual rights of many humans. From an environmental perspective, many human cultures could be considered 'invasive' species in some contexts,[9] as they tend to erode the integrity of the biotic community, which violates Aldo Leopold's (2003) land ethic (Callicott 1993; Freeman 2015). This rationale for environmentalists to respect the rights of nonhuman animals is also endorsed by Donaldson and Kymlicka (2011, 158): "Amongst the different types of entities within the ecosystem, some beings have a subjective existence that calls for distinctive moral responses, including respect for their inviolable rights. In fact, ecologists already accept this idea; after all, they would not recommend the therapeutic culling of human beings in order to protect a vulnerable ecosystem. . . . We believe a similar principle can and should apply to animals."

Animal rights advocates want to protect all sentient individuals (even those who

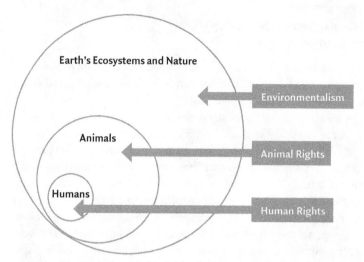

FIGURE 1 Ideal Relationship Model for the Human Animal Earthling Identity
Notice that no one is outside of nature in my ideal model, and no human is outside of the animal kingdom. Human rights are encompassed within animal rights, and animal rights are encompassed within environmentalism, making animal rights the bridge between humans' rights and nature's rights. There is no category of nonhuman animals who are solely part of human society, meaning ideally no animal would be domesticated and all would be free/wild (although humans may choose to provide care for injured or orphaned nonhuman animals, and nonhumans may rescue and support us as they wish, sharing *mutual* interactions).

eat endangered individuals), while environmentalists are willing to kill nonendangered individuals (especially invasive species) to protect ecosystems and species (especially endangered species) (Kemmerer 2015a). This alludes to some philosophical tensions that exist between animal ethics and environmental ethics, especially the tension over whether to privilege *nonhuman* individuals versus whole species (Faria and Paez 2019; Sagoff 1993). I emphasize *nonhuman* here, as mainstream environmental philosophies often assume an anthropocentrism that implicitly takes individual human rights for granted, while unfairly dismissing the rights of individual *nonhuman* animals (often ones who are more innocent and less culpable in causing environmental degradation than many humans).[10] To strengthen environmental ideology, my previous scholarship (Freeman 2015; 2010b) has suggested that environmental organizations resolve a contradiction between their claim to be holistic in valuing the well-being of *species/groups* and how their rhetoric expresses concern for the suffering and lives of certain *individual* animals (if they are human, endangered, or charismatic megafauna).[11] Ironically, their rhetoric perpetuates the human/animal and culture/nature dualisms that are at the core of the very environmental problems they seek to remedy. Therefore, I recommend that animal rights should be conceived as implicit in environmental ethics (see figure 1).

The following subsections explore how and why each movement should embrace or respect both other movements (human rights, animal protection, and environmentalism), acknowledging any specific tensions that exist and offering some resolutions and inspirations for how to work together.

HOW THE HUMAN RIGHTS MOVEMENT CAN EMBRACE ANIMAL RIGHTS AND PROTECTION

Some primary tensions to foreground here are that, from a mainstream anthropocentric perspective, it may appear to social justice activists that anyone who works on behalf of nonhuman animal welfare or rights has skewed or misguided priorities—that they have purposely or ignorantly overlooked the *social* justice causes they could be championing instead. This can indicate that the animal activists are so privileged that they are naïve to the struggles that many human minority groups still face, or worse yet, that they know but do not care (meaning they are either prejudiced or misanthropic). Those critiques may be true in some cases, and the upcoming section will address what the animal protection movement can do to confront and address their own biases. But those who belittle animal protection and its proponents for working on a 'lesser' cause and skipping over more important beings (humans) in the hierarchy should recognize the very basis of their critique (bias in favor of the human animal) is what necessitates activism on behalf of the nonhuman animals whom we humans exploit. The reason some humans need to help nonhuman animals is precisely because most of humanity views 'animals' and their interests as less worthy, a belief then used to justify their (ab)use for human benefit or profit. So even though some animal protection campaigns need to become more sensitive to human inequalities (as part of achieving the goal of total liberation), those examples should not be used as an excuse to continue to ignore or dismiss heinous injustices that most humans (whether in the minority or majority) perpetuate on nonhuman animals.

Another tension to confront is whether the continued inferiority of nonhuman animals helps ensure human rights, especially for the minority groups who have been denied the full privileges of humanity historically enjoyed by wealthy, white, cisgender, able-bodied Christian males in Western culture. It seems like it would be warranted for minority groups to worry that their special rights as humans, for which they still struggle, may be diminished if 'lowly' animals were seen as equally worthy or equally victimized. It is hard for animal rights to not seem like an insult to humans, especially those who have been discriminated against by being called 'animals.' But the goal of any social movement is not to pull oneself up to be better than someone else and earn privileges at their expense. A more socially beneficial goal is to dismantle oppressive hierarchies (and worldviews) that have enabled widespread injustice of many types of living beings.

Just as social justice activists understand that the constructed hierarchies that at-

tempt to justify oppression of certain humans are inherently unfair, those that justify oppression of nonhuman animals must also be seen as unfair. Thus, Donaldson and Kymlicka (2011) ask us not to dismiss the harm or death our actions cause
to other animals by justifying it as simply the price of human 'progress.' And if
members of other species cause us inconvenience or harm, killing them is not a
morally justifiable solution. Donaldson and Kymlicka (2011) suggest that to be fair
to everyone when making decisions, we must weigh the costs and benefits to all animals (human and nonhuman). As a guide for this inclusion, they suggest a political model (usually reserved for humans) as a familiar framework by which we can
organize our relationships and interactions with nonhuman animals—by considering domesticated animals in our communities as citizens, and wild/free animals as
sovereign beings (citizens of international nations). Working at the intersection of
sociolegal studies and critical animal studies, Dinesh Wadiwel (2009, 2015) proposes that the best way to end our violent domination against animals—what he argues constitutes a war—is not just to paternalistically look out for their welfare or
grant them 'rights' but rather to consider them sovereign beings. Philosopher Martha Nussbaum (2006) also offers a political prescription for nations to respect the
agency and autonomy of nonhuman animals to fulfill their potential, based on recognizing animal cognition and capabilities.

Another political viewpoint that justifies considering the rights of nonhuman animals alongside those of humans is the recognition that, under our current system
that offers nonhuman animals very few rights to their own liberty, some humans
will always be vulnerable to being reclassified as 'animals' (nonhuman) and losing
their protections under human rights laws (as has happened in military prisons).
Critical animal studies scholar Vasile Stanescu (2012, 70) proposes the need for animal rights laws that offer basic protection against abuse and imprisonment for anyone, stating: "The violence committed against the prisoners of Abu Ghraib reflects a
long history of showing conquered subjects as wild nonhuman animals who must,
for their own protection, be 'captured,' 'trained,' and 'domesticated.'" He is arguing that "the belief that nonhuman animals should be captured and trained serves
as a caesura in law that allows captured (human) subjects to be mistreated, to the
point of torture, in order to 'turn' them into humans" (70). In this way, the common and legally endorsed practice of domesticating nonhumans serves as a justification or model for taming the supposed animality in humans that the state deems
unruly, to make them more 'productive' to society. Similarly noting the legal vulnerability for minority human groups to be deemed 'animal,' intersectional activist Aph Ko (2015) argues that "anyone who falls outside of that category called 'human' . . . aka white-cis-wealthy-heterosexual-man, you are one step away from being
labeled 'sub-human' or 'animal' and thus, experiencing violence legally."

Many scholars have noted how all oppression is connected (or at least dependent on multiple factors) and must be dealt with in an intersectional way. To be

more inclusive, intersectional approaches must not only take into account race, ethnicity, gender and sexual orientation, class, ability, nationality and citizenship, religion, etc. but also species. Philosopher and spiritualist Will Tuttle (2014, 305) edited a book of essays that connects issues of injustice toward *all* beings, explaining: "In many crucial ways, our mistreatment of nonhuman animals is the core injustice that creates the basic structural context in our culture that makes the many faces of social injustice to humans inevitable." By this he means that animal agriculture, in particular (but also other common practices whereby we use other animals for our own pleasure), psychologically drives human conflict and injustice as it teaches us to repress our natural sensitivities to be respectful and kind toward others, as we "are injected with a cultural program of violence toward defenseless and enslaved animals, and the ripples of that radiate as exclusivism" (21), which feeds various forms of entitlements and alienation from other people.

In his anthropological analysis, sociologist David Nibert (2014) also argues that nonhuman animals' domestication (he calls it "domesecration") by humans is the root cause of our social inequalities within human culture: "It is impossible to resolve the pressing problems of our world without addressing the subjugation of other animals. Human use of other animals has undermined the development of a just and peaceful world for all species, and their continued oppression—especially for use as food—constitutes one of the most significant threats to both human rights and environmental sustainability" (149). The thesis of Nibert's 2013 book *Animal Oppression and Human Violence* is that the ranching and pastoralist practices adopted by various human cultures worldwide, whereby large animals became seen as sources of wealth, caused widespread violence not just toward nonhumans but toward humans, especially "devalued" groups like women and indigenous peoples who also then began to be seen as property (2). Resulting harms against humans include "invasion, conquest, extermination, displacement, repression, coerced and enslaved servitude, gender subordination and sexual exploitation, and hunger" as well as disease epidemics (5). Additionally, since the exploitation of animals enabled the expansion of capitalism, it fueled the entangled oppression of humans and other animals as part of elites' "desire for material gain" (5). Nibert believes economics is the primary motivation driving most oppression.

These views about animal farming being a root cause of injustice parallel anthropological arguments made by Jim Mason (1997) in *An Unnatural Order* and Carol Adams (1991) in *Sexual Politics of Meat* that humans (especially men) should not see themselves historically as a violent, predatory, dominant being who has always killed and eaten nonhuman animals. We can tell a different, more egalitarian origin story for our species for the tens of thousands of years the human diet was more herbivorous, not only in the prehunting era but especially the pre-agricultural eras before accumulation and masculine domination viewpoints led to economic inequality, oppression of women, war, and slavery. Animal activist David Cantor

(2014, 31) proposes changing our humanist ideology to a new animalist ideology via a name change from *Homo sapiens* to *Homo complexus*, to encourage us to go from seeing ourselves as a "killer ape" to a "tyrannized peaceable ape narrative."

Part of why humans have largely chosen to identify with a historical narrative of being an apex carnivore more than a herbivore is anxiety over being reduced to mere prey by a carnivorous animal. Lee Hall (2010, 93) claims, "The greatest challenge we face is imagining humanity without the master role. Is it our fear of free animals' power (over our children, our dogs, our cows, the back yard at night, the woods our government claims for the people, our own bodies) that keeps us from imagining another identity for ourselves?" She contends that our fear of free-living animals (a desire for self-preservation) is at the heart of our motivation to control them, and that is why we have a history of domination. Research on terror management theory informs this, as experimental psychologists have found that when humans are reminded of their own mortality, they are more likely to distance themselves from and devalue 'animals.' This is hypothesized to be because humans see 'animals' as more vulnerable to being killed, hence they want to feel unique and special among species (Becker 1973; Goldenberg et al. 2001). This poses a challenge for activists, like myself, who want to encourage humans to identify with their own animality. Scientists and animal advocates Marino and Mountain (2015) have studied this mortality anxiety research; they suggested that one way to potentially reduce humans' existential angst over our status as a mortal animal is to transform our exalted view of ourselves and our relationship with nature: "The only viable future for humankind lies in achieving some level of acceptance of our own mortality and developing a more humble, and ultimately more satisfying, relationship to our fellow animals and the natural world" (17).

Besides our psychological reticence to acknowledge that we are just another mortal animal, humans may not want to embrace their animality due to the history of 'animal' being deployed (mainly by the dominant white culture) to purposely discriminate against and demean racial or ethnic groups and attempt to morally justify their oppression. This poses a challenge for animal rights advocates today in asking all humans to proudly see themselves as animals (or better identify with the plight of nonhuman animals), causing a tension between the animal rights and human rights movements. In the next section, I seek further explanations and remedies that may inspire unification and increased understanding.

Tensions and Connections between Racism and Speciesism. Showing sympathy for both critical race studies and critical animal studies, some scholars highlight how the concept of 'animal' has functioned as a way to marginalize and discriminate against not only nonhuman animals but also people of color. Vegan and antiracism activist and blogger Aph Ko (2015) explains: "The category of human is anchored to the fictional superiority of whiteness, and the category 'animal' is anchored to the fictional inferiority of anything labeled non-white." She goes on to clarify that the 'ideal' human category is comprised of "white, man, able-bodied, Christian, cis-heterosexual, wealthy, while the animal/subhuman category is comprised of nonwhite, persons with disabilities, non-christian, trans/queer/non-binary, low income" (Ko 2016).

Ko (2015) contends that the concept of 'animal' is socially constructed and defined by dominant human groups who created it "to objectify certain bodies so that their violations and abuses are seen as normal, and even justified." One of the most horrific and obvious violations of someone's rights is enslavement. Regarding historical slavery in the U.S. South, Ko (2015) argues: "Slavery wouldn't even be possible without speciesist thinking—one way white people justified the enslavement of black people was by trying to show how black people were animals." This is documented in Marjorie Spiegel's 1996 book *The Dreaded Comparison: Human and Animal Slavery*, which demonstrates the painful similarities between the abuses against enslaved people of African descent in the eighteenth and nineteenth centuries and enslaved nonhuman animals then and now (the latter being in the farming, entertainment, and research industries). She demonstrates the grotesque similarities in the torturous equipment of control and restraint used in slavery, cruel transport methods, separation of family members, rape and sexual violation, marketing of bodies for sale, hunting and capture, secrecy of the abuses from the public to maintain support, and use of religion and superiority narratives for moral rationalization of this oppression. To expose the abuses of enslavement, abolition movements formed on behalf of both human and nonhuman animals who were/are enslaved (Spiegel 1996).

Political scientist Claire Jean Kim (2015) explains the interwoven concepts of race and species in her book *Dangerous Crossings*. She argues that race and species are "synergistically related" (18) because "differences are co-constituted" (16) and must be dismantled simultaneously, rather than being perceived as two distinct causes: "Animalization has been central not incidental to the project of racialization. . . . Race has been articulated in part as *a metric of animality*, as a classification system that orders human bodies according to how animal they are—and how human they are not—with all of the entailments that follow" (18). Yet conflicts sometimes arise between racialized human groups and nonhuman animal protection groups (largely white or nonracialized), such as over hunting or meat-eating practices of a certain human cultural minority group, or when an animal rights campaign compares human and nonhuman tragedies. Rather than each group seeing the situation narrowly through the optic of their own cause and disavowing the other, Kim (2015) suggests using a multioptic view that follows an "ethic of mutual avowal" (20) whereby you recognize ways in which your struggles are connected or mutual.

To do so, both animal and civil rights groups should denaturalize race through considering imperial histories and also "denaturalize species difference and consider the history and contours of human supremacy" (Kim 2015, 15). Interrogation of the social construction of humanness is essential not only to animal rights but also to civil rights:

> In the end the effort to gain full humanity by distancing from nonhuman animals, like the effort to achieve moral considerability for animals through racially fraught, racism-denying analogies, is a misbegotten project: it has not succeeded and cannot succeed because race cannot be unsutured from species and dismantled while species categories motor on in force. Rather, these two taxonomies, intimately bound with one another, must be disassembled together in our efforts to meaningfully and radically rethink the category of the human. (286–287)

Similarly, Syl Ko argues it is unproductive for antiracist groups to reinforce the human/animal divide to gain rights for people of color by emphasizing their humanity: "As long as these notions of 'the animal' and 'the human' are intact, white supremacy remains intact. For this reason, I have advised against the strategy of 'humanizing' groups of color or gaining protections for vulnerable groups on the basis of their humanity" (in Ko 2015). Aph Ko (2015) recommends that instead of trying to align with the dominant group and gain their approval, antiracism groups should support the marginalized 'animal' instead: "I'm arguing if we don't side with the animals, we're siding with white supremacy, a system that is invested in anti-blackness."

Fayaz Chagani (2016) puts these sentiments into a postcolonial perspective and advocates for postcolonial scholars to recognize the problems inherent in "humanizing" the colonized humans as a basis for determining their worth, at the expense of other animals: "Decrying the 'dehumanizing' practices that accompany (neo-) colonialism preserves and entrenches the domination of the rest of the living. As a basis for critiques of injustice, dehumanization sets the category of the 'human' as the threshold of ethical and political considerability." Anthropocentric bias in postcolonial studies overlooks how nonhuman animals are also imperialized and colonized subjects of violence (Chagani 2016). Even though green postcolonial scholars Huggan and Tiffan (2010) champion nonhuman animals, many ecocritical postcolonial scholars still undercut nonhuman animals and nature when they value them primarily as a means to human ends, according to Chagani (2016).

Similarly, environmental communication scholar and social activist Emily Plec (2015) contends that the exclusionary ideology of human exceptionalism should be interrogated by today's social justice activists because it has functioned to privilege white humans as exceptional and superior. She explains why antiracist activism should also be antispeciesist: "The parallels between the discourse of human exceptionalism and white supremacist rhetoric are not coincidental, with many critics of speciesism employing arguments that parallel the positions of plantation owners and other opponents of abolition" (144).

Ko (2016) recommends that fellow antiracist activists avoid saying, "Black people experience racism and, therefore, are treated like animals." She clarifies that this phrase, "treated like animals," is "redundant simply because racism is *already* entangled with speciesism. What black folks are experiencing isn't 'like' non-human animal oppression . . . it is a layer *of* it." Other points of awareness for civil rights groups include Kim's (2015) suggestion that, in the context of American culture, animal rescue efforts (such as the rescue of companion or farmed animals during Hurricane Katrina in New Orleans) should not be perceived as favoring the lives of nonhuman animals over human minority groups, as that "reduces nonhuman animals to instruments for measuring degrees of anti-Blackness" (286). Both humans and nonhumans deserve rescuing in times where they were abandoned and made to feel their lives and well-being were less important than wealthy, white humans. "Defending Black humanity does not logically require reinscribing the subordination of nonhuman animals" (Kim 2015, 286).

Because white supremacy has always had a vested interest in maintaining its superiority over minority groups, they are untrustworthy on issues of nonhuman animals too; thus Ko (2015) advises, "We shouldn't trust white supremacy telling us that animals are beneath us, because guess what, this system also believes that we, as black people are beneath them. Why are we siding with white supremacy when it comes to their opinions on animals?" Ko's recommendation for activists is to strike at the roots of oppression: "We can't just attack expressions of white supremacy like police violence, mass incarceration, etc. We have to attack its framework that justifies white superiority and the inferiority of everyone else, which is largely hinged upon who is human and who is animal."

Sociologist David Pellow (2014) notes that white supremacism's reliance on privileging a certain kind of 'human' connects the animal and earth liberation movements with the human liberation movement. He argues that activists in these movements who go up against the "dominant social order" (11) face threats or marginalization as 'extremists' or 'terrorists': "The 'terrorist' label imposed on these movements reveals not only repression against a politically radical 'other' but also a momentary designation of these movements as politically *racial* others—people who are criminalized because their ideas and actions are at odds with white supremacy and human supremacy" (11). When one is radicalized, one is racialized, so that even white activists are identified more with the subhuman or animal than the human.

Plec (2015) acknowledges the difficulties inherent in addressing the entanglement of interlocking oppressions between humans and nonhumans: "To escape the racist (and sexist) wedding of people of color (and women) to animals, we had to lift and distinguish ourselves, leaving the animals—with all their instructive otherness and similarity—firmly pressed below. So pulling racism and speciesism back together hurts for what it implies" (144). Despite the discomfort in comparing humans and nonhumans, Will Kymlicka (2013) suggests that we must explore the continuities between oppression in the human and animal case because we need to learn about a new relationship, since we are so "impoverished in examining human animal relations" in the academy and in society.

Kim's (2015) solution is for all activists to recognize that the fate of human minority groups and nonhuman animals is tied up together, as the category of 'human' has always been about excluding groups in ways that attempted to justify their discrimination as lesser beings. Therefore, "the project before us is not an *extensionist* one (expanding the definition of the human to allow a few racialized groups or preferred ape species in) but rather a *reconstructive* one (reimagining humans, animals, and nature outside of systems of domination)" (Kim 2015, 287). In speaking to progressive activists, Ko (2015) suggests that "we should use our own experiences with white supremacy and patriarchy as a launching pad to build coalitions with other oppressed groups because remember, the goal of coming together isn't to highlight how we're the same or different, it's to dismantle the systems that oppress us all very differently."

In doing so, Maneesha Deckha (2012) contends that posthumanist, ecofeminist scholarship on animal issues should deepen its intersectionality to be less gender-myopic and further embrace postcolonial perspectives foregrounding both *race* (interrogating how whiteness informs the human/animal binary) and *cultural difference* (interrogating how colonial logics and "civilization discourses positioning Western culture as superior to non-Western cultures" still influence discussions of human-animal relationships) (530). The next subsection expands on the latter, postcolonial and speciesist perspectives.

Connections between Indigenous Rights and Animal Rights. Philip Armstrong (2002) suggests that both postcolonial and animal scholars should embrace diversity among 'othered' groups—human and nonhuman animals—and show "respect for local differences" (416), seeking cross-cultural and cross-species understanding: "Encountering the postcolonial animal means learning to listen to the voices of all kinds of 'other'" (417). Armstrong (2002) contends that animal studies and postcolonial studies should inform each other because the latter recognizes that the human/animal dichotomy and notions of human supremacy largely derive from European colonialism, and many indigenous cultures directly challenge these Western values of domination. Similarly, Billy-Ray Belcourt (2015) argues that decolonization must center around "non-speciesist human-animal intra-subjectivities" (8) found within indigenous mythologies that view animals as kin. Belcourt, a member of North America's Driftpile Cree Nation, asks animal activists and scholars to avoid just accepting the white settler-colonial state as a normative 'given' to work within on reforming (as he claims Donaldson and Kymlicka do in *Zoopolis*). Instead, in a quest for total liberation, we must make central the "unsettling of the colonial history through which settler-colonial life-ways are already Indigenous death-ways" (Belcourt 2015, 2). This involves "re-theorizing domesticated animal bodies as *colonial subjects*" and "capitalist subjects" (3) who were forced to labor within "industrialized, colonized, and vacated spaces (such as [factory] farms, urban apartments, and 'emptied' forests)" (3). Belcourt (2015) argues for a "decolonial animal ethic" that is also a *land ethic* where the very notion of animality would be re-created by "repatriation of land to Indigenous peoples" (4) and abolition of speciesist spaces such as zoos, research labs, and slaughterhouses. Adding to Andrea Smith's (2010) "three primary logics of white supremacy—slaveability/anti-black racism, genocide, and orientalism" (1), Belcourt (2015) offers a fourth logic—anthropocentrism: "Anthropocentrism, I argue, is therefore, the anchor of speciesism, capitalism, and settler colonialism. This logic holds that settlers (as reifications of whiteness) are always already entitled to domesticated animal bodies as sites of commodity/food production, eroticism, violence, and/or companionship" (4). As an example of connecting white supremacy, anthropocentrism, and colonialism, Belcourt views animal agriculture as a capitalist scheme requiring privatization of land and removal of indigenous bodies, and is thus a political space where "speciesism intersects with the logic of genocide" (5). Adding to this, David Nibert (2014) outlines how European settler ranchers, "cattle kings" (152), viewed Native Americans and free-living animals as impediments to personal profits, pushing them farther West or eradicating them—a practice, in part, still sanctioned today via government wildlife killing programs largely at the behest of ranchers, many of whom are grazing their domesticated animals on public lands for very low costs, despite the ecological problems it causes.

Colonial extermination and land theft are predicated on an anthropocentrism, or speciesism, that excludes not only nonhuman animals but also non-European peoples from the privileges imbued by the criteria of being 'human.' Despite the presence of indigenous peoples who cultivated, utilized, conserved, and lived on the land, British colonizers, in particular, arrogantly viewed lands like North America, New Zealand, and Australia as being "terra nullius" (Connell 2007, 199): belonging to no one and thus fair game to be claimed as land now owned by the crown. In a similar vein, colonizers did not view nonhuman animal species as having the right to remain in their native territory: "Well into the twentieth century, acclimatization societies in Australia and New Zealand still operated with the explicit aim of fostering the replacement of native fauna with that of the imperial homelands" (Armstrong 2002, 416). Exploiting the perceived primacy of their own perspectives on right and wrong, colonizers conveniently dismissed the territorial rights of indigenous people and their longstanding kinship with the land simply because these societies didn't have the same economic system of property rights, private ownership, and notions of "proprietary interests" (Connell 2007, 199) recognized within European law. Similarly, I would add that wildlife does not legally codify ownership of land in an economic sense, and thus their land rights are dismissed. While westerners more often view land in economic, individualistic, and dominionistic terms, indigenous cultures more often view land in terms of a relationship that socially constitutes their community, something that is arguably more in keeping with environmental conservation. Connell (2007) quotes the common saying: "In the European system, people own the land, while in the Aboriginal system, the land owns the people" (200).

Therefore, land rights are a social justice issue, as they are pivotal to cultural identity and the survival of Aboriginal cultures, according to Australian Aboriginal rights activist Mick Dodson (1997). The specific geographic landscape where an indigenous group of people lives is vital to their cultural identity. Thus, once colonizers forcefully disconnect Aboriginal peoples from their ancestral lands, the culture often can't survive displacement to a foreign space, which is why relocation often results in poverty and social alienation (Dodson and Wilson 1997). Future sections in this book will expound on the related problem of humans culling 'overpopulated' wildlife or relocating them to new territories.

In trying to find out more about the relationship between humans and nonhumans in North America prior to colonization in the late 1400s, Rita Laws (2014), a Choctaw tribal member, notes how history (and thus current Indian cultural identity) is distorted by the loss of 80–90 percent of Native peoples due to foreign diseases alone. Laws is proud to note her own precolonial ancestors were largely vegetarian, living a long life span, making clothing and shelter from nonanimal sources, and eating mainly plant-based foods they cultivated such as corn, beans, pumpkins, acorns, and berries. But European settlers encountering what looked like a "Garden of Eden" (99) often did not even recognize the Choctaws' agricultural achievements because the crops looked 'wild' and uncultivated—the same way they viewed the Native people (Laws 2014). Colonial history fails to give credit to the original American crop farmers—"nearly half of the plant foods grown worldwide today were cultivated first by New World Indians" (97)—and their sophisticated civilizations before the European invasion (Laws 2014; Nibert 2014). Many American Indian societies leaned toward plant agriculture more so than meat-eating due to a "lack of domesticated food animals, horses, guns and iron-making technology" prior to European introduction (Laws 2014, 99). Similarly, Linda Fisher (2011), a tribal member of the Ojibway Nation, also contends people native to North America ate a nourishing diet comprised of mostly plants, with meat eaten sparingly and hunting being minimal and not wasteful before the settler-colonial influence on their diets (based on the introduction of domesticated animals and guns that fostered the mass killing of bison). Fisher laments how North American settlers created a meat-centered diet that now involves factory farming of animals, which exploits workers, farmed animals, and the environment and harms human health, including that of her tribal members. She sees the current conception of American Indian culture and its heavy association with animal hunting and hides as foreign to her precolonial ancestors' respect for animal spirits and land conservation.

A limitation of my book is that much of the scholarship upon which I draw is from the Global North, where I reside, which biases the book in ethnocentric and colonial ways (Connell 2007). I look forward to the more globally diverse and nuanced scholarship that will emerge as posthumanism, critical animal studies, ecocriticism, and postcolonial studies further develop their bourgeoning merger, as Chagani (2016) proposes.

HOW THE ANIMAL RIGHTS MOVEMENT
CAN EMBRACE HUMAN RIGHTS

Activists in the animal rights movements do not always acknowledge the way ethnicity, race, gender, and species inequities are closely entangled, which can cause them to privilege fighting speciesism over fighting racism, sexism, homophobia, or economic injustice. Emily Gaarder (2011, 154) explains that within this viewpoint of the animal rights movement, "Expressing 'human' concerns about gender, race, or class is considered divisive to the movement, and even selfish. Focusing on one's own concern for liberation, voice, or equality is unacceptable when animals suffer the greatest oppression of all." Coalitions with other movements should not have to always favor animal rights as the most central issue, and the efforts for social change should be mutual. In support of the latter, Gaarder (2011) hopes that another competing framework within the animal rights movement will prevail—an inclusive one that views animal rights as an interdependent movement to end the instrumentalization of anyone. This framework "names the oppression of animals as part of a broad, intersecting web of inequality that encompasses gender, race, class, and environmental concerns. It suggests, for instance, that patriarchal and racist thought give rise to the same ideas that justify the devaluing of animals and the use of their bodies for instrumental means. This framework considers the participation of diverse groups of people within animal rights as an important aspect of the relational web" (154). I share this recommendation in my book on vegan advocacy (Freeman 2014), in which I suggest that appeals to support those who are farmed and fished must be embedded within a larger justice-based appeal to combat the "human superiority complex" (256) and all its resulting discrimination toward certain human and nonhuman species.

In a speech given on "Animal Rights, Multiculturalism and the Left," political philosopher Will Kymlicka (2013) addresses some of the charges leveled against animal protection advocates by many progressives, which impede supportive alliances among movements. Some animal campaigns are accused of being uncritically racist, sexist, or culturally imperialistic in that they "perform whiteness" and reinforce hierarchies that dominant Western perspectives are the 'humane' standards that other 'barbaric' cultures or cultural minority groups should follow. To reduce this, Kymlicka recommends that animal protection groups, especially animal welfare groups, be wary of putting the focus on cruelty, as the laws are already inequitably set up to punish minorities or individuals for what are seen as 'aberrant' and cruel cultural practices in comparison to a white Western norm. In contrast, laws often immunize majority practices by Western institutions or industries that harm animals. While not advocating for cultural relativism, Kymlicka (2013) suggests that animal protection advocates acknowledge and create a dialogue around perceived racial or cultural bias and also focus more on animal rights (rather than welfare) issues that go beyond a cruelty frame and begin to critique mainstream, institutionalized oppression in an attempt to be postcolonial and posthumanist. Additionally, all other movements on the political left have undergone a self-critique to address their privileges (around race, gender, class, religion, etc.) and embrace an intersectional perspective, and the animal rights movement must do the same in becoming multicultural. Kymlicka (2013) hopes that liberals support the animal rights movement in this process rather than alienating its adherents or using it as an excuse to dismiss their cause.

Vegan social justice activist and scholar A. Breeze Harper (2010, 35) notes that eco and animal campaigns can come across as a "white thing," as the activists themselves are predominantly white, which not only makes their campaigns less effective with some communities of color but may keep the movement from being as diverse as it should be. People of color may be concerned about animal and environmental protection issues but may not feel as welcome in these movements or may not see it as a priority if they are working to overcome discrimination of their own community, viewing all these causes as separate. Harper finds that the rhetorical delivery of animal rights and environmental campaigns is "often entrenched in covert whiteness and white privilege that are collectively unacknowledged by white-identified people engaged in them" (35); she recommends a more culturally sensitive message to help white activists connect to people of color or the working class. Otherwise, the appeal to consume ethically can come across as elitist, colonialist, and ignorant of the problems and struggles faced by many people of color or the poor. This can include an acknowledgment that people with fewer resources likely face additional obstacles that make it harder for them to practice veganism and green consumerism. Thus, it is best to avoid the reductionist campaign message that being green or vegan is "easy" and "simple."

In resolving conflicts that sometimes arise between a human minority group and an animal protection group, Kim (2015) supports the goal of both movements mutually avowing each other through a multioptic empathetic lens. To do so, she suggests that whites especially should not deny that race and its legacy of inequality and discrimination is a component that is valid to consider and that their own demands about how to treat nonhuman animals can come across as imperialistic, following a historical pattern of white people telling people of color what is right and how to live. Animal protection groups also need to be judicious about comparing an animal rights abuse to a human rights abuse (e.g., human slavery, the Holocaust) to avoid using the latter merely as a tool by which to gain attention for their own cause (implying that discrimination of the racialized human group is resolved, and they are not continually made to feel subhuman). This may impede forming alliances.

In a conference paper I presented on PETA's "Holocaust on Your Plate" vegan campaign, I concluded that comparisons between nonhuman murder with that of human slavery, concentration camps, and human genocides are best made by members of the group who was or is oppressed (Freeman 2007). I do have sympathy for expressing these parallels (in limited instances and with care) as part of a needed attempt to ask humans to identify with their own animality, thereby deconstructing the human/animal dualism that justifies oppression of the animal 'other.' Critical animal studies scholar Steven Best (2014) also does not think the Holocaust or slavery comparisons should be ruled out, so long as they are historically informed, factually accurate, and culturally sensitive (recognizing that racism still exists), and they acknowledge the legitimate differences while also emphasizing the important similarities. But some people who are offended by well-meaning analogies between humans and 'animals' are offended based largely on speciesist views that ultimately enable the killing, as they do not believe that nonhuman animals are very important or deserve to be free as humans do (and do not want to see themselves as animals) (Best 2014; Freeman 2007). In those cases, Best (2014, 32) argues "we must not accept blanket rejections of the validity of 'animal slavery' and 'animal holocaust' terminology, such as [that] voiced in blatantly speciesist ways."

Best contends that animal rights should not be considered a new abolition movement that replaces the 'old' abolition movement against the historical enslavement of humans, but as a "continuous and coherent struggle against slavery in modern society. It advances a positive aspect of human nature that manifests in increasingly inclusive ethical systems, the universalization of rights, and thereby the expansion of liberties, democracy, equality, and community" (Best 2014, 38). This acknowledges that while enslavement of nonhuman animals is globally pervasive (and largely legal), mass enslavement of the human animal persists in current times and is also globally prevalent, albeit illegal. Some of the basic legal appeals used successfully in the human slavery abolition movement inspire legal scholars working on behalf of nonhuman animal rights today. For example, Gary Francione (1996) argues we must abolish the legal status of nonhuman animals as human property. And Steven Wise (2000; 2005), through his Nonhuman Rights Project, is working in the U.S. state court system to argue for personhood status for individual captive chimpanzees and elephants (based on habeas corpus rights not to be held captive against their will).

Because of their contention that white male supremacy is the root cause of systemic violations against anyone deemed subhuman or 'animal,' Aph and Syl Ko (2017) suggest that animal rights efforts will be most effective if coordinated together with (or from within) the antiracism movement. Through the Sistah Vegan Project, Harper (2015, 37) attempts to provide a connection and culturally resonant message that encourages women of color to acknowledge how "our antiracist and antipoverty praxis must promote a break from addictive, ecocidal, uncompassionate consumption." In addition to the Sistah Vegan blog and vegan conferences that partner with the Black Lives Matter movement, some other spaces for black vegan community have formed as a supplement/complement to the mainstream vegan movement in the United States, such as black vegetarian societies and festivals and Aph Ko's Black Vegans Rock website. I have noticed that animal rights conferences have started to address white privilege as an internal issue and create more awareness of how the movement can become not only more racially and culturally diverse but also more culturally open, self-aware, and self-critical, and it can build bridges to sincerely support anti-oppression movements.

Intersectional scholar and activist Anthony Nocella (2014) provides guidance on how people (particularly white, able-bodied activists from animal and environmental movements) can be an ally to human rights activists working on racial and disability injustice causes. Be an ally by engaging with humility, sincerity, and accountability for your own role in oppression. Be willing to speak up to call out prejudices from members of your own groups when they arise. When joining social justice movements, do so without an agenda to promote your own cause. Instead, be willing to listen, self-reflect, learn, support, serve, follow, and build trust.

HOW THE ANIMAL RIGHTS MOVEMENT CAN EMBRACE ENVIRONMENTALISM

In her anthology on finding common ground between animal and earth activists, Kemmerer (2015a) notes that both movements share an interest in protecting habitat, expanding our moral circle, and eradicating speciesism and anthropocentrism. Additionally, some of the goals of deep ecology's philosophical viewpoint (Devall and Sessions 1985) are in sync with that of animal rights philosophy, in that they both challenge human entitlement and ensure that the needs and interests of nonhumans are not subordinated to human interests (L. Hall 2010).

Lee Hall (2010) argues that the animal rights movement should ideally envision more wild animals (what she often calls "free-living" animals) and less captive ones for humans to save, yet animal advocates often focus on the latter. Environmentalists sometimes think that animal protection goals are overly sentimental or unrealistic, and Hall contends that animal advocates must not construct a world where the goal is for humans and other animals to avoid all suffering and risk, as those are an inherent part of nature. Instead, she recommends that animal rights campaigns represent nonhuman animals with dignity instead of perpetuating a stewardship narrative where they are represented as weak victims who need human heroes to rescue or care for them. Making nonhumans dependent upon humans limits their freedom and creates unequal relationships. The popular use of animal imagery that emphasizes human mercy or their cuteness can diminish human respect for them; it is preferable to show them out in nature as fellow adults who are part of "free living communities" (31). She suggests that the animal protection movement shift its focus to protecting free-living nonhuman animals and their habitat instead of campaigning for more space for captive farmed animals, which just further displaces wilderness.

In my first book, I recommend that animal activists' vegan campaigns not only emphasize justice for farmed animals and fishes but also emphasize environmental responsibility, especially how hundreds of millions of free (wild) animals are impacted by our animal-based diets (Freeman 2014). This includes us polluting animals' habitats, usurping their freshwater or land, or killing them via drowning (as 'bycatch' in nets) or via human hunters who view some species as predators competing for the fishes or pasture animals whom farmers and fishers want to kill and sell in the market. Hunting by humans is a point of contention between animal protection advocates and some environmentalists. Ecologically speaking, while *farming* of animals is unnatural, *hunting* by carnivores and omnivores is something that is a natural and inevitable practice for the cycle of life. Thus, within the animal rights movement, I think we could start opening up to the fact that hunting by certain human omnivores (even though it involves killing) should not always be considered unethical if necessary in some regions for subsistence and sheer survival of human families (as omnivorous and carnivorous animals do to provide for basic nutrition) and in a quick and more primitive way (i.e., not with steel leg-hold traps or explosives) (Freeman 2014). I am not advocating commercial hunting and fishing that encourages excess killing to accumulate bodies to profit in the marketplace. The ethicality of hunting is something that each human society will need to address culturally to determine how necessary any form of animal hunting or fishing truly is to their survival, and globally we can work toward equitable (organic) plant-based food distribution to help eliminate the need for animal killing (Freeman 2010a). This viewpoint allowing limited subsistence hunting and fishing (seeing the human animal as not only herbivorous but also omnivorous when needed) is more flexible than animal advocates usually are but more restrictive than environmentalists usually are on the issue of hunting. I think it could provide a needed path for cooperation between animal rights and environmental movements. I will discuss the human practice of hunting for recreation or to supposedly control animal populations in the next section.

HOW THE ENVIRONMENTAL MOVEMENT
CAN EMBRACE ANIMAL RIGHTS

In the procurement of food for human society, the type of killing that is most ethically problematic and in defiance of animal rights and ecological principles is farming and commercial fishing (to sell animals in the marketplace) because it is not done by other mammals, is domineering and perpetuates a humanist mind-set over nature, and is excessive and often unsustainable (Freeman 2015). In particular, humanity's development of animal agriculture about ten thousand years ago normalized structural violence against nature and nonhumans (and often human groups too), reducing them primarily to commodities to own, control, or manage, and making many free-living animals seem like pests and competitors, "justifying the mentality of speciesism: that humans are inherently superior to animals" (Tuttle 2014, 286).

Much evidence exists acknowledging the unsustainability and environmental destructiveness of humans farming animals and commercially fishing them, in terms of land use, wilderness destruction, freshwater use, fossil fuel/energy use, biodiversity loss, pollution of water and air (including greenhouse gas emissions), incidental killing of billions of 'nontarget' sea animals, and killing of wildlife deemed as 'competitors' or 'pests' (Anderson 2012; Andersen and Kuhn 2014; EAT-Lancet 2019; FAO 2006; Kemmerer 2015b; Pew 2007; Poore and Nemecek 2018; Singer and Mason 2006). Yet the mainstream environmental advocacy groups (at least in the United States) do not tend to prioritize campaigns advocating for plant-based diets, as was the theme of the documentary *Cowspiracy: The Sustainability Secret* (Andersen and Kuhn 2014; Freeman 2010a). Their food-based campaigns instead tend to emphasize eating local, organic, nongenetically engineered foods. When they do highlight the unsustainability of current agribusiness or fishing practices that produce animal flesh, dairy, and eggs, their solutions tend to favor simply cutting back (rather than eliminating these foods) or switching to 'sustainably raised' animal products or 'sustainable seafood' species (Freeman 2010a; Laestadius et al. 2013).

Laestadius et al. (2016) critically investigated the motivations environmental movement staff have for not openly advocating for a shift to a plant-based diet, and it included their own meat consumption habits, workplace culture that did not emphasize veganism, and a sense that dietary campaigns are not part of their mission and also may not be strategically effective or appealing. Regarding the latter point, my own sense is that environmental groups may be reticent to align themselves with what is largely seen as an 'animal rights' issue (for fear of offending supporters/members who hunt or are more religious and do not want to see themselves as fellow 'animals'). Some of these concerns can be addressed by my previous section's discussion of how some subsistence hunting may be necessary to procure human food in some regions, and other discussions in this book about the overlap between human and nonhuman animal rights. But, either way, there is a need for the environmental movement to be more self-reflective and ask for the kind of major changes, such as veganism, that are necessary for humans to live within the earth's ecological capacities (Anderson and Kuhn 2014; Laestadius et al. 2016), and to show moral continuity in respecting all animals (as they do the human animal) (Freeman 2010a; Kemmerer 2019).

Besides animal-based diets, another issue that causes tension between environmental and animal rights advocates is how to deal with free-living animal species deemed 'overpopulated.' Environmentalists or natural-resource government agencies often propose hunting/culling of 'overpopulated' species as part of ecological 'wildlife management' practices to maintain a healthy population for those or related species (Kemmerer 2015b). Gallo and Pejchar (2016) found that common wildlife management practices, especially geared toward supporting 'overpopulated' species that hunters prefer, are not based on sound science and can be counterproductive to the ecosystem. Lee Hall (2010) notes that a solution that is both supportive of environmentalism and animal rights is to ensure that the free-living animals have adequate space to thrive and migrate (i.e., reduce urban sprawl or human development), and to reintroduce natural predators into the ecosystems to maintain balance, as they tend to prey on weaker animals (rather than having human hunters take the biggest individuals for a trophy). From an ethical perspective, Hall argues that it is unfair to employ any methods toward free-living nonhumans that we would not employ to restrict our unsustainable and extensive human population growth (such as forced sterilization).

Throughout his book on the ethics of species, philosopher Ronald Sandler (2012) claims that sentient beings deserve compassion, while compassion is not something we need to give to nonsentient beings (even though we should still consider their interests). Thus, I propose that an environmental ethic that respects individual animal rights (human and nonhuman) would view plant species, natural objects, and ecosystems holistically, governed by utilitarian notions of the greater good for animal species. Here, natural objects are cared for largely to provide healthy environments for sentient beings (animals). As environmental philosopher Dale Jamieson (2002) notes, both the animal rights and environmental movements share a desire to protect habitat, so he proposes that nature be valued primarily as a home for animals who are valued more intrinsically as individuals. I agree with Jamieson's suggestion that environmentalism find ways to value nonhuman animals as they inherently value the human animal. This means that humans would attempt to solve environmental problems in ways that respect the lives and welfare of individual animals,[12] even ones who are not members of an endangered species. Animal rights philosopher Tom Regan (2002) argues that instead of primarily hoping that the practice of privileging *group* interests will benefit its individual members, privileging the care of *individual* members can lead to a greater good for the whole group; environmental philosopher Gary Varner (1998) takes a similar ethical position based on biocentric individualism.

When it comes to resolving perceived conflicts between nonnative or 'invasive' species and native individuals or ecosystems, environmentalists could embrace an animal rights ethic that protects individual sentient beings, as they do for the human animal (who also may be ecologically problematic) (Faria and Paez 2019). Providing guidance, Donaldson and Kymlicka (2011) argue that for introduced exotic animals or feral animals, "extermination campaigns are not an acceptable response" (225), since that is the "animal equivalent of ethnic cleansing" (211); any calls for relocation of these individuals should only be considered if it is proven that they are truly destructive. In support of fair treatment, these authors contend: "It is unfair to have a zero tolerance policy as regards animal risks to humans, while completely disregarding the risks we impose on them. . . . Any viable scheme of co-existence in shared territory requires mutual restraints and mutual accommodations" (Donaldson and Kymlicka 2011, 244–245). Almiron and Tafalla (2019, 8) agree that rather than investing so much effort in culling animals, environmentalists should invest more in enabling humans to curtail our own population and our own destructive practices (e.g., eating animals, driving cars). The authors critique the environmental movement's speciesist choices by saying: "It seems easier to demand that animals sacrifice their entire lives than to renounce human caprices."

Our moral obligation is to find creative ways to minimize harm to all parties and coexist. Using a political model, Donaldson and Kymlicka (2011) call for us to treat wild animals as sovereign beings (akin to having international citizenship) and to treat 'liminal' animals (wildlife who live in close proximity to or within our human communities; in North America that includes species such as pigeons, coyotes, raccoons, moose, mice, feral cats, deer, songbirds, etc.) as denizens/residents, following a multicultural appreciation model that inspires peaceful coexistence.

To balance human rights and environmentalism, the practice of protecting individual rights should not preclude governments or societies from placing responsible restrictions on human behavior in accordance with what is deemed beneficial to preserving the whole ecosystem, as deep ecology principles suggest (see Devall and Sessions 1985), but regulations should be enacted in ways that are not unfairly restrictive of each human's personal expression and basic liberties; we must ensure that we combat environmental racism/injustice.

The environmental justice movement, as currently constituted, aims to protect humans from environmental toxins and exploitation, which is indicative of the special privileging of humankind inherent in human rights causes. While cruelty toward nonhuman animals may be peripherally condemned by human rights advocates (including the environmental justice movement), this respect for animal *welfare* (especially for domesticated animals) is not generally extended to a respect for nonhuman animals' *rights* to bodily integrity, life, and liberty. In fact, the use of nonhuman animals as resources has often been seen as a human right.[13] So the animal rights movement has historically been distinct in protecting the basic liberty of all animal individuals, including condemning any domestication, enslavement and imprisonment, or use of animals for human purposes, particularly when it is not vital to human survival (Nibert 2013).

Human self-interest may currently view the lower status of other animals as a benefit because it justifies our farming and eating them or simply culling them to resolve any conflicts. But if humans begin identifying with fellow animals and seeing themselves as citizens within the broader animal kingdom, Donaldson and Kymlicka (2011, 254) contend that it would make the needed switch to a plant-based diet psychologically appealing to us: "We may hope that one day, humans will not view prohibitions on eating animal flesh as a burden or sacrifice, because people will not think of themselves as the sort of people who want to engage in that behaviour. In this way, changing moral sensibilities redefine our sense of self, and hence our sense of self-interest." If humans embrace an animal rights ethic, it may serve to logically enhance the environmental movement's efforts to get humans to identify with wildlife, natural habitats, and ecosystems.

HOW THE ENVIRONMENTAL MOVEMENT CAN EMBRACE HUMAN RIGHTS

A burgeoning subset of the environmental movement is the environmental justice movement, which foregrounds ways that human rights should guide environmental policy; it advocates that any environmental degradation, toxins, or health risks be equitably distributed among the human population globally, as currently that burden has fallen more heavily on poor people and people of color (Bullard 2005). Additionally, there is a need to protect indigenous human communities and cultures from being destroyed by industrial activities. Environmental justice would advocate that all humans, especially those with class privileges, more fully experience the risks and costs of our polluting collective actions; this equitable burden-sharing might encourage everyone to move toward healthier, more sustainable policies and lifestyles to reduce toxins (Sandler and Pezzullo 2007).

Yet environmental scholar Julian Agyeman (2013, 4) notes that, historically, the broader sustainable development and green movements have an "equity deficit" as they did not properly interrogate economic discrimination against human minority groups or adequately acknowledge the social needs and welfare of humans in their sustainability policies (see also Sandler and Pezzullo 2007). Agyeman (2013) refers to the combination of social justice and sustainability principles as "just sustainability," which is defined as "the need to ensure a better quality of life for all, now and into the future, in a just and equitable manner, while living within the limits of supporting ecosystems" (5).

Pellow (2014) notes that the environmental justice movement is mainly comprised of people of color and the working class, while the radical earth and animal liberation groups are populated more with white, middle-class, heterosexual male activists. But there are many core ideas that connect them: "In fact, the ideas that radical animal and earth liberation movements express in their public and internal movement conversations are almost entirely reflective of concepts contained at the heart of the Principles of Environmental Justice," which is a founding document of the U.S. environmental justice movement (256). Nonprofits such as Green 2.0 are attempting to increase racial diversity in the larger environmental movement. Green postcolonial scholars Alex Hunt and Bonnie Roos (2010) view the concept of justice as the bridge that unites efforts for environmentalism and postcolonialism; postcolonial activists can acknowledge how colonial practices have unjustly impacted nature and humanity (especially racial minorities), and Western environmental activists can become more racially and culturally sensitive in their mind-set and approach (Hunt and Roos 2010).

TOTAL LIBERATION FOR ALL SPECIES:
BRINGING TOGETHER RACE, ETHNICITY, GENDER, AND SPECIES

Some academic and advocacy groups are promoting intersectional perspectives on total liberation of species. Such open-access academic journals as *Journal of Critical Animal Studies* and *Green Theory and Praxis* try to promote total liberation, focusing on the intersectional analysis of human social justice, nonhuman animal protection, and environmentalism, which demands more than just theorizing about injustice; it encourages applied scholarship that promotes and supports direct action groups. Pellow (2014, 6) defines total liberation as an effort to "understand and combat all forms of inequality and oppression," based on four pillars: "(1) an ethic of justice and anti-oppression inclusive of humans, nonhuman animals, and ecosystems; (2) anarchism;[14] (3) anti-capitalism; and (4) an embrace of direct action tactics." In this solidarity effort, Pellow warns earth and animal liberation activists to be self-aware enough of injustices toward humans to avoid "imperialistic values," oversimplified notions of purity and "universal truth," or the implication that efforts on behalf of nonhumans represent "the ultimate freedom movement" or the "final frontier" of social change, which overlooks the continued oppression of many human groups (255).

Building on Best's (2010) total liberation concept, Colling, Parson, and Arrigoni (2014) promote "revolutionary decolonization" for humans and other animals, which embraces both a personal and sociopolitical transformation by which we each must liberate our own consciousness (the colonized mind-set and identity) as well as collectively taking "revolutionary actions against the structures of colonialism" (58). As part of this, the authors seek "groundless solidarity" (64) where all resistance struggles mutually support one another, which includes human solidarity with nonhuman animals as fellow agents of resistance. The authors say those in privileged positions should lend support to liberate other animals and any oppressed community without being imposing—allowing liberated beings some autonomy to define their own communities and relationships. This is part of Colling et al.'s (2014) belief that total liberation must engender "a relationship framework of mutual aid" (70).

A human group that has been overlooked within many advocacy movements is people with disabilities. Just as ecofeminism and environmental justice movements have served to intervene in the environmental and animal protection movements to challenge racism and sexism within the movements, there is a nascent eco-ability movement developing to challenge ableism (Nocella 2014). Eco-ability simultaneously challenges binaries of human/animal, domestic/wild, and normal/abnormal. Sociologist and community organizer Anthony Nocella (2014) has developed eight values of eco-ability: difference and diversity; holistic transformation through dialogue and education; inclusive social justice and a total liberation movement; intersectional, solidarity, and alliance politics; opposition to oppression and domination; engagement in critical theory and practice; techno-digital justice; and a collaborative and interdependent web of life.

Values are also an integral part of Best's (2014, xii) understanding of total liberation of species, which is "an ideal, a vision, and a goal to strive for, one that invokes visions of freedom, community, and harmony." We must understand the relationship among human, animal, and earth liberation movements, "building bridges around interrelated issues such as democracy and ecology, sustainability and veganism, and social justice and animal rights" (xii).

Taking a holistic approach to ecological and social change, Will Anderson (2012), a deep ecologist who co-founded Greenpeace Alaska and Green Vegans, proposes that we need to create a "new human ecology" where humans replace our anthropocentric identity with a biocentric identity to build a humane and sustainable future. This relies on veganism and ending "hunter fisher and animal agriculture predations" and other "neopredations" (xxvi) (i.e., building highways, warming the atmosphere, etc.) that harm animals and the environment. Anderson outlines seven results that the new human ecology must achieve: (1) healthy land and sea ecosystems requiring little human intervention; (2) an organic vegan lifestyle; (3) social and economic justice with transparent institutions; (4) immediate negative human population growth; (5) economic systems that are sustainable and not reliant on endless growth; (6) an increase in empathy, love, and compassion toward all beings and ecosystems; and (7) sustainable and equitable consumption of goods and services. He argues that the urgency of ecological problems requires all human cultures to adopt these standards, but we need to start with our own identity and behaviors first. We are required to "rethink who we are, change our perspective and worldviews, and trade in some of our most cherished behaviors for better ones" (31).

To bring all movements together around common values, consider that a popular bumper sticker for environmentalism instructs humans to "live simply so that others may simply live," while a bumper sticker for animal rights might, rather, instruct humans to "live and let live."[15] Although distinct, both slogans emphasize protecting the lives of others through a restriction on human excess, whether it is in our use of natural resources or in our unnecessary interference in the lives of other animals. These suggestions to be less selfish overlap with human rights principles of justice and an ethic of care by instructing us to be fair and empathetic toward others, such as the motto that might be found on a bumper sticker for human rights: "treat others as you would want to be treated." Thus, I propose that human rights, animal protection, and environmentalism are all social *justice* movements in some sense, as they all advocate that humans be *just*, and that we should meet our survival needs in ways that are responsible, moderate, and fair—recognizing that we must share the earth. This includes humans avoiding excess exploitation of anything (natural 'resources' like plants, water, land, etc.) or exploitation of anyone (animals) as a resource.

CHAPTER TWO

Posthumanist Philosophies Challenging the Human/Animal Dualism

Most people do not see themselves as animals, considering that to be a wholly different category than humankind—there are minerals, plants, animals, and then there are humans. In over two decades of advocating for nonhuman animals, I have discovered that the hegemonic distinction between human and animal serves as a primary boundary that constrains and impedes an average Westerner's consideration of animal rights as a valid ethical position. A harmonious conversation about animal issues splits at the point where I, as advocate, compare injustice toward nonhuman animals to that toward humans. At this point speciesism comes into play, and I have lost my audience, as the listener claims that caring about humans' interests takes priority. This is indicative of the general acceptance of animal *welfare* viewpoints in favor of better treatment of domesticated and 'useful' animals as opposed to animal *rights* viewpoints that reject the very practice of domestication and use. This leads me to believe that arguments on behalf of animal rights often lead nowhere unless we deconstruct the human/animal dualism that lies at the heart of speciesism.

I argue in this chapter that advocates should prioritize notions of *humanimality* or, in other words, how humans might rhetorically construct themselves as animals. Yet this is a challenge for activists, as Western society is built on humanist principles that celebrate humanity's specialness and define it in opposition to animality. So the question becomes, How can animal advocates talk about humans and other animals in ways that are posthumanist yet resonate with the public?[1] In answering this question, I draw on posthumanist scholarship to critically analyze how these humanist tensions not only affect, but also exist within, animal rights philosophy itself, likely weakening arguments in favor of animal rights. My goal is to improve the logical basis upon which this philosophy informs animal rights advocacy.

I begin by examining how humanist terminology makes it hard to rhetorically avoid speciesism and embrace humanimality. I then analyze the paradoxes involving animal activists' deployment of humanist adjectives like *humane* and *ethical*, as well as tensions over whether animal rights strategies should promote humanity's similarity to other animals or take a new tack toward embracing the diversity among all animals. This involves not only deconstructing the human/animal binary but also the related binaries of nature/culture and similarity/diversity to unify these dualistic concepts in strategic ways.

I suggest that animal advocates should more humbly represent humans as social animals who are uniquely prone to excess, explaining the biological need for humanity's complex ethical systems (in comparison to other social animals) as opposed to viewing human morality solely as a magnanimous cultural choice. Rather than continuing to primarily craft messages saying "they are like us," animal advocacy messages should begin to promote the idea that "we are like them" in many ways that are worth acknowledging. However, the challenge in this focus on humanimality and expanded notions of identity is to find a way to respect the diversity represented in the animal world (among groups and individuals) so as to avoid creating new hierarchies or revised notions of 'the animal other.' I conclude by presenting a blended approach as a solution to better understanding the humanimal / nonhuman animal relationship.

The Problem of Humanist Terminology
INCONSISTENT DEFINITIONS OF THE TERM ANIMAL

Animal advocates must struggle with using the very central term *animal*. As Mary Midgley (1988, 35) observes, *animal* has two definitions with differing connotations: a "benign" one that includes humans; and a "negative" one that not only excludes humans but represents what is "unhuman, the anti-human." This links the human/animal and nature/culture dualisms. Similarly, social anthropologist Tim Ingold (1988, 4) explains the two opposing conceptualizations of animality as (1) a "domain or kingdom" (which includes humans—a scientific taxonomy that takes into account ecological connections/dependence) and (2) a "condition" (which excludes humans and is "opposed to humanity"). In the latter conceptualization, human culture is separated from nature, which is seen as the nonhuman's domain. This antihuman condition of being an 'animal' represents the distinction between 'natural' behaviors devoid of values or reasons and the process humans go through to become enculturated and overcome this animality. Steven Best (2014) renounces the dualisms that situate humans with culture and 'animals' with nature:

> Humans overestimate their own rationality as they underestimate the rationality of animals. Whereas humans have reduced animals to biology and thus denied animals culture, so too, focusing only on the voluntarist facets of their own [human] behavior, they have failed to grasp the biological dimensions of human culture. Much light can be shed on human behavior once we renounce cosmic narcissism and abandon the dualist and speciesist mindsets that block our

understanding of other animals and ourselves and alienate us from other species. (127)

Even though humans may understand they are technically part of the animal kingdom, to call a human an *animal* is largely considered an insult. English scholar and animal advocate Joan Dunayer (2001, 2) explains, "Nonhuman animal terms insult humans by invoking a contempt for other species. The very word *animal* conveys opprobrium. *Human*, in contrast, signifies everything worthy." When someone says "humans *and* animals," she notes, they commit a "verbal ruse" (11) denying the benign definition of animal that includes humans in the animal kingdom. I find the grammatically incorrect yet common phrase "humans and animals" is even used by animal rights campaigns, due to a combination of assumptions about the distinction and the connotation of *animal* as an affront to audience members' superior status as humans (Freeman 2014). Indeed, there is a long history of those in power using animal labels to belittle human groups for purposes of hierarchizing, marginalizing, and oppressing (Adams 1990; Spiegel 1996). Calling a human an *animal* also invokes an implicit belief in the evolution of species that categorizes humans as primates. Animal advocates may be unwilling to risk offending religious viewpoints grounded in a humanism that views humans as closer to a divinity than to apes, as the evolution versus creationism debate is highly politicized in places like the United States.

STRUGGLE FOR NONSPECIESIST TERMINOLOGY

Given the problematic double meaning of the word *animal*, it is challenging to find a nonspeciesist term to denote the proper respect for nonhuman animals. Other animals could be called *nonhuman animals*, as I choose to use in this book, or *other-than-human animals*, as both of these labels possess the benefit of reminding humans that they too are animals—humanimality is foregrounded every time *nonhuman animal* is invoked. However, these labels still mark them as an 'other' in negation to the dominant term *human*, much like *nonwhite* may imply a racial hierarchy. Activists sometimes refer to nonhuman animals using the term *being*, as in *sentient being* or *living being*, but this still does not carry the weight of *human being* as far as indicating an implicit dignity. Indeed, while the phrase "human dignity" is common, its counterpart "animal dignity" is rare.

Instead of finding a new term for other animals, humans could redefine themselves by including the word *animal* in their own description, calling themselves *human animals* instead of just *humans* to remind themselves of their mutual status as animals; this may help eliminate the use of the term *animal* as an insult toward humans. But *human animal* is awkward and inconsistent in the sense that we do not refer to other specific animal species by adding the term *animal* to their name (e.g., we do not say *dog animals*, *fish animals*, etc.). Alternately, humans could simply refer to all animals as *persons* and distinguish them, humans included, based on species names when needed. It does, however, seem like some new terms are required to properly denote the new value humans should be placing on what philosopher Jacques Derrida (Derrida and Roudinesco 2004, 63) refers to as "the multiplicity of living beings" and animals' status as members of one group. Some might find the term *infrahuman* too clinical, so perhaps *humanimal* is the best neologism proposed yet, as it reveals that the term *animal* is literally a part of *human*.[2] Advocates should carefully phrase existing words to increase respectfulness toward other animals and foreground how language has been used to covertly privilege humans.[3] But the creation of new terms also seems necessary to circumvent the speciesism inherent in a discourse built to reflect the human/animal dichotomy at the heart of the Western worldview.[4]

INABILITY TO DEFINE HUMAN BORDERS

In the debate over definitions of *animal*, Derrida prefers to embrace complexity instead of homogeneity, emphasizing that there are many differences that could be characterized as "uncrossable borders" among all animals, even among humans (Derrida and Roudinesco 2004, 66). This diversity cannot be reduced to just one definitive border between humans and all other animals: "There is not one opposition between [man] and [nonman]; there are, between different organizational structures of the living being, many fractures, heterogeneities, differential structures" (66). Archaeologist Peter Ucko (1988, ix–xvi) echoes this claim that the borderlines are indistinct, even between mammals and other animals: "Contrary to the normal assumption, the borderline between humans and animals, or more specifically between humans, and birds, fish or invertebrates, is anything but obvious, clear and immutable." In fact, Derrida states it is very difficult to identify any trait that is uniquely "proper of [man]" or exclusive to humans, "either because some animals also possess such traits, or because [man] does not possess them as surely as [he] claims" (Derrida and Roudinesco 2004, 66).

Other scholars have noted this same futile humanistic struggle for humans to find a line they can draw in the sand based on one uniquely human characteristic. Anthropologist Elizabeth Lawrence (1995), for instance, details the many allegedly 'human' traits throughout history that failed to be proven exclusively human, such as: making tools, teaching cultural practices, practicing rituals, having unique personalities, being aware of death, building and transforming nature, creating art, practicing altruism, possessing language, and experiencing wonder.

While language use was once considered a hallmark of humanity, Derrida also acknowledges nonhuman language. He explains how human language is related to that of other animals through the notion of *différance* (the fluidity and interconnectivity of meaning that relates to and relies on myriad other meaningful concepts):

> I am thinking in particular of the mark in general, of the trace, of iterability, of différance. These possibilities or necessities, without which there would be no

language, *are themselves not only human*. It is not a question of covering up rup-
tures and heterogeneities. I would simply contest that they give rise to a single
linear, indivisible, oppositional limit, to a binary opposition between the human
and the infra-human. And what I am proposing here should allow us to take
into account scientific knowledge about the complexity of "animal languages,"
genetic coding, all forms of marking within which so-called human language,
as original as it might be, does not allow us to "cut" once and for all where we
would in general like to cut. (Derrida 1995, 284–285)

For Derrida, the trait of language that might represent this border between species
is analogous to a cut in the subject, or who can be defined as a subject and not an
object. This cut, designating a sense of which subjects' interests and perspectives
matter, can be marked wherever humans choose, and he lobbies for the cut to include nonhuman animal languages.

But should philosophers keep looking for a place to cut or even continue asking
what makes humans different from other animals? Mary Midgley (2004) answers
"no" to this by acknowledging we are all complex beings who share many qualities, so searching for one differentiating factor is reductionist and futile. She proposes that fellow philosophers instead ask what the best thing about human life is
and answer according to traits that other animals may also possess. That concern is
important as a start to discursively shift the scholarly questions and the purpose of
constructing these truths so that the answers are productive rather than destructive
and enable community as opposed to separation or marginalization. Scholars and
advocates should begin exploring how all species are unified and in what ways primary differences can be viewed as strengths.

PROBLEMS DEFINING THE
MORAL BOUNDARY BETWEEN SPECIES

While there are not distinct divisions separating *all* humans from all other animal
species in ways that are morally relevant, there are scientific debates over what divisions should define "species" as a category (Sandler 2012). Some popular criteria for species categorization include being able to reproduce, having an evolutionary lineage (phylogenic), sharing similar genetics, and sharing an ecological/
regional niche. But philosopher Ronald Sandler (2012, 6) chooses a broader definition that designates a species as a group of biologically related organisms distin-
guished from other species by their "shared form of life." This means that species
boundaries have no ethical significance (not on an objective basis), including that
of *Homo sapiens* (Sandler).

Philosopher Daniel Elstein (2003) also contends that the broader categorical
concept of *species* is a contested and arbitrary social construction. He cites Charles
Darwin's belief that *species* was an indefinable category where differences between
animals were more a matter of degree than kind. Elstein claims that, although these

degrees of difference represent varying gaps between species, there is no clear way to determine how much of a gap is of moral significance.

Yet in defining moral significance, Elstein (2003) argues that it is a common logical fallacy for people to say that distinctions are based on some physical or biological trait, when it is really *mental* traits that they prioritize. *Physical* traits (such as ability to mate, DNA similarities, or physical resemblance) do not sufficiently warrant the exploitation or mistreatment of a species, while *mental* traits (such as language use, intelligence, or sentience) form the real basis for why people say species divisions matter morally. In a rather radical idea, Elstein proposes reducing the myriad of animal species down to four different (but not mutually exclusive) "moral species concepts" that are based on an animal's mental ability to: (1) plan for the future, (2) experience boredom, (3) suffer pain, and/or (4) feel emotions.

The morally relevant traits specified in Western animal rights philosophy are broader versions of these mental traits. For example, Peter Singer (1990) claims that the true moral distinguishing factor is being sentient, and Tom Regan (1983) proposes it is being a conscious subject of a life. These mental traits still necessitate a hierarchy, to some extent, where categories of animals are deemed (by humans) to be sentient and conscious enough to warrant fair treatment as a subject; for example, mammals and birds may qualify, while krill or insects may not. This hierarchy reveals the complications of hegemonic power in the creation of truth (Foucault 1980). Humans can engage in an ideological struggle to define who counts as morally significant beings, yet it is always humans (and certain groups more than others) who maintain the power to redefine mental traits in ways that could just continue to serve instrumental interests and maintain human privilege. This could even be done under the guise of animal protection, since discourse can continually be constructed and reconstructed to enable a comforting appearance that humans are treating 'the other' morally.

Human society especially privileges the mental trait of morality—a 'civilized' trait that is generally assumed to be a unique product of human culture rather than other animal societies or nature. In the next section I explore how animal advocacy rhetoric could appeal to ethics (perhaps including the notion of being 'humane' toward other animals) without reinforcing the problematic nature/culture and human/animal divides.

Ethicality and the Nature/Culture and Human/Animal Binaries
RHETORIC AND THE MISUNDERSTANDING OF VIOLENCE

A paradox exists in the lofty, 'humane' moral values that humans claim to have (and to which animal activists appeal) and the way that 'human kindness' is often not reflected in humans' actual relations with other animals. Humans' actions toward other animals seem largely based on self-interested rather than altruistic values. This reality challenges the notion that humanity is humane. Dunayer (2001) suggests that the word *humane* is both speciesist and unjustified, as it implies that kindness is an inherent part of each human's nature, yet many examples can be given of individual humans failing to show compassion. She also critiques the common use of the phrase *human kindness*, as if the two words naturally fit together, whereas the phrase *animal kindness* seems foreign and senseless to the ear.

Because humans have a high opinion of their moral values, in comparison to the supposed lack of morality in other species, if they had to bear witness to or admit the harm they actually cause other animals (such as in factory farming), it would propagate cognitive dissonance. Derrida predicts that the "industrial, scientific, technical violence" humans impose on other animals must and will change, albeit over centuries, because it will become "more and more discredited" and "less and less tolerable" (Derrida and Roudinesco 2004, 64) as it becomes visible. Further emphasizing visibility and perceptions, he theorizes that a driving force of such change is that this violence "will not fail to have profound reverberations (conscious and unconscious) on the image humans have of themselves" (64). He asks interviewer Elisabeth Roudinesco, "If you were actually placed every day before the spectacle of this industrial slaughter, what would you do?" (71), and Roudinesco replies that she would not eat meat anymore and would live somewhere else because she prefers not to see it. Her answer illustrates an earlier point Derrida makes about humanity's need to avoid acknowledging the violence: "No one can deny seriously, or for very long, that [men] do all they can in order to dissimulate this cruelty or to hide it from themselves, in order to organize on a global scale the forgetting or misunderstanding of this violence" (Derrida 2002, 394).

Our rhetorical denial of routine violence and oppression assumes that humans feel guilty about their collective mistreatment and murder of other species, if interpreted as such; therefore, *visibility* of violence is to be avoided in both images and words, requiring careful framing of the way humans view their interactions with other animals. Critical animal studies scholar Dinesh Wadiwel (2009, 2015) argues that our systemic violence against nonhuman animals constitutes a war that we mask within the 'peaceful' discourse of Western political sovereignty (which in itself is based on privileging humans over 'animals' and nature), including welfare laws against violence deemed gratuitous. He explains "the civil political space hides forms of intense domination of animal life through apparatuses that do not, at least on the outside, betray the form of war" (289). Within this notion of Western sovereignty, factory farming has "enabled death on a scale that has hitherto been completely unimaginable," prompting Wadiwel to ask: "How else can we explain the complete impotence of ethics, 'humane' thinking, and the rights framework before these horrors, without recourse to understanding how victory in war leads to an intoxication of power that guarantees a total and unending defeat of the loser through other means? It is a victory so absolute that it becomes merely everyday, apparently lacking any resistance, without politics" (289). Industrialized slaughter is banal under the protection of legal legitimacy, as "the law aims to establish a covenant of continuing freedom and plunder for the victors of war: an unending flow of pleasures, an economy of greed" (289).

The intentional misunderstanding of violence is practiced rhetorically through strategic use of the word *murder*. One way humans avoid feeling guilty, according to Dunayer (2001, 4), is by constructing the notion that "unjustified killing is murder only if the victim is human." She claims that humans "prefer to couch nonhuman exploitation and murder in culinary, recreational, and other nonmoralistic terms" (4). Ecofeminist Carol Adams (1990) also acknowledges humans' rhetorical tricks meant to deny oppression and violence in food choices. She argues that terms like *meat* and *veal* create an "absent referent" (42) in which the individual nonhuman victim of oppression as well as the human perpetrator are purposely removed from the concept. But what is the benefit of hiding this abuse if humans seek to truly be 'humane'? According to Dunayer (2001), "Speciesism is a lie, and it *requires* a language of lies to survive. Currently, our language denies the harm that humans routinely inflict on other animals; linguistically, both the victims and the perpetrators have disappeared" (ix). The answer, then, is that it satisfies a psychological need to believe oneself to be *humane*, and the need for this positive self-perception likely takes privilege over actually doing the hard work of living up to one's morals.

This reveals the complexity of the humanist tension in relation to animal ethics, since these scholars must conceive of humans as *being* a moral species to presume people need to deceive themselves linguistically in order to continue being speciesist, yet it is a paradox that humans are *not* inherently moral enough to live up to the term *humane*. As I analyze this circularity, the human claim of morality begins to look as if it might be a façade for arrogance, in which language (like the very term *humane*) is used as the veneer. Yet animal ethics and advocacy rely upon the idea that if activists rhetorically challenge people to acknowledge the harm they cause other animals, such as Anderson's (2012, xxvi) use of the explicit term "neopredation" to describe humanity's routine polluting and destruction of habitats, it *would* activate an innate morality. While people's improved behavior might be enacted primarily for purposes of egoism and self-esteem, the advocacy rhetoric reveals a belief that altruism should also be a motivating factor (Freeman 2014).

THE PARADOX OF HUMANE-KIND

I argue that the notion of human morality results in a conflict for animal advocacy whereby the very idea that humans should treat nonhumans better may be humanist. In other words, promoting an essentialist and superior view of the human being may privilege humans with a certain ethical status presumably not found in other animals. Because animal advocates claim that species differences are more a matter of degree than kind, I contend that if they were to be truly morally consistent, instead of supporting an implicit paternalism toward other animals, they would have to expect all other animals to have ethical standards and responsibilities too (albeit based on the animal's individual capacities and free will and not necessarily a contractarian notion of exact reciprocity). This poses a rhetorical conundrum for animal rights activists over how to call for ethical behavior without eliciting elitist notions of 'humanity' in opposition to an implied brute animality. But when it comes to the supposedly humanist notion of morality, if society conceives of moral principles as deriving from nature and not just human culture, then it logically follows that morality might also naturally apply to many social animal species.

Recent research contends that social species *do* have general expectations for cooperative and moral behavior within their group. Animal ethologist Marc Bekoff and philosopher Jessica Pierce (2009) find that humans are not the only animal to develop morality and justice, as other social animals practice fairness, empathy, altruism, and trust in their own ways with varying levels of complexity. These scholars coined the term *animal morality* to describe the prosocial behaviors that they believe are a product of both biological and sociocultural factors. They describe morality as specific to each species and note that individual animal behavior may vary in how well each chooses to observe these group standards, indicating animals exhibit a sense of free will and are not just guided by instinct.

The claim that humans are not the only moral animal could be left at that; however, I will additionally explore the idea of a 'natural' universal morality that applies to individuals of most animal species, transcending the notion of morality being limited to the culture of social or 'higher' animals (and its implication that humans must therefore be the highest and most moral animal due to their choice to privilege cultural rather than natural tendencies). As nature and culture conflate here, I examine human ethics by deconstructing it within the nature/culture dualism.

THE NATURE VERSUS CULTURE DEBATE
IN ETHICS FOR HUMANITY

Consider that human ethics generally values the compassionate tendency of humans to protect the weak or innocent, such as children or the sick, from predation and exploitation by the strong. This protection from exploitation is the basis of social justice movements and, on the surface, appears to be in opposition to the harshness of a simplistic 'survival of the fittest' view of nature. Yet humans' ethical prohibition against causing harm is legally limited to harm in *excess* of what is necessary for one's survival (consider self-defense arguments in murder trials or in justifying war). This is a principle in line with other animals' practices in nature that ensure ecological balance. Despite ethical standards in human society, clearly many humans do practice exploitation of the weak, often to excess (consider child pornography, slave labor, scams aimed at the elderly, factory farming, clear-cutting of forests, genocide/extinction, etc.). In fact, at the risk of essentializing, I argue that the one relevant trait that does distinguish the human species among most other animal species is its ability to do most things (both good and bad, productive and destructive) in *excess* of what is necessary for survival.

Throughout history, philosophers have acknowledged humans' propensity for excess, and they have discussed this tendency in both positive and negative terms. For example, Aristotle noted that humans could be the most wicked, cruel, lustful, and gluttonous beings imaginable (Linzey and Clarke 2004, 7). Neoplatonist philosopher Porphyry believed animals are sentient, rational beings who "likewise have vices, and are envious; though their bad qualities are not so widely extended as in [men]: for their vices are of a lighter nature than those of [men]" (Walters and Portmess 1999, 39). English philosopher Thomas Hobbes, too, said that language allows humans to benefit from society and laws but that humans can also use speech for misdeeds, like lying and teaching bad behavior, so that "[man] errs more widely and dangerously than can other animals" (Linzey and Clarke 2004, 19). Hobbes posited that humans are also more destructive for unjust reasons than other animals: "So just as swords and guns, the weapons of [men], surpass the weapons of [brute] animals (horns, teeth, and stings), so [man] surpasseth in rapacity and cruelty the wolves, bears, and snakes that are not rapacious unless hungry and not cruel unless provoked, whereas [man] is famished even by future hunger" (19). Implying that there are also natural guidelines outside human ethical systems, Michel de Montaigne argued that "animals are much more self-controlled than we are, and keep with greater moderation within the limits that Nature has prescribed" (106).

As humans seek to move beyond natural limits, they create additional choices that lead to excess. German philosopher Johann Herder blamed this on humans' sense of free will: "Whilst animals on the whole remain true to the qualities of their kind, [man] alone has made a goddess of choice in place of necessity" (Linzey and Clarke 2004, 35). French philosopher Jean-Jacques Rousseau admired humans' free will to resist instinct and choose behaviors, specifically behaviors that lead to self-improvement. But to Rousseau this free will was also the "source of all human misfortunes," which "producing in different ages his discoveries and his errors, his vices and his virtues, makes him at length a tyrant both over himself and over nature" (Linzey and Clarke 2004, 33). Rhetorician Kenneth Burke described a human as one who is corrupted by his/her pursuit of perfection to ascend in hierarchies and is given to excess in this pursuit; Burke especially noted humans' excessive use of symbols and tools (Foss, Foss, and Trapp 1991, 207).

Feminist scholar Rosalind Coward argues humans' excesses create hierarchies and social inequalities at an unnatural level, while "in animal societies there's a startling absence of complex accumulation and unequal distribution of resources" (in Linzey and Clarke 2004, 96). The source of humanity's excess can be traced back to the advent of agriculture (Mason 1997). The domestication of animals about eleven thousand years ago transitioned many human beings to a more sedentary, agricultural way of life. Agricultural surpluses created divisions of wealth. In order to protect this wealth, patriarchal warrior cultures developed, creating oppressive systems of control labor such as slavery and imperialism. While forager societies often viewed other animals with wonder, respect, and partnership (not that some of these societies did not cause extinction or suffering), herder/agrarian societies were more likely to disempower animals in order to control and demystify them. Thus, many societies came to view domesticated animals as commodities and wild animals as competition and pests (Mason 1997).

If humans are characterized by excess, which can lead to both comfort and poverty, charity and harm, then I think an ethical system becomes socially and ecologically necessary for purposes of restraint. Western male philosophers have often lauded humans' ability to think abstractly because it leads to free will, which leads to the ability to control and choose behaviors. According to previous quotes by Montaigne, Herder, and Rousseau, they implied control is a positive ability to demonstrate restraint in the face of both the "sins" of excess choice in a human society and a supposed animal instinct born from nature. Ancient Western philosophers valued temperance and restraint as ethical virtues, including restraint in food choices (Singer and Mason 2006, 3). Yet, while humans have the ability to individually show restraint in the face of choice, some claim that humans, as a whole, excessively decrease choice in environmentally problematic ways. For example, food writer Michael Pollan (2006) claims that humans are "homogenizers" who use science to simplify natural complexity, such as with monoculture crops that decrease natural diversity.

Environmental philosophers often credit human ethics to biology and evolution, arguing that ethical behavior is natural, and what is natural is, therefore, good. Aldo Leopold (2003, 215) conceives of ethics as biological, where there is naturally a "limitation on freedom of action in the struggle for existence." J. Baird Callicott (1993) believes this was influenced by Darwin's evolutionary theories of humans as social animals that need to create kinship. Callicott argues that ethics would have preceded reason in humans' evolutionary process because humans needed to have complex linguistic skills that came from being social, and being social requires some limitations on individual freedoms. Darwin, along with philosophers David Hume and Adam Smith, contended that ethics rested on feelings and sentiments, which were found in the animal kingdom. Darwin said that natural selection privileges those individuals with feelings, as they would be more likely to produce offspring who behave in socially acceptable ways. This echoes sociobiological theories claiming cooperation is more natural than competition among highly social animals, such as humans (Ridley 1996; Kropotkin 2004). Thus Callicott (1993, 129) argues that nature is not immoral, as "intelligent moral behavior is natural behavior." Holmes Rolston (1993) also argues for a natural ethic where right is determined by an ability to sustain life rather than just sustaining pleasure. He says that the "is/ought" principle, usually seen as specious, can make sense in nature because as humans use science or experience to describe how nature functions and explore nature's intricate relationships and harmony, they discover that what is often or frequently is what *ought* to be. It is, then, hard to know where facts end and values begin.

I contend that, because the human practice of exploiting or harming other animals to excess goes against harmonious or ecological principles often found in nature, humans' ethical system of promoting compassion and protective justice is actually largely based on 'natural' principles: both the principle of cooperation to garner social support and the principle of moderation for ecological balance. I believe our fundamental ethical principles are, or should be, based on the idea of taking only what we need for our basic survival, complementing the principles of deep ecology (see Devall and Sessions 1985), with any excess acts of harm constituting exploitation and a breach of ethics.

Ultimately, this moderation is what most other animals (not just social animals) already practice, making all animals equally subject to these same ethical guidelines; this notion of equality avoids the humanist tendency to imply that humans should be kind to other animals because humans are ethically superior beings. Thus I argue that while humans can admit that their ethical system may be highly complex and impressive when compared to that of other animals, this high level of sophistication appears to be necessary to restrain humanity's special propensity for excessive harm. Therefore, when advocates promote animal rights on ethical grounds, they should avoid the word 'humane' and take care not to insinuate that all ethical principles are limited to the realm of humanity or that the human animal is more advanced. Perpetuating a construction of the human species as 'humane-kind' might unintentionally reinforce the problematic human/animal dualism and related notions of human superiority that lead not only to discrimination against nonhuman animals (and racialized human groups unfairly deemed 'subhuman') but also to condescending notions of paternalistic stewardship.

Yet one tension in my conclusion above is that it might imply animal rights should be garnered by emphasizing the likeness between human and nonhuman animal traits, in this case a capability for ethical behavior. Applied more broadly, if one admits that humans or other animal species might generally exhibit more 'positive' traits (as in a morally relevant mental trait) than other animals, does that imply some animals are more worthy of rights or fair treatment than others who are different, particularly disadvantaging those who are less like humans? The next section will explore this concern that the likeness model, popular in social justice rhetoric, is ultimately humanist and therefore self-defeating in combating speciesism.

Dilemmas over Whether Animal Rights Strategies Should Promote Similarity with Humans or Diversity

CONTRADICTIONS BETWEEN ANIMAL RIGHTS AND HUMANISM IN PROMOTING SIMILARITY

Inconsistencies associated with humanism and animal advocacy rhetoric cause some posthumanist scholars to critique the philosophical basis of animal rights, while they remain sympathetic to the need to end modern institutionalized violence toward nonhumans. Critical theorist William J. T. Mitchell advises scholars to study humanism as essential to a critique of speciesism: "'Speciesism' is ritually invoked in the denigration of others as animals while evoking a prejudice that is so deep and 'natural' that we can scarcely imagine human life without it. The very idea of speciesism, then, requires some conception of 'the posthuman,' an idea that makes sense, obviously, only in its dialectical relation with the long and unfinished reflection on species being that goes by the name of humanism" (in Wolfe 2003, xiv). An analysis of humanism fits with the contention that a focus on humanimality and an interrogation of human *privilege* (not just the mistreatment of the animal 'other') should become central to animal activism.

But in considering animal rights philosophy, Derrida contends that the concept of animal rights is flawed so long as it models itself after a juridical concept of human rights; the notion of human rights is based on a humanist "post-Cartesian human subjectivity" that has led to the very oppression that animal activists seek to end: "Consequently, to confer or to recognize rights for 'animals' is a surreptitious or implicit way of confirming a certain interpretation of the human subject, which itself will have been the very lever of the worst violence carried out against nonhuman living beings" (Derrida and Roudinesco 2004, 64–65). He claims that rights are so conflated with humanism that they cannot serve as the basis for ending nonhuman animal exploitation. This is why, even as critical as he is of industrialized exploitation, he talks about animal rights from the perspective of an outsider, saying: "I have sympathy (and I insist on that word) for those who revolt against the war declared on so many animals" (67). In merely expressing "sympathy" for activists' desires to challenge violence, Derrida clarifies his doubts about the efficacy of activist communication strategies that rely on an implicit humanism and a legal notion of rights.

Prominent animal ethics philosophers Singer (1990) and Regan (1983) propose theories that could be considered humanist in their focus on how animals are similar to humans. Taking this stance, Cary Wolfe (2003, 8) notes the irony that animal rights' anthropocentrism ends up "effacing the very difference of the animal other that it sought to respect." It is true that the tensions between the priorities of similarity and difference are essential to the paradox present within animal rights. Thus feminist scholars Lynda Birke and Luciana Parisi (1999, 57) determine that "the tension between our similarity and our difference from other animals, moreover, informs much of the political and philosophical tension around debates on animal rights."

To clarify a misconception, Ingold (1988) states it is not anthropocentric to show how a particular human trait, even a positive one, is unique to the human species, as every species is also likely to have something unique about it. It is anthropocentric, however, to compare nonhumans to humans and expect nonhumans to have the same capacities before respect is granted, which is something that some animal ethics philosophers do. This anthropocentrism is especially explicit in animal ethicist Paola Cavalieri and Peter Singer's (1994) *Great Ape Project*, in which they propose that nonhuman primates serve as a bridge species who deserve to have their rights recognized before other animal species because apes and humans are most closely related.[5] But on a broader scale, the suggestion by scholars (Clark 1988; Lawrence 1995; Derrida and Roudinesco 2004) that there are few, or no, traits that humans possess that are not also possessed by at least some other animal species is also anthropocentric, albeit more implicitly.

However, before chastising animal rights philosophers and activists for implicitly promoting humanism, one might determine whether the activist's line of argumentation is based more on the desire to build nonhumans up in the 'noble' likeness of humanity (expanding humanity to include other animals) or based more on the desire to nudge humans down off their self-constructed pedestal, encouraging them to embrace, instead of shun, their innate animality (expanding animality to include humans). The issue is really a matter of directionality, and I argue that the distinction between the two approaches is key. The latter approach of encouraging humans to embrace their animality is less humanist and therefore more morally tenable to posthumanist scholars, and it fits Aph and Syl Ko's (2017) suggestion that we not side with the white supremacy historically presumed in the construct of 'human'. Strategically, however, asking humans to embrace their animality is less commonly done, presumably for the utilitarian reason that it more directly challenges current ideologies about human supremacy and comes across as more threatening to the status, esteem, and 'dignity' of the very humans who must be convinced. While advocacy that focuses on humanimality might have more philosophical veracity, I recognize that on the level of a media sound bite, it may fail to easily resonate with the public in meaningful ways and thus takes more rhetorical skill to construct.

EMBRACING HUMAN ANIMALITY

Thinking long-term, if animal activists fail to convince humans to respect their animality instead of despising it, humans may never treat other animals (or even all human groups) with appropriate respect. Philosopher Giorgio Agamben (2004) notes that humanity is currently based on how much humans control the animal within themselves, as Western metaphysics defines humanity in opposition to animality. This relates to a politics of excluding someone who must still simultaneously be included. The animal is held in an ambiguous space that is both external and internal, where he/she is subject to exile and death without remorse (Agamben 2004).

Another approach to privileging humanimality is through recognizing that wisdom (a valued mental trait) can be obtained via the body by all animals in ways that are not restricted to a human-centered rationality reliant on a limited, linguistic or phonetic notion of language. David Abram (1997), an environmental phenomenologist, suggests that if we began to privilege the body as a source of communicative knowledge, we could deconstruct the mind/body dualism that parallels the human/animal and subject/object dualisms. Abram encourages humans to begin to reaffirm their bodies and physical senses as a communicative site of gaining wisdom about the entire natural world instead of just relying on human-based symbolic communication and limiting knowledge to anthropocentric realms. By embracing the 'primitive' sensual communication most humans have lost, they would expand their knowledge by beginning to relearn and value what other species are communicating. If the body were not viewed as separate from, and inferior to, the mind, then humans would not use the supposed superiority of the human mind's ability to reason abstractly as an excuse to reduce other life to mere bodies devoid of wisdom. In Abram's (1997) view, the body, even that of nonhuman animals, should be enlivened as a subject rather than mechanized by being reduced to an object.

Abram's (1997) perspective is useful for redefining intelligence in a nonanthropocentric sense and associating it with all animals, thereby increasing humans' appreciation for the wisdom that can be gained from reading the world in ways more common to nonhumans or 'primitive' human culture than industrialized human culture. I think this could also restrain animal activists from claiming that nonhuman animals are 'voiceless,' encouraging an acknowledgment that nonhuman animal communication is silenced in one sense and often unheard or misinterpreted in another. I suggest that to recognize the nonhuman animal voice, activists should attempt to include nonhuman communication in advocacy campaigns.[6]

Asking humans to begin to respect the body's wisdom and to embrace their animality is perhaps a philosophically rigorous approach to promoting animal rights, but it is not as pragmatic as the humanist approach of simply proving that many nonhumans are similar to humans. The latter strategy recognizes that because people place a high value on supposedly human traits (such as intelligence, kindness, emotional sensitivity, symbolic communication, education, artistic talent, and spirituality), it is only reasonable that animal activists appeal to the fact that nonhuman animals also *share* some of these traits when trying to convince humans to have higher respect for other animals.[7] This tactic of emphasizing like traits was used successfully to pass basic human rights laws for historically oppressed groups of humans (Bormann 1971; Campbell 1989). Therefore, Derrida's and Wolfe's suggestion that animal rights philosophies should be less humanist and should avoid this human rights or likeness model of social justice is unsettling and challenging to conventional activist wisdom about achieving social progress for oppressed groups.

PROMOTING DIFFERENCE AND DIVERSITY

A philosophical problem with the tactic of emphasizing that nonhuman animals share many valued 'human' traits is that it runs the risk of reducing other animals to lesser categories of 'subhumans.' Wolfe (2003, 53) explains that different species cannot be expected to possess "qualities, potentials, or abilities that are realized to their fullest in human beings." This could leave nonhuman animals forever stuck in the role of diminished or immature humans, just as humans would always be a diminished version of cats, gorillas, birds, fish, or any other species, and just as women were once considered diminished forms of men. Sandler (2012) warns us not to use human capacities as the benchmark for what abilities matter most in other species or make someone inherently valuable: "There is no non-question-begging reason why the capacities that are crucial to our form of life (or the form of life of any other species, for that matter) should be the standard for whether members of other species have inherent worth" (44). This is because each individual has capacities that are not better or worse than ours but rather appropriate to them and their species in terms of being what they each need to be able do to survive.

Activists and philosophers may also find it counterproductive to insinuate that nonhumans are close to being humans but are just underdeveloped. Dunayer (2001) posits that, from an evolutionary perspective, species should not be ranked as more or less 'primitive' against the benchmark of humans serving as the 'advanced' species. She clarifies, "species don't evolve toward greater *humanness*, but toward greater *adaptiveness* in their ecological niche" (13), which is reflected in the fact that Darwin did not believe in ranking species as higher or lower.

The case against promoting similarities (whether it be by expanding humanity or animality in either direction) leads to the somewhat counterintuitive argument of promoting *differences* in order to gain equality for other animals. On the surface this flies in the face of reason since their differences from humans have been highlighted as an excuse to discriminate against them. However, toward gaining equality, an acknowledgment of difference does not have to equate with an admission of inferiority. While other species are different, they are by no means failed or lesser versions of humans. In exploring the idea of embracing differences, it is useful to acknowledge that the advanced stages of some human social justice movements in the United States have also moved in this direction, as they now promote diversity and multiculturalism. The problem that the human rights approach had in gaining equality by emphasizing the similarities between human groups (i.e., men and women, whites and blacks, or heterosexuals and homosexuals) was that the historically oppressed groups were then forced to assimilate into the dominant group's world and live by the standards set by white, Western, heterosexual males. Just as many activists in the civil rights movement do not advocate for complete colorblindness, under the premise that it would wipe out some distinguishing and valued cultural traits and generally disrespects difference, so too the animal rights movement should not expect people to be blind to the many splendid cultural and biological variances among animals.

David Pellow (2014) argues that respect for diversity must be part of the movement for total liberation of species. In discussing how we should negotiate borders between humans, species, and ecosystems, he clarifies: "Challenging these borders and arguing for equality is not the same as collapsing them entirely and arguing for sameness. If activists do this—and they do sometimes—this violently erases uniqueness, varied experiences, histories, and biographies" (253). I agree that any activist should ask the public to respect differences. Additionally, diversity in both human society and the natural world is not limited to groups or species but applies to *individuals* within groups/species as well (for example, dogs do not all have the same personalities), or else it promotes reductionist biological essentialism (Clark 1993).

But as a caveat to abandoning approaches that favor inclusion/similarity, American women's rights activists and those who worked for the abolition of human slavery in the United States did not have to concede that women and people of color were not as smart as white men (which was the generally constructed fallacy that historically justified their lower status) by arguing that they deserved rights anyway because America valued diversity (Bormann 1971; Campbell 1989). Many would rightly agree that activists for these causes need not concede this, as the capabilities of women and people of color are obviously more likely to closely resemble the capabilities of others of their own species than those of nonhumans. But does this mean that animal rights activists must concede that, in comparison to humans, nonhuman animals are not as smart (or communicative or ethical or sensitive) while claiming that these differences should not matter anyway? Many may not want to nor feel it is truthful to fully concede that humans and other animals are so completely different.

Blending Similarity and Diversity

Ultimately, I propose the best position to these dilemmas is a blended one that embraces both the fundamental commonalities that provide kinship in a broad sense and the specific differences that provide diversity in an individual sense. While people may come to value nonhuman animals and respect diversity, the concern is that they will still prioritize fellow humans over other animal species if they do not see some similarity that connects all animals together and gives them a reason to value other species just as they value their own species. Consider Gary Steiner's (2008, 137) suggestion that "we must learn to identify with animals, to see ourselves in them and them in ourselves, in order to appreciate their plight and their prospects" as part of his proposal for conceptually expanding humanity's moral community and identity to include other animals as kin.

As a shared trait, or what Kenneth Burke calls a "consubstantial" (Foss, Foss, and Trapp 1991, 192) unifying trait that creates a mutual identity, I suggest that Regan's (1983) idea of being a conscious "subject of a life" may be the best option. Subjective consciousness is broad enough to include many animal species yet still allows for diversity within and among species. It could be compared to the consubstantial trait of *personhood* that has allowed (in theory) for equality among races, genders, and ethnicities, while still allowing for diversity. Singer's notion of sentience is quite similar and could also work, as long as the focus expands beyond concerns over bodily suffering and emphasizes individual *life* and personhood. Perhaps if animal rights campaigns encouraged people to embrace diversity and their own animality, it would mitigate some of the problematic humanism inherent in building off a human rights model.

The ideas of critical theorists Gilles Deleuze and Félix Guattari (2004) seem to support this notion of blending human-animal relations, as they argue that animals serve to rupture notions of identity and sameness. In their article "Becoming Animal," they use the Nietzschean idea of "becoming over being" to emphasize animal-becoming as a way to free humanity from its humanistic straitjacket. Deleuze and Guattari privilege dynamic notions of expansion, multiplicity, mutuality, heterogeneity, and rhizomes over orderly notions of classification, identification, essentialism, and linear progression. Becoming is considered 'real,' in that it contains difference and acknowledges how everything is implicated in everything else. Similarly, Donna Haraway (2008, 19) prefers to see humans as "becoming with" animals: "I am who I become with companion species, who and which make a mess out of categories in the making of kin and kind." This complicates traditional notions of identity by saying it is something determined primarily by our relations with other animals.

I believe these scholars' ideas pose an even larger rhetorical challenge than do my previous discussions of combating speciesism, as they challenge how we think rather than what we think. Instead of just asking people to incorporate the animal other into a new and expanded identity of fellow conscious beings, as I have in this chapter, these scholars ask people to understand themselves outside of a defining notion of "self." Rather, people should understand themselves more openly via their dynamic relationships with all beings (something so ontologically radical I can scarcely describe or conceive it). I hope to see scholars undertake this challenge to demonstrate how notions of "becoming over being" might inform a radically different posthumanist advocacy rhetoric. Overall, I see the value of animal advocates undertaking the challenge of embracing the deconstructive principles of diversity, difference, and complexity. But to avoid total relativism, their rhetoric must maintain some sense of unity and kinship (between all animals) that respects ethical standards based on overarching principles, like avoiding unnecessary harm and valuing sentience. This encourages humanities scholars and human rights activists to admit that natural/instinctual tendencies and ecological principles have some merit in influencing human behavior and, conversely, that there is a 'humanity' or culture in what was once thought to be a separate 'animal' realm of nature.

Rather than primarily talking about nonhuman animals, animal advocates must rhetorically problematize the fragile borders of humanity and species through deconstruction of speciesist language so that humanimals begin to feel pride in their animality. This requires transformation of language to reconstruct new identities because humanimals will likely experience instability from the deconstruction of deep-seated binaries that once provided familiar and stable boundaries. A quote from Derrida (2002, 372) is applicable here: "Crossing borders or the ends of [man] I come or surrender to the animal—to the animal in itself, to the animal in me and the animal at unease with itself." To put the humanimal at ease with itself, I contend that advocates and scholars must construct the posthuman in ways that blend the retention of moral integrity and rights with the introduction of a humbler and more integrated place among fellow beings who all must live sustainably within nature's ethic—hence the basis for the human animal earthling identity in this book.

CHAPTER THREE

Pilot Study: Identifying Shared Values in Rights Declarations for Humans, Other Animals, and Nature

To begin to identify which values seem central to human rights, animal rights, and environmental causes, I conducted a pilot study of global rights declarations and charters. I will build on this chapter's legal/rights-oriented study later in the book with a discourse analysis of major advocacy organization campaigns, as both studies will ground my prescription of core values for the 'human animal earthling' identity. Rights declarations are a useful site of initial study, as they represent the universal values and goals of coalitions (of NGOs and quasi-governmental organizations like the United Nations) that collectively debated and negotiated their claimant groups' priorities for needed and deserved improvements to their lives and well-being. These declarations identify major problems facing living beings and propose solutions or at least affirm basic standards for decent and fair treatment. Because these global charters are declarative and succinct in nature, each term and goal was presumably the result of much careful consideration and is thus a meaningful representation of collective beliefs.

Methodology and Sample

I searched for common values articulated on behalf of humans, other animals, and nature in the discourse of key global rights declarations, choosing the following six declarations as my sample texts:[1]

- **The United Nations Universal Declaration of Human Rights** was adopted in December 1948 by the United Nations (UN) General Assembly to affirm every human's rights as a result of the atrocities of World War II (United Nations General Assembly 1948).
- **The Universal Declaration of Animal Rights (1989)** was conceived by French intellectuals and eventually drafted by the International League of Animal Rights in Geneva. Proclaimed in a ceremony before the UN's Educational,

Scientific, and Cultural Organization (UNESCO) in October 1978, it has not been officially adopted by the UN. It was inspired by the UN's Declaration of Human Rights. Many of the drafters were scientists, as it draws upon scientific progress in evolutionary biology to propose "a moral code based on respect for life in its universality" (Neumann 2012, 95). The principles were revised in 1989, and I use the latest version for my sample.

- **The Universal Declaration of Animal Rights (2001)**, drafted by Uncaged in the UK (an organization that recently evolved into the Centre for Animals and Social Justice), was adopted in December 2001 and signed by over seventy-five animal protection organizations worldwide. It was based on the UN Declaration of Human Rights, halfway to its 2048 centennial, upon which date they hope the UN will adopt this animal rights declaration (Uncaged 2001).

- **The Principles of Environmental Justice** was adopted in October 1991 at the First National People of Color Environmental Leadership Summit. The preamble asserts, "To begin to build a national and international movement of all peoples of color to fight the destruction and taking of our lands and communities, [we] do hereby re-establish our spiritual interdependence to the sacredness of our Mother Earth; to respect and celebrate each of our cultures, languages and beliefs about the natural world and our roles in healing ourselves" (People of Color Environmental Leadership Summit 1991).

- **The Earth Charter** was adopted in 2000 by the Earth Charter Initiative, a coalition that originally began as a UN initiative. The Earth Charter is a "declaration of fundamental ethical principles for building a just, sustainable and peaceful global society in the twenty-first century." Recognizing that social justice and ecology are interdependent, it is an "inclusive, integrated ethical framework" formed through "cross-cultural dialogue on common goals and shared values" (Earth Charter Initiative 2000).

- **The UN World Charter for Nature** was adopted in October 1982 by the UN General Assembly based on a concern that "the benefits which could be obtained from nature depended on the maintenance of natural processes and on the diversity of life-forms and that those benefits were jeopardized by the excessive exploitation and the destruction of natural habitats," thus recognizing "the need for appropriate measures at the national and international levels to protect nature and promote international co-operation" (United Nations General Assembly 1982).

In analyzing these declarations and charters, I asked the following descriptive research questions:[2]

- RQ1. Who matters and what terminology do they use to describe these significant entities?
- RQ2. What is valued as good/right/ideal?

- RQ3. Which of these values overlap between causes and, thus, are more universal?

RQ1: WHO MATTERS?

To identify the entities that the charters hope to help, they range from individuals to the broader community of life (see table 1). The human rights declaration and the animal rights declarations (especially the one from 2001) focused mainly on individuals, with the former limiting that to humans and the latter to "human and nonhuman animals," as it sought to emphasize kinship and continuity with "all animal life." The 1989 animal rights declaration also expanded beyond the animal realm to include nature by alluding to species and habitat. The three *environmental* charters tended to have an understandably broader focus not only on "people" but also "other living things," "living beings," and "life-forms" that make up "the natural world" or the "community of life."

All the environmental declarations expressed great concern for the health of the natural world, but largely based on sustaining *human* life now and for "future generations." While the Earth Charter also reflected this utilitarian respect for nature, it also made the unique recognition in principle 1.a. that "Every form of life has value regardless of its worth to human beings." This Earth Charter incorporated all species, frequently invoking collectivity and kinship through use of terms such as "the human family," "the Earth community," the "community of life," and "Earth as home." The Principles of Environmental Justice used spiritual language, describing "our Mother Earth" as "sacred." The UN World Charter for Nature often focused ecocentrically on life-support "systems" and "processes," even though it was anthropocentric in many respects, using terms such as "civilization" and "mankind." All rights declarations include an inherent respect for "human dignity," but it was only the animal rights declarations that attempted to extend this level of respect to nonhuman animals.

Regarding nonhuman animals, the UN World Charter for Nature and the Earth Charter sometimes mentioned "animals," but separately from humans. The only *environmental* charter not to specifically mention "animals" was the Principles of Environmental Justice, as it focused more on peoples and cultures who have been colonized and oppressed, and it tended to lump nonhuman animals in with nature (presumably) under phrases such as "other living things" or "other life-forms." The oldest declaration, the UN Human Rights declaration, was predictably anthropocentric by design, not mentioning nonhuman animals or nature either, focusing primarily on individual humans embedded in their human communities. So, when this declaration frequently referenced "all" or "everyone," this inclusivity was limited to humanity.

TABLE 1 References to Who Matters: Terminology Used by the Various Rights Declarations

UN WORLD CHARTER FOR NATURE (1982)	EARTH CHARTER (2000)	PRINCIPLES OF ENVIRONMENTAL JUSTICE (1991)	UNIVERSAL DECLARATION OF ANIMAL RIGHTS (2001)	UNIVERSAL DECLARATION OF ANIMAL RIGHTS (1989)	UN UNIVERSAL DECLARATION OF HUMAN RIGHTS (1948)
• Every form of life	• Earth our home	• Our Mother Earth	• Individuals	• Individuals	• Everyone
• Life-forms	• Earth community	• Our lands and communities	• Nonhuman animals	• Living beings	• All
• Life-support systems and processes	• Larger living world	• Our cultures	• Human and nonhuman	• Life	• Human
• Nature	• Community of life	• People(s)	• Fellow creatures	• All animal life	• Human beings
• Living resources	• Biosphere	• Native peoples	• Kinship of all animals	• Animal	• Men and women
• Civilization	• Human family	• People of color	• Natural world	• Species	• Community
• Man/mankind	• Peoples of the earth	• Natural world		• Human	
• Animals	• Humans	• Other living things		• Man	
• Future generations	• Animals	• Other life-forms		• Nature	
	• Living beings	• Future generations		• Habitat	
	• Resources				
	• Future generations				

TABLE 2 Values Represented as Good/Ideal in One or All of the Various Rights Declarations

LIFE-SUPPORTING	RESPONSIBLE	FAIR	UNIFYING/CONNECTING	PLEASURABLE
• Protection	• Respect (for life, human and animal dignity, sacredness of Mother Earth)	• Democratic participation	• Community	• Flourishing
• Care	• Moral progress	• Equality	• Family	• Beauty
• Peace/nonviolence	• Ethics	• Liberty/freedom	• Kinship	• Happiness
• Life	• Duty	• Emancipation	• Universality	• Expression
• Health and well-being	• Courage	• Justice	• Multiculturalism	• Pursuit of aspirations
• Biodiversity	• Moral consistency/integrity	• Self-determination	• Understanding	
• Uniqueness	• Compassion	• Dignity	• Love	
• Interdependence	• Humaneness	• Diversity	• Partnership	
• Human development	• Reprioritizing lifestyles	• Inclusivity	• Solidarity	
• Security	• Leadership	• Mutuality	• Coexistence	
• Safeguarding	• Moderation	• Open-mindedness	• Expression	
• Sustenance	• Frugality	• Compensation/reparation	• Capacity for sentience and/or reason	
• Balance	• Precaution	• Humility		
• Harmony	• Conservation	• Healing and recovery		
• Sustainability	• Recycling	• Recognition		
• Clean	• Restraint	• Shared wealth		
• Pure/natural	• Accountability	• Access to resources		
• Ecological integrity and vitality and stability	• Gratitude			
• Regeneration	• Legacy			
• Capacity	• Education/wisdom/learning			
	• Long-term planning			

RQ2: WHAT IS VALUED AS GOOD/RIGHT/IDEAL?

I categorized all the dozens of values promoted in the declarations into five broad values categories: life supporting, responsible, fair, unifying/connecting, and pleasurable (see table 2).[3] Every cause (environmentalism, animal rights, and human rights) had values in each of these five categories.

In considering differences among causes, environmentalism created the lengthiest and most diverse list of values unique to it, while values unique to the human rights declaration were largely limited to valuing *human development and expression*.[4] The only values unique to the animal rights declarations were the need for humans to be *courageous* and *open-minded* in acknowledging the feelings and capacities of other animals (hence their emphasis on valuing *sentience*). While the sentience of human and nonhuman animals was often acknowledged in various declarations as a basis for being concerned about welfare and nonviolence, it did not seem to garner the nonhuman animal any equality or closer connection to the human animal except in the animal rights declarations. This is indicative of the fact that all causes may value *life, nonviolence,* or *fairness* but apply it in a hierarchical fashion (inequitably) to various beings. This is why I do not just ask *what* is valued (RQ2) but also *who* is valued (RQ1).

RQ3: WHICH OF THESE VALUES OVERLAP
BETWEEN CAUSES AND, THUS, ARE MORE UNIVERSAL?

The values present in (universal to) all three causes were:

- life and health
- nonviolence, coexistence, and peace
- protection
- justice
- respect
- liberty
- equality
- recognition (of rights)
- dignity
- sentience/capacity for feeling
- education[5]

Of the universal values, *respect* is more like a modifier for other values (as in "respect for what/whom?") or a verb that encourages recognition of the other values. In fact, in considering what actions or resulting states of being the declarations condemned as wrong, I would describe them as any action that showed a *lack of respect* for others (nature or all animals)—disrespecting their physical health and well-being, their equal rights and opportunities and liberties, or our shared resources. Thus, all three causes condemned actions that represented a denial of the dignity or inherent value of others:

- **Unfair Actions:** unjust, oppressive, discriminatory, exploitative
- **Irresponsible Actions:** excessive, destructive, wasteful
- **Physically Harmful Actions:** cruel, contaminating, violent[6]

Discussion: Recommendations for Values
Befitting the Human Animal Earthling's Identity

After identifying the overlapping values found in rights declarations on behalf of humans, nonhuman animals, and nature, in this section I answer the following prescriptive and analytical research questions:

- RQ4. Which values are most applicable to a human animal earthling's identity?
- RQ5. In what way do these values need reframing to be less anthropocentric or more sentient or biocentric in their application and scope?

RQ4: WHICH VALUES ARE MOST APPLICABLE TO A HUMAN ANIMAL EARTHLING'S IDENTITY?

A human animal earthling identity should reflect the values that all three causes have in common, so I started the list (see table 3) with those universal values (from RQ3) and then added in some central values that may be unique to each cause (or only two causes) but are important to facilitating a well-rounded viewpoint respecting and protecting all forms of life. To be comprehensive, I also considered the actions that rights declarations universally condemned as wrong and then identified the opposite as the value (putting it in an affirmative). That led me to determine that *compassion* deserves to be on the universal values list since there is much condemnation of cruel and insensitive treatment of individuals. In considering the opposites of the 'irresponsible' actions category from the environmental declarations, I found values such as *responsibility, moderation, care/carefulness,* and *sharing* to be implied. While these latter values were not explicitly mentioned in all declarations, my goal is to use universal commonalities as a starting point and then blend in core values found in either human rights, animal rights, or environmental causes so my final values list is holistic and representative of the concerns of all these causes.[7] While the previous list of ideals (table 2) had approximately seventy-five values, I cut the number in half to make my final list more manageable and cohesive (table 3).

When the animal rights cause is considered with environmentalism, they both call for *humility* in human recognition of their *kinship* with *nonhuman life*, requiring that humans *moderate* exploitative practices. For example, the Earth Charter says: "The spirit of human solidarity and kinship with all life is strengthened when we

TABLE 3 Pilot Study: Proposed Values Most Befitting a Human Animal Earthling

LIFE-SUPPORTING VALUES	RESPONSIBLE VALUES	FAIR VALUES	UNIFYING/ CONNECTING VALUES
• Peace/nonviolence	• **Respect** (for life, sentience, diversity, nature, ecology)	• **Equality**	• Community
• Protection		• **Liberty**	• Kinship
• Life		• **Justice/fairness**	• Inclusivity
• Health and well-being	• **Responsibility**	• Sharing	• Interdependence
• (Bio)diversity	• **Care/carefulness/ caring**	• Reparation	• Reciprocity and trust
• Purity and naturalness	• Courage	• Humility	• Sentience
• Ecological integrity and vitality	• Moderation	• Open-mindedness	• Compassion
	• Sustainability		• Understanding
	• Accountability		• Love
	• Moral integrity		• Cooperation/ teamwork
	• Far-sightedness		• Humor
			• Imagination

NOTE: Bolded values are ones that were promoted by rights declarations on behalf of humans *and* nonhuman animals *and* nature.

live with . . . humility regarding the human place in nature." Additionally, environmentalism and human rights both recognize the *interdependence* of all life in an ecological *community* dependent on *peaceful, responsible,* and *sustainable* human practices, where humans take *accountability* for *reparations* to heal natural systems and social inequities.

I especially think the values under the 'responsible,' 'fair,' and 'unifying' sections (in table 3) are indicative of the self-transcendent and intrinsic values that psychological research tells us will lead to prosocial and pro-environmental behaviors (Crompton and Kasser 2009). In fact, I note that many of the values in the 'responsible' and 'fair' categories concentrate on willing restraint; environmentalism calls for human societies (particularly wealthy, industrialized societies) to stop being as excessive and selfish with resources, and human rights and animal rights also call for humans to restrain their ability to be dominating and exploitative toward individuals.

To additionally promote self-transcendence, I expanded the 'unifying' values section that connects humans within a larger social and ecological *community of interdependent* beings, where we all benefit from the support that comes from *cooperation* and *reciprocity*. I added in the value of *trust* as inherent to *reciprocity* (mutual give-and-take between all members of an ecosystem) so that my list would include all eight of the cross-cultural values that Kidder's (1994) research demonstrated were important to foster social justice.

The 'unifying' notion of similarity and collectivity can sometimes be considered at odds with individuality and *diversity*; granted, my list does lean more toward collectivity (*kinship*) than individuality (except, perhaps, in its emphasis on respecting sentient individuals and their freedom), but it represents the reality that a just and sustainable humanimality is a more collective/community-focused society than we currently have now (especially in Western consumer cultures). It represents a need to increase *teamwork* and *sharing* of resources rather than accumulation and self-gratification. In my recommendations, the value of *liberty* is aimed more at animals (humans included) being liberated from oppression or exploitative use as a means to an end, rather than meaning freedom for humans to do whatever they want regardless of its effects on others.

Notions of integrity appear frequently, not only the need for *ecological integrity* in the 'life-supporting' section, but also *moral integrity* and *accountability* in the 'responsible' section, and the need for *reparation* in the 'fairness' section. Reparation requires humans to restore the *vitality* and *purity* of ecological systems that we have damaged or contaminated and to make amends to individuals (human and nonhuman) for harm and inequalities caused by violence, discrimination, colonization, and oppression. *Imagination* combined with *open-mindedness* will help us envision new ways of being and relating to the natural world. To relinquish our species privilege (and race, gender, and class privileges) will require *courage* and the will to combat the inertia of cultural norms and economic power structures.[8]

The 'pleasurable' values section (from table 2) isn't a necessity in terms of justice and rights, and it could be seen as a self-enhancement value of "hedonism," so I eliminated pleasure as its own category for table 3. But pleasure is something that any sentient individual seeks for mental well-being, so I included some aspects of it within the unifying category. For example, pleasure is experienced through the fulfillment that comes from *loving* and *caring* for others and being loved and cared for in return. This incorporates a feminist ethic of care that acknowledges that many ethical actions are motivated more by feelings of care and affiliation than by a sense of duty or responsibility (Kheel 2008). I added *humor* to this section because it is a well-developed trait of humans that represents part of our better nature; if used productively, humor can facilitate connection with others and increase *cooperation* by diffusing tensions in conflicts or problem-solving.

RQ5: IN WHAT WAY DO THESE VALUES NEED REFRAMING TO BE LESS ANTHROPOCENTRIC OR MORE SENTIENT OR BIOCENTRIC IN THEIR APPLICATION AND SCOPE?

One of the major challenges is not just to cultivate a more benevolent/caring social identity, as most cultures already tend to rank benevolence as the premier value (Bardi and Schwartz 2003). The challenge is to ensure that humanity envisions this benevolence/caring as applying to many forms of life, not just to humankind, one's immediate kin, local environment, or private property. In this way, the self-transcendent value category of "universalism" is necessary to extend altruistic or caring notions beyond one's immediate group, especially beyond our human species. As Crompton and Kasser (2009) note, an anthropocentric identity must be

TABLE 4 Recommended Terminologies for Referencing Who Matters

← MOST INCLUSIVE/BROAD ─────── MOST EXCLUSIVE/NARROW →			
ALL EARTH'S ANIMATE AND INANIMATE INHABITANTS	ALL ANIMALS (HUMAN AND NONHUMAN)	ALL ANIMALS BESIDES HUMANS	THE HUMAN ANIMAL ONLY
• Earthlings • Community of life • All living things • All forms of life • The living world • The natural world • Nature • The environment • Ecosystems • All species • Future generations*	• Living beings • Animal kingdom • Everyone* • All animals • All of us, we • Cultures* • Individuals • Person(s)*	• Nonhuman animals • Other animals • Fellow animal species • Nonhuman animal cultures* • Nonhuman animal societies and communities	• Humans • Human beings • The human animal • Humanimality • Human cultures • Human society

* I recognize these are nontraditional uses of these terms to be more inclusive of nonhuman species. Therefore, when using these terms in novel ways to promote novel thinking and to deconstruct nature/culture and animal/human dualisms, they may need explanation to broaden the notion of whom they represent.

challenged so that other animals and nature become part of humanity's in-group, essential to developing an "environmental identity" (Clayton 2012).

To cultivate a human identity as human animal earthlings, social movements should promote a less human-privileging core justice ethic that begins to situate the human more humbly as an animal who has unfairly exploited rather than shared the communal resources of our home planet (see Diamond 1992; Mason 1997; Nibert 2013). Thus, social movements should build critical rhetoric around values of justice and responsibility that make humans feel accountable for solving the life-and-death problems we have caused the animal kingdom. To care enough to be accountable would require that we also value our own moral integrity and take pride in living our values by being responsible global citizens. Citizenship engenders a sense of a global community and interdependence upon each other as earthlings.

Respect for life is also a core value of all movements, and this respect needs to be inclusive of all living beings, but we may respect different forms of life in different ways. Fellow sentient animals can be valued inherently as individuals, while plants, natural objects, and living systems can be valued more instrumentally (or holistically) as groups that support the lives of sentient beings (Jamieson 2002). In a strictly ecological sense, sentience is not a valid reason to privilege any living being (Taylor 1993), but I am attempting to blend ecological, human, and animal ethics by using animal rights (based on privileging sentience) as the logical bridge between the human and nonhuman world, as discussed in chapter 1.[9] To delineate who matters, see table 4 for a list of terms that can be used to inclusively and respectfully refer to various beings.

Humans should note our kinship with the animal kingdom while also embracing the diversity and uniqueness inherent among not only species but individual members of species (Bekoff and Pierce 2009), as diversity is valued in culture and nature; diversity is important to the civil rights movement and also to environmentalism, as in biodiversity. The animal rights movement has not emphasized diversity as much, but I think it should begin to play an important role in defeating the anthropocentrism inherent to privileging only the other animals who most resemble humans. We should respect fellow animals for their similar sentient capacities but must also appreciate their splendid and impressive differences, as they are not diminished versions of humans (Freeman 2010b).

Social movements can raise the status of nonhuman animals in the process of promoting ecofriendly, moderate lifestyles, by noting that we should follow nonhumans' cultural example of living sustainably and avoiding excess, gluttony, and waste. In this way, human animal earthlings can be framed as team players on planet earth; here we practice reciprocity by returning the favor of living in a simpler and more natural way, as other animal societies do, that justly allows other sentient beings to flourish as well. This view of other animals as wise, sustainable, and ethical role models is a useful part of furthering our respect for them while also practicing humility so we do not exalt our own ethicality to justify human superiority, as discussed in the previous chapter.[10]

In Conclusion

This chapter's pilot study begins to identify shared motivations around which anti-exploitation movements can strategically ally in support of the broader goals of justice and protection of life. This means designing campaigns (on any issue) that cultivate a unified, core set of intrinsic social values (table 3) meant to foster a more responsible and benevolent human culture—one that values human rights yet transcends anthropocentrism.

I believe values that foster this human animal earthling identity for humanity start by respecting life—the lives of fellow sentient individuals and the natural living world on which all sentient individuals depend. By recognizing our ecological interdependence on all species as well as our special kinship with those animals who emotionally experience our world as we do, it helps us to feel a sense of care and responsibility for our home planet. This sense of community should engender a will to share our planet and be fair to our fellow earthlings—by creating more equitable and cooperative societies, by letting animals live freely in their habitats, and by reciprocating the sustainability and moderation displayed by nonhuman animal cultures and nature. In this way, I think the slogan for the human animal earthling might read "Share our home planet: support life, take care, and play fair."

CHAPTER FOUR

What Values Human Rights Organizations Appeal To

In reading this chapter, you will learn about the many types of heartbreaking injustices humans face worldwide, but you will also be inspired to discover shared values and the ways social movement organizations and societies are working to improve people's lives. This chapter essentially describes the collective values advocated in the 2017 web discourse of the five human rights organizations in my sample: Amnesty International, Anti-Slavery International, CARE, Human Rights Watch, and Minority Rights Group International (see appendix A for more details on methodology). By examining their main campaign messages, I first identify the beings on whose behalf they advocate, to demonstrate which human and nonhuman beings most merit our care and protection. I then share examples of the many concepts, traits, behaviors, and entities that they highlight as *good/ideal* (something that is presumably valued by the organization and the public) and, conversely, the ones they highlight as *bad or problematic* (something to be avoided or reformed). The chapter ends with a discussion of the groups or social norms that human rights organizations explicitly or implicitly blame as the source of the problems. The items that are characterized as good or bad in this chapter will later be compared to the ones identified in the web discourse on animal protection and environmental organizations in upcoming chapters; this is toward the end goal of identifying overlapping values between all three causes that can serve as the basis of a human animal earthling identity.

Who Merits Care and Protection

Campaigns of the five human rights organizations in my 2017 sample naturally show concern for humanity, and within this, they all emphasize special support for:

- those who are living in poverty
- women and girls

- children
- migrants, refugees, and immigrants

Other human groups who are ubiquitously featured in campaigns include minorities who face discrimination and those people who are the most disadvantaged. Minority groups can include:

- people of color
- indigenous cultures (mentioned by Amnesty International and Minority Rights Group)
- members of the LGBTQ community (mentioned by Amnesty International, Human Rights Watch, and Minority Rights Group)
- those with disabilities (mentioned by Minority Rights Group and Amnesty International)

Among the most disadvantaged are:

- the poor (many of whom live in the Global South)
- women and girls (a special focus of the organization CARE)
- civilians facing poverty or violence in a conflict zone
- underpaid or unpaid workers (millions of enslaved adults and children were especially a focus of Anti-Slavery International and Human Rights Watch)

All these categories above overlap and are not mutually exclusive. For example, an impoverished Muslim woman and her children who are refugees in a European camp after fleeing the war in Syria may face additional disadvantages, such as sexual violence, discrimination, exploitation, insecurity, unsanitary living conditions, and poor mental and physical health.

Additionally, political prisoners, activists, and journalists receive support from Amnesty International when they face oppression, detention, or harassment (often from authoritarian governments) for speaking out against injustice. CARE is unique in mentioning both farmers (especially female farmers) and future generations of humans. *Nonhuman beings* are not often mentioned in human rights campaigns, but CARE sometimes shows concern for trees, crops and agricultural land, and farmed animals on whom poor families rely for part of their income or food.

Common Values: What Matters Most

In their appeals to the public to support their campaigns, human rights organizations not only show concern for certain groups they think the public should care about, they also promote common values that societies tend to support. In table 5 I list the main concepts, traits, entities, and behaviors that many of the organizations value as good or ideal. In providing examples of the most ubiquitous and emphasized values, I have categorized them (as I did in the pilot study) into values related to supporting: life and well-being, fairness, responsibility, and unification.

TABLE 5 What Is Valued as Good or Ideal in Human Rights Organizations' Campaigns

VALUED AS GOOD OR IDEAL BY HUMAN RIGHTS CAMPAIGNS	MORE POPULAR: MENTIONED BY A MAJORITY OF GROUPS	SOMEWHAT POPULAR: MENTIONED BY SEVERAL GROUPS
LIFE-SUPPORTING VALUES	· *Human health / good health* · *Access to basic needs (food, water, shelter, medical care, jobs)* · *Life / saving lives* · **Humanitarian assistance** · **Security and stability** · Livelihood and ability to earn an income	· Safety · Clean and sanitary living conditions · Nourishment / nutritious food · Reproductive rights for women (family planning and access to contraception and abortion services)
FAIR VALUES	· **Human rights** · *Freedom (including freedom of choice over one's body, beliefs, and actions)* · *Democratic inclusion of all groups in decision-making* · **Justice (including fair trials and a criminal justice system that punishes offenders)** · **Equality (especially gender equality)** · **Land rights** · Providing legal representation/ support to those experiencing injustice · Assisting those in greatest need · Privacy rights · Self-determination and informed consent · Restitution and reparations for harm	· **Protection of the vulnerable** · **Freedom of speech and everyone having a voice** · **Fair and/or equal allocation of resources** · **Independence (free from conflicts of interest)** · Diversity, multiculturalism, and/or pluralism · Inclusion · Peaceful protest and activism
RESPONSIBLE VALUES	· *Education (especially for girls)* · **Accountability for consequences** · Transparency and openness · Responsibility · Effective advocacy to achieve change / enact solutions	· Acknowledgment of humans' inherent value · Peaceful/harmonious relations and coexistence · Honesty · Tolerance of others' differences · Taking action · Speaking up to the powerful/politicians · Political will and commitment to address and solve problems · Legal declarations and treaties (like UN treaties) · Enforcement of international law, including international oversight
UNIFYING VALUES	· **Human dignity** · **Peace, nonviolence, and harmony** · Working together · Love	· **Sense of identity** · Cultural rights and traditions · Sharing knowledge · Being part of a movement, network, or community
OTHER VALUES		· Certainty · Leisure time

NOTE: Bolded and italicized words indicate ubiquity (all five groups mentioned the item); bolded words indicate importance (it was repeatedly emphasized by one or more groups).

TABLE 6 What Is Represented as Problematic or Bad/Wrong in Human Rights Organizations' Campaigns (Nonvalued Concepts, Traits, Entities, or Behaviors)

PORTRAYED AS BAD OR WRONG BY HUMAN RIGHTS CAMPAIGNS	MORE POPULAR: MENTIONED BY A MAJORITY OF GROUPS	SOMEWHAT POPULAR: MENTIONED BY SEVERAL GROUPS
RELATED TO PHYSICAL OR MENTAL HARM	· *Rape and sexual violence* · *Violence* · *Death* · **Killing people/murder** · **Death penalty / execution by government** · **Torture or abuse** · **Poverty** · Suffering · Hunger, malnutrition, and starvation · Trauma · Insecurity	· Human genocide · Terrorism · Domestic violence · Homelessness · Overworking employees · Overcrowding · Constraint (physical) · Weapons
RELATED TO UNFAIRNESS	· *Discrimination* · **Enslavement and forced/unpaid labor** · **Injustice** · Forced marriage / child marriage · Unfair detention and imprisonment by government · Imprisonment, bondage, or confinement · **Displacement of people, including land-grabbing** · Hazardous or unsafe working conditions · Cruel, degrading, or inhuman treatment or conditions · **Impunity from rightful punishment**	· **Exploitation / taking advantage of the weak or vulnerable** · **Marginalization and exclusion of groups** · Patriarchy and oppressive customs · Isolation and segregation · Racism/xenophobia · Intolerance · Treating humans like animals · Human rights violations/abuses, including crimes against humanity · Paying low wages · Environmental damage · Violating/breaking laws · Weak/corrupt justice system · Lack of law enforcement · Unfair/weak laws · Government corruption · Government persecution or domination · Censorship · Surveillance
RELATED TO IRRESPONSIBILITY	· Risky or dangerous behavior · Deception and lying	· **Hypocrisy** · Covering up abuses and crimes · Neglect, including neglect by government · Indiscriminate harm
OTHER	· **War and conflict** · Climate change	· **Contamination and pollution** · Ignorance · Uncertainty · Instability

NOTE: Bolded and italicized words indicate ubiquity (all five groups mentioned the item); Bolded words indicate importance (it was repeatedly emphasized by one or more groups).

These categories overlap and are not mutually exclusive. I also contrast this with examples of what many of the organizations highlighted as bad or problematic, organized within similar categories—physically or mentally harmful, unfair, or irresponsible (see table 6).

Within these upcoming paragraphs that flesh out the values listed in the tables, *italicized terms reflect items that were valued as good* by a majority of the organizations in my study and/or emphasized as good by some. I discuss 'bad' items from the table alongside items valued as 'good' to show how the good and bad were conversely used to reinforce each other (e.g., saving life versus killing; freedom versus bondage or repression; clean and safe versus dirty and toxic). Similar to the organization of the table, I organized the following subsections around the main categories of values deemed to be good, those supporting: life, fairness, responsibility, and unification.

DISCUSSION OF VALUES SUPPORTING LIFE

In their section on the environment, Human Rights Watch emphasizes a core concern for the lives and well-being of humans: "As the world urbanizes and industrializes, and as effects of climate change intensify, environmental crises will increasingly devastate the lives, health, and livelihoods of people around the globe." This fits with the Human Rights Watch tagline: "protecting rights, saving lives." As demonstrated in the humanitarian campaigns that all five organizations promoted to ensure people get adequate food and medical care, they prioritize *saving human lives*. The killing of humans is the ultimate crime, especially civilians and other innocent people, such as the killing and persecution of the Rohingya, an ethnic minority, by security forces in Myanmar, as criticized by Minority Rights Group, among others.

On the basis that government executions are "cruel, inhuman, and degrading," Amnesty International has an anti-death-penalty campaign in which they oppose capital punishment "regardless of who is accused, the crime, guilt or innocence, or method of execution," whether done via beheading, electrocution, hanging, firing squad, or lethal injection. Amnesty points out that some governments use capital punishment as a political tool, such as mass executions of human prisoners unfairly accused of being spies in Saudi Arabia or blasphemy laws in Pakistan that enable the killing of religious minorities such as Hindus and Christians. Executing innocent people also occurs in democratic systems: "Since 1973, 150 U.S. prisoners sent to death row have later been exonerated," according to Amnesty International.

In order to save human lives, all organizations advocate for *meeting people's basic needs*, including food, water, shelter and homes, medical care, and, tangentially, their needs for a source of income, education for children, and sanitary facilities. This coincides with providing *humanitarian assistance* to those in need, such as civilians in a war zone, refugees, or victims of a famine or natural disaster. CARE's disaster relief efforts help provide for people's basic needs during crises, such as an earthquake in Nepal; a hurricane in Haiti; droughts in Mozambique, Ethiopia, and Malawi; and conflicts in Yemen, South Sudan, Syria, Mali, Democratic Republic of the Congo, and Gaza. Hunger is a huge issue threatening human life; CARE decries the high levels of malnutrition that still exist in the developing world (stating that 98 percent of hungry people live in developing countries), noting the long-term adverse effects of food insecurity on families: "Children born to malnourished mothers are at increased risk of disease and death. Chronically malnourished children face lifelong consequences in reduced mental capacity, lower retention in school and reduced lifetime earnings." CARE explains how climate change affects agriculture and threatens the survival of people, especially those in poverty without the resources to recover from the droughts, heat waves, or floods. CARE worked with Latina women in the highlands of Ecuador who could no longer grow crops year-round since the climate is increasingly colder. As part of climate adaptation, they were trained on how to build low-cost greenhouses, strategically plant trees to create a slightly warmer microclimate in the garden, and collect the mist on a screen as a local source of water.

Freshwater is a life necessity for hydration, sanitation, and agriculture; CARE notes that "having access to basic clean water and a decent toilet saves children's lives, gives women a leg up in earning money and ensures a good food supply." In their water programs, CARE advocates for women, especially in impoverished communities, to be included in a locality's policy decisions about water allocation and management, noting that if women and girls do not have to spend hours each day hauling water, they have more time for school or income-generating projects.

Livelihood and ability to earn a living. To enable people to sustain themselves and not be at the mercy of needing constant aid, they need a career, a job, or the ability to provide sustenance for their families, such as by growing their own food. Anti-Slavery International tells a success story of a young Nepalese woman who escaped from bonded/forced labor and was given a loan that enabled her to go to school to train to be a beautician; now she owns her own beauty shop and is able to provide a home for her family. And in support of entrepreneurship, CARE has a donation package where donors can help a Syrian refugee start a business. Many of CARE's packages include giving individual farmed animals to people in developing countries to use as a source of food or income.

Medical care is mentioned as a basic human need by Amnesty International, which demands that political prisoners get medical treatment for illnesses and injuries, often caused by prison beatings or neglect (including preventable infections from cuts and ingrown fingernails). In addition to urgent medical care, people need ongoing health care and medicine to prevent diseases, reduce suffering, and ensure their health and well-being. Poor children worldwide are particularly vulnerable to dying of preventable causes, such as malaria and malnutrition. CARE mentions the need to cut child mortality rates, as they have in Bangladesh, by providing "low-cost interventions, such as adequate nutrition, bed nets and skilled health workers." Several organizations mention the need for *reproductive care for women*. CARE laments that every day eight hundred women and teenage girls die from "preventable health complications with childbirth," mostly in developing countries, because "the world is failing to help." Thus CARE advocates for "access to quality sexual, reproductive and maternal health as a fundamental human right." This includes women exercising their reproductive rights, as CARE notes that family-planning abilities directly connect to a woman's social, economic, and physical status. They mention an interesting family-planning statistic: that if a woman is able to have fewer than four children, spaced at least three years apart, the chances of survival increase for both mother and child.

Physical well-being includes mental health. Part of the strategy of Anti-Slavery International is to provide psychological support as a vital part of recovery for formerly enslaved people, as many forced laborers suffer the trauma of rape, beatings, and separation from family. Minority Rights Group highlights how a legacy of cultural repression, hate crimes, and assimilation pressures for minorities and indigenous peoples has profound impacts, from "disproportionate levels of suicide and mental illness to impoverishment and lower life expectancy." Reconnecting minorities with their heritage often strengthens their sense of identity and community, and serves as an empowering force as they gain further recognition and social and political visibility.

Security, safety, and stability. At a macro level, to increase security and stability, society would need to mitigate war and human-induced climate change; human rights organizations often mention these harmful forces as two of the biggest causes of uncertainty and instability. On a micro level, every human needs to feel safe from physical harm and violence. Amnesty International works to protect people from torture and abuse at the hands of governments. One of the many reports they have issued is called *Beating Justice: How Fiji's Security Forces Get Away with Torture*, detailing how "uniformed officials on Fiji's islands have inflicted severe beatings, rape, and other sexual violence, attacks by police dogs, shootings and other forms of torture and ill-treatment or punishment in violation of international law." Abuse isn't just from government forces but can also happen at the hands of employers. In their campaigns against bonded ("debt") labor, Anti-Slavery International documents how some brick kiln owners in India treat their forced laborers: "violence against the workers, including beatings and abductions of family members, is common, especially when labourers seek help. Women are particularly vulnerable to abuse and sexual violence." Human Rights Watch calls on the UN Security Council to focus on ending sexual violence against women that is so prevalently used as a tactic by soldiers and terrorist groups like Boko Haram and ISIS; thus the UN should promote greater involvement of women in peace-building efforts.

Violence also occurs in the home. CARE reports that one in three women are abused in some way by a husband or male family member, resulting in long-term psychological and physical trauma. They featured a hopeful story about a Rwandan man explaining how he overcame his abusive patterns after participating in CARE's violence prevention program. He used to beat his wife because she had borne only daughters, not sons. But he stopped blaming her and asked for forgiveness, and now he and his wife support each other and share household tasks, and he teaches his kids to avoid any violence.

Another aspect of safety is the human desire for sanitation and cleanliness—not having home or work conditions that are dangerous, dirty, overcrowded, or contaminated. Amnesty International explains how deplorable the conditions are in some prisons, like the Maroua prison in Cameroon in 2014, which was so crowded with men detained without trial that they had to take turns sleeping and could not stretch their legs. One detainee described being in a cell with several men who died in front of him because they were beaten so badly. On average, eight prisoners die a month from poor and inhumane conditions. Workers in industries also face unsafe conditions. Human Rights Watch celebrated that the UN worked to pass a treaty to protect children and adults who labor in African countries in gold mining and are exposed to mercury pollution. Existing in a clean and nontoxic space increases people's comfort and, more importantly, their health and well-being.

DISCUSSION OF VALUES SUPPORTING FAIRNESS

Because I selected human rights organizations for this study, it is self-evident that *human rights* are valued by all these organizations; they condemn any crimes against humanity. Among other things, this section will give further evidence of specific types of human rights that are heralded, such as various types of *freedom*, including freedom of choice over one's body, beliefs, and actions. One of the most vital freedoms is to avoid enslavement. Yet despite being illegal, enslavement of humans is a widespread global problem present in every country, affecting millions. Anti-Slavery International explains the horrors involved in various types of modern slavery: bonded labor—a debt-based servitude where in some cases "entire families are forced to work for nothing to pay off generational debts"; forced labor like in agriculture, sweatshop factories, or domestic/household jobs, including exploitation of migrant or immigrant workers; child labor; descent-based slavery based on ethnic or caste discrimination; and forced prostitution and sex trafficking, especially of women and girls. Anti-Slavery International explains how slavery often involves coercion and detainment: "They are not allowed to work for anyone else. Violence and threats can be used to coerce them to stay, and in some cases they are kept under surveillance—sometimes under lock and key."

In addition to slavery at the hands of cruel individuals and businesses, another restraint on bodily freedom is perpetrated by governments; Amnesty International details unfair imprisonments worldwide by repressive governments who arbitrarily arrest people (for political or discriminatory reasons) and/or fail to provide them with a *fair trial or adequate access to legal representation*. In these cases, people are unfairly detained, and their core freedoms denied, without any legal recourse. Amnesty International advocates that people write to the media and governments to apply public criticism to free political prisoners. Sometimes it is people with disabilities who are put in bondage, such as being locked up in institutions, literally put in shackles—a practice that Human Rights Watch explains is denounced in the UN Convention of the Rights of Persons with Disabilities.

As part of respecting *self-determination*, innocent people should be able to give permission and *informed consent* for any practices someone induces them to participate in. One troublesome practice mentioned by several organizations is child "marriage," where against her will, a girl (not yet an adult and some not even having reached puberty) is married off to a grown man. In most countries, this practice would constitute pedophilia and rape and is therefore illegal, but certain cultures still practice child marriage even if it is technically illegal (largely in parts of Africa and Asia, but certain states in the United States allow teens to marry). CARE estimates that thirty-nine thousand girls suffer these forced marriages every day, to the detriment of their mental and physical health and well-being: "Child brides have a diminished chance of completing their education and are at a higher risk of being physically abused, contracting HIV and other diseases, and dying while pregnant or giving birth." Anti-Slavery International argues that perpetrators intentionally mislead people about this sexual exploitation of minors by calling it "marriage" to give it a respectable label rather than calling it what it is—enslavement of girls.

Another important freedom is *freedom of speech*. In Amnesty's 2016 *State of the World's Human Rights* report overview, they highlight that five years after the aspirational Arab Spring demonstrations of people power, "governments are using increasingly calculated means to crush dissent, not just in the Middle East, but globally." For example, "In Turkey and across the former Soviet Union, leaders increasingly abandoned respect for human rights altogether, as they strengthened their control of the media and further targeted their critics and opponents." In Crimea, the Tartar people openly oppose Russian occupation but face repression and are harassed into silence by Russian authorities. Amnesty's office in East Asia started a #ConnectionDenied campaign on behalf of the North Korean people whose government keeps them isolated and forbidden from accessing and sharing information: "No one should be denied their basic human rights to connect with their loved ones and to the outside world." Every human deserves to have his/her voice heard, and it is for this reason that Minority Rights Group has a Minority Voices Newsroom that serves as a digital library of media stories produced by minority and indigenous communities for circulation by the mainstream media; wider distribution of minority-produced media brings added attention to their languages as well as to their religious and cultural traditions, which are being lost in a globalized world. Women need more of a voice in the public sphere as well; an extreme example is mentioned in the section on women's rights on Human Rights Watch's website detailing how women in Saudi Arabia are fighting for the right to speak for themselves and make their own choices and not have to be represented by or obtain permission from a "male guardian" (a legal stipulation severely limiting women's freedom of choice, movement, and equal access to resources).

Protection of the vulnerable. In addition to protecting people from suffering due to lack of necessities (such as from poverty, war, or natural disasters), the human rights organizations want to protect people from being victimized, abused, and exploited at the hands of brutal people or organizations. In Anti-Slavery International's 2017 Anti-Slavery Charter, they advocate for closing gaps in legal systems that allow unscrupulous people to exploit the vulnerable (i.e., the poor, children, people with disabilities, immigrants, and women and girls); governments and NGOs should commit to empower the vulnerable and promote access to dignified work. Amnesty International's website section on torture explains vulnerability: "If you are poor or belong to a group suffering discrimination, it is more likely you will face torture and you'll have fewer ways of defending yourself. For example, women, children, members of religious or ethnic minorities, or political opposition groups." Human Rights Watch's online section on children's rights explains children's vulnerability: "Young and immature, they are often easily exploited. In many cases, they are abused by the very individuals responsible for their care." Children also need protection from being forced to work long hours in hazardous conditions (like Indonesia's child tobacco workers) or forced to become soldiers in armed conflict. Children can be vulnerable not just at the hands of unethical people but by unfortunate and unintentional larger global forces, like global warming; Human Rights Watch explains how children in particular can be disproportionately vulnerable to the negative effects of climate change, as their minds and bodies are developing, and they are more prone to become sick if their parents cannot provide them with enough clean water and food due to an unstable climate (as documented in Kenya).

People are also vulnerable to being displaced from their home territories, especially minority and indigenous groups. The right to remain where you're from (on the land you cultivated or historically have known) gets discussed as *land rights* by many of the human rights organizations. Minority Rights Group's report *State of the World's Minorities and Indigenous Peoples* critiqued the "land grabbing" that was increasing, particularly in Africa, Asia, and Oceania, often for purposes of natural resource extraction. This excludes people from food sources, livelihoods, and spiritual sites. Minority Rights Group also discusses the ongoing struggle of the Garifuna community in Honduras, who have been forcibly evicted from their communal lands for decades; their land has been "appropriated" for mining and oil extraction, palm oil plantations, and, recently, tourism projects along the pristine coastline. Tourism and also the establishment of wildlife conservation areas are reasons that the seminomadic Maasai people in Tanzania are being prohibited from the ancestral lands on which they graze cattle and access traditional medicinal plant species and water sources.

This land-grabbing demonstrates the need for *inclusion of all groups in decision-making processes so they are fair and democratic*: the Garifuna community leaders should be consulted before their communal lands are sold, and the Maasai should be included in decisions about conservation areas and to establish how they can coexist. CARE works to empower women, especially female farmers (as most working women in developing countries work in agriculture), to form groups to get involved in community decision-making about the land and water policies that affect them. Democratic inclusion relates to supporting *multiculturalism and diversity*, which, perhaps ironically, can be hard due to globalization forces that promote assimilation for minority groups, especially through mainstream media and dominant languages like English. Minority Rights Group laments that in the next hundred years, "between 50 and 90 percent of the world's 7,000 mostly indigenous languages will have died out."

People value *fair and equal access to resources*, which is part of the larger category of *equality*. CARE lists equality as one of their core values, explaining that "every human being" has equal value and thus should be respected and honored. They especially work on promoting gender equality in a patriarchal world. To empower women and address inequality also requires fighting poverty and reducing climate change impacts, as scarce resources frequently mean that the female children in a family may be "the last to eat and the first to be kept home from school." CARE advocates for women to own the land they farm (women produce half the world's food but own less than 2 percent of the world's land), to have the freedom to earn a living and get an education, and to go where they like in public, as do men. Women tend to be paid less than men across most industrial sectors, and CARE notes how in the agricultural sector in developing countries, female farmers are paid less than men, are excluded from agricultural organizations, and carry a disproportionate share of household workloads; these inequities create a gender gap in tapping women's full potential contributions to food security.

All organizations seek to fight discrimination and protect people from the harm and violence it enables. Amnesty International explains that discrimination is based on a prejudice toward people you do not identify with—someone you look down on as being different or 'less than you.' Some governments justify discrimination, such as gender discrimination, in the name of "morality, religion, or ideology." For example, female victims of sexual violence by terrorist groups or soldiers in Afghanistan can unfairly face criminal prosecution for "moral crimes" or be murdered in "honor killings," according to Human Rights Watch. Related to racial discrimination, xenophobic reactions to immigrants can foster racism. Minority Rights Group describes how immigrant populations in Europe tend to be segregated to the edges of major cities, where their work options are limited to menial jobs and those jobs native populations avoid. For example, black people in Europe face much higher unemployment rates than white people or, when employed, are often overqualified for the jobs they get.

Discrimination can be a major driver of persistent poverty, and impoverished people are more vulnerable to being enslaved into debt bondage, according to Anti-Slavery International: "Bonded labour exists because of the persistence of poverty, widespread discrimination making large groups of people vulnerable to exploitation, and the existence of people who are prepared to exploit the desperation of others." The discriminated social groups get trapped in debt and poverty in large part because they are denied fair access to educational and justice resources.

Discrimination against lesbian, gay, bisexual, and transgender people is a worldwide problem. Human Rights watch explains that such discrimination includes "torture, killing and executions, arrests under unjust laws, unequal treatment, censorship, medical abuses, discrimination in health and jobs and housing, domestic violence, abuses against children, and denial of family rights." They list recent examples, such as President Trump's discriminatory policy preventing transgender individuals from (any longer) serving in the U.S. military; U.S. doctors performing irreversible genital surgeries on intersex infants to presumably make them more "normal" and "lovable," rather than letting the child make that decision later in life; and Russian police brutality against gay men in Chechnya (roundups, beatings, detentions, and humiliation).

In asking for fair justice systems, Anti-Slavery International advocates for child and adult victims of enslavement to not be treated as criminals by police because they were forced to commit crimes like prostitution, pickpocketing, petty theft, drug cultivation, or begging, or because of any illegal immigration status. To combat this injustice, Anti-Slavery International has a program to train European Union officials to prosecute traffickers, not their victims. The organization also makes it a policy to provide legal support and empowerment to people impacted by slavery so they can claim their legal rights and seek reparations and compensation from abusers. In the case of government torture, Human Rights Watch and Amnesty International advocate for legal compensation, redress, and rehabilitation for victims and justice (prosecution) for perpetrators. Many organizations lament lax government laws and enforcement that enable criminals/abusers to operate with impunity. In supporting international justice systems, Amnesty International says its three main tenets are justice, truth, and reparation. The notion of justice can go beyond just criminal justice. For example, CARE defines "social justice" as the idea that "all people, everywhere in the world, have the right to a life of dignity. This means a life free from poverty, violence, discrimination, or human rights violations . . . where all people are included in society and can claim their rights to healthcare, shelter, and education regardless of how poor or rich they are." With a similar focus on justice being based on respect and compassion, the executive director of Human Rights Watch, Kenneth Roth, advocates for following the golden rule (as stated in their 2017 world report), when he implores that in a political climate filled with strongmen, repression, and unresponsive governments, we need to "affirm the basic value 'we should treat others the way that we would want them to treat us.'"

The last value I'm categorizing under "fairness" is independence. While we might commonly think of independence as meaning personal autonomy (the opposite of interdependence), in this case, the human rights organizations mention it in relation to the ethicality of their own organizations remaining *independent / free from conflicts of interest* that could bias their programs and priorities toward vested (moneyed) interests or politically partisan interests. In this way, they demonstrate integrity, trustworthiness, and credibility by acting solely on behalf of their target audiences/beneficiaries rather than investors or authorities.

DISCUSSION OF VALUES SUPPORTING RESPONSIBILITY

Responsibility is something human rights organizations expect from citizens, governments, corporations, and even their own organizations. They emphasize that they *work effectively to enact change and solve problems* to demonstrate they are not wasting resources, and thus it is efficacious for us to join their efforts. In the call-to-action in their campaigns, human rights organizations shun apathy and promote the notion of everyone making a difference and *taking action to help those in need*; this includes the public *speaking up to powerful interests and politicians* on behalf of justice and rights. Politicians are responsible for reforming the law and enforcing it, but that requires *political will*. Amnesty International claims that the two major reasons that people get away with grotesque human rights violations is due to "a lack of political will to investigate and prosecute people suspected of committing crimes, and weak criminal justice systems" that require public pressure to strengthen. For example, Amnesty asks supporters to "speak out for defenders" in South America, in support of hundreds of environmental activists, many of whom are indigenous people, who have been harassed, threatened, attacked, unfairly jailed, and even killed because they "work against powerful political and economic interests to protect the resources without which none of us would be able to live."

Sometimes responsibility is about governments doing their part in "burden sharing" to resolve global issues, whether it be in reducing greenhouse gas emissions, ending armed conflicts, or taking in refugees. In discussing responsibility for Syrian war refugees, Amnesty International insists that "Europe has a duty, both moral and legal, to welcome those fleeing conflict and persecution. This is not a responsibility to be outsourced or pushed back on other countries." Similarly, Human Rights Watch implores Indian authorities to "abide by international legal obligations" and not forcibly return any Rohingya refugees to Burma, and for China to halt forced returns of North Korean detainees, as, in both cases, returned refugees would face imminent danger. Responsible governments should also work toward *peace and coexistence*, which means that we all must hold nations accountable for reckless arms trading that fuels conflicts and indiscriminate harm, according to Amnesty International; they also note that states must take precautions and minimize harm, especially to civilians during war, as a humanitarian principle. To support the international human rights system, states must "protect *international gov-*

ernance and universal standards and oversight," including enforcement of international treaties and participation in the International Criminal Court, which prosecutes criminals when nations abdicate their responsibility to do so. International oversight is especially necessary to prevent genocide, according to Mark Lattimer, executive director of Minority Rights Group: "International isolation is a known risk factor for genocide or mass killing. If governments are increasingly evading international scrutiny, this is a serious concern."

Human Rights Watch deems government *accountability* for genocide, war crimes, and crimes against humanity an essential element to achieving international justice and respect for human rights. The 2016 Amnesty International report *State of the World's Human Rights* Asia-Pacific overview laments that governments seek to shield themselves from accountability for the criticisms they are facing, especially on social media, as young people speak out for their rights. In talking about the effects of war on children in particular, such as in Iraq, Amnesty emphasizes that states should be accountable for helping children recover: "If there are resources for the war, there must also be resources to deal with the consequences of war."

It is also the responsibility of *corporations* to treat people with care and avoid unnecessary harm. Businesses should avoid risky and dangerous behavior that threatens lives, like emitting greenhouse gases and other types of pollution and maintaining unsafe working conditions. Highlighting hypocrisy, an Amnesty International news segment on so-called sustainable palm oil critiques the industry's misleading marketing that conceals their unsafe labor practices in Indonesia, which put adult and child workers at physical risk from heavy labor and pollution hazards. Human Rights Watch has a business section on its website to "expose harmful practices by multinational corporations that can devastate communities" and "show how government failures and predatory business practices can combine to heap misery on the poor." They give an example of sweatshops in Asia, asking us to sign a petition for increased *transparency and honesty* from major fashion retailers about worker protections in the garment industry supply chain. Anti-Slavery International also exposes garment factory worker abuses, with a focus on prisonlike conditions and forced labor of girls and young women in Indian sweatshops: "Many workers suffer appalling ill health, brought on by poor diet, poor hygiene in the hostels, and the hazards associated with working with cotton," including lung problems such as tuberculosis; some workers die from a lack of health care.

All the human rights organizations emphasize the responsibility of societies to *educate children, especially girls.* Organizations work on overcoming the economic and social obstacles that keep children out of school, such as children needing to work to help impoverished families, girls getting pregnant or being forced into becoming child brides, or facing discrimination based on their ethnicity or gender (deeming them unworthy of social mobility opportunities). For example, Anti-Slavery International is attacking descent-based slavery in Niger through education: "For centuries, people from the slave-caste have been denied access to education, so this

is the first time children of these communities have benefited from formal school-
ing. . . . Education has given the children an understanding of their rights and
the confidence and ambition to follow careers in the future." They highlight that
no girls of this caste from these Niger villages have been forced into marriage, as
they normally would have if they were not in school. And microloans given to local mothers to start businesses helped bring some funds to these schools that facil-
itated building local wells so that children (particularly girls) were not taken from
school to retrieve water for their families.

CARE's section on education has a motto: "educate a girl—change the world,"
as educated girls grow up to lead healthier, more productive lives, helping their
families and communities do the same (see photo 1). In developing countries,
CARE works with boys, men, women, and girls to overcome the multiple barriers that keep girls out of school, such as lower social status, early marriage, chores,
hunger, and school safety and sanitation (access to bathroom facilities and men-
struation hygiene products).

Discrimination in education is not just a problem in developing countries. Minority Rights Group explains how the Black Lives Matter movement in the United
States has exposed the "sub-standard education" for poor students of color and
the lifetime negative effects it has on their future economic well-being. High drop-
out rates and the "school-to-prison pipeline" are a phenomenon facing black and
brown youth in the United States as the presence of police officers in schools has
expanded. Grassroots solutions include building trust between communities and
the police as well as actively addressing the host of disparities experienced by many
African Americans that foster disenfranchisement.

DISCUSSION OF VALUES SUPPORTING UNITY

Human rights organizations champion the notion of having respect for human dignity as a unifying trait all human beings deserve. CARE foregrounds their organization's "unshakeable commitment to the dignity of people," which they foster in
their mission to "save lives, defeat poverty and achieve social justice." Anti-Slavery
International promotes the inherent value of human beings by stating that people
should not be "sold like objects, forced to work for little or no pay" or be "at the
mercy of their employers." Human dignity is implied in messages that lament when
humans are treated like objects or "animals." For example, Amnesty International
quotes a Malawi girl with albinism saying, "We are not animals to be hunted or
sold," as she describes how painful it is for her to have people put a price tag on her
and tell her they could sell her body parts for ten thousand dollars. Amnesty has a
campaign to protect people with albinism from abductions, murder, and mutila-
tions caused by some superstitious people wanting to use their body parts in rituals.
And Anti-Slavery International tells Moulkheri's tragic story in Mauritania, where
she was "owned" because she is part of a slave caste; the owners raped her and did
not let her care for her last baby because she had to go take care of goats instead, so

her baby died out in the hot sun and was found being eaten by ants. Moulkheri said, "I had to bury her myself, with my hands; I felt like I was burying an animal instead of my child." Another enslaved woman of this caste in Mauritania described how she had to sleep with the farmed animals, with very little cover. These stories illustrate a lack of basic dignities afforded human beings, such as self-determination, shelter, and a proper burial. Access to appropriate toilet facilities is also mentioned as a basic right by Amnesty International in their "Living with Dignity" section on people with disabilities. Human Rights Watch shares a story of a Syrian teenage girl in a wheelchair who testified before an EU committee to demand "better access to bathrooms and basic services" for Syrian refugees held in Greece (fortunately, she and her family ended up getting asylum in Germany). The organization works to "ensure that all migrants are treated with dignity."

Another Syrian teenage girl who felt that she had to "leave herself behind" was touched by receiving a letter from a former refugee (through a "letters of hope" program from CARE) because it made her feel like she existed and someone acknowledged her. CARE's home page features a story about children standing in solidarity with refugees by sending them heartfelt letters that say "I love you." Love, in opposition to hatred or apathy, is sometimes mentioned by organizations as a way to show that people matter. They also acknowledge the importance of family bonds and being with loved ones by describing the pain families feel when they are separated by detention, enslavement, or migration.

The need for *peaceful and harmonious relations among people* is emphasized by the majority of human rights organizations, as opposed to conflict, violence, discrimination, and exclusion. Minority Rights Group works to "promote peaceful coexistence and sustainable social change" and offers evidence that "the inclusion of minority communities leads to stronger, more cohesive societies." To embrace multiculturalism, we must respect the importance of people's *sense of identity*, which is closely aligned with their cultural traditions and sense of community. Amnesty International notes that indigenous people "often share a key value—the close association between their identity, their way of life, and their lands" for which they serve as guardians for the next generation; thus, land and cultural rights should be respected. Allowing people to openly express their beliefs and self-identity is vital to inclusion and coexistence. For example, Minority Rights Group observes that the Ahmadi Muslim minority in Pakistan must conceal their identity and religion to avoid being accused of blasphemy and potentially killed by the government for practicing their version of Islam. And Human Rights Watch notes that LGBTQ individuals should not be persecuted or discriminated against for "who they are" and should be able to be safely open, not closeted about their identity.

Another unifying value is the idea that we all should *work together for positive social change*; the organizations emphasize how they *partner and collaborate with* other groups (from other NGOs and social movements, to marginalized and impacted communities, to government and industry groups); not surprisingly, human rights organizations encourage us to *be part of a social movement, network, or community* working to effectively enact social justice.

Responsibility for Problems

In my analysis, I took note of what entities the human rights organizations directly or indirectly blame for causing or allowing harms and injustices. While some organizations sometimes mention specific groups causing harm (such as criminals, terrorists, abusive or violent men, unfair employers, or other unscrupulous people), the focus is more often on harmful social norms and institutions. The most prominent institution that we expect to protect us and uphold justice is government (in particular, nation-states), so human rights organizations' campaigns highlight where governments are corrupt, oppressive, or neglectful in fulfilling their duties to society. And with the exception of CARE's campaigns, industries and corporations are a common target of blame, particularly for exploitation of workers and lands, greed, or deceptive practices. Sometimes governments are complicit in this industry exploitation, especially if politicians are influenced or corrupted by corporate money interests; extractive industries are singled out quite often. Larger social forces also perpetuate discrimination, including patriarchal and racist (including colonialist) social norms that tend to favor males, the wealthy, the able-bodied, heterosexuals, and members of the dominant race and religion (gender inequality is a focus of CARE and Human Rights Watch, while cultural appropriation and suppression is a focus of Minority Rights Group). Overall, the implication of the campaigns is that we need to work together as an organized and effective force to remedy the socioeconomic and political factors that enable injustice.

Summary

The five human rights groups in my 2017 sample (Amnesty International, Anti-Slavery International, CARE, Human Rights Watch, and Minority Rights Group International) had online campaigns that aim to prevent harm to humans most at risk, especially vulnerable people, including women, children, the poor, indigenous people and other ethnic minority groups, refugees, LGBTQ communities, and those who are enslaved. While the focus primarily on humans does not comprise a "total liberation" framework for all species (Best 2014), the campaigns do advocate for liberation and justice by targeting weak or corrupt governments, exploitative industries or employers, and discriminatory societal norms that perpetuate inequity and injustice. Values common to all the human rights organization include human health, access to basic living needs, human rights, individual freedoms, democratic inclusion of all groups in decision-making, and education (including equitable opportunities for women and girls). To form the human animal earthling identity, I'll incorporate these values, set in the context of a more biocentric set of values, in the final chapter.

CHAPTER 5

What Values Animal Protection Organizations Appeal To

In this chapter you will learn about the vast exploitation and suffering of nonhuman animals, but you can take some solace in discovering ways that animal protection organizations are appealing to humans to change destructive patterns so that animals can recover, live freely, and thrive. This chapter essentially describes the collective values advocated in the 2017 web discourse of the five animal protection organizations in my sample (see appendix A for details on the methodology): Animal Equality International, International Fund for Animal Welfare (IFAW), People for the Ethical Treatment of Animals (PETA), Sea Shepherd Conservation Society, and World Wildlife Fund (WWF). The sample includes a mix of groups that focus on animal rights (Animal Equality, PETA, and Sea Shepherd), animal welfare (IFAW), and wildlife conservation (WWF and Sea Shepherd). By examining their main campaign messages, I first identify the beings on whose behalf they advocate and who merit our care and protection (specifically which animal groups—human and/or nonhuman—and other beings). I then share examples of the many concepts, traits, behaviors, and entities that they highlight as good/ideal (something that is presumably valued by the organization and the public) and, conversely, the ones they highlight as bad or problematic (something to be avoided or reformed). The chapter ends with a discussion of the groups and social norms that animal protection organizations blame as the source of the problems. The items that are characterized as good or bad in this chapter will later be compared to the ones identified in the web discourse on human rights and environmental organizations in upcoming chapters, toward the end goal of identifying overlapping values between all three causes that can serve as the basis of a human animal earthling identity.

Who Merits Care and Protection

As highlighted in table 7, animal protection organizations talk broadly about all kinds of living beings and include human and nonhuman animals, sometimes together, when they use terms such as "animals," "sentient beings," "individuals," "all life," or "biodiverse life." Anyone who could be considered an individual sentient being (whether human or not) is deserving of protection. Some of the more mainstream organizations list living entities along with humans, but with the latter separated out and described as "people" (namely, IFAW saying "animals and people" and WWF saying "people and nature"). All organizations express concern for the well-being of all humans, with children getting some specific attention from IFAW, communities living near wilderness (such as indigenous communities) being highlighted by IFAW and Sea Shepherd, and "vulnerable" people being mentioned by WWF. Not surprisingly, the animal rights organizations make fewer distinctions across the human species than expressed by the human rights organizations in their campaigns and much more differentiation across nonhuman species.

Across the board, all animal protection organizations display a particular concern for:

- wildlife, whether free or in captivity
- mammals, both 'wild' and domesticated species, and
- human beings (humans are of course a mammal, but, with the exception of PETA and Animal Equality, organizations did not refer to humans as mammals or as 'animals')

Mammals, especially large or iconic species, are more commonly portrayed than other scientific categories of animals, especially more so than amphibians or insects (who were only really mentioned in campaigns by PETA). WWF lists all categories of animal species when they quote overall extinction rates. Birds are included in campaigns of IFAW, Animal Equality, and PETA (with the latter two animal rights groups mentioning farmed birds more so than wild birds). The only reptiles that garner attention are sea turtles, who are an endangered species mentioned by the majority of organizations. Endangered species (a subcategory of wild animals) are a popular category, especially for IFAW, WWF, and Sea Shepherd. Marine animals are popular with all organizations, but that is often limited to marine mammals (namely whales, dolphins, and seals). But fishes, sharks and rays, cephalopods and other nonmammal aquatic species tend to be highlighted only by animal protection organizations with animal rights ideologies (Animal Equality, PETA, and Sea Shepherd). Those same rights organizations also show concern for animals trapped in captivity, namely in zoos and aquariums (and, for Animal Equality and PETA, animals used in research labs). These three animal rights organizations also express concern for the well-being and rights of animals used for human food in agriculture and aquaculture. WWF discusses fishes and farmed animals sometimes in terms of ecological utility but also in terms of human utility—namely, continuing to serve as a source of protein for a growing human population. Domesticated animals are a focus for Animal Equality and PETA (farmed animals and companion animals) and IFAW (companion animals only), who often note that these animals are victims of abuse and neglect by human owners/caretakers.

TABLE 7 Who Merits Care and Protection

As explicitly addressed in animal protection organizations' campaign materials based on their missions and areas of advocacy focus. This indicates areas of emphasis, priorities, and/or terms used and is not meant to imply certain organizations do not care at all about those entities they didn't speak directly about.

WHO MERITS CARE AND PROTECTION	ANIMAL EQUALITY INTERNATIONAL	INTERNATIONAL FUND FOR ANIMAL WELFARE	PEOPLE FOR THE ETHICAL TREATMENT OF ANIMALS	SEA SHEPHERD CONSERVATION SOCIETY	WORLD WILDLIFE FUND
All animals (can include humans)	X	X	X		
Sentient beings	X	X	X	X	
"Animals and people"		X			
"People and nature"					X
"Individuals"	X	X	X	X	
All life; every living thing				X	X
Future generations				X	
Biodiverse network of species; diverse life				X	X
Endangered species / vulnerable species		X		X	X
"Ecologically, economically, and culturally important species"					X
(NONHUMAN) ANIMAL-SPECIFIC CATEGORIES					
Wildlife	X	X	X	X	X Iconic species
Farmed animals	X		X	X Fishes	
Companion animals	X	X	X		

Victims	X	X	X		
Captive animals	X		X	X	X
Animals in research labs	X		X		
Mammals	X Pigs, cows, sheep, fur-bearing animals, great apes, marine mammals	X Large land mammals like apex species; marine mammals	X Both domesticated and wild species (especially those in captivity)	X Marine mammals	X Elephants, tigers, snow leopards, polar bears, panda bears, whales, seals, dolphins, deer, orangutans, rhinos
Birds	X Chickens, turkeys	X	X		X
Fishes and marine animals	X Fishes	X	X	X Marine wildlife, sharks, fishes, endangered species	X
Amphibians			X		X
Reptiles	X Sea turtles	X Sea turtles	X	X Sea turtles	X Sea turtles
Insects			X		
NATURE-SPECIFIC CATEGORIES					
The environment	X		X	X	X
Habitat	X	X	X	X	X
Parks/reserves	X	X			X
Nature					X
Fragile/vulnerable ecosystems				X	X
Biodiverse ecosystems				X	X
A living planet					X

TABLE 7 Who Merits Care and Protection (continued)

WHO MERITS CARE AND PROTECTION	ANIMAL EQUALITY INTERNATIONAL	INTERNATIONAL FUND FOR ANIMAL WELFARE	PEOPLE FOR THE ETHICAL TREATMENT OF ANIMALS	SEA SHEPHERD CONSERVATION SOCIETY	WORLD WILDLIFE FUND
HUMAN-SPECIFIC CATEGORIES					
Humans	X	X	X	X	X
Children		X			
Vulnerable human communities					X
Human communities living near wildlife, including indigenous peoples		X		X	
Activists				X	

In the nature-specific category, the majority of animal protection organizations express the importance of protecting the environment and, in particular, wildlife habitats. WWF and Sea Shepherd are the two organizations that focus more on environmental protection, especially of "fragile" and "biodiverse" ecosystems. WWF emphasizes "a living planet" and the need to support nature parks and reserves (with the latter also being mentioned by IFAW).

Common Values: What Matters Most

In their attempts to appeal to public support for their campaigns, animal protection organizations not only show concern for certain groups they think the public should care about, but they also promote many common values that societies tend to support. In table 8, I list the main concepts, traits, entities, and behaviors that many of the organizations valued as good or ideal. In providing examples of the most ubiquitous and emphasized values, I categorized them (as I have in previous chapters) into values related to supporting life and well-being, fairness, responsibility, and unification. These categories overlap and are not mutually exclusive. I also contrast this with examples of what many of the organizations highlighted as bad or problematic, organized within similar categories—things that are physically or mentally harmful, unfair, or irresponsible (see table 9).

Within these upcoming paragraphs that flesh out the values listed in the tables, *italicized terms reflect items that were valued as good* by a majority of the organizations in my study and/or emphasized as good by some. I discuss 'bad' items from the table alongside items valued as 'good' to show how the good and bad were conversely used to reinforce each other. I organized the sections around the main categories of values deemed to be good, those supporting life, fairness, responsibility, and unification.

DISCUSSION OF VALUES SUPPORTING LIFE

All animal protection organizations in this study emphasize the need to *save the lives of animals* (especially nonhuman animals, but also humans). WWF's mission broadly emphasizes providing for "every living thing, including ourselves," saying they must "save a living planet," with their biggest goal being to save wildlife. In describing the various beings whose lives they protect, IFAW explains: "We rescue individuals, safeguard populations, and preserve habitats," indicating that animals matter as individuals, while plants are protected as part of larger ecosystems that provide needed habitat for animals. IFAW has campaigns to end the illegal hunting of wildlife such as tigers and elephants, and the commercial hunting of seals and whales. Sea Shepherd Conservation Society protects all marine animals, including fish, and is well known for their efforts against the Japanese whaling industry; their website estimates that Japan has killed more than 14,000 whales in the last three decades since the International Whaling Commission banned commercial whal-

TABLE 8 What Is Valued as Good or Ideal in Animal Protection Organizations' Campaigns

VALUED AS GOOD OR IDEAL BY ANIMAL PROTECTION ORGANIZATIONS' CAMPAIGNS	MORE POPULAR: MENTIONED BY A MAJORITY OF GROUPS	SOMEWHAT POPULAR: MENTIONED BY SEVERAL GROUPS
LIFE-SUPPORTING VALUES	· *Life and saving lives (animals)* · *Health and well-being of animals* · *Health and well-being of humans* · Sustainability and healthy ecosystems · Biodiversity · Rehabilitating and releasing wild animals · Protecting animals · Protecting and valuing habitats and the environment · Safety and security	· **Providing domesticated or rescued animals with their basic needs (food, water, shelter, vet care)** · Protection from the elements (for any animal) · Humane actions / being humane · Sanctuaries; providing sanctuary · Naturalness · Preciousness / uniqueness / rarity · **Regeneration of endangered species populations** · Species longevity on earth
FAIR VALUES	· Mobility (ability for animals to move about freely) · Strong animal protection laws · Strong enforcement of laws; catching and prosecuting criminals	· Animal rights · Equality and equitable ethical standards applied toward nonhuman animals · Acknowledging the desires, interests, and needs of sentient beings · Respect for animals · Animals escaping or being freed from captivity · Wildness and animal freedom · Inclusion of animal and eco-protection considerations in decision-making · Inclusion of local people in decision-making · Justice and fairness · Government and corporate responsiveness to and respect for the public's interests · Following and respecting the law

RESPONSIBLE VALUES	• Investigating and exposing animal abuses • Educating the public and raising awareness of issues • Taking action and speaking up • Fighting for rights • Effective activism/advocacy • Quality science and research • Resolving conflicts and solving problems • Making a difference • Conscientious consumerism (shopping/eating cruelty-free and green)	• Going vegan; consuming vegan (non-animal-based) products • Protesting and demonstrating • Being part of a social movement • Commitment • Political will • Efficiency (such as in use of resources) • Precaution / being careful • Investing in the future / planning • Having enough resources for animal protection and advocacy efforts • Transparency and openness • Moral consistency • Coexistence • Responsible caretaking of animals
UNIFYING VALUES	• Collaborating with and joining others / building partnerships and coalitions • Respect for sentience • Compassion and kindness • Keeping families together (including mother animals and their babies)	• Respecting maternal bonds and parental love for offspring • Companionship / friendship • Interdependence • Love and devotion • Engaging communities and the public • Intelligence in animals

Note: Bolded and italicized words indicate ubiquity (all five organizations mentioned the item); bolded words indicate importance (it was repeatedly emphasized by one or more organizations).

TABLE 9 What Is Represented as Problematic or Bad/Wrong in Animal Protection Organizations' Campaigns (Nonvalued Concepts, Traits, Entities, or Behaviors)

PORTRAYED AS BAD OR WRONG BY ANIMAL PROTECTION CAMPAIGNS	MORE POPULAR: MENTIONED BY A MAJORITY OF GROUPS	SOMEWHAT POPULAR: MENTIONED BY SEVERAL GROUPS
RELATED TO PHYSICAL OR MENTAL HARM	• *Killing or slaughtering of animals (human and nonhuman)* • Death • Cruelty and abuse • Deprivation • Misery and sadness • Pain and suffering, especially when unnecessary • Disease • Species decline or population loss • Extinction of species • **Degrading and destroying nature and habitat (land or sea); deforestation**	• Emotional trauma • Skinning someone • Crying and screaming • Fear • Frustration • Use of force • Rape and forced impregnation of female animals • Separating babies from mothers • **Poor or unnatural living conditions** • Overcrowding • Commercial hunting and fishing • Natural disasters • Destructiveness
RELATED TO UNFAIRNESS	• **Wildlife crime (poachers and traffickers)** • Factory farming; animal farms and slaughterhouses • Cages, pens, and nets • Imprisonment / entrapment of animals	• Kidnapping / capturing / abducting animals • Enslavement of animals • Zoos and aquariums • Animal research labs • Injustice and disrespect for animal life and autonomy • **Captivity / bondage / chains** • **Exploitation of animals or nature** • **Objectification or commodification of a living being** • Treating animals as disposable • Stealing from someone (including their babies, milk, eggs, or skin) • **Taking advantage of the vulnerable** • **Illegal hunting and fishing**
RELATED TO IRRESPONSIBILITY	• Pollution • Dangers, risks, and threats • Climate change (human-caused) • Apathy (ignoring problems; complicity; disregard of animals) • Ignorance • Profit-motivation • Hiding abuse / cover-ups • **Wastefulness**	• Selfishness • Shallowness • Misrepresentation / deception • **Irresponsible and neglectful practices (including unsustainable)** • Weak or neglectful governments • **Scarcity of resources (and human depletion of resources)**

Note: Bolded and italicized words indicate ubiquity (all five organizations mentioned the item); bolded words indicate importance (it was repeatedly emphasized by one or more organizations).

ing, while Sea Shepherd activists have documented saving 3,651 whales between 2005 and 2013.

In terms of saving animal lives, PETA cites some statistics of industries that kill animals, including the 1 billion animals killed annually for leather worldwide, and 9 billion chickens killed for their flesh and 305 million hens used for their eggs, and later killed, in the United States alone. PETA's vegan starter kit claims "going vegan saves lives," potentially saving one hundred animals per year. Similarly, Animal Equality's web section on food encourages us to save up to ninety-five animals a year through adopting a vegan diet, appealing to our moral desire not to harm or kill animals for trivial reasons: "Most of us already believe that animals should not be harmed unnecessarily, yet eating animal products harms and kills animals and is unnecessary for human health." They lament that hundreds of millions of animals are killed just because we like how they taste, explaining that more than 56 billion farmed animals are killed worldwide each year, not including "the fish and other sea creatures whose deaths are so great they are only measured by the ton." Animal Equality visually highlights the murder of animals by featuring animal corpses, often bloody, shown stabbed by humans in bullfighting rings or hanging from meathooks in slaughterhouses. PETA's website features many animals killed in agribusiness, such as dead hens living with live hens in egg-industry cages; male chicks dying in the garbage by the hundreds at hatcheries; goats dead on an organic dairy farm; chickens raised for meat whose legs collapsed under the weight of their bodies (making it impossible to reach the food and water bins); fish dead in nets or on the decks of ships; and cows, pigs, and birds in various stages of dismemberment and consciousness at slaughterhouses (see animal farming photos 2–4, 8–9, 13–14).

The *health and well-being of nonhuman animals* is important to all the animal protection organizations. This includes not only physical and mental well-being and healthy living conditions but also the avoidance of suffering, especially unnecessary suffering for trivial reasons, which relates to the popular goal of *protecting animals, especially from cruelty and abuse*. In prioritizing which animal issues to work on, PETA focuses on "the four areas in which the largest numbers of animals suffer the most intensely for the longest periods of time: in the food industry, in the clothing trade, in laboratories, and in the entertainment industry." Similarly, in fulfilling Animal Equality's vision of "a world where animals are respected and protected," they focus campaigns on "sparing the most amount of animal suffering" to prevent "a life of misery and an untimely death on farms, in laboratories, and in slaughterhouses." Their website displays examples of extreme suffering from investigations conducted on a chicken meat farm in the UK, a slaughterhouse in Mexico, an egg farm in Mexico, bullfighting events across Spain, and a Spanish mink farm, often involving animals suffering while dying. For example, they describe "the misery suffered by animals on fur farms, and their agonizing deaths: by gassing, electrocution or being simply skinned alive." Previewing a variety of issues, PETA's website emphasizes the cruelty humans impose on nonhuman animals for specious reasons: "Every day in countries around the world, animals are fighting for their lives. They are enslaved, beaten, and kept in chains to make them perform for humans' 'entertainment'; they are mutilated and confined to tiny cages so that we can kill them and eat them; they are burned, blinded, poisoned, and cut up alive in the name of 'science'; they are electrocuted, strangled, and skinned alive so that people can parade around in their coats; and worse."

Within their concern for animal health and welfare, several animal protection organizations mention *rescuing animals and/or providing for their basic needs (responsible caretaking)*. IFAW's mission is to "rescue and protect animals around the world," noting that they "provide hands-on assistance to animals in need, whether it's dogs and cats, wildlife and livestock, or rescuing animals in the wake of disasters." To further describe their concern for all types of animals needing support during natural disasters, IFAW explains: "While many natural disasters cause great financial hardship and can tragically result in loss of human life, animals are often forgotten in the chaos. Even though wildlife has adapted to extreme situations to some extent, they can often be victims of injury or desperately lacking food and shelter as a result of the disaster. Domesticated animals, dependent on human caretakers for survival, are often left to perish." In support of responsible caretaking that ensures "animals are happy and healthy because their basic needs are met," IFAW established a concept called Adequate Guardianship where "every dog and cat should get enough food, water and basic veterinary care. Equally, every animal should have access to shelter, exercise and companionship." This includes dogs who live on the street but receive some support from humans living near them.

Sea Shepherd Conservation Society has a campaign against the capture of dolphins in Taiji, Japan, for the aquarium industry, speaking forcefully in opposition to this cruelty: "Since the early [1960s], an insidious trade of intelligent, self-aware sentient beings has been growing like a malignant cancer within human society. It is a slave trade that has been the cause of unimaginable misery and has claimed the lives of thousands of dolphins. This cruel industry has spread across Europe and Asia with hundreds of marine aquariums operating, many of them with grossly inadequate facilities." Similarly, PETA provides an example of an unhealthy and unnatural living environment for wild animal species in describing SeaWorld's "abusement parks" that house marine animals in "lonely isolation or with incompatible tankmates," where animals are "denied everything that is natural and important to them," causing stress, monotony, boredom, and often premature death. PETA gives similar grim descriptions of the cramped and filthy conditions animals endure in many circuses, zoos, and fur farms, where they live in deprivation. PETA's description of animal experimentation labs also highlights the loneliness and boredom animals experience in the "barren cages" but also emphasizes their mental and physical anguish: "All they can do is sit and wait in fear of the next terrifying and painful procedure."

PETA's sections on animals used in the fashion and food industries feature many examples of animal suffering, such as untreated open wounds (e.g., from rough handling of sheep and goats during shearing or from pecks and bites from crowded cage-mates) or medical procedures performed without anesthesia (e.g., castration, branding, tail docking, debeaking, or dehorning), causing farmed animals to scream in pain and suffer for days. Industries that kill reptiles and fur-bearing animals for their pelts and skins cause much suffering in order to slaughter them in ways that result in an unblemished pelt for sale, including electrocution, head bludgeoning, and skinning them alive. PETA explains "snakes are commonly nailed to trees and their bodies are cut open from one end to the other as they are skinned alive, in the belief that live flaying keeps the skins supple." They document the unhealthy and unnatural living conditions for each type of animal farmed, saying, for example, that "ducks and geese raised for their flesh spend their entire lives crammed in dirty, dark sheds, where they suffer from injury and disease and are deprived of everything that is natural and important to them." PETA contrasts this with the freedom that ducks would have flying hundreds of miles each day in their natural habitat when migrating as well as coupling and mating for life. Images show ducks in cages and humans force-feeding geese with pipes down their throats for the foie gras industry.

Another way to ensure animals' well-being is to *rehabilitate and release wild animals or provide sanctuary and lifetime care for wild animals who cannot live on their own.* IFAW's rescue team focuses on "saving individual animals in crisis, rehabilitating them, and releasing them to the wild," giving examples of elephants, rhinos, tigers, and raptors. When rehabilitated animals cannot be released due to inability to survive on their own or in "areas with too many human settlements to make local release appropriate," such as the case with orphaned elephants near Kaziranga, India, IFAW finds them permanent sanctuary. This is not just for land animals—IFAW rescues stranded marine mammals off the coast of Cape Cod and expresses a commitment to the establishment and development of sanctuaries for whales. WWF also works on species recovery in the wild, highlighting Asian species such as pandas, tigers, and river dolphins.

Humanity's health and well-being are valued along with nonhuman animals by animal protection organizations. WWF's website shows activists wearing "save the humans" T-shirts, and their organizational description emphasizes that people are at the center of their work because they want to "ensure nature's ability to provide—for the sake of every living thing, including ourselves." WWF summarizes how wildlife conservation also contributes to human health and well-being by providing "breathable air, clean water, food, fibers, building materials, medicines, energy, fertile soils, climate regulation, transport, and recreational and spiritual values." In WWF's online climate change section, it laments how a warming climate will degrade humans' quality of life: "Coastal home values drop as insurance premiums rise; drought reduces feed for American farmers' cattle and water for their crops; more pollen and dust in the air aggravates asthma and allergies in kids and adults alike." WWF notes that climate change matters because it impacts humanity in terms of our security (destabilizing agricultural production and displacing vulnerable people, especially frontline communities prone to flooding); our economy (investing in clean energy to create jobs and a more stable climate); and our freshwater (reducing availability of water for agricultural and urban use). They explain how we must adjust to feed a growing population of humans with the planet's limited land and freshwater resources, by reducing over a billion tons of food waste, growing food more sustainably, and distributing it to reach the 800 million malnourished people who need it.

PETA also discusses the need to reduce world hunger; they argue that shifting away from animal agribusiness and fishing and toward plant-based diets will make better use of resources to produce more food for humans globally, and it will also end unsafe working conditions in slaughterhouses and improve overall human health. PETA's vegan guides tout a nutritious plant-based diet as a way to help prevent or reverse common life-threatening diseases.

WWF's campaign for freshwater ecosystems stresses the need for cities and communities to address water scarcity and quality issues, warning that more than a billion people lack access to water and double that number lack sanitation, which causes disease and is a leading killer of humans worldwide. They also express concern for the millions of people who rely on fish as a source of protein and livelihood. The Sea Shepherd Conservation Society critiques how open-net salmon farms threaten not only fish and wildlife but also local tourism in British Columbia and the rights and livelihoods of indigenous people in the area who oppose the salmon farms. Additionally, out of respect for human life and the heroism of activists, Sea Shepherd named one of their sea turtle campaigns "Operation Jairo" to memorialize a Costa Rican activist, Jairo Mora Sandoval, "who was brutally murdered on May 31, 2013, while attempting to protect leatherback turtle nests."

IFAW seeks solutions that balance the needs of "animals and people who live in communities around critical animal habitats," noting that both groups need help: "In most regions where we find intense animal suffering or population loss, we also find people who are struggling for their very survival." For example, in the area surrounding the Mansas National Park in India, a protected tiger habitat, IFAW has installed hundreds of fuel-efficient stoves that reduce the need for humans to go out searching for firewood in tiger territory.

Of course, you cannot save the lives of animals and ensure their well-being without protecting habitats and the natural world. Most land species live in forests, which are biodiverse areas, and WWF blames most of the world's deforestation on expanding agriculture, including the production of soybeans as animal feed for the meat and dairy industries; the Amazon has lost 17 percent of its forest cover in the last century, mainly to clear trees for farms and ranches. Agriculture is also a primary threat to freshwater habitats, which are home to half of the known fish species, many of which are facing steep declines. WWF claims that "more than half of the world's wetlands have disappeared since 1900, and fewer than 70 of the world's

177 longest rivers remain free of man-made obstructions" like dams. WWF also explains that because the oceans are "a life support system for Earth and a global commons that provides us with free goods and services, from the food we eat to more than half of the oxygen we breathe," we must protect the oceans from "the removal of living resources," loss and damage of habitats, pollutants, and release of its stored carbon.

To protect ocean bays in British Columbia, the Sea Shepherd Conservation Society has an anti-fish-farming campaign called "Operation Virus Hunter" that critiques open-net salmon farms for being "breeding grounds for disease organisms which multiply and load surrounding waters with viruses, parasites, and bacteria—pathogens that transmit easily from captive to wild fish," threatening wild salmon populations. The loss of wild salmon threatens species, such as whales, who rely on them for food. Additionally, pollution from the millions of captive salmon pours into the marine environment, causing algae blooms that can be toxic to aquatic life. Their campaign images feature a dead fish, baby captive fish with small wounds on them from lice, and salmon crowded in pens in a beautiful bay surrounded by mountains.

An important aspect of healthy ecosystems and supporting life is ensuring biodiversity and stemming the tide of mass extinction of species. The mission of WWF is to "conserve nature and reduce the most pressing threats to the diversity of life on Earth." The oceans contain the most biodiversity of species, most of which have yet to be discovered. WWF explains that because oceans are downstream from everywhere, they bear the brunt of a growing human population's collective footprint: "In the last four decades, populations of marine mammals, birds, reptiles and fish have declined on average by half, with some dropping by nearly 75 percent." Largely due to unsustainable fishing practices, there has been "a decline in the abundance of fish stocks, between 50–90 percent depending on species." WWF also notes how human food production (both land and sea) significantly contributes to the loss of biodiversity in populations of mammals, birds, amphibians, reptiles, and fish, which have declined by 52 percent. Humans are the cause of the current species extinction rates, which are at least 100–1,000 times higher than normal.

Some groups work to protect specific endangered species, such as IFAW's campaign to save tigers across Asia. The tiger population has plummeted by 97 percent because of humans illegally hunting them and encroaching on their habitats, causing deforestation. And Sea Shepherd has a campaign to save the most endangered marine mammal in the world—the vaquita marina porpoise, of which there are potentially only thirty individuals left in Mexico's Sea of Cortez. These small porpoises are "being wiped out faster than they can reproduce," mainly from getting caught in fishing gill nets. Sea Shepherd also features campaigns to save endangered species like sea turtles, whales, totoaba bass, sharks, and seals. To prioritize biodiversity, Sea Shepherd declares "there is nothing more important than to save a species from extinction." In that effort, their ships patrol the Galápagos Island corridor against poaching because the area boasts the "richest living marine diversity in the world."

DISCUSSION OF VALUES SUPPORTING FAIRNESS

A fundamental basis for treating someone fairly is to have respect for them. The animal protection groups often express *respect for animals through acknowledgment of their interests, needs, and desires.* IFAW's guiding ideas recognize that "animals have intrinsic value and are sentient beings." And Animal Equality frequently asserts that animals have inherent value, not instrumental value, such as saying "sheep are individuals with their own interests and desires, not producers of scarves." In their section on animals used for food, they advise us "to stop thinking of them as just resources, and to start viewing them for who they are: individual sentient beings whose lives deserve to be respected and valued." PETA laments that the pet trade "treats animals as mere moneymaking commodities to mass produce and peddle for profit," with females treated like "breeding machines" who are killed when no longer economically productive.

Sea Shepherd Conservation Society prioritizes marine animals' interests and the international environmental laws that protect them above any particular human culture's or nation's beliefs or interests: "Our clients are whales, dolphins, seals, turtles, sea-birds, and fish. We represent their interests. . . . We are not anti-any nationality or culture. We are pro-Ocean and we work in the interests of all life on Earth. We only oppose criminals and criminal operations." Sea Shepherd often showcases impressive facts about marine species, such as emphasizing the longevity of the sea turtle's life span on Earth (well surpassing our species) and how sea turtles have a rich family heritage, being born and then having their babies on the same beaches where their parents and grandparents were born. PETA also highlights positive attributes of various species that make them special and deserving of better treatment, especially animals we normally disrespect, such as farmed animals, reptiles, rodents, and insects: "Ants, cockroaches, wasps, and bees are fascinating animals who play a vital role in the ecosystem and provide many beneficial 'services,' including pollinating fruits and vegetables. . . . Ants, wasps, and bees cooperate with their colonies and hive-mates to find food and defend their homes against predators. Cockroaches are extremely adaptive and have been on Earth for approximately 400 million years."

For a few of the animal protection groups studied, respect for animal interests can overlap with the concept of *animal rights and equitable ethical standards applied to our treatment of nonhuman animals.* PETA's section "Why Animal Rights?" explains that the concept of animal rights is not just a philosophy but a social movement that "challenges society's traditional view that all nonhuman animals exist solely for human use" and emphasizes animals' "inherent worth." It is animals' ability to suffer that gives them the "right to equal consideration" of their interests. Also, in support of fair treatment, Animal Equality's section on animal experimentation emphasizes that equal moral standards should be applied to avoiding harms to nonhuman animals that we no longer subject upon humans: "The majority of society would be against experimentation on humans against their will even if this would lead to great advances in the search for vaccines and cures. The same criteria should also apply to other animals since they, just like us, are sentient and the emotions and sensations they feel matter to them just as much as ours do to us. Like us, they don't want to die and want to enjoy a free life." Animal Equality articulates the rights of animals to own their own bodies (skins, fur, wool coats, etc.) and babies, as the description of each type of animal farming critiques the separation of mothers from their babies. In support of not stealing from someone else, Animal Equality's clothing campaigns remind us that fur "pelts belong to the animals" and "leather is wearing someone else's skin."

Most animal organizations express *respect for wild animals to live wild and free*. And for both 'wild' and domesticated animals, *sufficient mobility and the ability for animals to move about freely* was valued over confinement or bondage (see photos 5 and 6). Animal Equality's section on using animals for entertainment declares that practices like zookeeping, circus acts, bullfighting, rodeos, and horse racing "keep animals in captivity and use them against their will for human entertainment . . . forcing animals into confinement to suffer and die for our entertainment." Similarly, PETA's website section on Animals Used for Entertainment visually and discursively emphasizes restrictions that imprison land and marine animals such as tigers kept in cages, elephants chained by the legs, horses hitched to carriages on city streets, and dolphins trapped in tanks. Animals stuck in aquariums would normally swim freely for miles each day in their own territory but are now kept in cramped tanks where they have no privacy or escape from unwanted interactions with humans. PETA tells the story of Lolita, an orca who was abducted from her family in the ocean at age four. Since then she has spent over forty-five years alone at the Miami Seaquarium, languishing in the nation's smallest orca tank; Lolita's owners refuse to set her free to a sanctuary or to return her to her family, despite decades of campaigning by activists.

Sea Shepherd's campaign against marine aquariums refers to the capture of hundreds of dolphins in Taiji, Japan, as an "evil slave trade that must be abolished." In Taiji, activists have gone to jail for freeing cetaceans from fishermen's nets. Nets are often featured in Sea Shepherd imagery, such as activists freeing live animals from illegal gill nets used to catch endangered totoaba bass in Mexican waters near California. These nets not only kill the bass, but they indiscriminately kill endangered vaquita porpoises, sea turtles, sharks, dolphins, and at least one whale. In total, Sea Shepherd documented over a thousand dead animals found in these nets between 2015 and 2017, but activists were able to free more than seven hundred living animals.

PETA documents how scientific laboratories breed primates in commercial facilities (taking newborn babies away from screaming mothers only days after birth) or abduct them from their wild habitats in Asia. Investigations reveal that "trappers often shoot mothers from trees, stun animals with dart guns, and then capture the babies, who cling, panic-stricken to their mothers' bodies." Then these traumatized primates are "usually confined to barren steel cages—a far cry from the lush forests and savannahs where they would otherwise live."

IFAW encourages the building of migration corridors for wildlife to roam between protected park areas, reminding us that "elephants, tigers, whales and most other large wildlife species customarily travel each year, through spaces vast enough to enable them to adapt to changing seasons and maintain healthy populations." Therefore, "if we want a world in which there is a place for wild animals, then as we create development plans for people, we must also preserve critical habitat for wildlife." In support of this viewpoint, IFAW's section on education shows literacy efforts with kids in Malawi to "keep animals wild," where kids express that "wild animals belong in the wild."

Fairness extends to decision-making processes that take into account animal and environmental concerns. IFAW provides research to international governing bodies and nation-states to advocate for the consideration of animal welfare in international agreements like CITES and for uniform welfare standards within each country. WWF advises that we must share the earth with animals, which requires us to reduce our impact on the planet, such as by building a more sustainable food system that "complements nature and protects wildlife." To ensure that animals are not left out of decision-making, WWF elevates wildlife's worth by using the "best science, policy influence, market-based strategies, and communications to quantify and enhance the value of wildlife for key stakeholders and expand constituencies and funding for wildlife conservation." To prevent deforestation, "WWF helps countries, like Myanmar and Belize, assess the value of their natural resources and the services they provide, such as forests that absorb carbon and provide habitat for endangered wildlife," so forest protection can be factored into decision-making and policies. They do the same to protect freshwater ecosystems and put water higher on government agendas, stating that they aim to "change how water is governed and [to] embed the value of nature into business planning." Because wildlife is negatively impacted by climate change, WWF suggests that we ensure "our own responses to climate change factor in the health and wellbeing of the habitat and resources on which they depend."

Fair and inclusive decision-making is a two-way street, and animal protection organizations must also consider affected local human communities. With its tagline "together possible," WWF works with local communities to protect wildlife "to ensure a future that includes healthy wildlife populations and sustainable economic growth." IFAW stresses that wildlife conservation approaches must be more comprehensive than just saving land, so they work with local communities on finding mutually beneficial solutions, such as maximizing the benefits of having large wildlife species like elephants or whales as neighbors and the potential livelihood opportunities from wildlife-watching tourism. Similarly, when working on dog and cat welfare issues, such as with the Sagamok First Nation in Canada, IFAW likes to engage community members in participatory workshops where they can all come up with long-term sustainable plans that "improve the lives of both animals and people."

A large focus of ensuring justice for animals involves enacting *strong animal protection laws and enforcement by governments, including catching and prosecuting criminals.* PETA's campaigns often ask the public to urge legislators to protect animals, such as the millions of mice and rats used in experimentation who are not protected under the U.S. Animal Welfare Act. In Jalisco, Mexico, Animal Equality introduced an initiative to make cruelty to farmed animals, who number around 187 million, a felony crime. They also introduced a petition with Compassion in World Farming to ensure that the UK will maintain the legal recognition of animals as sentient beings when the UK exits the European Union.

In the United States, the animal agribusiness lobby has been successful in some states in pushing through "ag gag" legislation that criminalizes journalists and activists who document and expose abuses on farms. PETA works to combat this corporate legislation on the grounds that "eyewitness investigators provide authorities with crucial evidence and empower them to hold abusers accountable to the law, and they've helped officials achieve landmark criminal indictments and convictions of abusers across the country."

IFAW works extensively on wildlife crime and warns that the trade threatens biodiversity through species loss and also "causes needless suffering to animals, as well as humans." Elephant populations are threatened by the ivory trade, so IFAW works to prevent the "violent crime" of poaching of elephants for their tusks by helping to investigate crimes and train wildlife law enforcement officers in Kenya. IFAW helps protect tigers from extinction through legislation and poaching prevention efforts supporting rangers in India, Russia, and China. For example, they removed almost 2,800 snares that were positioned to kill Amur tigers and leopards in the forests of Hunchun, China. Images in this website section on wildlife crime show men holding elephant tusks and tiger pelts (some with the tiger's head still attached).

Sea Shepherd actually considers it a mandate to "assume a law enforcement role as provided by the United Nations World Charter for Nature" and uses their ships to engage in direct action to "protect endangered marine species and ecosystems" from illegal operations. They actively follow and interrupt Japanese whaling efforts and help South American governments increase wildlife crime detection. Sea Shepherd instituted a K-9 dog unit in Colombia that has resulted in the apprehension of wildlife smugglers and their contraband, which includes both live and dead animals and parts. They also provide anti-poaching staff to the Galápagos National Park Service to patrol the waters around the biodiverse Wolf and Darwin Islands as well as provide telecommunication equipment to detect suspicious movement of fishing vessels in the marine reserve that has "resulted in the apprehension of several purse seiners and dozens of longliners." Illegal fishing is an issue also taken up by WWF, which says "overfishing, illegal fishing, bycatch, poor governance, and lack of monitoring and enforcement are challenging the health of the ocean, where species, as well as entire ecosystems are being lost," in particular mangrove ecosystems.

Sea Shepherd campaigns provide examples of taking weak or corrupt governments to task, such as calling out the Canadian government for failing to remove foreign-owned salmon farms that pollute the ecosystems and threaten native salmon populations in Canadian bays, including First Nation territories. In Costa Rica, Sea Shepherd asks the public to pressure the government to further protect endangered sea turtles from being killed for their eggs and meat. And they oppose "research" whaling sanctioned by the Japanese government and were the first to sue Japanese whalers in U.S. courts for piracy and violent tactics against Sea Shepherd activists. The Japanese government is quick to throw activists in jail for freeing whales and dolphins from fishing nets in Taiji. In response, the Japanese and Costa Rican governments have persuaded INTERPOL to issue red notices against Captain Paul Watson as a "terrorist" to have him arrested and silenced for his direct actions protecting marine animals.

DISCUSSION OF VALUES SUPPORTING RESPONSIBILITY

To be responsible, broadly speaking, animal protection organizations advocate for *active resolution of conflicts and problem-solving (nonviolently)*, rather than being passive or apathetic. To be part of the solution, it is important for each of us to *make a difference in the world and have a positive impact*. IFAW focuses on effective advocacy: "We promise supporters and policy makers effective animal protection solutions delivered with intelligence, compassion and integrity." Sea Shepherd emphasizes the impactful nature of their unique advocacy approach: "We are one of the few global environmental organizations that focuses primarily on direct action," and their mission statement specifies, "We use innovative direct-action tactics to investigate, document, and take action when necessary to expose and confront illegal activities on the high seas." Action images show their boats and activists taking personal risks to interfere with industrial activities, and statistics document their impact in terms of lives saved, media gained, and supplies donated. Emphasizing the power of committed activists more so than money, they exclaim: "What Sea Shepherd has accomplished over the last twelve years demonstrates what people of passion can accomplish with few resources despite heavy multi-government opposition." Animal Equality's campaign page encourages each of us to engage in vegan outreach on college campuses through leafleting and virtual image technology as an effective way to get young people to reduce their consumption of animal products and save lives.

A primary vehicle for making a difference is to *take action and speak up, such as fighting for rights collectively as a social movement*. All organizations encourage people to get involved with their organization's collective efforts and to take action. For example, PETA suggests that viewers "take a stand against cruelty to animals." Actress Emily Deschanel narrates a PETA video on dairy industry cruelty to cows and their babies where she urges us to "stand up for all mothers." Other PETA action items urge viewers to write letters, such as to car companies to demand welfare improvements in Brazil's leather industry, and to mayors to ban workhorses in their cities, and to filmmakers to "voice your objections" to using chimpanzees and other wild animals as actors. IFAW expresses its absolute commitment to ending seal hunting through a variety of activism methods: "Until Canada's commercial seal hunt ends forever, we will fight against it: documenting its cruelty, presenting our evidence to the authorities, researching, educating, lobbying for legislative change and working to shut down markets for seal products." And Sea Shepherd expresses a similar commitment to abolishing whaling, claiming: "We will never quit." *Public protest* is also touted by some organizations, featuring their activists holding signs out on the street. Animal Equality conducts unique and gripping public vigils where their activists stand together in silence, each holding a dead animal victimized by industry.

To be effective long-term, activists must *create political will for change.* This can come through building "trusted relationships and partnerships" in solving problems, as WWF notes, and by encouraging collective action from current and future generations of people who can pressure their legislators to do the right thing. The drive to raise public awareness of issues and public concern for animals is ultimately part of developing this political will.

All animal protection organizations promote *educating the public and raising awareness,* which often includes *investigating and exposing animal abuse or issues.* To expose college students to the hidden world of factory farming, Animal Equality features iAnimal virtual reality videos on the life of a calf, a pig, and a chicken. "Our team of investigators documented cruel but standard conditions across seven countries in order to take you to a place the meat industry tries to keep secret." For example, when students put on the iAnimal video mask, they get immersed in the virtual-reality film *42 Days in the Life of a Chicken,* which helps people "experience life and death through the eyes of a factory farmed chicken." A testimonial from a female viewer expresses how horrified she was by what she saw and the birds' screams she heard, commenting: "People need to be aware, and they're not. . . . You should watch this before you eat meat, because I don't think you would eat it."

Animal Equality also conducts undercover investigations that "bring to light shocking images that reveal the institutionalized suffering humans inflict on other animals. This work to expose the animal industries is essential to show the consuming public and policy makers how farmed animals are bred and killed." One 2016 exposé of a dairy farm in Somerset, England, reveals a male worker kicking and throwing around mothers and baby cows, yelling curse words at them (mostly female slurs), and telling them he hates them. Male calves are shot dead in front of their mothers. Some cows hobble around lame. The video commentary focuses on the routine emotional trauma and physical strain the cows endure, being repeatedly impregnated and separated from their calves "so that we can drink the cows' breast milk." Dulce Ramirez of Animal Equality says, "Society has a right to know how what they are consuming is produced so that they can make compassionate decisions." PETA also conducts many undercover investigations that reveal hidden animal abuses in entertainment, farming, and research industries worldwide, usually with grotesque imagery of animals suffering and crying out for help. For example, they provide visual evidence in laboratories of "mutilated rabbits," "monkeys driven mad," and laboratory workers abusing animals. At the end of these videos, PETA often instructs viewers to educate others by sharing this information and telling friends. Another way to reach the public with compelling images of animal exploitation is through media exposure. Sea Shepherd touts the success of its reality television series *Whale Wars* (which profiled Sea Shepherd's exciting direct action on the high seas) and documentaries like *The Cove* and *Blackfish* to expose the killing of marine mammals, "which sent SeaWorld's attendance and share prices plummeting as well as the failure of expansion plans by marine aquariums in Vancouver and California."

Sea Shepherd also conducts shark awareness education in Galápagos schools. "We believe that kids are the Ocean Defenders of the future. The survival of sharks and other species depend on these young people's understanding and respect for the animals' vital role in the world's ecosystem." IFAW's wildlife conservation efforts also include education. With kids, they emphasize compassion for animals and habitat protection, such as their "born to be wild—saving the majestic tiger" program. Videos show kids around the world exclaiming, "We don't want a world without tigers!" With adults, IFAW educates consumers, such as those in China, about the violence behind elephant ivory and tiger parts and promotes PSAs to tourists, affirming that "animals are not souvenirs." To encourage kids to become animal advocates, PETA produces separate websites and special materials aimed at educating children (PETA kids) and teenagers (peta2).

To educate the public accurately requires truthful communication that *shares honest information based on quality science and credible research*, avoiding deceptive messages and manipulation. One of IFAW's guiding ideas is that "policy should be based on sound science within an ethical framework for animals." And they point out how industry marketing is not based in sound science: "Currently the government of Canada sanctions the killing of grey seals, claiming that mass killings will benefit commercial fisheries. However, there is no scientific evidence to support these claims." Similarly, with the seal hunt in Namibia, "Science does not support the argument that Cape fur seals negatively impact fisheries." IFAW also helps expose the sham of "scientific whaling" in Japan. To reveal the falsehoods, they assert that Japan, Norway, and Iceland "hunt for profit, not out of necessity or for science as some claim." Sea Shepherd affirms this by saying, "Japan pretends this killing is legal because it is 'researching' the whales, even as it profits from the sale of their flesh."

PETA's "SeaWorld of Hurt" campaign exposes the misinformation that aquariums give to consumers and reminds us these are for-profit entertainment facilities, not the conservation or education organizations they claim to be. PETA also helps consumers differentiate between a legitimate sanctuary and zoos masquerading as sanctuaries when they really breed, sell, and exhibit animals for profit. PETA's animal experimentation section claims "testing on animals is bad science: it's unreliable and unnecessary," based on the fact that "animal studies teach us nothing about the health of humans because animals of different species absorb, metabolize, and eliminate substances differently from humans."

A responsible society also *invests in and plans for the future, thinking about long-term viability and following only sustainable practices.* WWF commends nations who signed the Paris Agreement to significantly curb greenhouse gas emissions, businesses that are "making investments in clean energy," and communities that are "redesigning their roads, buildings, airports, and railroads to make them climate resilient." WWF mentions projects in Central Asia and Nepal that help communities mitigate and adapt to climate change while protecting habitat, biodiversity, and forests (trees trap carbon dioxide). But WWF also notes irresponsible actions, such as President Trump rolling back climate and environmental protections.

Animal protection organizations often highlight irresponsible industrial activities, such as the fishing industry polluting the oceans with fishing gear that entraps, which then often kills, sea animals and birds. IFAW's Marine Mammal Rescue and Rehabilitation team saves seals off the coast of Cape Cod from long-term injuries or "a slow and painful death" when they get entangled in fishing equipment. Seals are also harmed by human activities in other ways. While investigating the Canadian seal hunt in 2017, Sea Shepherd documented that climate change is visibly melting the ice in Canada's Gulf of St. Lawrence that breeding harp seals need to survive, noting that "thousands of baby seals are drowning as the ice melts from underneath them."

To be ecologically responsible means *using resources efficiently and wisely* to avoid scarcity, waste, and excess. PETA's vegan appeals include the environmental benefits of avoiding animal agribusiness, as meat wastes water and is an inefficient use of land, causing deforestation and greenhouse gas pollution. Commercial fishing kills not only the intended species but also coral reefs, ocean floors, and "bycatch" animals as collateral damage. Sea Shepherd documents the pollution caused by open-net salmon farms, where "they let tons of waste fall through the nets per day into once-pristine bays and channels because this is cheaper than dealing with their sewage," and notes how inefficient it is to feed these farmed salmon other fish wild-caught by commercial fishing operations, "starving one ocean to pollute another." WWF promotes a transformation in fishing practices to be sustainable, as currently "most commercially important stocks [of white meat fish] are overfished. Some species are classified as vulnerable or even endangered, and could completely disappear within fifteen years if serious management is not implemented."

WWF's section on food warns us that "we are literally eating the planet" because we are beyond carrying capacity, using one-third of the world's land to grow food and consuming "1.6 times what the earth's natural resources can supply." Yet food demands are expected to double by 2050 as the human population skyrockets to 9 billion. While animal rights organizations promote plant-based foods as a solution (changing consumer demand), WWF tends to rely more on supply-side solutions, recommending using resources more efficiently, reducing waste, and farming and fishing more sustainably. They note the environmental problems caused by the beef and dairy industries (i.e., excess use of land, water, and energy; pollution of waterways; greenhouse gas emissions), so they work to engage these farmers in more sustainable practices.

Part and parcel of the environmentally responsible practices and long-term thinking described above is *being careful and taking precautions*, avoiding risky or potentially reckless actions that could eventually threaten life. This caretaking is mentioned explicitly in IFAW's guiding ideas that say conservation decisions should be guided by the precautionary principle within an ethical framework for animals, along with considering biological and ecological sustainability principles. PETA shows how precautions can also be taken with domesticated animals. Because companion animals are vulnerable to abuse and neglect, PETA urges us to "proceed with caution" when placing dogs and cats in a forever home, by carefully screening applicants to find a "responsible, compassionate animal guardian," rather than making decisions rashly just to get animals in any household.

To be responsible, we must be able to *coexist with animals*, living together peacefully in shared spaces on the planet. IFAW's section on sustainable solutions for wildlife and people lists various ways they resolve human-wildlife conflicts, such as reducing ship strikes of whales and facilitating wildlife migration corridors. In a few cases of elephants in conflict with local villages, such as in the Ivory Coast and Malawi, IFAW had to relocate the entire group of elephants to prevent the governments from culling the elephant communities or fencing them into tiny areas. But relocation is considered a last resort, and animals remaining in their natural territory is preferable. PETA has a "Living with Wildlife" section on their website that provides ideas for how homeowners can live harmoniously near insects, rodents, raccoons, and rabbits without resorting to lethal 'pest control' methods. PETA urges us not to denigrate these animals as 'pests' but to see them as individuals who also want and deserve to live in the area. Thus, we should choose compassionate solutions such as securing trash bins, repelling insects with scents, and employing a humane mousetrap to release live mice and rats outside our homes.

Most animal protection organizations, especially animal rights groups, promote *conscientious consumerism and cruelty-free shopping* as an important way to demonstrate personal responsibility. IFAW informs consumers of the unnecessary killing in Canada's seal hunt: "Tens of thousands of baby seals are brutally slaughtered on the ice so their skins can be sold for luxury products." PETA overtly reminds the public that as consumers we have a moral responsibility to buy cruelty-free products to avoid causing animal suffering: "The everyday choices we make—such as what we eat for lunch and the kind of shampoo we buy—may be directly supporting some of this abuse. But as hard as it is to think about, we can't stop animals' suffering if we simply look the other way and pretend it isn't happening." When it comes to getting a companion animal, PETA urges consumers not to buy animals from a breeder or pet store, especially not 'exotic' wild animals, and to instead adopt domesticated animals from a rescue organization and have them spayed or neutered. These responsible practices avoid causing the killing of other individuals for lack of homes. PETA's "animals used for entertainment" section is filled with pleas for consumers to boycott these captivity and entertainment facilities and choose to support legitimate sanctuaries and animal-free circuses instead. Similarly, Sea Shepherd aims to get consumers to stop buying tickets to dolphinariums, saying the only thing that motivates these industries and their shareholders to change is money, not moral arguments.

Animal rights organizations PETA and Animal Equality heavily promote *consumers going vegan and avoiding wearing or eating products that have animal-based ingredients* as a vital part of conscientious consumerism. Animal Equality works extensively on promoting veganism as a way to "choose a life based on kindness and justice." These moral appeals assure us that by "not taking part in their exploitation we can personally prevent thousands of animals from being harmed and killed on our behalf." PETA exposes how food labels such as "organic," "humanely raised," and "free-range" attempt to fool well-meaning consumers yet don't protect animals from suffering. PETA concludes: "There is only one truly humane label, and it's vegan." At the end of their numerous videos on fishing and farming (for both food and clothing), PETA makes a pitch for viewers to buy vegan products to avoid supporting cruelty. The "Glass Walls" video narrated by vegan musician Sir Paul McCartney concludes by saying, "Make the compassionate choice. Leave meat, eggs, and dairy off your plate." PETA makes appeals for cruelty-free fashion, assuring us that "compassion is in fashion," telling consumers to "save a sheep—don't buy wool," and choose "fake snake, mock crock, and other animal-friendly options" instead of leather.

DISCUSSION OF VALUES SUPPORTING UNITY

The values in this section celebrate what brings us together (both among and between species) in coalitions, families, friendships, and shared ecological systems. Some of the animal protection organizations promote *respecting and recognizing common traits shared between animal species (human and nonhuman), especially sentience*. Animal Equality's Choose Veganism website discusses the similar sentience between human and nonhuman animals: "Animals are sentient beings like us. They are able to feel emotions and sensations such as pain, pleasure, fear or stress, and like us they are individuals with their own needs, desires and an interest in living." Their section critiquing zoos, circuses, and aquariums ends with the inclusive phrase: "We should all be able to enjoy freedom, human or not." PETA president Ingrid Newkirk has often said: "When it comes to pain, love, joy, loneliness, and fear, a rat is a pig is a dog is a boy. Each one values his or her life and fights the knife." IFAW's education program in Malawi includes a video with kids explaining that they know humans are animals, and like us, animals have the same basic needs. These kids from around the world also express affection for animals, like tigers, saying, "I love animals." *Love and devotion* are highly motivating, unifying values. Animal Equality emphasizes love and caring as emotional incentives to pledge to go vegan: "Because I love animals and care about the environment, I pledge to reduce or cut out milk, meat and eggs in my diet." As demonstrated in many examples given already in this chapter, animal protection organizations, Animal Equality and PETA especially, often make moral appeals for people to *be compassionate and kind toward others*, rather than being divisive, violent, selfish, or apathetic. PETA uses the word "compassion" a lot in urging people to be vegan and cruelty-free consumers, and asks people to "live in harmony with" wild animal neighbors by solving any wildlife conflicts compassionately rather than through lethal or inhumane means.

One way to be kind to fellow sentient beings is to *respect familial bonds and allow families to stay together*. In discussing animal agribusiness, Animal Equality and PETA emphasize the cruelty of farmworkers separating babies from mothers as a matter of course, year after year (especially for those females used as a breeding sow or a dairy cow). PETA's video on "dairy farm cruelty" describes the trauma a mother experiences having her calf traumatically torn away from her each year, after another round of artificial insemination, so her baby's milk can be taken for the human market. And a chicken raised for flesh, born in a hatchery, "will never be allowed contact with his or her parents, let alone be raised by them." In describing captivity facilities like zoos and aquariums, animal rights organizations will often mention how families are torn apart and individuals must unnaturally live with whomever the facility owners deem to be their tank- or cage-mates. PETA describes the "terrifying" process that some marine mammals in aquariums endured when they were "kidnapped" from the wild and taken away from their mothers. And PETA's profiles of many different species of animals often highlight the animals' commitment to family, such as how Canada geese mate for life and are "devoted to each other," raising babies together and working as a team with the whole flock, who look out for one another and mourn losses of flock members. *Companionship and friendship* are sometimes mentioned by animal protection organizations, usually in relation to animal friendships within species (such as those that form at a sanctuary) but also between species, especially the bond between humans and their companion animals, such as cats or dogs. PETA urges us to make a "lifetime commitment" to providing "plenty of love and attention" to pets as our "best friends."

Another theme in the animal protection discourse is the benefit of *collaborating with others to form partnerships and coalitions, acknowledging our interdependence, both so-*

cially and ecologically. Sea Shepherd acknowledges ecological interdependence by exclaiming, "If the ocean dies, we all die, so this is an investment in our own survival." Similarly, WWF emphasizes our shared reliance on salt- and freshwater ecosystems, saying, "Both people and wildlife depend on the health of our oceans," adding that "all life needs water. It is the world's most precious resource."

Social interdependence is summarized by WWF's tagline "together possible," because they emphasize forming partnerships with governments, businesses, civil society, and academia to "challenge the threats to nature" and "protect life on our planet." WWF president Carter Roberts says, "Only by working together can we create solutions to the most vexing problems we face." Sea Shepherd engages in several partnerships to advance their ocean campaigns, including working with First Nations people in British Columbia to fight Norwegian-owned salmon farms polluting the area, and helping the government of Mexico, researchers, and NGOs to protect the endangered vaquita porpoise. IFAW attempts to unify the animal welfare and conservation movements by "demonstrating that healthy populations, naturally sustaining habitats and the welfare of individual animals are intertwined." They highlight the need for collaborative efforts by saying, "We work closely with communities to find solutions that benefit both animals and people." An example of a partnership is IFAW's tenBoma anti-poaching program in Kenya: "TenBoma, meaning ten houses, is inspired by an African community security philosophy that if ten houses look out for each other, the broader community is safer." They use this model to partner with law enforcement agencies and local communities to "create a coordinated system of eyes and ears" to prevent wildlife poaching. To imply there is strength in numbers and build a community of activists, PETA encourages the public to "join the millions of other compassionate people who are working to create a kinder, better world for animals," reassuring us that "together, we can make a difference."

Responsibility for Problems

In my analysis, I took note of what entities the animal protection organizations directly or indirectly blame for causing or allowing harms and injustice. Hunters are criticized by almost all the organizations, especially for killing marine mammals, with PETA and Animal Equality being the only organizations to critique legal hunting of land animals. Illegal hunters (poachers) and other wildlife criminals receive condemnation, especially from groups focused on wildlife. The animal rights organizations, in particular, are more critical of governments with weak criminal justice systems, and they also denounce all industries who use or exploit captive animals. Wildlife-focused groups (Sea Shepherd and WWF) blame a growing human population and our collective unsustainable practices, including agribusiness and fishing, for causing mass extinction and climate change, with WWF especially underscoring society's excessive use of limited resources. PETA and Animal Equality also consider society a big part of the problem, based on speciesist attitudes that lead to our discrimination against nonhuman animals. And these animal rights groups also call out consumers who fail to shop or eat cruelty-free, whereas IFAW only singles out consumers as problematic if they buy illegal wildlife parts. Less frequently, the animal rights organizations also blame those who throw their weight around to exploit or maintain their power over the less powerful, including suppressing activists who are trying to rescue animals from this domination.

Summary

The five animal protection groups in my 2017 sample (Animal Equality, IFAW, PETA, Sea Shepherd Conservation Society, and WWF) have online campaigns that aim to prevent harm to wild animals (especially mammals and endangered species), their habitats, and the broader environment as well as to safeguard human well-being and, in some cases, the rights and welfare of domesticated animal individuals. Animal protection campaigns are the closest of all social causes to promoting "total liberation" of species (Best 2014), although there is room for animal advocacy to more frequently include social justice issues for humans and put more emphasis on environmentalism. Campaigns promote liberation and justice as they often target hunters (mostly illegal hunters—poachers) and wildlife traffickers. Animal rights groups tend to confront weak law enforcement, exploitative industries (including agribusiness, fishing, and companies who keep animals in captivity), and speciesist attitudes in society. Wildlife groups tend to focus on mitigating unsustainable practices by powerful entities and a growing human population. Values common to all the animal protection organizations include saving animal lives and protecting the health and well-being of human and nonhuman animals, but many also emphasized compassion, sustainability, biodiversity, animal freedom and mobility, respect for sentience, awareness raising, action and engagement in social change, strong legal protections, and conscientious consumerism. I'll incorporate these values as central to forming the basis of the human animal earthling identity outlined in the final chapter.

PHOTO 1. Social entrepreneur and author Dominique Alonga mentors high school girls in Rwanda in the library she helped stock at White Dove Global Prep. She also founded Imagine We Rwanda publishing house to allow Rwandan children to publish their own stories and see themselves represented in literature. Photo Credit: Josh Estey / CARE. Copyright © 2019 CARE. All Rights Reserved.

PHOTO 2. Chickens on a 'free-range' industrial farm in Spain try to push through a wire fence to avoid a farmworker's grasp. Credit: Jo-Anne McArthur / Animal Equality

PHOTO 3. Bulls hung and bleeding out while another is stunned before slaughter at a slaughterhouse in Turkey, suffering the fate of billions of land animals globally. Credit: Jo-Anne McArthur / We Animals

PHOTO 4. Barramundi raised in crowded tanks at a fish farm in South Australia. I wanted to include a photo of fish because they are killed in the highest numbers for food globally, whether in land-based aquaculture shown here, open-net ocean fish farming, or commercial fishing, discussed heavily in the book. Credit: Jo-Anne McArthur / We Animals

PHOTO 5. Tourists point at Kiska, an orca whale kept alone on display in a tank at Marineland Canada. Kiska was kidnapped from Icelandic waters as a baby, and all her own babies (born in the entertainment industry) died at a young age, according to the Whale Sanctuary Project, which could potentially offer Kiska a better home with pod-mates. Credit: Jo-Anne McArthur / We Animals

PHOTO 6. Captive orangutan at a zoo in Australia. In the wild, orangutans are one of many (endangered) species and cultures in Indonesia who are losing their homes to industry deforestation (palm oil in particular). Credit: Jo-Anne McArthur / We Animals

PHOTO 7. Destruction of a rainforest in Indonesia: the Singkil peat swamp, Leuser Ecosystem, August 14, 2016. Credit: Paul Hilton / RAN (Rainforest Action Network)

PHOTO 8. Aerial views of CAFO (concentrated animal feeding operation) pig farm and manure lagoon in North Carolina. In September 2018 photojournalists from We Animals documented the aftermath of Hurricane Florence, which caused the death of at least 3.4 million farmed animals and widespread environmental devastation from breaches in toxic manure lagoons. Credit: Jo-Anne McArthur / We Animals

PHOTO 9. Farming of cows exacerbates the climate crisis and other environmental issues as well as infringing on the cows' individual autonomy. For example, the cows shown here with severely enlarged udders are kept at a large dairy farm near Haifa, Israel, separated from their babies. Each has a number branded on her back. Credit: Jo-Anne McArthur / We Animals

PHOTO 10. Students in El Salvador planting citrus trees at their school with the international nonprofit Fruit Tree Planting Foundation (FTPF) to improve school lunches and serve as an outdoor classroom to demonstrate sustainable practices for the environment. Photo courtesy of FTPF

PHOTO 11. Yenzekile Mathebula and Leitah Mkhabela, members of the predominantly female Black Mambas Anti-Poaching Unit in South Africa that utilizes nonviolent means, here shown protecting rhinos. Credit: Jo-Anne McArthur / We Animals

PHOTO 12. Siphewe Sithole teaching local schoolchildren during a classroom visit, part of the Black Mambas community education conservation program in South Africa. Credit: Jo-Anne McArthur / We Animals

PHOTO 13. Pigs driven to the slaughterhouse in crowded transport trucks in the heat of summer. Photo taken during a Toronto Pig Save witnessing vigil, Canada. Credit: Jo-Anne McArthur / We Animals

PHOTO 14. A Melbourne Pig Save activist provides water to a thirsty pig on a transport truck in Australia, moments before his or her impending slaughter. Credit: Jo-Anne McArthur / We Animals

CHAPTER SIX

What Values Environmental Protection Organizations Appeal To

In this chapter you will learn about the key problems that environmental organizations address, including the climate crisis, biodiversity loss, destruction of forests, overfishing, factory farming and industrial agribusiness, pollution, threats to human life and welfare, and environmental justice issues, especially those affecting low-income communities and indigenous groups globally. The organizations also propose a variety of hopeful solutions in their quest to create a just, peaceful, and sustainable future. This chapter describes the collective values advocated in the 2017 web discourse of the six environmental protection organizations in my sample (a mix of groups from more conservative to radical, some covering all types of issues, and some advocating for specific ecosystems or against specific issues like extinction and global warming): Friends of the Earth International (FOE), Greenpeace International, Nature Conservancy, Oceana, Rainforest Action Network (RAN), and 350.org. By examining their main campaign messages, I first identify the beings on whose behalf they advocate, to demonstrate who they indicate merits our care and protection (specifically which natural entities and which human and nonhuman animals). I then share examples of the many concepts, traits, behaviors, and entities that they highlight as good/ideal and, conversely, the ones they highlight as bad or problematic. The chapter ends with a discussion of the groups and social norms that eco-protection organizations blame as the source of the problems. The items that are characterized as good or bad in this chapter will later be compared to the ones identified in the web discourse on human rights and animal organizations in upcoming chapters, toward the end goal of identifying overlapping values between all three causes that can serve as the basis of a human animal earthling identity.

Who Merits Care and Protection

By referencing table 10, you will see that the six environmental organizations all care about human beings (usually referred to as "people"), and they all express various degrees of concern for nonhuman animals (particularly mammals, birds, and endangered species) and ecosystems, particularly forests and marine environments. Many environmental protection organizations inclusively express concern for "all life" on earth, or they might specify different life-forms by saying "people and . . ." (people and nature; people and wildlife; people, plants, and animals). When it comes to nonhuman animals, organizations address them broadly as "wildlife" or "endangered species," and more specifically by species. Birds are mentioned by four organizations, some focusing on seabirds. When reptiles are shown, it is typically sea turtles, an iconic and beloved endangered species. Mammals are the most popular type of animal discussed in campaigns, with large, iconic, threatened species getting the most attention, such as elephants, rhinos, primates, bears, and big cats. Marine mammals such as whales, dolphins, and seals are mentioned by Greenpeace and Oceana—organizations that focus the most on ocean life. Those organizations and the Nature Conservancy also discuss issues with fish species dying off, but it was often put in an instrumental context of fish being a protein source for humans. The marine protection organization Oceana covers a wider variety of aquatic species, including sharks, rays, salmon, octopuses, and crustaceans. Despite how prolific and important insects are to our ecology, they are not popular in environmental campaigns, with the exception of bees, whom Greenpeace and the Nature Conservancy highlight. The Rainforest Action Network (RAN), despite having a panther in their logo, talks much more about the human animal than nonhuman animals, although they did highlight some threatened forest mammals like orangutans. FOE and 350.org also focus more exclusively on humans than nonhuman animals, while Greenpeace tends to do the opposite.

Environmental organizations display frequent humanitarian concerns for how certain communities will be more heavily impacted by the destructive environmental patterns that are largely perpetuated by industrialized nations or industries in general. Perhaps this sense of environmental justice is why 350.org mentions a need to protect "innocent people" impacted by the climate crisis. Almost every environmental organization expresses a concern for indigenous people, especially those living near exploited wilderness areas, as Native peoples are often considered a particularly vulnerable group deserving of protection from continued marginalization. The word *vulnerable* is used to describe other people put at risk, including the poor, people in developing countries, children, and frontline communities (such as coastal communities facing rising sea levels). FOE is the only organization to give attention to how refugees, women, activists, and journalists face particular threats, while the Nature Conservancy and Oceana put some emphasis on the value of scientists. Local communities facing environmental issues get attention from many environmental organizations. This can include local or small-scale farmers and fisherfolk, who often generate sympathy in opposition to industrial-scale food producers. Most of the environmental organizations want to preserve the environment for "future generations," and while that may theoretically include all kinds of

TABLE 10 Who Merits Care and Protection

As explicitly addressed in environmental protection organizations' campaign materials based on their missions and areas of advocacy focus. This indicates areas of emphasis, priorities, and/or terms used and is not meant to imply certain organizations do not care at all about those entities they didn't speak directly about in these terms.

WHO MERITS CARE AND PROTECTION	FRIENDS OF THE EARTH	GREENPEACE	NATURE CONSERVANCY	OCEANA	RAINFOREST ACTION NETWORK	350.ORG
All life; Life in all its forms		X	X		X	
People and planet	X				X	
People and wildlife			X			
People and nature			X			
Animals, plants, and people		X	X			
Our earth		X				
Keystone species				X		
Native species	X					
Ocean/marine life				X		
NATURE-SPECIFIC CATEGORIES						
Nature			X			
Natural resources			X			
The environment		X				
Habitats			X			
Ecosystems	X	X	X		X Diverse	
Vulnerable ecosystems; Environmentally sensitive regions				X		X
Wilderness					X	
Forests	X	X Ancient, rainforests	X		X Rainforests	X

TABLE 10 Who Merits Care and Protection (continued)

WHO MERITS CARE AND PROTECTION	FRIENDS OF THE EARTH	GREENPEACE	NATURE CONSERVANCY	OCEANA	RAINFOREST ACTION NETWORK	350.ORG
NATURE-SPECIFIC CATEGORIES (CONTINUED)						
Oceans			X	X		
Coral reefs			X			X
Wetlands				X Mangrove		
Streams		X				
Grasslands			X			
(Our) land			X			X
(Our) water		X	X			X
Trees			X			
Plant species		X	X			
Soils		X	X			
Ancestral lands	X					
UNESCO World Heritage Sites, priceless landscapes		X				X
(NONHUMAN) ANIMAL-SPECIFIC CATEGORIES						
Endangered species		X	X		X	X
Animals or animal life			X		X	
Wildlife	X	X	X			
Mammals		X Polar bears, elephants, orangutans, tigers, rhinos, jaguars, sloths, monkeys, gorillas, bonobos, cows	X Elephants, rhinos, bears, horses, bison, sloths		X Rhinos, orangutans, elephants	X Polar bears

Marine mammals		X Whales, walruses, dolphins	X Whales	X Whales, dolphins, seals
Sea animals (nonmammalian)		X Fish	X Fish (as a protein source), sharks	X Fish (as a protein source), salmon, sharks, octopuses, rays, crustaceans
Birds		X Seabirds	X	X Seabirds
Reptiles			X Sea turtles	X Sea turtles
Insects	X Beetles	X Bees, spiders	X Bees	
HUMAN-SPECIFIC CATEGORIES				
Humans / people	X	X	X	X
Future generations	X		X	X
Indigenous people	X	X	X	X
Poor people	X		X	X
Vulnerable people	X Refugees			X
People in developing countries	X Global South		X	X
Children	X	X	X	
Frontline communities; People in coastal regions			X	X
Innocent people				X
Local communities	X		X	X
Farmers (small or local)	X		X	X
Fishermen (small or local)		X		X
Cultures	X	X		X
Enslaved workers			X	
Scientists	X	X		X
Activists	X			
Journalists	X			
Women	X			

species, the context seems to imply that the most important future generations to worry about are those of our own children.

Of course, environmental organizations, in particular the Nature Conservancy and Greenpeace, focus heavily on nature-specific categories. All organizations mention the need to protect "ecosystems," especially vulnerable ones. Forest ecosystems, particularly rainforests due to their biodiversity, are a focus of all groups except Oceana. Oceana's mission is to protect various aquatic ecosystems (e.g., oceans, coral reefs, and wetlands). The Nature Conservancy and Greenpeace both discuss the need to protect plant species and soils. These two organizations, along with 350.org, also talk about responsible management of land and water. FOE's discourse on nature is less about specific beings or types of species and more about broader concepts of biodiversity and "natural resources." The notion of nature as a "resource" is also used by the Nature Conservancy but tends not to be used by Greenpeace.

Common Values: What Matters Most

In their attempts to appeal to the public to support their campaigns, environmental protection organizations not only show concern for certain groups they think the public should care about, but they also promote many common values that societies tend to support. In table 11 I list the main concepts, traits, entities, and behaviors that many of the organizations valued as good or ideal. In providing examples of the most ubiquitous and emphasized values, I categorized them (consistently as I have in past chapters) into values related to supporting life and well-being, fairness, responsibility, and unification. These categories overlap and are not mutually exclusive. I also contrast this with examples of what many of the organizations highlighted as bad or problematic, organized within similar categories—things that are physically or mentally harmful, unfair, or irresponsible (see table 12).

Within these upcoming paragraphs that flesh out the values listed in tables 11 and 12, *italicized terms reflect items that were valued as good* by a majority of the organizations in my study and/or emphasized as good by some of them. I discuss some of the 'bad' items alongside items valued as 'good' to show how the good and bad are conversely used to reinforce each other (e.g., biodiversity versus extinction; safe versus toxic). I organize the sections around the main categories of values deemed to be good, those supporting life, fairness, responsibility, and unification.

DISCUSSION OF VALUES SUPPORTING LIFE

At the core of what environmental organizations do is *save and preserve life*, including human and nonhuman animals (especially endangered native animal species), as organizations want to ensure the *survival of wildlife* and nature. Greenpeace's primary goal is "to ensure the ability of the earth to nurture life in all its diversity." The following quote comprises many of the values we will explore in this section: "Greenpeace is campaigning for a future that will allow our forests to thrive—filled

TABLE 11 What Is Valued as Good or Ideal in Environmental Protection Organizations' Campaigns

VALUED AS GOOD OR IDEAL BY ECO-PROTECTION ORGANIZATIONS' CAMPAIGNS	MORE POPULAR: MENTIONED BY A MAJORITY OF GROUPS	SOMEWHAT POPULAR: MENTIONED BY SEVERAL GROUPS
LIFE-SUPPORTING VALUES	• Life (saving lives, preserving and protecting life and nature) • Protection of habitats and ecosystems • Biodiversity • People having basic needs met • Human health and welfare • Nature as productive and providing sustenance and livelihoods • Safe/stable climate • Sustainable/better future	• Clean/safe water and air • Safety and security • Nonviolence • Welfare for farm animals • Survival (of wildlife, including endangered species) • Thriving • Healthy ecosystems • Restoration of forests and native plant and animal species • Reserves / sanctuary areas
FAIR VALUES	• People power • Accountability • Justice/fairness • Fair democratic participation (especially including impacted communities in decision-making)	• Human rights (including freedom of speech) • Giving a voice to local people • Equality (including economic justice and environmental justice); social justice • Reparations • Cultural diversity (in human world) • Human dignity • Respect • Respecting rights of indigenous peoples and forest communities • Land rights of indigenous peoples for ancestral territories • Inherently valuable or unique wildlife/places/nature

TABLE 11 What Is Valued as Good or Ideal in Environmental Protection Organizations' Campaigns (continued)

VALUED AS GOOD OR IDEAL BY ECO-PROTECTION ORGANIZATIONS' CAMPAIGNS	MORE POPULAR: MENTIONED BY A MAJORITY OF GROUPS	SOMEWHAT POPULAR: MENTIONED BY SEVERAL GROUPS
RESPONSIBLE VALUES	• *Finding concrete, creative solutions* • *Effectiveness in actions and in achieving goals* • *Capturing or sinking carbon* • Limiting/reducing greenhouse gas emissions • Clean, renewable energy sources • Resilience/adaptability • Mobilizing and building a social movement; collective action to pressure the powerful to improve • Public protest (peaceful) • Commitment • Sustainable/green lifestyles • Conscientious consumerism • Food security (including diversity of food crops) • Science-based evidence / truth • Honesty/transparency	• **Education about issues / raising awareness; education of children** • Exposure and monitoring of wrongdoing • Making a difference • Taking responsibility (either for change or for harm caused) • Everybody taking action / engagement • Courage/boldness • Climate justice • Divesting funds in dirty industry • Making sense and using reason; knowledge • Integrity / keeping promises • Guardianship and stewardship of the land and ocean • Sustainable agriculture and sustainable fishing industry (including small-scale fishing and farming) • Protein for people (especially fish) • Enforcement of laws • Strong forest protections • Efficient and wise use of natural resources • Repairing / cleaning up ecosystems
UNIFYING VALUES	• *Working together / forming partnerships / collaborating*	• Compassion / having a heart • **Valuing people and planet over profits (prioritizing life)** • Peace • Interdependence • Coexistence • Humans living in harmony with nature • Common ground / solidarity / consensus

NOTE: Bolded and italicized words indicate ubiquity (all six organizations mentioned the item); bolded words indicate importance (it was repeatedly emphasized by one or more organizations).

TABLE 12 What Is Represented as Problematic or Bad/Wrong in Environmental Protection Organizations' Campaigns (Nonvalued Concepts, Traits, Entities, or Behaviors)

PORTRAYED AS BAD OR WRONG BY ECO-PROTECTION CAMPAIGNS	MORE POPULAR: MENTIONED BY A MAJORITY OF GROUPS	SOMEWHAT POPULAR: MENTIONED BY SEVERAL GROUPS
RELATED TO PHYSICAL OR MENTAL HARM FOR LIVING BEINGS	• Extinction and species loss; declining wildlife populations • Pollution/polluting • Toxins (including chemicals) • Hunger/malnutrition/starvation • Disease and health problems • Degradation or destruction of ecosystems; unhealthy ecosystems • Deforestation • Extreme weather / natural disasters	• Death or killing (especially of humans or endangered animals) • Violence, including militarization and use of weapons • Poisoning/polluting freshwater sources • Contamination, especially plastic trash • Animal cruelty, including intensive confinement of farm animals
RELATED TO UNFAIRNESS	• Poverty • Land-grabbing / displacement of human communities	• Food scarcity/insecurity • Social inequality/injustice • Human rights violations • Threatening/intimidating activists, journalists, or farmers, including imprisoning/detaining them • Corrupt government or abuse of power • Impunity • Illegal fishing and hunting (poaching) • Illegal or destructive logging • Exploitation of people and resources • Commodification (of forests or biodiverse areas) • Oppression of local communities • Slavery / unpaid labor • Climate refugees • Top-down leadership; elite control; monopolies and oligopolies

TABLE 12 What Is Represented as Problematic or Bad/Wrong in Environmental Protection Organizations' Campaigns (Nonvalued Concepts, Traits, Entities, or Behaviors) (continued)

PORTRAYED AS BAD OR WRONG BY ECO-PROTECTION CAMPAIGNS	MORE POPULAR: MENTIONED BY A MAJORITY OF GROUPS	SOMEWHAT POPULAR: MENTIONED BY SEVERAL GROUPS
RELATED TO IRRESPONSIBILITY	• *Deadly/risky/threatening practices* • *Climate change* • *Fossil fuels / dirty energy* • *Greenhouse gas emissions* • **Wastefulness and inefficient use of resources** • Animal agriculture as damaging, especially factory farming of animals • **Greed (corporate)**	• **Dirty extraction practices** • **Investing in fossil fuels / dirty industries** • Causing irreparable and/or long-term harm • **Industrial-scale commercial fishing** • Meat and dairy consumption by society (high levels are unsustainable) • Monoculture and GMOs • Destructive corporate crop plantations • **Profit motives** • Cover-ups / deception / misleading info • Denial of issues (climate change denial) • Hypocrisy or shallow rhetoric • **Ineffective/false solutions** • **Depletion of natural resources, includes overfishing** • **Overconsumption** • Increasing demands and pressures on natural resources • Unsustainable food choices • Ignorance

Note: Bolded and italicized words indicate ubiquity (all six organizations mentioned the item); bolded words indicate importance (it was repeatedly emphasized by one or more organizations).

with unique wildlife and able to sustain local people and economies whilst cleaning the air of carbon: a future with no deforestation." RAN explains the centrality of rainforests in providing livelihoods and oxygen for millions of humans and serving as "the last home for rapidly disappearing animal life." They highlight the Sumatran orangutan, pushed to "the brink of extinction" by deforestation due to conflict palm oil.

To describe the magnitude of the extinction threat facing wildlife and the need to create migration routes for them as temperatures change, the Nature Conservancy cites expert warnings that "one-fourth of the Earth's species will be headed for extinction by 2050 if the warming trend continues at its current rate." 350.org cautions that in addition to threatening wildlife, climate change threatens human lives too: "One degree is the difference between life and death for thousands of people."

Oceana shows concern for animal life through critiquing the deaths of millions of marine animals as bycatch: "unintentionally caught and killed by indiscriminate fishing gear," including "certain fish species, whales, dolphins, sea turtles, and sea birds." They express special interest for these animals as "ecologically important" and endangered species, noting that irresponsible fishing practices are undermining efforts to rebuild their populations. A healthy marine habitat is essential as fish nurseries and as homes for "keystone species" like "marine mammals, sea turtles and sharks." Oceana reassures us that defending marine habitats from "destructive fishing practices and pollution protects all marine life, from top predators to tiny zooplankton." In support of the importance of all species, FOE describes ecological rights as the right for a beetle to survive, implying that even those we would consider the humblest of creatures have the right to live.

Interwoven with concern for living beings is the implication that for people and wildlife to survive, *habitats and ecosystems must be protected*, thus preservation is a prevalent focus of many environmental organizations. For example, the Nature Conservancy's mission is to "conserve the lands and waters on which all life depends," and RAN's mission is to "preserve forests, protect climate, and uphold human rights," and Oceana's tagline is "protecting the world's oceans."

Protection means that *ecosystems should be clean and healthy*, including remaining free of contamination. Oceana identifies ocean pollution as a core problem: "Mercury, antibiotics, oil, and climate-changing gases threaten marine wildlife, habitat, and human health." Plastic pollution is also a "massive and growing threat," as over five trillion plastic particles float in the oceans. Oceana explains that "plastics never go away" but just break down into microplastic particles that attract chemical toxins and get eaten by fish, working their way up the food chain. Additionally, marine life dies by getting entangled in or ingesting plastic; an accompanying image of a sea turtle with plastic stuck on him illustrates their point.

Healthy ecosystems must also be free of destructive practices that reduce the richness of its *biodiversity*. Oceana repeatedly uses the word "biodiversity" as a primary goal: "Protecting important marine habitats is critical for maintaining healthy oceans and restoring biodiversity." The Nature Conservancy's vision is for "people act to conserve nature" to create "a world where the diversity of life thrives." In the United States, forests provide "habitat to more than 4,000 forest-dependent wildlife and plant species, 27 percent of which are at risk of extinction." Rainforests in particular are biodiverse, as they house "half the world's plants and animals." And coral reefs house one-fourth of all marine species and provide nurseries for fish and protection from predators, so the Nature Conservancy warns us that "scientists estimate that unless we take immediate action, we could lose up to 70 percent of coral reefs by 2050" due to rising ocean temperatures causing coral bleaching.

A popular ecosystem targeted for biodiversity protection is *forests and their species restoration*. FOE's web section on biodiversity explains that forests are "amongst the most species-diverse habitats on earth," but the health and biodiversity of remaining forests is "declining rapidly." They lament that "half of the world's forests have disappeared," with further deforestation triggered by "privatization, trade liberalization and increased exports of meat and crops, such as soy and palm oil." Greenpeace champions forest protection to preserve biodiversity and defends the rights of forest communities. They call for an end to deforestation by 2020 because "around the world, lush tropical forests are being logged for timber and pulp, cleared to grow food, and destroyed by the impacts of climate change. Four-fifths of the forest that covered almost half of the Earth's land surface 8,000 years ago have already been irreplaceably degraded or destroyed." RAN's rainforest protection campaigns focus on "the biggest global drivers of deforestation"—agribusiness (largely farming of animals and their feed crops), the palm oil industry, and the pulp and paper industry. They successfully worked with the retail/supply chain to pressure well-known publishers, clothing brands, and food manufacturers to get Indonesian rainforest deforestation out of their books, fabrics, and (palm-oil-based) snack foods.

Several environmental organizations propose *reserves and sanctuaries* as part of the preservation solution. The Nature Conservancy prides itself on land preservation. In 2016 they lauded the signing of the Great Bear Rainforest Agreement between First Nations and the British Columbia government in Canada, as it "permanently conserves 19 million acres" of Pacific coastland, where "9 million acres are off-limits to logging" and the rest is managed by "stringent harvest standards." Yet the Nature Conservancy's risk assessment identifies that of natural lands at highest risk for development globally, only 5 percent are legally protected, so they suggest that future land-use planning and development concentrate on conservation. For example, the Nature Conservancy describes their successful projects in the midwestern United States, Kenya, and Argentina to conserve grassland habitats, home to native plants, hundreds of bird species, and iconic mammals such as elephants and rhinos. RAN highlights a campaign to save "one of the world's highest plant and animal diversity regions" that needs preservation—the Leuser Ecosystem in Indonesia—as "it is the last place on Earth where tigers, orangutans, rhinos, elephants and clouded leopards all share this same habitat." Also citing the forests' and peatlands' benefits to local communities and climate stability, RAN asks us to protect Leuser from loggers, poachers, mining operators, and pulp and palm oil plantation owners (see photos 6 and 7).

Greenpeace is campaigning for a marine sanctuary in the seas off the North Pole to "ban oil drilling and destructive fishing in Arctic waters." Arctic wildlife are "under threat," such as polar bears losing the ice upon which they hunt, rest, and breed. In fact, Greenpeace suggests we "zone off" 40 percent of the world's oceans, especially fish breeding grounds or regions where fish species are "already at the breaking point," as a necessary recourse for ocean recovery. They explain that ocean sanctuaries are "large areas where you don't take anything, break anything, or pollute anything," and "it is by far the most significant thing we can do to be the change we want for the seas." The images on their website feature fishing boats, a man swimming in plastic-polluted water, and an underwater activist at a coral reef holding a sign saying, "Save our seas!"

It's not enough that humans just survive; environmental organizations want *people to thrive in terms of their well-being and health,* which requires that families and communities have access to the living essentials they need (i.e., healthy food, clean water, sanitation, medical care, homes, and jobs). 350.org warns that climate change and its extreme weather, droughts, and fires pose a hardship on farmers and contribute to human hunger. The food crisis is increasing, as more than 860 million people go hungry, which FOE blames on the industrialization and commoditization of food and farming; they see agroecology as the answer. Oceana proposes ocean conservation as the answer: "Restoring the ocean could feed one billion people a healthy seafood meal every day."

FOE expresses concerns that "destructive energy sources" and the environmental and social conflicts they drive are causing pollution, health problems, premature deaths, unsafe and insecure jobs, and the collapse of local economies." Similarly, RAN outlines the threats to humans from coal and power companies, including contaminated drinking water, forced resettlement, destroyed livelihoods, violent treatment of environmental protesters, and increased risks from droughts, storms, and rising sea levels. Because sea level rise "displaces people" and "increasing intensity of storms kills people," while at the same time rising temperatures cause species migration and extinction, 350.org proposes that "keeping fossil fuels in the ground is the best way to protect people from untold destruction" and to "protect important habitats and livelihoods."

Part of protecting human health is maintaining *clean and safe water and air.* 350.org campaigns against dirty energy, including stopping the building of a mega-coalmine (Adani) in Australia, with locals protesting that "coal kills" and calling coal a "dirty, dangerous fuel" that "kills our hope for a safe future." Also in support of clean energy, Greenpeace warns that, due to the coal industry's "polluting stacks and toxic ash dumps," it "threatens our most basic needs: clean water to drink, clean air to breathe, and a safe climate." In addition to causing smog and acid rain, "the coal industry also uses enough fresh water to meet the basic needs of one billion people," so the industry not only pollutes water, it wastes it. Greenpeace has a whole web section entitled "detox" that outlines the need to eliminate "hazardous, persistent and hormone-disrupting chemicals" that "poison our water." They call on industries, such as companies producing garments and electronics, to detox our rivers and "build a toxic-free future."

Part of promoting life is ensuring humans live in a *nonviolent* society, enjoying relative *safety and security*. Shifting to 100 percent renewable energy is "the key to security and wellbeing for all," according to Greenpeace. They share their vision that "today's children will be the first to live in a world totally powered by these clean, safe and secure energy sources." Greenpeace uses the words "clean, safe, secure, and renewable" repeatedly. Ending nuclear contamination and threats has been a longtime campaign issue for Greenpeace, as "much of this nuclear waste will remain hazardous for hundreds of thousands of years, leaving a poisonous legacy to future generations." They use the Fukushima nuclear reactor disaster as an example of how it impacted hundreds of thousands of people's lives and how unsafe these power plants are, and Chernobyl, where thousands of Russians "still endure very visible and painful effects" from the "nightmarish" nuclear accident. To support increased safety, Greenpeace also calls for nuclear disarmament to prevent catastrophic war casualties, and because the people who live near two thousand nuclear weapons test sites "have suffered from cancers, still births, miscarriages, and other health effects."

Nature is often mentioned as a productive source of human sustenance and livelihoods. To show preservation as an investment, Nature Conservancy is mapping the value of nature, in particular ocean wealth, not just in dollars but in "production functions" to report ecosystem services, "in terms of jobs, food security, risk reduction, and visitor numbers." Coral reefs in particular "provide amazing resources for people, including food and income that sustains 500 million people, medicines, and protection from storms." On land, the Nature Conservancy protects forests so they "continue to provide their life-giving services for people and nature." The Nature Conservancy explains that rainforests provide food, water, medicine, and air for everyone, plus they regulate the earth's temperature and weather patterns, provide critical habitat for one-third of the world's species, and are central to the livelihoods and cultures of indigenous peoples and local communities. In the United States alone, forests store and filter "half of the nation's water supply" and "provide jobs to one million forest product workers," generating billions of dollars in recreation-based economic activity.

FOE describes environmental rights in terms of "access to the unspoiled natural resources that enable survival, including land, shelter, food, water and air," and notes that forests "provide livelihoods for many local communities and indigenous peoples," who number over a billion. In agreement, RAN explains that "for decades, frontline and Indigenous communities in Indonesia and around the world have relied on rainforests to support their lives and provide their livelihoods." Greenpeace also details how rainforests are vital to the various tropical regions of the world. The Congo forest functions as the "lungs of Africa" and "provides food, fresh water, shelter and medicine for tens of millions of people." Deforestation in Indonesia's biodiverse forests is not only threatening the lives of "orangutans, elephants, tigers, rhinoceroses, more than 1,500 species of birds, and thousands of plant species," but also "the lives of millions of Indonesians who depend on the forests for food, shelter and livelihoods are also changing beyond recognition as the forest disappears." Greenpeace reminds us that not only land but oceans are bountiful: "Every day the oceans give us the air we need to breathe; the weather to grow crops; water to support the smallest to the largest animals on earth and 80 percent of all species; vast ice flows to help regulate our climate; millions of jobs; and a lifetime of pleasure." Oceana works on policy changes to "restore ocean biodiversity and abundance" to "deliver more seafood to the future."

Environmental organizations emphasize the welfare of individual humans more than the *welfare of nonhuman animals*, yet several organizations allude to the suffering of animals used for food. FOE describes factory farming as causing "intolerable animal cruelty," and Greenpeace similarly critiques the mass production and crowding of land animals on industrial farms. Oceana criticizes the farming of salmon in overcrowded pens, showing pictures of the farmed fish suffering bloody wounds from sea lice. They note these bloodsucking parasites "make life miserable for farmed and wild fish alike," while the pesticides used to kill the lice are toxic to other marine life.

In terms of animal welfare issues caused by commercial fisheries, Oceana expresses concern for sharks "left to die" after having their fins hacked off for the shark fin trade, and for "Risso's dolphins, pilot whales, hammerhead sharks, and seabirds" who are "unlucky victims of pelagic longlines," where they are "left on the hook for hours or even days to drown or bleed to death." And Oceana explains how the fossil fuel industry harms "marine mammals, sea turtles, fish and other wildlife" through the practice of seismic air-gun blasting to explore for oil and gas beneath the ocean floor: "The air guns are so loud that they can disturb, injure and even kill marine life." They describe how piercing and incessant the blasts are for days or weeks on end, which "could injure as many as 138,000 whales and dolphins and disturb millions more."

In the end, environmental organizations are trying to build a *sustainable, better future* to support life in the long run, which, they often emphasize, requires a *stable climate*. Greenpeace's mission is to "force the solutions which are essential to a green and peaceful future." Greenpeace claims "a stable climate is a vital foundation for all life on Earth," but climate change is "putting millions at risk," as the sea level rises and "heatwaves, droughts, and fires are becoming more ferocious." Similarly, FOE sees "climate change and the global energy crisis" as threatening the "lives and livelihoods of billions of people." 350.org declares "we believe in a safe climate and a better future—a just, prosperous, and equitable world built with the power of ordinary people." To make that happen and "create a sustainable future for our world," 350.org encourages us to mobilize to pressure organizations to divest in fossil fuels and pressure governments to "help build a new more equitable, low-carbon economy."

DISCUSSION OF VALUES SUPPORTING FAIRNESS

To support justice, governments and corporations must be held accountable for unfair and unsustainable practices and policies, but environmental organizations know they must not trample over people's rights by unilaterally trying to push through their organization's conservation initiatives. Instead, they must work with communities on solutions to "balance the needs of people with nature," as the Nature Conservancy puts it. Thus, you see messages supporting *people power*. RAN lists "people power" among their values and in their tagline: "We use people power to challenge business as usual and we win." And Greenpeace implies people power, not corporate power, when they emphasize their "financial independence from political or commercial interests," as they do not take donations from companies or governments. FOE claims the current destructive energy system is unsustainable and unjust based on a power imbalance, with "corporate and elite power and interests outweighing the power of ordinary citizens." FOE uses the clever name "Reclaim Power" for its campaign to "usher in a people-centered clean energy revolution," working together to "fight for justice for affected communities."

People power relies on *participatory democracy for fair and inclusive decision-making, involving local communities and giving them a voice*. Part of FOE's mission is "to secure the empowerment of indigenous peoples, local communities, women, groups and individuals, and to ensure public participation in decision-making." Because RAN believes "Indigenous peoples are the best stewards of rainforests," they advocate for indigenous peoples' "right to Free, Prior and Informed Consent regarding decisions implicating customary rights on traditional lands" and provide community grants to foster that grassroots leadership. 350.org suggests that climate justice entails "listening to the communities who are getting hit the hardest and following the leadership of those who are on the frontlines of the crisis." And the Nature Conservancy is committed to "supporting the voice and vision of local communities to co-develop innovative conservation solutions" and "prioritizing collaboration with low-income communities" in its cities initiative.

Regarding gender inclusivity, Oceana works to get policymakers to include the input of fisherwomen in fisheries' decision-making, as they observe that "policymakers tend to ignore fisherwomen, even though they are the ones who often feed and educate their children." In farming, FOE similarly finds that women "sustain traditional knowledge about the diverse uses of locally-found plants for nutrition and health, yet they are consistently denied access to land, and technical and financial assistance." Therefore, FOE asserts, "for agroecology to achieve its full potential, there must be equal distribution of power, tasks, decision-making and remuneration between men and women."

RAN emphasizes the importance of "upholding human rights" in their mission statement and discourse. RAN specifically calls out the "conflict palm oil" industries in Indonesia and Malaysia for perpetuating child labor and slave labor conditions on some plantations and for forcefully removing local people from their lands. To emphasize the exploitative nature of these industries, RAN states, "Where workers are exploited and their rights ignored, it's common to find that environmental regulations are also being violated." With part of their mission being "respect for human rights and peoples' rights," FOE's home page condemns human rights violations toward farmers and activists: "Friends of the Earth International denounces massacre of peasant farmers in Peru—six farmers murdered in land grab for palm oil plantations" and "Honduran students on trial for peaceful protest."

Many environmental organizations, emphasize equality and social justice issues (especially economic justice, environmental justice, and climate justice). Among their values, RAN lists racial justice, social justice, and systemic change for institutional systems of injustice; they post a statement of anti-oppression principles and apply a "racial equity analysis" to their own work to self-reflectively check their own implicit biases in order to be more inclusive. RAN explains that racial injustice is a "fundamental system of injustice that informs every aspect of society," so their organization cannot remain neutral and must directly address racial inequity to "avoid perpetuating unjust systems." FOE's vision is a society "founded on social, economic, gender, and environmental justice, free from all forms of domination and exploitation, such as neoliberalism, corporate globalization, neocolonialism, and militarism." Part of environmental justice is food sovereignty, in which people, not a corporate oligopoly, "determine and control their own food production systems." Impoverished people around the world rely on small or subsistence farms, so FOE asserts that it's unjust for international trade policies to "allow large transnational corporations to enter Southern countries and force small-scale local farmers out of business and off their land." Greenpeace agrees, explaining that because "a greedy elite are industrializing, commodifying, and controlling every aspect of our food system," we must seek an "eco-farming revolution" with "people and farmers at its heart" that would "fight poverty and promote food sovereignty."

In the wake of hurricanes and natural disasters, FOE calls for climate justice, explaining: "The most affected are the vulnerable in society, the economically impoverished." They propose that the climate crisis requires "the people's solutions" based on equity and community ownership, such as "food sovereignty, agroecology, community forest management, public community-based water management, and energy sovereignty." FOE believes energy sovereignty ("the right of communities to choose their sustainable energy sources") is one of the keys to achieving climate justice because it is unfair that "over a billion impoverished people in the world have no access to energy," when they will be "hit the hardest by climate change impacts." In the spirit of true sharing, FOE proposes that "all people must share an equitable amount of resources within ecological limits."

The Nature Conservancy also discusses climate justice issues, warning that "tens of millions of people in low-lying areas, especially in developing countries," could become climate refugees as sea levels rise. One of 350.org's primary principles is "we believe in climate justice." Part of what makes climate change an injustice, especially from the perspective of Pacific island nations working with 350.org, is realizing "at the rate that the developed world is digging up and burning fossil fuels, climate change will continue to have disastrous impacts on those who have done the least to cause these problems." This is part of the environmental justice movement because "the poor and vulnerable are hit first and worst," such as in extreme weather events, like Hurricane Sandy, as low-income neighborhoods in New York were in high flood zones. Thus, 350.org calls for New York mayor Bill de Blasio to divest the state's pension funds from dozens of oil and gas company stocks.

Several environmental organizations discuss holding harmful entities (such as governments, industries, or criminals) accountable for reparations and legal penalties. Greenpeace says it exists to "expose environmental criminals, and to challenge government and corporations when they fail to live up to their mandate to safeguard our environment." FOE critiques corrupt governments that have "rewritten laws to give legitimacy to their heinous rights violations, providing legal cover for rights abuses" against environmental activists, community defenders, and journalists. They also denounce criminal business practices, such as illegal logging. Regarding crime prevention, Oceana spends more time supporting responsible fisheries management than punitive measures, but they do sometimes mention the need to stop illegal fishing and prevent the laundering of illegally caught fish into the legal seafood market (consumer fraud).

"Environmental rights are human rights," FOE asserts, so they advocate for laws supporting "the right to claim reparations for violated rights, including rights for climate refugees and others displaced by environmental destruction, the right to claim ecological debt, and the right to environmental justice." To get industrialized nations to be accountable for their "climate debt" in causing the bulk of the climate crisis, FOE "pressures governments in the North to commit to the necessary emissions cuts, as well as the necessary financial transfers for mitigation and adaptation in developing countries." Essentially, FOE promotes "rights for people and rules for business."

Respect for humans is a prominent value, such as respecting human dignity. RAN mentions human dignity several times in its vision and values statement, and FOE's mission and vision statements also mention human dignity several times. Part of the vision FOE expresses is "a society of interdependent people living in dignity." Organizations also express respect for cultural diversity. In its list of core values, the Nature Conservancy includes "respect for people, communities, and cultures" as well as "commitment to diversity," which mentions being inclusive, sensitive, and fair to local cultures. They describe their approach to conservation as "human rights-based," incorporating "traditional knowledge and cultural values." Many environmental organizations also privilege *respecting indigenous communities' rights, especially land rights.* RAN explicitly supports "Traditional and Indigenous Peoples' rights, including the right to sovereignty, self-determination, reparations," and traditional land rights to prevent further land grabs. FOE also asserts, "We support forest-dwelling communities in upholding collective and traditional land rights." And there are many forest-dwelling communities that need support. For example, Greenpeace acknowledges that the Amazon rainforest is "home to 20 million people, including hundreds of indigenous peoples." The Nature Conservancy recognizes that 18 percent of global lands, representing "much of the Earth's biodiversity," belongs to indigenous people and local communities, who are "uniquely positioned as conservation leaders" due to their "vast experience in environmental stewardship."

Most of the environmental organizations also express *respect for the inherent value of nature and wildlife—appreciating the uniqueness of living beings and special places worth protecting.* RAN states that biodiversity and wildness have "intrinsic value." For example, RAN celebrates the Indonesian rainforests as "some of the world's most culturally and biologically diverse ecosystems" with "irreplaceable wildlife," such as "the Sumatran rhino, Sumatran elephant, and the Sumatran and Bornean orangutan." They use the term "irreplaceable jewel" to describe the Leuser Indonesian rainforest ecosystem they are trying to protect from extractive industries.

In protecting various ecosystems globally, the Nature Conservancy will often identify what makes the places special, such as rainforests nurturing "thousands of plants and animals found nowhere else on Earth"—species that are "the Earth's most interesting and rare." They specifically highlight the "largest remaining tropical forest on our planet" by declaring that "no other place is more critical for human survival than the Amazon Rainforest" because it serves as home for so many human and nonhuman species, one-quarter of the world's freshwater, and trees that store billions of tons of carbon. Greenpeace also heralds the diversity within the world's largest rainforest, the Amazon, home to a quarter of all known land species: "The jaguar, the pink river dolphin, the sloth, the world's largest flower, a monkey the size of a toothbrush, and a spider the size of a baseball," with many more species yet to be discovered. Greenpeace marvels that the second largest rainforest on earth, the Congo forest, "is home to many critically endangered species including forest elephants, gorillas, bonobos, and okapis," and 39 of its mammal species and 3,300 plant species are found nowhere else on earth.

And in the "beautiful but fragile" Arctic region, Greenpeace describes this ecosystem as "vitally important" and its wildlife as "incredible," including "majestic polar bears, blubbery walruses, mysterious narwhals and graceful seabirds."

Greenpeace champions the oceans, in particular, as they house the most life in all the universe and are "so rich in diverse, beautiful, weird and wonderful, large and small species," such as the blue whale, "the largest animal our planet has ever known," plus potentially millions more species that have yet to be discovered.

To protect the world's most special places, 350.org has a campaign asking UNESCO to "protect culture not coal," stating that the international body should demand that governments comply with the Paris Agreement and stop coal plants from being built near UNESCO World Heritage Sites, such as the Sundarbans forest in Bangladesh, Lamu Island in Kenya, and many ancient places in Turkey.

DISCUSSION OF VALUES SUPPORTING RESPONSIBILITY

To be responsible is to take charge in solving problems, and every environmental organization discusses ways they are *finding creative, concrete solutions to environmental problems*. Since humans have polluted and overfished most of the world's oceans, Oceana's solution is to increase the ocean's biodiversity and abundance through more responsible and efficient fishing practices and marine habitat protection. Greenpeace says it exists "because this fragile earth deserves a voice. It needs solutions. It needs change. It needs action," and their mission says they "expose problems" and "force solutions" essential to a green future. Every issue that FOE's website profiles features problems, solutions, and "what we're doing" to solve the problem.

Environmental organizations sometimes call out industry or governments for proposing "false solutions." Trade and investment policies that attract corporate agribusiness are a false solution to create food security "geared for creating profits for them," not local communities. Another ineffective solution is "'carbon sink' schemes and other proposals that replace forests of biodiversity with tree plantations." In these vital next few years to "prevent runaway climate change," FOE encourages people to work together and demand system change to "fight dirty energy and false solutions." While the nuclear industry proposes itself as a climate-friendly energy solution, Greenpeace reveals this as a false solution, detailing how many trillions of dollars nuclear energy costs and how it needs subsidizing, which "squanders the resources necessary to implement meaningful climate change solutions." Greenpeace declares that renewable energy is the "real solution to climate change."

All organizations emphasize that *activist tactics should be effective at achieving goals*, which is part of a broader results-oriented message that we all need to *make a difference by having an impact*. In solving problems, environmental organizations often emphasize efficacy to bolster confidence in the competency and the utility of actions they propose for individuals. One of the Nature Conservancy's values is to produce "tangible, lasting results," offering "innovative solutions to complex conservation problems at scales that matter and in ways that will endure." They also provide ideas for how individuals can "make a difference," saying "small acts of empowerment can have big results." Similarly, Greenpeace's oceans section encourages everyone to take action, with a subsection labeled "we can all do something" including phrases like "if each of us did just one thing, we could change the future." In an effort to have a tangible impact, Greenpeace seeks to eliminate problems, not just manage them, saying it isn't enough to merely "point the finger," so instead they "develop, research, and promote concrete steps towards a green and peaceful future." They assure people of the efficacy of their collective action strategies, saying "together we are winning" in the fight against dirty energy, and "protecting forests is one of the quickest and most effective ways to prevent climate change."

Oceana expresses confidence in their agenda to win policy victories and strategic campaigns that achieve practical solutions with measurable outcomes. They note their accomplishments by saying Oceana has "won more than 100 victories and protected more than one million square miles of ocean." They also motivate consumers to "make a difference right now," such as ending plastic pollution, by saying, "Vote through the ballot box and with your wallet." In the wake of the Trump administration's pro-oil stance, RAN encourages a renewed fight to prevent the Keystone XL oil pipeline project in the United States by reminding people of the "power of grassroots organizing" that successfully pressured President Obama to reject the pipeline, saying: "In 2015 we proved that when we fight, we win. Now it's time for another round." And 350.org assures us "the worldwide movement to stop climate change and resist the fossil fuel industry is growing stronger every day." They provide examples of steps forward, including the decline in global carbon emissions, the reduction in building coal plants, and the growing popularity of electric cars.

An effective approach is to *provide credible scientific evidence and to use reason and common sense*. The Nature Conservancy often highlights their use of the "best available science" and innovation, such as "science-driven solutions" to "slow the rate of climate change." By science, they do not seem to mean biotech and chemicals but rather careful research on which solutions would work the best and most efficiently, such as restoring natural areas as carbon sinks, where scientific research bolsters a "nature-based solution." RAN says they "provide cutting-edge research and analysis." And Oceana also emphasizes their use of fact-based science and experts to achieve results. They advocate for "science-based fishery management" that establishes "science-based catch limits" to protect habitat.

Many environmental organizations encourage citizens to *mobilize as part of a social movement, collectively act to pressure the powerful to change, exhibit courage and boldness, and show commitment to a cause*. On their home page, RAN declares that they "take action against companies and industries driving deforestation and climate change." In their palm oil campaign, RAN describe how they "put mounting pressure on these companies," including meeting with executives, conducting nonviolent direct actions at headquarters, "calling out bad actors," brand jamming, and coining the now popular term "conflict palm oil." In protesting the Keystone XL pipeline, RAN's strategy is to follow the funding and "take bold, courageous action to stop the construction of this horrible pipeline." In "fighting for people and planet," RAN affirms their commitment to "doing what is necessary." But they don't do it alone; they are part of "a global network that supports and works closely with front-line communities."

Greenpeace motivates collective action by expressing urgency: "We really have to change; we have only a limited time to act. Join us as we fight to end polluting coal, oil, gas and nuclear projects," and "our oceans need all of us to work together to build a network to protect them." In mobilizing, Greenpeace emphasizes numbers, saying they speak for 2.8 million supporters and encourage "many millions more than that to take action every day." They describe the variety of activist methods they deploy to "promote open, informed debate about society's environmental choices," including research, lobbying, quiet diplomacy, and nonviolent conflict. FOE led a "Reclaim Power" climate justice campaign in October 2017 that mobilized activists across five continents for a "day of action" to highlight the climate emergency, fight dirty energy, and build a "diverse and effective global movement to stop climate change."

With a network across 188 countries, 350.org uses online campaigns, grass-roots organizing, and mass public actions to "stand up to the fossil fuel industry" and its financial backers. They use strong language such as "take back the power" and "climate change is one of the biggest problems humanity has ever faced," causing a "ravaged planet," "devastated people," and "corrupted governments." To support mass mobilization, 350.org asserts that "world leaders are incapable of solving this problem on their own. We need to get out in the streets and make our voices heard—that is how we demonstrate our power as a movement and that is how we force our government to make the right decisions."

Peaceful protesting is part of some environmental organizations' activist toolkit. All these organizations use nonviolent activist tactics, even if they engage in protests or direct action. Greenpeace's website features many pictures of people protesting, such as the home-page image with an oil rig in the background of Greenpeace's *Arctic Sunrise* boat, where activists display signs that say "People vs Arctic Oil." Because they are "committed to nonviolence," they mention that everyone participating in a Greenpeace action is trained in "nonviolent direct action." RAN also features many images of protesters, especially against fossil fuel, agribusiness, and Wall Street companies, often juxtaposed on their website with images of the destructive industry activities (i.e., smokestacks and clear-cut forests). 350.org chapters worldwide organize many protests, from signs that read "clean coal is a myth," to "protect water," to "break free from fossil fuels." *Educating the public and raising awareness of issues* is another responsible activist tool. Like many of the environmental organizations, Greenpeace urges citizens to educate the community and tell their friends about solutions, from ecological farming to ocean protection. FOE even has schools of sustainability across the globe where local people share information on environmental solutions and mobilization tactics.

Environmental organizations *monitor and expose wrongdoing*, while *asking for honesty and transparency from government and industry*. 350.org assures us that there is scientific consensus that burning fossil fuels leads to global warming, and they decry the deceptions perpetuated by industry to create doubt: "The fossil fuel industry has pumped millions of dollars into creating uncertainty. Exxon joined an industry-wide attack on the truth to protect profits." 350.org's #ExxonKnew campaign showcases evidence of Exxon's deception campaign to fund think tanks to spread doubt and misinformation about climate change, even though Exxon executives knew for decades the damage they were doing. 350.org wants an investigation to hold Exxon accountable, as they "robbed the world of a generation's worth of time to reverse climate change."

Oceana has a "Global Fishing Watch" to "shine a light on suspicious activities like illegal fishing" and increase transparency. They also expose how this illegally caught fish is often mislabeled to consumers, citing a study where a third of seafood tested was mislabeled. To prevent this seafood fraud, Oceana advocates for policy changes that require DNA testing and tracing of fish sources to "bring transparency to the seafood supply chain." In terms of wrongdoing and raising awareness, RAN noted it was "one of the first U.S.-based organizations to make the connection between the destruction of rainforests and grazing land for beef cattle in the early 1980s." But they worry that meat has become so central to billions of people's lives, yet many of the environmental, public health, and ethical consequences of these large meat-producing companies' practices "remain largely undocumented." RAN warns that if meat production and consumption go unchecked, it will lead to increased displacement of small-scale farmers, poverty, climate risks, and loss of species.

A big focus is *taking responsibility (both for harms caused and for making needed improvements); everyone should actively take responsibility and be engaged*. I've categorized this section into responsibilities of various entities, including individual citizens and consumers, society at large (with emphasis on government and corporate responsibility), and food producers.

To take responsibility, *citizens and consumers should live sustainable/green lifestyles and practice conscientious consumerism*. The Nature Conservancy's climate change campaign has a "how you can help" section that suggests citizens offset their carbon footprint, sign a climate pledge to pressure leaders to stick to the Paris Agreement, purchase green energy and electric or hybrid vehicles, telecommute, and eat a low-carbon diet. Regarding diet, the Nature Conservancy explains that "a third of all food emissions in the U.S. come from red meat and dairy products, while chicken and vegetables have up to ten times smaller footprints per serving, so small diet switches can make a big difference." Because it takes six hundred gallons of water to produce a hamburger, the Nature Conservancy's water campaign suggests that consumers eat less red meat, such as "skipping meat for one meal a week." Other responsible water choices include conserving energy, using nontoxic and biodegradable cleaning products, avoiding pesticide use, cleaning up streams, and planting trees.

Ocean-friendly consumer lifestyle choices offered by Greenpeace include not littering, using nontoxic products, avoiding plastic, reducing your greenhouse gas emissions, avoiding unsustainable seafood, and pressuring businesses. Greenpeace assures consumers that since fishing is a business, "consumers are a powerful force," and they list specific fish species not to buy and suggest we ask questions of retailers: "If the shop owner or waiter can't tell you what fish it is, where it's from, and how it is caught, just don't buy it." And because Greenpeace details how "more meat threatens the planet" with rainforest deforestation, greenhouse gas emissions, and water pollution, they suggest consumers "reduce meat and dairy consumption," along with other tips to buy local, organic, fresh, whole produce; plant food gardens; and provide healthy food in schools. Similarly, FOE urges us to "change consumer behavior on meat eating," and their global map of agroecology projects includes some vegan and meat-reduction initiatives.

To save the oceans, Oceana instructs citizens to "vote responsibly and share your voice with politicians regularly," and instructs consumers to eat sustainable seafood, reduce energy use, safely dispose of hazardous materials, use fewer chemical fertilizers, and clean up beaches. To reduce plastic ocean pollution, Oceana asks consumers to recycle, "pledge to break free from plastics," and avoid the use of plastic bags and straws.

To take responsibility, *society at large (especially corporations and government)* should practice *stewardship and responsible guardianship of the land and seas*, including *efficient and wise use of resources*. The Nature Conservancy frequently emphasizes increasing pressures from a growing human population: "Global demands for food, energy and material goods are putting unprecedented pressure on our planet." The Nature Conservancy often focuses on conserving nature and implementing sustainable land- and water-management strategies to meet these demands, rather than discussing population stabilization. With water shortages and water pollution issues, they propose green infrastructure, healthy watersheds, upstream land management, and reforestation in order to improve water quality. FOE's forest campaign calls attention to neoliberal policies and the "increased demand for meat, exotic timber, and crops such as soy and palm" that are causing forests to rapidly disappear, suggesting we must "drastically reduce our energy consumption, paper use, and the export of grains to feed cattle." Regarding the *enforcement of laws*, FOE asks governments to "step up" and "make a courageous comeback" in policymaking and investments that support small farms rather than corporate agribusiness.

To take responsibility, *food producers should practice sustainable, small-scale agriculture and fishing*. FOE supports small-scale "peasant and family farmers" as well as "artisan fisherfolk" that use "traditional knowledge for sustainable management" of lands and seas. They denounce "factory and livestock farming" and note that "meat is at the center of some of our world's greatest ecological and public health threats: deforestation, habitat destruction, water scarcity, climate change, water pollution, diet-related disease, antibiotic resistance, animal cruelty, and more" (see photos 8 and 9). In addition to asking consumers to reduce meat consumption, FOE promotes farming of animals in "grass and pasture-based systems that work in harmony with nature" and reduce the need for growing "thirsty grains for feed." To deal with the massive problems caused by corporate-dominated industrial farming and fishing, Greenpeace mainly emphasizes conscientious consumerism and the establishment of marine sanctuaries, but they do instruct the fishing industry to "start fishing better" and "stop the destructive wasteful and overfishing practices." They instruct farmers to stop factory-farming animals and propose an "eco-farming revolution" based on *crop biodiversity and natural farming methods*, where chemicals are not used as fertilizers or insecticides. Similarly, FOE sees the corporate promotion of genetically modified crops as a false solution to the food crisis and instead supports agroecology—where fisherfolk and peasant farmers lead a "political movement" toward *food security and sovereignty*, such as using their own native and heritage seeds for crop diversity.

In support of systemic change, RAN also mentions the need to "shut down factory farms" due to greenhouse gas emissions, social inequities, extinction of species, and rainforest destruction, noting "commercial agriculture is driving 71 percent of tropical deforestation." At a 'reducitarian' summit promoting a reduction in global meat consumption, RAN spokespersons touched on the need to make healthy plant-based foods "accessible and affordable for all, especially low-income neighborhoods." The Nature Conservancy provides a visual metaphor to illustrate how large agriculture's footprint is, saying global cropland is about the size of South America, and animal grazing land encompasses an area the size of Africa. They also note that "agriculture is the largest single user of water." Their solution to meet growing demands for food is to use scientific and technological approaches to "sustainable intensification," implementing management practices that improve efficiency of inputs and conservation and cleanliness of water. The Nature Conservancy sees farmers and ranchers as "good stewards" and the "greatest allies in conservation," so they work with ranchers in the United States "to implement strategies that maintain beef supplies while sustaining and improving grazed lands." They also mention that China's growing demand for "more dairy, meat, and poultry products" is causing rainforest destruction in Brazil where most soy is grown as animal feed, prompting the need for a sustainable soy trade.

Some organizations perceive *fish as a needed protein source for humans*. Oceana identifies overfishing as a core problem, as we "take too many fish out of the water" and deplete fish populations, yet we are "squandering potential sources of food," while "destructive and wasteful fishing practices threaten animals and damage the sea floor," so they propose establishment of science-based catch limits, a reduction in bycatch, and protection of marine habitats. This dovetails with a problem facing humanity—the need to "produce 70 percent more food to meet the coming hunger needs" of a human population projected to reach nine billion by 2050. Oceana argues that there is not enough arable land and fresh water to feed these additional billions, so they propose responsibly caught fish as the perfect animal protein to feed over a billion people a day because it is affordable, healthy, and doesn't require the land or water resources that beef does. With similar concerns and suggestions, the Nature Conservancy warns that demand for seafood is expected to double in the next several decades, and they offer fishing-management strategies to "sustainably produce enough fish to meet this demand while maintaining healthy oceans with sharks, whales, turtles, and other important marine life."

Every environmental organization in this study, not only the clean energy organization 350.org, has a section on their webpage dedicated to *mitigating human-caused climate change, via reducing greenhouse gas emissions and switching to clean, renewable energy sources.* Greenpeace proposes "quitting coal" and switching to "100 percent renewable energy." Because the warming oceans are causing flooding, intensification of storms, coral reef bleaching, and alteration of animal habitats, Oceana proposes a switch to clean energy sources and a ban on expansion of "dirty offshore drilling." They highlight that oil drilling is a risky business that destroys pristine habitats and coastal communities: "Where we have drilled, we have spilled." FOE notes that intensive agriculture also exacerbates climate change because it is "highly dependent on oil" both to grow food and in distribution by "jetting food around the globe."

Divesting in fossil fuel companies is a climate strategy promoted by 350.org and RAN. 350.org applies moral pressure on organizations that serve the public good (like governments and nonprofits) to cut their ties with the fossil fuel industry to avoid contributing "to the veneer of legitimacy that enables them to keep expanding operations," essentially withdrawing the industry's "social license to operate." RAN also has a "defund extreme fossil fuels" campaign, with theirs aimed at big banks who pump hundreds of billions of dollars into various fossil fuel companies. They call out leading financial institutions for supporting business as usual "in direct contradiction of [the] global consensus" to limit global warming. RAN does herald some progress in the last two years, where many big banks are beginning to reduce their lending to the coal industry, but RAN calls for a more accelerated divestment.

All environmental organizations mention the need to *capture carbon and protect carbon sinks.* 350.org often touts the benefits of "keeping fossil fuels in the ground." Greenpeace says instead of mining, fracking, and drilling for oil and gas, we must "keep most of these dirty fuels in the ground" and regrow forested areas as carbon capture. RAN also uses the phrase "keep it in the ground." The Nature Conservancy also champions forests as well as grasslands and wetlands as a major carbon sink that sequesters a portion of fossil fuel emissions. They propose that 30 percent of the climate change goals established in the 2015 Paris Climate Convention can be achieved through "nature-based solutions—such as stopping deforestation and restoring coastal ecosystems." Oceana explains how "oceans absorb about one-third of the planet's atmospheric carbon dioxide," but the increased emissions have created imbalance and caused ocean acidification that damages coral reefs.

If local people have more control over the production of their food, they can be more *resilient to climate change*, according to FOE. The Nature Conservancy also discusses the need for farming to be more resilient in the face of a warming climate, growing heartier crops and maintaining productivity under extreme weather conditions. They also research coral reef resistance against bleaching to establish factors that promote reef resilience in a warming ocean.

DISCUSSION OF VALUES SUPPORTING UNITY

The need to *work together, collaborate, and form partnerships* is emphasized by all environmental organizations, which overlaps with previous sections on participatory democracy and mobilization for collective action. RAN encourages people to come together "to create a stronger global movement to protect our planet." The broad-based movement is based on "building relationships with impacted communities" and "working in solidarity" with them as allies. RAN emphasizes fairness and inclusiveness in these coalitions, where they equalize power, actively listen, and show respect for allies by helping amplify their voices; humility is implied while diversity is valued. Working with an international group of NGOs, Oceana's campaign to stop plastic pollution seeks to mobilize people around shared values in our shared world: "We are trying to make this movement as big as possible and we want you to join! We share the common values of environmental protection and social justice, and these shared values guide our work in building the world in which we wish to live."

Collaboration is aided by *building solidarity through finding some common ground and consensus* among differing groups. "Working together in solidarity" is part of FOE's mission, and they want to find ways to "build alliances with diverse movements." The Nature Conservancy notes that nature unites us; despite all the diversity and divisions in the United States, "we can find common ground in conservation" as "nature is essential to everyone." On the issue of climate change, the Nature Conservancy expresses how crucial it is to "make energy policy less divisive, and to work on coalescing broad bipartisan policy leadership behind the climate solutions we know work." They want to "rally people around the world," exclaiming, "Together we have the power to limit the effects of climate change." In discussing the coalition to stop the Keystone XL pipeline, RAN emphasizes its inclusion of "people from all walks of life," including "First Nations, ranchers and farmers, environmentalists, and youth fighting for their future." 350.org encourages people working together to fight climate change, but it must be all types of people in a "diverse coalition" comprising "not just environmentalists, but students, business owners, faith groups, labor unions, universities and more." This diversity creates the strength needed to stand up to governments and industry: "We're stronger when we collaborate." Greenpeace expresses flexibility and openness to work with any company or government that is willing to change and work toward mitigating environmental threats, so long as they are sincere and their actions actually benefit the environment.

Several organizations mention our *ecological interdependence and the need for humans to live in harmony with nature.* Greenpeace notes that all of us, "animals, plants, and people," depend on the world's forests as well as the oceans: "You and I are alive right now because of the oceans." Greenpeace takes an inclusive stance on how pollution on land and sea harms all species. RAN values promoting "interdependence with healthy natural systems" and maintaining the "abundance of life in all its forms." RAN also emphasizes how social justice causes are interdependent and systems of oppressions intersect. FOE showcases how human rights and environmental rights are interdependent, as "people's livelihoods, their health, and sometimes their very existence depend upon the quality of and their access to the surrounding environment."

Living in harmony relies on *peaceful coexistence.* Greenpeace incorporates peace into their mission and seeks to "promote peace, global disarmament, and nonviolence." Most organizations imply the concept of peaceful coexistence, as discussed in previous sections, via their commitment to nonviolent tactics; the protection of nature and individuals from unwarranted, life-threatening harm; the desire for humans to work together and for people and wildlife to coexist; and the broader goal of creating a peaceful, just, and green future. FOE sums it up nicely in their vision of "a peaceful and sustainable world based on societies living in harmony with nature."

Being compassionate and having a heart is implied through the altruistic sentiments expressed by environmental organizations throughout this chapter that we should care about nature, wildlife, and especially people. This relates to the conviction in much of the environmental discourse that *people and planet (life) should be prioritized over profits.* FOE laments that transnational agribusiness seems to serve and feed corporations, not people, while conversely "agroecology values the life of people and planet over profits." RAN also uses the phrase "profits put over people and planet" to show that extractive or destructive industries "are some of the worst polluters and the most unsafe for workers," showing a callous disregard for all types of living beings. To denounce corporate greed, 350.org's home page has an image of a climate change activist holding a sign that says "The Oil Companies Don't Care about People."

In order to express how ecosystem health is more valuable than money, Greenpeace shares a philosophy: "When the last tree is cut, the last river poisoned, and the last fish dead, we will discover that we can't eat money." And when they estimate it may take $15 million a year for governments to protect 40 percent of the oceans as marine sanctuaries, Greenpeace suggests that "safeguarding the world's most essential asset" is a more important and vital use of this money than spending it on luxury items.

Responsibility for Problems

In my analysis, I noticed when each of the six environmental organizations place blame or responsibility for problems on particular entities or practices. The most popular target is the fossil fuel industry and dirty energy systems, which is the sole target of 350.org as a climate organization. But any corporations or industries that pollute or "put profits before people and planet" are problematized, especially by Greenpeace, FOE, RAN, and Oceana (with the latter singling out the plastics industry). Industrial-scale fishing operations and farms are included as polluting or destructive industries, including factory animal farms as well as soy and palm oil plantations (the latter especially by RAN). It is interesting to note that the Nature Conservancy does not tend to place blame on anyone and focuses instead on companies and farmers improving management of land and water.

Compared to other environmental organizations, FOE and 350.org put more emphasis on governments who are either weak or corrupt and violent, with Greenpeace also condemning corporate-influenced governments and environmental threats posed by militarism. International commerce and trade systems are a focus of FOE, which critiques unjust trade laws (as a larger critique of neoliberal capitalism), while Oceana focuses on ending *illegal* trade in seafood. As a leverage point to create change, 350.org and RAN have campaigns that target banks and any businesses that sponsor or invest in destructive industries. At a broader level, sometimes it is just the collective destructive practices (such as those that produce greenhouse gas emissions) that are problematized, along with the growing human population (mentioned by the Nature Conservancy) and overconsumption and greed (mentioned by Greenpeace and 350.org).

Summary

The six environmental protection groups in my 2017 sample (FOE, Greenpeace, Nature Conservancy, Oceana, RAN, and 350.org) have online campaigns that aim to support life and prevent harm to all living beings, especially ecosystems (particularly forests and oceans) and people (particularly indigenous groups, local frontline communities, small-scale farmers and fisherfolk, and future generations). Wild animal species are also a point of concern, especially land and marine mammals, fishes, birds, bees, sea turtles, and endangered species in general (including plants). Because they focus on defending so many species from exploitation, the environmental organizations are already largely working for "total liberation" of species (Best 2014), but they often overlook the rights of nonendangered animals and domesticated animals in particular. Environmental groups do promote liberation and justice with campaigns that often target polluting and wasteful industries such as fossil fuel companies and industrial fishing and farming operations (and their financial investors) but also governments that are corporate-corrupted or violent. Values common to all the environmental organizations include the need for effective advocacy that makes an impact and working together to achieve solutions, such as stabilizing the climate, protecting biodiversity, cleaning up toxins to restore the health of ecosystems, and putting the interests of people and planet before profits. I'll incorporate these values, blending in concern for individual sentient beings, to form the human animal earthling identity outlined in the final chapter.

CHAPTER SEVEN

Finding Common Ground
among All Three Causes

This chapter synthesizes the results of my study of human rights, animal protection, and environmental organization campaigns (as discussed respectively in chapters 4, 5, and 6). Here I compare and contrast similarities and differences among the discourses of the three causes to find broad areas of agreement in issues, subjects/beings of concern, and values. This answers research question 3: Which values overlap between movements and are more universal? This chapter also comprises an overview of what virtues the three causes promote in terms of identifying ideal human character traits, as that will ultimately inform the human animal earthling identity I propose in the final chapter. To begin to consider areas of future collaboration between social movement causes, I detail shared issues they address and responsible parties they commonly target.

Who Matters Most to Social Movements

Table 13 outlines the commonalities I found for "who matters" to each of the three social movement causes (human rights, animal protection, and environmentalism) in terms of whose interests they advocate for and whom they mention as important to consider. The most common group for whom all three causes show concern is humans. In this broad category of humanity, organizations within each of the three causes also specify vulnerable human groups that need more help and consideration, including children, the poor, indigenous peoples, and the local human communities who live in any area experiencing a conflict or injustice. If you narrow it down to human groups that were a concern for at least two of the causes, then it was usually the human rights and environmental movements showing concern for women, minority groups, enslaved workers, and small-scale farmers. Sometimes the concern is just for any group of humans that is innocent and therefore does not merit harm or injustice. Although the animal protection movement does talk about human well-being (each of the five animal organizations expresses concern for people), they are the social movement that focuses on humans the least.

The only other entities that are universally of concern to all causes are "the environment" and individuals. "Individuals" is another more general way to refer primarily to humans, but the term's vagueness means it can sometimes include other sentient beings like "animals." The "environment" is mentioned to some extent by each cause, with human rights organizations mentioning it the least. The animal and environmental protection causes are the ones that also talk more generally about all life, future generations, natural resources, and the planet. The references to living beings, all life, and individuals are particularly inclusive terminology because of the ability of these terms to include many diverse species while specifying what we appreciate most about them (that they are unique beings who are alive and struggling to survive on this planet).

Besides humanity and specific human groups, "the environment," and "individuals," I did not categorize anyone else (any nonhuman animal species or specific nature entity) as being a universal concern for all the causes, mainly because most human rights organizations tend not to mention nature or other animals and none emphasize them. While those nonhuman beings are not within the purview of human rights concerns by definition, there are opportunities to incorporate them more as fellow victims of many of the same risks humans face or just generally as part of a healthy, thriving ecological community. In table 13, any entity listed under the categories of nonhuman animals (e.g., wildlife, mammals, birds, etc.) or nature (e.g., ecosystems, habitats, parks, etc.) represents the interest shown for those nonhuman entities solely by environmental and animal protection organizations.

It is telling that even though animal protection and environmental organizations focus more on nonhuman beings (animals and nature) than human beings (with the exception of some very human-centered environmental groups), these social movements still demonstrate care for humanity generally and vulnerable human groups specifically. However, human rights organizations do not show that same courtesy—extension of concern to nonhuman beings—which is, in part, a reflection of our current anthropocentric culture that privileges human interests above all other species. Anthropocentrism gives human protection organizations the freedom to overlook the harms faced by other animals and nature (without experiencing much criticism) while it discourages animal and environmental protection organizations from excluding the 'most important' species—humans—for fear of seeming misanthropic, myopic, uncaring, elitist, or 'tone-deaf' to human struggles.

To play devil's advocate to my anthropocentrism critique, one could argue that every movement appeals to concerns about humans primarily because they are all targeting human audiences and thus the topic is salient and relatable (not necessarily because they deem humans more important). Additionally, animal and environmental causes naturally encompass humans as fellow animals and earthlings

TABLE 13 Who Matters: Entities Deserving Protection, According to Two or More Social Movement Causes

WHO MATTERS	UNIVERSAL: MENTIONED BY ALL THREE SOCIAL MOVEMENT CAUSES	POPULAR: MENTIONED BY TWO SOCIAL MOVEMENT CAUSES
GENERAL CATEGORY	• Environment • Individuals	• All life / living beings • Earth / the planet • Future generations • Resources (especially natural resources)
HUMAN CATEGORY	• Humans / "people" • People living in poverty • Children • Indigenous groups • Local communities • Activists • Vulnerable people	• Women • Minority groups • Innocent people • Small-scale farmers • Enslaved workers
NONHUMAN ANIMAL CATEGORY		• "Animals" • Wildlife • Endangered species • Mammals (on land and sea, especially large iconic mammals) • Farmed animals • Birds • Sea turtles • Fishes • Sharks • Bees
NATURE-SPECIFIC CATEGORY		• Nature • Biodiverse ecosystems (especially forests and oceans) • Wildlife habitats • Nature parks and reserves

(so they are inherently part of their cause), while the cause of protecting humans is, by its very definition and design, already specific just to one species (so including other animals and nature is optional for human rights organizations). But total liberation of species pertinent to a human animal earthling identity calls for frequent acknowledgment of the inherent value of the more-than-human world—outside of any benefits that protecting nature and other animals might also offer to humanity—prioritizing appeals that are biocentric rather than anthropocentric.

Values Common to All or Most Social Movement Causes

I synthesized the most popular and emphasized values promoted as "good or ideal" by the three causes to identify which values these social movements have in common (see table 14), organizing them into values categories of life supporting, fair, responsible, and unifying. Overall, social movements value the establishment of responsible and democratic programs and long-term policies that save lives and improve the well-being of animals (human and/or nonhuman), nature, and/or ecosystems so these entities can thrive now and into the future in healthy and diverse ecological and social environments. Additionally, when it comes to human societies, social movements seek to uphold respect for human rights and diversity, democratic principles of people power, fair and nondiscriminatory policies and practices, and accountability for the powerful or lawbreakers who cause unwarranted harm to living beings.

Some of the same trends present in table 13 are noticeable in table 14; animal protection (especially animal rights) and environmental protection are not as emphasized as human protection and therefore rarely fall within the "universal" category. One exception where an environmental value was universal is in the *life-supporting values category* where clean and safe environments (including a stable climate) are part of keeping humans healthy and somewhat secure. In places where I abstracted the common sentiment expressed by the social movements regardless to whom it was directed (e.g., life preservation, respect and acknowledgment of inherent value, equality, strong legal protection, togetherness, compassion, or freedom), that means it was applicable to both the human and nonhuman animal (e.g., freedom over one's body represents the human rights campaigns against human enslavement as well as the animal rights campaigns against animal enslavement and captivity; togetherness and companionship are valued by all social animals). But for context, I often kept the value more specific and segregated according to whom it applied (e.g., 'human health and well-being' is universal to all three social movement causes, and I listed it separately from 'animal health and well-being,' which is advocated primarily just by the animal and environmental protection movements, as is the protection of *habitats* and *wildlife* populations).

The *fairness values category* reveals universal support for justice, democracy and inclusion, respect (which is based on an acknowledgment of the inherent value or specialness of various living beings), equality, and strong laws and law enforcement. Specific types of rights are popular with environmental and human rights groups that advocate for social justice and land rights for humans; animal protection and human rights groups advocate for individual freedom rights for sentient beings (involving bodily freedom from enslavement and confinement, self-determined agency, and freedom of expression). Being fair also involves helping those who need it most (which is a utilitarian ethics sentiment), repaying innocent people you unjustly harmed (restitution), and protecting cultural diversity (valuing different groups in an equitable way).

The *responsible values category* is heavily influenced by encouraging civic engagement to document and solve problems in order to work collectively to make the world a better place (which is perhaps not surprising for social movements to em-

TABLE 14 Common Values among the Social Movement Causes (Human Rights, Animal Protection, and Environmentalism)

VALUED AS GOOD OR IDEAL	UNIVERSAL: MENTIONED BY ALL THREE SOCIAL MOVEMENT CAUSES	POPULAR: MENTIONED BY TWO SOCIAL MOVEMENT CAUSES
LIFE-SUPPORTING VALUES	• Life (protecting/saving life) • Human health and well-being (emotional and physical) • People having their basic needs met • Secure, safe, and clean environment and living conditions (including a stable climate)	• Animal health and well-being (emotional and physical), especially welfare of domesticated animals • Protecting wild animals • Restoring wildlife populations (aiding endangered species) • Protecting habitats and ecosystems (maintaining healthy habitats) • Biodiversity • Sanctuaries and wildlife reserves • Enabling people's livelihoods (especially via protecting nature)
FAIR VALUES	• Justice and fairness • People power and participatory democracy—inclusion of local people and all affected stakeholders in decision-making (animal protection groups want eco and animal interests to be considered) • Respect (for humans and laws; and for animals, according to animal protection groups) • Acknowledgment of the inherent value of living beings (humans, animals, and unique species and places) • Equality (equitable application of standards and allocation of resources; social and environmental justice) • Strong laws to protect living beings (humans, animals, and nature) • Enforcement of laws; punishment for criminal offenders	• Human rights • Freedom over one's body, speech, labor, and mobility; self-determination • Land rights (especially for indigenous human communities) • Reparations/restitution for harms • Aiding those who need it most (protecting the vulnerable) • Cultural diversity

TABLE 14 Common Values among the Social Movement Causes (Human Rights, Animal Protection, and Environmentalism) *(continued)*

VALUED AS GOOD OR IDEAL	UNIVERSAL: MENTIONED BY ALL THREE SOCIAL MOVEMENT CAUSES	POPULAR: MENTIONED BY TWO SOCIAL MOVEMENT CAUSES
RESPONSIBLE VALUES	• Taking responsibility (for improvements; for caretaking) • Being cautious and careful to avoid harm • Education (especially educating children and the public about issues; raising awareness) • Transparency and openness; honesty • Effective advocacy; solving problems • Making a difference; everyone taking action • Collective action for social change; speaking up to the powerful • Public protest (peaceful) • Political will and commitment	• Being accountable for harm caused • Efficient and wise use of resources • Investigating and exposing abuses and wrongdoing • Using credible scientific evidence and research • Conscientious consumerism and green lifestyle choices (including veganism or eating fewer animal products, according to some animal and eco-protection groups) • Investment in a sustainable future (limiting pollution and greenhouse gases; stewardship of nature; sustainable, natural, small-scale agriculture)
UNIFYING VALUES	• Peaceful, harmonious relations; coexistence • Collaborating and forming partnerships • Compassion for living beings (putting life before profits)	• Human dignity (and a similar acknowledgment of animal sentience and intelligence) • Togetherness and bonds between families, companions, communities, and cultures (among various species) • Love • Ecological interdependence

phasize, as they are filled with activists doing just that). The value of education would not have made it into the universal category here if it was solely framed as the education of children in school (primarily a human rights concern), but if I combined classroom education with all social movements' concerns over educating the public about issues and needs so that citizens are knowledgeable and develop humane attitudes, then education is a universal value. Responsibility is also the category that values being careful not to put others at risk, being accountable for your actions, being a conscientious consumer, and not being wasteful with shared resources. To be responsible is also to be honest and open with others (especially having governments and corporations be transparent), a truthfulness value related to using credible scientific research instead of being deceptive and self-serving with information. Because there are so many examples of how to be ecologically responsible, they are not all mentioned by each cause (except environmental groups), so I aggregated several of them (that were common to animal and environmental protection groups) into the value of 'investing in a sustainable future.'

The *unifying values category* emphasizes both (1) the universal need to coexist peacefully and work together in our interdependence, and (2) the acknowledgment of some shared traits that we might recognize in one another to feel a sense of community or solidarity (intra- and interspecies). The universal value of showing compassion for other living beings is commonly expressed by social movement organizations (even if they do not all use the word "compassion" as often as animal protection groups do), primarily to tell corporations or greedy people that they need to prioritize the lives and well-being of others over making a profit (based on empathizing with fellow beings).

Virtues That Social Movements Admire Most

In examining the values articulated as good or ideal by all three social movement causes, I parsed out values that could also apply as *virtues*—character traits of a good or ethical person. The two most popular and emphasized virtues indicate that all the causes would view a virtuous person as someone who is fair and responsible first and foremost. They all agree that a virtuous person must also be caring, respectful, and committed to and engaged in making the world a better place. Demonstrating integrity and being compassionate, honest, wise, open, and generous (altruistic) are also popular virtues among most groups.

Some social movement causes promote virtues that other social movement causes do not tend to prioritize as overtly but certainly are not against. For example, compassion and generosity are not emphasized as much by environmental advocacy groups, perhaps because these traits are ones used more for dealing with animals (humans included) and indicate a sense of charity toward individual sentient beings. The animal advocacy groups do not tend to emphasize accountability, trustworthiness, prudence, and peacefulness as often. This indicates that the human and environmental advocacy groups more frequently discuss the need to take precautions not to pollute environments or harm humans as well as to hold governments and corporations accountable for the harm caused (whereas the animal groups may rely more heavily on behavioral changes from consumers). Peacefulness can be implied as being a trait the animal groups support because they advocate nonviolence (which is the premise of vegan advocacy in PETA and Animal Equality campaigns), but human and environmental advocacy groups more overtly associate 'peacefulness' with avoiding destructive warfare. The human rights groups do not emphasize the need for activists to be courageous as much, but they do emphasize love more than the other movements do, especially in their focus on kids and families.

Opportunities for Collaboration among Social Movements

Looking at the shared issues these various causes tackle and overlapping 'guilty parties' that they target as being responsible for harms can help identify potential projects for intermovement collaboration. Consider the common issues and problem areas below.

SOME COMMON ISSUES THAT TWO OR MORE OF THE SOCIAL MOVEMENTS ADDRESS

I've listed these in alphabetical order below:

- Animal agribusiness (especially factory farming)
- Climate crisis
- Commercial fishing
- Displacement of human groups; land-grabbing
- Environmental injustice (disproportionately harming the poor)
- Extinction and species loss
- Habitat destruction, including deforestation
- Human rights violations
- Human starvation
- Poaching (illegal hunting of animals, sometimes endangered)
- Pollution of land, air, and water (including rivers and oceans)
- Unjust, exploitative, or corrupt businesses or governments
- Waste or misuse of shared resources that need conserving

All these issues, in a broad sense, deal with healing and preventing serious and often life-threatening harm to a variety of living beings. Lethal harm is literally 'over-kill' in many cases: hunting and/or breeding and killing billions of animals to sell their bodies; destroying forests, aquatic ecosystems, and other home habitats; suffocating the livelihoods of endangered species to the point that each day more individuals of their kind cease to exist; allowing millions of impoverished human beings to starve instead of sharing ample food supplies; and spreading deadly toxins that contaminate living spaces.

The major long-term harms threatening all living beings are environmental:

1. Pollution of environments that degrade their ecological ability to function productively, especially human-caused greenhouse gas emissions warming the planet
2. Failure of humans to conserve and sustainably use shared resources like freshwater or land needed by future generations of species
3. Loss of biodiversity causing myriad unknown and often deleterious ecological consequences that multiply deaths and degrade the ability of other species to thrive over time

Social movements also address harm to individual sentient beings, in this case immediate but nondeadly injustices, namely, violations of the rights of animals (humans included) to live freely as self-determining beings fully integrated into their native or preferred societies/cultures, each with equal opportunities to enjoy the benefits of life common to fellow members of their community, without being oppressed by the powerful. Benefits include having a healthy home (shelter or territory) for purposes of affiliation, protection, growth and development, and facilitation of livelihood and sustenance. The next section summarizes whom the social movement organizations tend to blame for causing these injustices, long-term environmental harms, and the death of billions.

COMMON SOURCES OF PROBLEMS: PARTIES RESPONSIBLE FOR HARM

Social movement organizations disperse the responsibilities for harm among many entities, but these universally include the most powerful institutions on the planet— governments and corporations. Corporations often put profits above all other concerns, which can lead to exploitation of living beings. Governments can be corrupted by business interests, and/or by their own greedy leaders, or by a society of citizens where dominant groups seek to discriminate against certain minority or historically disadvantaged groups (or an apathetic society that just does not care enough to advocate for equal rights for all its members). In all these cases, it is a misuse of power that 'enriches' some by disadvantaging others, largely for self-interested reasons.

The environmental and animal protection movements often mention other parties responsible for harm, and only one of them is criminal or is intentionally doing harm—namely, those who illegally trade in wildlife and poach wild animals. The other culpable parties are hard to pinpoint, as they are just larger social forces of daily practice, in which people in many societies are collectively acting in ways that seem innocent and routine on an individual level but are destructive in aggregate: buying food, vehicles, clothing, electronics, and other products; driving or flying to destinations; eating animal products and GMO foods multiple times a day;

using and discarding packages and items (including plastics); having babies; using energy and water in their homes, yards, and commercial buildings; expanding their local spaces with new homes and roads, etc. When these daily practices are multiplied among millions or billions of people, and the practices are each somewhat harmful to the environment or wildlife, the collective negative impact is massive. Some animal protection and environmental organizations highlight that consumers should conduct daily practices consciously to use green/renewable/ecofriendly products or cruelty-free/vegan products, thereby lessening the collective impact (although they often acknowledge that current systems might not make it easy for people to be green). But the fact that the human population keeps growing and consumption levels (consumer lifestyles) increase globally means the strain and harm to ecosystems and animals (human and nonhuman) is multiplying to catastrophic and unsustainable levels. So while, much of the time, campaigns put the blame on *them* (powerful targets like corporations, governments, and criminals), social movements must also put some of the blame on *us* as individuals and as a society (as less-responsible consumers and citizens who must jointly demand and enact systemic sociopolitical reform).

COLLECTIVE PROBLEM-SOLVING

Examining these harms and culprits offers opportunities to identify where all three social movement causes can work together on similar problems, sometimes with similar targets of reform. For those advocacy organizations that are willing to target consumer behavior and lifestyle, they can enact conscientious consumption campaigns on fair (cruelty-free and fair-trade), clean, and green foods and products as well as educate the public on daily sustainable practices to conserve resources. To expand this into a government or corporate campaign, it would help individuals make better choices if governments and systems were reformed to facilitate fair, clean, and green practices and products to be the default option for consumers and citizens (making these options more affordable, convenient, and easily accessible for widespread adoption).

One area where more attention must be paid by all movements is in stabilization and eventual reduction in the human population growth rate, instead of just viewing this growth as a given that we must accept. All three causes can enact educational and policy-driven programs aimed at reducing birth rates (without trampling on human rights), especially in consumer cultures. This can be achieved by promoting adoption of children, empowerment and education of girls and women, and widespread access to affordable contraception and reproductive health-care services.

To target a fundamental underlying problem in governance, the movements could also enact a joint campaign to support democracy and people power and to remove corporate interests in politics and elections; this would involve engaging citizens in voting for politicians who will stand up for fairness and ecological responsibility. Another campaign aimed at the powerful could have all three causes either holding a relevant government or a leading corporation or industry accountable for making massive reforms in a key sector—such as agriculture, fishing, or energy. Included in this joint campaign could be protective policies that help not only the environment but also the rights of humans and other animals. It should also have a climate stabilization component, a biodiversity component, and a social justice component so it connects our greatest problems to needed solutions, demonstrating their interconnectedness.

A collective approach to fighting human hunger would require a multipronged approach that combats poverty drivers, but it should include an agriculture and food distribution program that enables more people worldwide to consume and to grow nutritious organic crops (which are climate-friendly and animal-friendly foods) as well as to protect their local ecosystems to better support their long-term ability to thrive and make a living in that area.

Another joint campaign could revolve around protection of wildlife and habitats to prevent habitat fragmentation and destruction, extinction of species, and criminal trade in wildlife parts. This should involve the leadership of indigenous groups and any local communities who live within or near these habitats. This local leadership would not only ensure that campaigns were culturally appropriate with local buy-in but also that environmental justice concerns were upheld in the process of helping wildlife.

Because social discrimination is a pervasive issue causing mass injustice, exploitation, and poverty, all social movement campaigns on any issue must be cognizant of promoting tolerance and cultural diversity to avoid reinforcing harmful stereotypes that disadvantage human minority groups, instead finding ways to empower and amplify minority voices. This could also include an awareness that humans should treat other animals fairly and with more respect, as they are inherently valuable beings in an interdependent global ecosystem, so their interests deserve to be included in campaigns. In general, it would be helpful to have campaigns that foster respect for all sentient beings and fight the exploitation of anyone being used as a mere tool or resource for another.

Summary

In reviewing areas of overlap between campaign topics and campaign values, the three social movement causes of environmentalism, animal protection, and human rights share some common ground that is ripe for fostering campaign coalitions and serving as allies for one another. On a fundamental level, all causes seek to prevent serious harm and to support the long-term health of living beings (including future generations) and our shared ecosystems, while fostering equitable relations in human society. Because environmental issues are fundamental to the well-being of all species, all social movements can team up in support of environmental protection causes such as biodiversity, climate change mitigation and adaptation, reduction of pollution and waste, human population stabilization, restoration of wildlife habitats, freshwater preservation, environmental justice and equitable sharing of resources, and sustainable agriculture. They could also work collectively to support democratic decision-making and fight government and corporate corruption to protect all vulnerable beings from exploitation, while transforming systems, especially economic systems, to start putting life before profits. Their campaigns can promote shared virtues such as fairness, responsibility, respect, caring, and commitment to enacting peaceful social change.

CHAPTER EIGHT

Insights from Interviewing Activists

This chapter features the highlights of interviews I conducted with nineteen activists regarding their views on social change campaigning, areas of overlap between causes, common core values, and collaboration strategies (see activist profiles in appendix B). To select activists to interview, I approached all sixteen international organizations that I used in my discourse analysis for this book and first attempted to interview the CEO/president of each, five of whom participated. In cases where that top executive was either unavailable or uninterested, I asked for a leader working in communication for their organization. I was able to conduct interviews with representatives (see the alphabetical list below) from all organizations except Anti-Slavery International, International Fund for Animal Welfare, Oceana, and 350.org.

Emma Daly, Communications Director, Human Rights Watch

Devadass Gnanapragasam, Deputy Director of Campaigns, Amnesty International

Ginette Hemley, Senior VP Wildlife Conservation, World Wildlife Fund

Ashfaq Khalfan, Director of Law and Policy, Amnesty International

Martin Lloyd, Senior Mobilisation Strategist, Greenpeace Netherlands

Ingrid Newkirk, Co-founder and President, People for the Ethical Treatment of Animals

Sharon Núñez, Co-founder and President, Animal Equality International

Erich Pica, President and CEO, Friends of the Earth USA

Maria Rohani, Social Movements Advisor, CARE USA

Carl Soderbergh, Director of Policy and Communications, Minority Rights Group International

Laurel Sutherlin, Senior Communications Strategist, Rainforest Action Network

Mark Tercek, President and CEO, Nature Conservancy

Captain Paul Watson, Founder and President, Sea Shepherd Conservation Society

I also supplemented this sample by including six additional activists at organizations that were not part of my book's discourse analysis but whose prominent leaders exemplify an intersectional approach to some degree—blending concerns for two or more causes (e.g., animals and nature, or humans and the environment, or human and nonhuman animals). These activists include:

Mustafa Ali, Senior VP, Climate, Environmental Justice, and Community
    Revitalization, Hip Hop Caucus
Frances Moore Lappé, Co-founder and Co-president, Small Planet Institute
Lori Marino, Co-founder and President, The Whale Sanctuary Project
Dawn Moncrief, Founder and President, A Well Fed World
Will Travers, OBE, Co-founder and President, Born Free Foundation
Zoe Weil, Co-founder and President, Institute for Humane Education

Between fall 2017 and summer 2018, I conducted separate hour-long phone interviews with eighteen of these activist leaders (Newkirk submitted her interview answers via email). While I selected most of these interviewees because of the social movement organizations (SMOs) they work for, I should disclaim that each interviewee speaks for her- or himself and cannot possibly represent all viewpoints shared by colleagues in their organization.

In this chapter, I present these activists' views on the benefits and challenges of the three causes collaborating together (animal protection, environmentalism, and human rights causes) and their advice on how to make collaboration work. To highlight social movement interdependence, activists discuss the commonalities between the three causes, including the common opponents they fight. In favor of designing campaigns that are mutually supportive and inclusive of all living beings, I list the top values that activists currently appeal to as well as values they wish society would prioritize, including tables of where these values overlap. To find further common ground, I outline the activists' assessments of the core attitudes, beliefs, or behaviors that serve as root causes of the problems their organizations address. To move forward, activists discuss how they have made accommodations to be more supportive of other causes while advocating for their own, and how they believe environmental, human rights, and animal protection campaigns could be more inclusive. I end with activists' terminology suggestions for whether they choose to refer to humans as 'animals' and why not, in most cases.

Collaboration among Causes: Pros and Cons

In this section, activists address the benefits of working together, the challenges collaborative work poses for social movement organizations, and ways to make it work.

BENEFITS TO CROSS-CAUSE COLLABORATION

The interviewees express many benefits about collaboration between environmental, animal, and human causes; many think providing mutual support makes sense because the causes are interconnected. "For me it's all connected," Ali explains. "We have to be protecting our public spaces. We have to be protecting public health. We have to be protecting animal rights. Because when we allow any of these to wane, then we know that there's a break in the chain." In an era that is so divisive, Ali feels it is vital to remind everyone that "we're all in this together." Some of the pragmatic benefits of alliance building are achieving greater reach and impact and leveraging more support. Sutherlin says, "It's smart not to keep ourselves divided and to leverage our resources and impact for everything they are worth." Hemley acknowledges, while there can be competition between groups for fundraising dollars, "I think that everyone is also seeing that donors and supporters really love collaboration, so it makes them all look good—not only look good but obviously more effective, which is the ultimate goal." Rohani believes activists must work more "accurately and successfully" by having environmental justice and human rights SMOs "working alongside each other," because for affected people, "environmental justice and social justice aren't two different experiences in their lives, right? They're often intertwined." Pica also recommends gaining strength in numbers when he says, "We need to build power to take on this exploitative system of injustice."

Working together can reveal common interests and motivations that SMOs may not have recognized before, fostering dialogue and better understanding of each cause and its activists. On an interpersonal level, some interviewees express that collaboration offers the opportunity to develop rapport, which helps humanize activists in other organizations and can facilitate long-term relationships.

Some interviewees mention how it can be more efficient for organizations working in the same community or region to tackle issues holistically, making a variety of interrelated improvements at once instead of in a piecemeal manner over time. To be less myopic, collaboration has the benefit of bringing in multiple perspectives on an issue to serve a wider set of stakeholders, spreading out care and consideration more equitably. Travers gives an example of a Born Free wildlife conservation project in Northern Kenya where the lioness sanctuary is surrounded on two sides by high human population density, and the local school, serving six hundred people, had no electricity or running water. Travers explains, "Those people could quite rightly turn around and say, 'Why is this nongovernment organization from overseas spending time and money on lions and elephants when this community is struggling as it is?'" Therefore, Born Free is working with the community to provide water, bring power to the classrooms, plant woodlands, and integrate environmental education into their schools. Travers sees this as mutually beneficial:

> Our logic in this is if people think that a wildlife organization cares about them, then they're more likely to be supportive of that wildlife organization and its wildlife agenda. And as long as we do that with integrity and sustainably and for the long-term, then we've built a collaborative coalition of ourselves and of local people and law enforcement agencies so that when or if bad guys turn up to do harm, that community is our first line of defense. Because they will say, "You

come here and you mess up our wildlife, you're messing up our relationship with an organization that has been standing beside us shoulder to shoulder."

And Travers is also working with a new charity that will organize all the services the community needs at one time "in a holistic, intelligent, and coordinated way" (e.g., solar power, water, education, health care, human rights), including wildlife and environmental needs, with one project manager. He maintains that if organizations "that are all working in one space, coming with different agendas" would just talk to one another, then they could "find more ways of working together than not."

CHALLENGES TO COLLABORATION BETWEEN CAUSES

The challenges interviewees identify fall into two areas: (1) ideological and (2) structural and pragmatic. In the latter category, a primary *pragmatic* challenge is the limited resources (staff, funding, time) that nonprofits have to put toward efforts to collaborate administratively on projects when they may already feel strained just to achieve their basic mission. Additionally, it may be impractical to work together if one's style of activism is too different or target audiences too distinct. For example, SMOs that are more conservative or radical on any spectrum (either in ideology or activism approach) may not be able to work well with organizations on the opposite end of the spectrum, and it may displease their supporting members who could perceive the alliance as either 'selling out' or radicalizing beyond their comfort level. Disagreement over tactics deemed as too aggressive can make some alliances impossible. For example, Watson notes that Sea Shepherd and Greenpeace (an organization he worked for at its founding) disagree over the definition of violence, as Watson argues that it isn't violent for Sea Shepherd to damage property/ objects if that saves lives, such as disabling whaling ships and fishing nets. "In 1986 we sank half of Iceland's whaling fleet and destroyed their whale processing plant because they were illegally killing whales," Watson explains. Sea Shepherd received a lot of criticism even from environmental groups, but Watson argues that they didn't sink the ships to please any particular humans: "We sank them for the whales. And if you find me one whale that disagrees with what we did, I promise you we won't do it again."

Another structural issue is that collaboration requires a unified campaign target, and some SMOs aim for government and policy reforms (systemic reforms) while others aim for consumer lifestyle changes (individual behavioral reforms, such as campaigns to promote veganism or recycling). For example, some SMOs may prefer to work at the corporate level to change the supply side of the marketplace (e.g., paper companies not purchasing rainforest tree lumber or home improvement stores not stocking those products) rather than consumer changes on the demand side (e.g., consumers boycotting paper made from rainforest trees).

SMOs also have different priorities that can impede consensus building toward a common goal, especially if all the organizations fail to see their issues as truly interconnected and therefore lack full motivation to work together or compromise.

Additionally, one's own preferred message may get diluted when seeking a universal message as part of a coalition, and the compromise might feel like too much of a sacrifice of your SMO's goals and identity. Sutherlin explains, "People have their different deeply seated beliefs and priorities, and a lot of people are really fervent about this being THE THING that matters. And so, getting people actually pointed in the same direction and actually building on each other's strengths rather than pulling in different directions and diffusing the momentum is challenging."

Interviewees mention several *ideological* challenges to collaboration. A primary difference between animal and environmental protection groups is over how to handle nonnative species that are causing problems for native species. Animal protection organizations favor humane solutions for sentient individuals, while environmental organizations allow for lethal solutions, sacrificing (nonhuman) individuals to benefit the larger system or species group. The issue of meat is also a point of contention, as animal rights groups again protect the rights and lives of individual animals and thus promote vegan diets, while animal welfare groups and environmental groups often opt for "less meat or better meat" messages, as Lloyd puts it, such as working with farmers and the fishing industry on less unsustainable or cruel practices.

Marino says an ideological impediment to collaboration is when there is asymmetry in an SMO's conflict-resolution approach and they inherently expect nonhuman animals to "take the fall" in any conflict between humans and nonhumans. She explains, "Human inconvenience is often met with the killing of other animals," and that's "just not good enough as a justification for killing." Daly admits, at HRW, when there are conflicts between animals and people, HRW will side with people, as that is their mandate; she is pragmatic in acknowledging they "can't protect everyone's rights," meaning that a human rights group is meant to focus on enforcing international *human rights* laws, even though that is admittedly a "narrower part of life" than other social movements address.

Ideological differences between human rights and environmental/wildlife groups include preservationist views of some environmentalists who believe park or wilderness areas need to be off-limits to human inhabitants or human use in order to protect wildlife and ecosystems; this is contrasted with human rights activists or some conservation groups who prefer that conservation areas be more accessible to local, indigenous people, seeing them as environmental stewards and equal stakeholders along with wildlife. Another barrier to collaboration is when environmentalists are fighting a destructive industry, but they cannot get the support of the workers if labor rights activists see the industry as a source of good jobs.

HOW TO MAKE COLLABORATION BETWEEN CAUSES WORK

In order for collaboration between causes to make sense, many interviewees mention that the SMOs involved must have a shared vision for success—a common goal with agreed upon objectives and tactics. And then everyone must remain pointed in the same direction, focusing on their similarities and common goal, building on each other's strengths, and not focusing on the inevitable differences that remain on other related matters. As Lloyd explains, "If everybody agrees on what success looks like, then we can work together and we can agree to leave the other stuff out of it." For example, Núñez, a vegan and animal rights advocate, says she can envision a coordinated campaign to encourage governments to reduce national meat consumption. Pica could also envision fellow environmentalists partaking in a meat reduction coalition with animal advocates.

Regarding interpersonal relations, some interviewees recommend being patient with other activists and checking your own ego so you can be more self-aware. Weil and Watson both suggest admitting your own hypocrisies, with Watson humorously adding, "If you've got a birth certificate, you're guilty of something!" Therefore, be understanding and respectful of other activists' different beliefs and ideas. Moncrief advises, in particular to fellow vegan activists, "Don't try to convert people." Similarly, Watson tells fellow animal activists to "lead by example" and offer vegan foods to those with whom you partner, without demanding they too become vegan. And Weil argues that when working toward a shared goal, it is not helpful to be "too principled" to work with some investor or group because they eat meat or have some other differing ideas. In order to form coalitions, she asks activists to actively seek and "find bridges," advising that "people have to be willing to listen to other people to work toward the common goals that one can find."

Some common mistakes that interviewees warn against include (1) fighting over whose cause is most important and (2) enacting narrow or single-minded approaches that ignore other stakeholders who are important to other causes. It is essential to also be respectful of human minority groups and avoid racist, sexist, homophobic, ableist, or other discriminatory messages in campaigns. Similarly, do not overlook the rights of human minority groups and local people affected by campaigns; seek their input and authentic partnership as stakeholders, following a bottom-up rather than top-down approach to campaign planning. And lastly, recognize that if your organization cuts a weak deal with opponents in a unilateral move, that can undercut larger shared goals of coalitions.

How Struggles Are Interrelated among Causes

In this section, activists discuss what values and goals unify the three causes as well as what common opponents and systemic oppressions they jointly combat.

COMMONALITIES AMONG CAUSES

The three causes of animal, environmental, and human protection are "inextricable" and exist as "strands of the same movement," according to Sutherlin. He explains they are all "really just one movement" because if you start with "a commitment to justice, equity, and ecological health," you come to the same conclusion about how animals, people, and landscapes should be treated. In further support of all three causes, Daly states, "All of us live on this planet, and we should have respect for the planet and for the people and creatures living on the planet," saying "law, dignity, and justice" underpin all three.

Moncrief notes that all social movements try to make the world a better place by countering corrupt interests and preventing harm. Núñez also sees SMOs focusing on the mutual goal of not harming others and avoiding discrimination based on differences. Similarly, Newkirk claims the common belief among causes is nonviolence and an aversion to oppression, prejudice, and exploitation. Pica echoes this shared focus on fighting unfair and inherently exploitative systems, instructing all SMOs to build solutions on a framework of justice—preventing humans from imposing their will over someone else (human, animal, or environment) or trying to take away their rights. In terms of human rights, Rohani notes that "the big intangible system that we talk about looks the same and it acts the same and it's often from the same roots," saying even if SMOs work on different issues, the systems of inequality are the same: "Maybe somebody calls its gender-based violence, maybe someone else calls it labor violation work, but at the end of the day those are similar systems of oppression." To emphasize how human and animal rights movements are connected in their struggle against oppression, Marino states: "Fighting child sex slavery is the same thing as fighting chickens being in cages, or pigs in gestation crates, or whales in tanks. I mean, it's all against the same thing."

Khalfan notes that all three causes resist powerful interests, promoting common values of altruism, compassion, and selflessness. With a similar acknowledgment for power imbalances faced by all types of beings, the common struggle is the vulnerable versus the powerful, Marino simply states. Ali also mentions privileging the vulnerable when he says we must "listen to the concerns of the most vulnerable communities." Fairness and compassion for others is emphasized by Travers, who sees SMOs all struggling to give individuals (including wildlife) choices over their lives, by freeing them from various states of captivity. Travers describes rights for human and nonhuman animals as being about "opportunities to live a life based on our values and choices."

A related commonality across all three causes is fighting cruelty to reduce individual suffering. And suffering can relate to environmental issues, as Travers explains that suffering is caused by a lack of caring for the environment. He notes there are long-term benefits to all of us having "viable, dynamic, evolving, and secure ecosystems." Watson emphasizes the importance of ocean health, in particular, to supporting all life on earth. Weil also sees health as a common goal of these interconnected causes as they attempt to "enhance a thriving, healthy, and humane life for all."

At a core level, all causes promote respect for life, according to Hemley, with ecological principles demonstrating the connection between the environment, animals, and humans. When supporting ecological conservation efforts, Tercek recognizes the need to also serve community-oriented objectives, as conservation will not work if it is at the expense of people living in those natural areas. And Daly further acknowledges this interdependence by noting that human rights crises end up fueling environmental degradation and vice versa. Similarly, Khalfan explains how human rights law recognizes how "environmental harm has clear negative impacts on the rights of humans." Soderbergh sees human rights and environmentalism as "totally integrated" because human health and food are reliant on a healthy, clean environment and a stable climate. He adds that wildlife will also be impacted by climate change, as animals will be climate refugees too.

Regarding the animal rights movement, Newkirk states that human rights are included within animal rights, since humans are animals. And Marino says we should all be for human and nonhuman rights: "A lot of people think that you're either for animals or for humans. But the fact is that if you're for both, you can still move in the same direction." And Watson sees animal rights as also being a natural part of the conservation movement: "We feel that a vegan lifestyle goes hand in hand with active conservation and environmentalism." Because Watson views veganism as something that "should be normal," it's natural that all Sea Shepherd ships' meals have been vegan since 1999. A supporter of veganism herself, Moncrief concludes that we must save the environment to protect human and nonhuman animals, and one route to help animals is by not eating them, as plant-based diets are the key to reducing environmental destruction and human hunger. Newkirk also acknowledges that animal agriculture is a problem that connects animal rights, environmentalism, and human health, and Núñez too notes how animal agribusiness is a driver of human hunger, poverty, and climate change.

Climate change is an environmental justice issue for humans who are affected in "stark ways," notes Rohani, as human health and livelihood rely on a healthy planet (she describes this as an "intrinsic relationship" between planetary and human health). Part of the wildlife protection movement, Hemley and Sutherlin both see climate change campaigns as having the potential to bring all three causes together with a mutual goal, as Sutherlin puts it, to "build diverse, dynamic, healthy communities." In fact, Greenpeace and Amnesty have started collaborating in support of renewable energy to combat pollution and climate change.

In essence, the overarching philosophy between all causes, according to Marino, is to encourage humans to follow the golden rule to do unto others (human and nonhuman) as you would have done unto you. Similarly, Daly supports the universal principle that we should "protect people from wanton, willful, or unnecessary pain and suffering." While saying this, she recognizes that protection from unnecessary harm probably should extend to animals and the planet as well.

In thinking fundamentally about SMOs' social change missions, Lloyd views their common interest as "securing space for civil society and democratic rights to protest." Similarly, Lappé believes democratic reform is a "movement of movements" that deserves prioritizing, considering the global attempts to concentrate power and undermine the power of citizens; she adds that people need to start enacting government regulations—laws not to be perceived as restrictions but as standards for ensuring health. And Tercek thinks that having each SMO encourage people to vote and be civically engaged is perhaps more useful than collaborating on specific issue campaigns. Gnanapragasam says Amnesty International was founded on the democratic principle of ordinary people coming together, "working in solidarity to build a better world."

SIMILAR OPPOSING FORCES

I asked interviewees about the entities responsible for the problems the SMOs are aiming to solve, inquiring what opposing forces all three causes have in common. The answers often include corporations, our economic system, governments, and discriminatory views.

Corporations. The most popular answer among more than half the interviewees is to mention corporations or industry as their main opponent, especially if those companies are exploitative of workers and/or polluting. To convey how some companies are dismissive of human and nonhuman life, Sutherlin observes, "It's certainly the case that the same corporations that are running roughshod over rainforests are also abusing their workers and exploiting their workforce, and that's not a coincidence, of course." Rohani agrees, saying, "The factories that are polluting the community's environment are also the factories where we're not seeing the type of labor rights that we need to keep folks safe." Lappé frames the main problem as corporate power being both concentrated and unaccountable. The only industries that multiple interviewees singled out as problematic for all three causes are animal agribusiness, extractive industries (in particular fossil fuels), and banks.

Economic System. While the previous category of corporations is part of the economic system, a third of the interviewees speak more broadly about systemic problems caused by the global financial system, capitalism, or big banks (including the World Bank). They characterize this economic system as incentivizing profits and exploitation and causing increased income inequality globally. Pica says, "In my opinion, all three of us are fighting against this system that's built on exploitation." He blames this exploitation on a neoliberal economic system with instrumental values:

> We're actually fighting against an economic system, largely originating in the United States right now, whose main purpose and goal is to turn people and things and animals, whatever you want, into commodities that are meant be kind of used and abused then thrown away for this ever-growing, for this ever-insatiable appetite for profits and wealth concentration. . . . What we're commonly fighting is a kind of political economy that only values, that mostly values, wealth generation at the expense of everything else.

Governments. Half the interviewees mention problems with governments, usually in relationship to governments that are too beholden to corporate interests and lobbying instead of the broader public interest. This can cause governments to be seen as corrupt or weak in enforcing protective laws and holding the powerful accountable. While Watson works in partnership with many governments, he also expresses frustrations with government "bureaucrats" (whom he refers to as "the most insidious group of people on the planet") who let red tape and rules keep charities and SMOs from being able to do their good deeds. And Travers argues that we may have well-meaning politicians who want to help social movements, but they get caught in the inertia of a political system that lacks integrity, as they become beholden to the constant need to campaign to get reelected and cannot enact meaningful legislative change. In this vein, Weil encourages campaign finance reform to help get money out of politics so it can work in the public interest.

Discrimination. Marino includes white supremacy among a list of other types of problematic discrimination caused by people failing to care for anyone they deem as 'beneath' them (she is generally problematizing this kind of hierarchical thinking). And Rohani notes that colonialism and capitalism are root causes of inequality, as those political and economic practices disenfranchised so many people and took away resources, such as land. The common opponent in any movement against oppression, according to Newkirk, is "those who misuse their power; those without any interest in understanding others' perspectives and experiences; and those who wish to profit, no matter the cost to others." A unique answer to my question about a shared opponent for social movements is given by Ali. He laments that well-intentioned but unreflective activists and scholars often use communities (particularly communities of color) for programs or research without building true, equitable, and lasting partnerships that really benefit those communities long-term.

Looking at all the responses more broadly, interviewees tend to identify the main culprit as undemocratic systems where power is concentrated, causing inequities, and where those powerful entities are less accountable to the majority of citizens—with misguided incentives that favor selfish interests (like profits) over people and planet. I would also characterize these as influential systems that are not designed to promote caring and support for living beings, and in fact are unjustly set up to 'benefit' from taking advantage of those with less power and rights. Lappé summarizes the problem as powerful entities viewing the world through the narrow lens of a "myopic short-term profit motive" that clouds decision-making so that it fails to actually "serve lives" in the long term.

Designing Mutually Supportive and Inclusive Campaigns

To help these three causes become allies and apply the benefits of mutual support or collaboration previously discussed, I use this section to highlight common values that the nineteen interviewees suggest SMOs employ and promote in campaigns, including recognition of foundational root causes of the problems SMOs fight. This is followed by practical advice from interviewees for activists in each cause about how they could adapt their campaigns to be more supportive of other living beings who face harm (beyond just their own constituents), fostering alliances of compassion and justice more broadly.

BENEFICIAL VALUES

In an attempt to identify values that all three causes prioritize, I asked interviewees to list top/primary social values that they (1) currently appeal to, or try to tap into, when reaching out to the public in campaigns (table 15) and (2) would like society to adopt (or values to prioritize if already existing) (table 16). To summarize their answers to both sets of values-questions, I would say that activists from all causes hope people will:

- Feel compassion and empathy for others;
- Show respect for them (for human dignity, animal sentience, and the inherent value of nature); and
- Feel a sense of community that promotes sharing, fair and equitable treatment, and harmonious coexistence.

The highest-ranking values among the activists interviewed are justice, compassion and empathy, equality, and respect. Part of respect and fairness is the notion that we should embrace diversity and be more inclusive, not discriminating against others (although those related values get listed by just a few activists). The value of community or interconnectedness is also popular. Some notion of solidarity, working together, and tolerance for differences is mentioned in response to both questions, which relates to the values of cooperation and harmonious relations.

Empowerment (giving voice, using your voice, enabling agency) is one of the most commonly expressed values in SMOs' current campaigns but is not mentioned as much by activists in terms of the top values that society needs to adopt. Perhaps this is due to the fact that empowering action is something social movements naturally foster in campaigning for change. But I also see empowerment as related to the value of responsibility (such as responsibility to take action), which is mentioned by a minority of interviewees each time. The following subsections and corresponding tables detail my inquiries into the top social values shared by various causes.

Values to Which SMO Campaigns Currently Appeal (see table 15). Fairness is the most popular value activists listed, and Lappé notes that "this sense of fairness runs very, very deep" in humans across cultures, so the unfairness of the "extreme inequality" we see today threatens to "break apart society." The other most popular values that are assumed to be important to people in SMO campaigns across causes are per-

TABLE 15 Values to Which Activists Appeal (out of Eighteen Participants)*

MOST POPULAR ANSWERS (mentioned by at least a third: 6+ people)	COMMON ANSWERS (mentioned by at least a fifth: 4–5 people)	LESS COMMON ANSWERS (mentioned by at least a tenth: 2–3 people)	UNIQUE ANSWERS
• Justice / fairness (9) • Empowerment / voice / agency (8) • Compassion / empathy (7) • Care / help / stewardship / protection (6)	• Respect (for people, other animals, and nature) (5) • Rights / freedom (5) • Dignity (4) • Democracy (4) • Solidarity / bringing people together (4) • Challenging corporate power (4) • Taking action (4) • Sharing (4) • Equality (4)	• Community / connection (3) • Responsibility (3) • Nondiscrimination (3) • Integrity (2) • Conservation (2)	• Acknowledgment / recognition (Ali) • Cooperation (Lappé) • Family bonds (Marino) • Honesty and trustworthiness (Weil) • Courage (Watson) • Veganism (Watson)

* The interviewee who was not asked this question was Khalfan from Amnesty International. Instead, Gnanapragasam answered these values questions on behalf of Amnesty International.

sonal agency and empowerment, compassion, and care/protection. At least a fifth of interviewees also prioritize the following values in campaigning: respect, rights and freedoms, democracy, dignity, solidarity, equality, sharing, and taking action, such as challenging corporate power.

To highlight that these are fairly universal values that people share, consider Tercek's and Weil's comments about conservation and animal protection. Regarding the rationality of protecting the environment, Tercek maintains that "what we're for is consonant with what people of goodwill and good intelligence should be for. I mean, we're not really asking anyone to do anything that's not in their best interest." Regarding animal protection, Weil sees compassion for animals as a common trait, but one that people frame differently: "I start from the assumption that we probably share very similar values. We may manifest them differently, so for example very few people will say 'I hate animals' or 'I don't think animals deserve compassion,' but the way people will interpret what their appreciation for or love of the animals means in terms of practical action is very different." This notion of how to frame common values more inclusively (to activate their applicability to human and nonhuman species) will be an important aspect of recommendations I outline in the final chapter of the book.

Values Worthy of Prioritizing in Society (see table 16). To advance social change, the top values that many interviewees say are worthy of society prioritizing are compassion (including empathy), equality, respect (for all beings), fairness, and interconnectedness or a sense of community. "If I were able to wave my wand and instill a value in people," Sutherlin explains, "it would be a respect for nature and a recognition that the diversity of life has a value in and of itself that we need to account for, and there doesn't need to be any other reason." Similarly, Watson wants society to prioritize biocentrism (instead of anthropocentrism), recognizing the value of other species, because "worms and trees and bees are more important than people because they can live without us, but we can't live without them." In asking humans to embrace humility, Watson argues that humans "aren't as intelligent as we think we are, as the intelligence of every animal is based on its ability to live in harmony with the ecosystem that it inhabits." When a whaler critiqued that viewpoint as ludicrous because "by that criteria, cockroaches are more intelligent [than humans]," Watson humorously replied, "You are beginning to understand what I'm trying to say!"

In thinking about human well-being, Pica believes well-being should not be built around a consumer identity—leaving us unsatisfied and always wanting more; instead, being part of an equitable society should ground our social identity: "There needs to be a different, more robust conversation about how do we define ourselves." He says this could lead to a "much richer, deeper kind of justice-oriented conversation" that wraps in concerns of rampant inequities of the "few benefiting over the many."

TABLE 16 Values That Activists Want Society to Prioritize (out of Eighteen Participants)*

MOST POPULAR ANSWERS (mentioned by at least a third: 6+ people)	COMMON ANSWERS (mentioned by at least a fifth: 4–5 people)	LESS COMMON ANSWERS (mentioned by at least a tenth: 2–3 people)	UNIQUE ANSWERS
• Compassion / empathy (8) • Equality and equity (7) • Respect (for people, other animals, nature) (6)	• Community / interconnectedness (5) • Justice / fairness (5)	• Sharing / coexistence (3) • Responsibility / accountability (3) • Human dignity (3) • Inclusivity / diversity (3) • Recognition (acknowledgment/ respect) (2) • Empowerment (2) • Harmony (2) • Working together / solidarity (2) • Nature and biodiversity as inherently valuable (2)	• Humility (Watson) • Biocentrism (Watson) • Ecological knowledge (Tercek) • Mutual understanding / tolerance (Tercek) • Freedom (Gnanapragasam) • Integrity (Rohani)

* The interviewee who was not asked this question was Khalfan from Amnesty International. Instead, Gnanapragasam answered these values questions on behalf of Amnesty International.

In support of developing a community orientation, Lappé reframes the notion of freedom and independence by connecting it with interdependence, saying, "Our individuality is developed through community," and we are "co-creating each other" through relationships. Further, she explains, "Our happiness is in our interdependence," and thus we should value and embrace our social nature. Along these lines, Daly suggests that "familiarity actually breeds understanding more than contempt" and has faith that humanity can change their discriminatory societal attitudes (such as those against LGBTQ people) if we foster social interactions between a wider variety of people: "Give people the ability to see what's common, what we have in common, rather than what makes us different."

CORE PROBLEMATIC ATTITUDES, BELIEFS, OR BEHAVIORS TO ADDRESS IN CAMPAIGNS

I asked activists to identify the kind of social attitudes or behaviors that fundamentally cause problems and impede positive social change, and they highlighted the following in rank order: discrimination and superiority, fear, selfishness, divisive misunderstandings and ignorance, unaccountability (naming and blaming), mass killing of animals, and authoritarianism and civic disengagement (see table 17).

Related to the largest problem identified—discrimination and misuse of power—Núñez believes the root cause of oppression is a "might makes right" attitude. To challenge the belief that humans have the right to dominate the planet, Travers explains: "It's almost as if it's the terms of the contract for living on this earth that we run it. And you know, as it stands, there's every prospect that we're going to run it into the ground, and self-extinguish ourselves and an awful lot of other lives with it." All the causal factors in table 17 represent larger, foundational forces and attitudes we could challenge collectively as general areas for coalition building (around democracy, equality, nonviolence, accountability, and altruism) that may transcend specific issues such as pollution or sexual violence.

MAKING ACCOMMODATIONS FOR OTHER SOCIAL MOVEMENT CAUSES IN YOUR OWN CAMPAIGNS

To avoid counterproductive campaigns that might unwittingly jeopardize or impede another social movement's cause, I asked activists to share how they have made accommodations (or how they suggest other SMOs do so) to be more inclusive of other issues or beings while advocating for their own cause. Here is a summary of answers categorized by social movement cause, followed by examples pertinent to all causes (such as respectful representations based on race, ethnicity, and gender).

For *Environmental Groups.* Travers recognizes that animal and eco groups should ensure that their wildlife protection projects produce real benefits for local human residents and include them. Sutherlin gives the example that human workers in Indonesia exploited by the palm oil industry felt left out of rainforest protection cam-

TABLE 17 Root Causes and Problematic Attitudes, Beliefs, or Behaviors (out of Eighteen Participants)*

DISCRIMINATION AND UNJUST USES OF POWER OVER "OTHERS" (9)

- Human superiority / dominance / exceptionalism; Anthropocentrism (belief in hierarchies / great chain of being) (Travers, Marino, Watson)
- Human entitlement to exploit others, colonize, or impose one's power over others (Travers, Pica, Sutherlin); 'Might makes right' attitude (Núñez)
- Oppression and rights violations (Núñez, Gnanapragasam); Discrimination against those who are different (Núñez, Gnanapragasam); Sexism / patriarchy / gender injustice (Rohani)
- Objectification of others so you can devalue them and fail to see them as individuals (Soderbergh, Travers)

DECISIONS BASED ON FEAR OR INERTIA THAT HOLD BACK PROGRESSIVE CHANGE (6)

- Denial and defensiveness / fragility (Moncrief); Fear of going against status quo of social norms (Moncrief, Newkirk); Seeing change as scary or difficult (inertia) (Moncrief, Newkirk); Hopelessness, complacency, and apathy (Hemley, Lloyd)
- Fear (Weil); Stoking fears about others (Daly)

SELFISHNESS AND GREED (6)

- Myopic, narrow-minded thinking; short-term thinking, like a corporate model (Weil, Sutherlin)
- Greed (Weil, Hemley); Selfishness (not caring about others and not being willing to make any sacrifices) (Moncrief)
- Profit motive (Lloyd, Pica, Sutherlin); Neoliberal economic system (corporate model) based on exploitation and wealth generation at the expense of everyone else (Pica, Sutherlin)

MISUNDERSTANDINGS THAT DIVIDE US (5)

- Divisiveness that keeps us separated so we don't see the connections between us and fail to work together (Weil, Tercek, Daly); Failure to understand each other (Weil, Tercek)
- Ignorance about ecology (lack of awareness about and respect for nature) (Watson, Tercek); Failure to understand that all species are interconnected and interdependent (Watson)
- False narratives about minorities and the poor (Ali)

PASSING THE BUCK; FAILURE TO TAKE RESPONSIBILITY (3)

- Lack of mutual accountability (Lappé); Accountability of corporations to shareholders only (Sutherlin)
- Blaming individuals, not unjust systems (Ali); Blaming and stigmatizing others (Soderbergh); Blaming and shaming (Lappé)
- Governments divesting in poor communities (Ali)

SYSTEMICALLY VIOLENT AND ECOLOGICALLY IRRESPONSIBLE TREATMENT OF ANIMAL LIFE (2)

- Killing animals; mass extinction of species (Watson)
- The popularity of inexpensive animal products for consumption; Continuing to produce and consume a lot of meat despite knowing the costs (Travers)

LACK OF DEMOCRACY OR PUBLIC ENGAGEMENT (2)

- Authoritarianism instead of democracy (Daly); Democracy / civic engagement being seen as a burden by society rather than a way of life (wrong attitude about democracy) (Lappé)

---

* The interviewee who was not asked this question was Khalfan from Amnesty International. Instead, Gnanapragasam answered these values questions on behalf of Amnesty International.

paign messages that only featured wildlife, like orangutans, as victims; therefore, with their permission, human stakeholders should also be a campaign feature and an equally sympathetic basis for appeals to the public. This fits with Soderbergh's recommendation that campaign images feature local humans along with nature and wildlife to avoid implying that humanity and nature are separate entities. He contends, "Environmentalists should not privilege nature over people but see their interests as mutual." Soderbergh further suggests that conservationists view local minority groups as an integral part of the natural area in terms of its protection, such as pastoral communities, like the Maasai, who traditionally traverse national or park borders in West Africa. "We have so much to gain in terms of indigenous knowledge of the lands and good stewardship and management," Soderbergh explains. "It's just crazy, especially in time of climate change, not to draw on that wealth of knowledge."

Similarly, in his work with Greenpeace, Lloyd finds it is important to collaborate with local and indigenous human communities before rolling out any public campaign in their area (such as protecting seals or the Arctic region), as the locals will have insightful ideas and, in some cases, may require help in transitioning to other, more productive ways to support themselves. Along the same lines, Khalfan suggests that conservationists must make provisions for local humans rather than just "setting aside land." Soderbergh notes how sad it is when conservation groups "have this picture of land and animals versus people," so then "boot indigenous communities off their land," which happened to the Batwa in the Congo to create a gorilla sanctuary. "Fundamentally, it's not the indigenous communities that are the threat to the lands and animals," Soderbergh explains. "Often the animals are there *because* the indigenous people are there," since the people are "good custodians." Hemley agrees that humans who rely on a certain wilderness area should be considered and consulted by wildlife organizations wanting to protect the area. She suggests an "integrated approach to conservation" is best, where some "sustainable harvesting" is allowed in protected areas in order not to disadvantage local human communities, as opposed to cutting off all use of a wilderness area. Activist debates over no-use versus wise-use are also a concern of Tercek, who acknowledges, "It's a messy, overlapping world of complicated trade-offs, I'm afraid." As such, he finds it counterproductive when some environmentalists take an abolitionist approach— for example, taking the purist stance of "no dams period," as the dam might then get built without the input of environmentalists.

To address a similar point about abolitionist campaigns but pertaining to animal agribusiness, Tercek—although a vegan himself—suggests that rather than simply promoting vegan-only campaigns for consumers, he finds it more useful for the Nature Conservancy to engage ranchers on how to make tangible improvements toward more ecologically friendly practices. He concludes, "These [ranchers] are good people who are great partners of the environment." Even though Tercek acknowledges that "it would be a good thing if more and more people around the world reduced meat consumption," ranchers might not be willing to work with his organization if he was promoting a plant-based diet instead of more sustainable meat, so he notes it can be "tricky" to try to do both.

In support of a sustainable meat product that doesn't involve living animals, Weil recommends endorsing the wide availability of "clean meat" (animal flesh grown from tissue cultures), as it is a pragmatic example of a systems-level change that would save more lives than has the consumer (vegan) campaigns for dietary reform: "We all eat and can come together and ultimately put an end to some of the most devastating environmental destruction, the most egregious cruelty to animals, and the largest problems with human health." A switch toward this clean meat would save the lives of domesticated and wild animals, as Weil notes that raising animals for human food causes an illogical cycle of unnecessary deaths: "We kill wild animals to protect livestock, who are going to be killed and eaten when nobody needs to eat them to begin with." Because Pica also recognizes "the most destructive elements of the food system are how we raise and treat animals," he suggests collaboration between environmental and animal advocates to fight confined animal-feeding operations. Núñez is not certain why most advocates for the environment or public health are not actively campaigning for changes to diet, given the significant ecological and health problems caused by consumption of animal products.

As a vegan activist, Moncrief has found language that fits with the popular 'reducitarian' (meat reduction) movement in environmental and public health circles: "If you are not going to be vegan, the more you do, the better. I'll say, 'Minimize, ideally eliminate' meat. So, minimize harm, maximize good." When speaking about individual-level change, she uses the term "eliminate," but on the global level she more pragmatically talks about "reduction" or "reversing the trends" in meat consumption. She asks reducitarian campaigns to keep their messages vegan friendly: "Don't use vegans as foils"; instead, use inclusive messages like "vegans are reducitarians too, but they've just gone all the way."

When a human community is having some issues (whether with wildlife or with needing more resources), Travers finds it ill-informed to promote trophy hunting or culling of wildlife as some kind of solution. He says we need to give animals "if not equal, then full consideration" with thoughtful, carefully informed decisions that "don't create callous, uncaring impacts on living creatures." If we treat animals as individuals (like Cecil the lion), that keeps us from implying they are nameless beasts that we can "use, abuse, or lose" as we wish. Travers explains that studies help us understand that "animals are indeed individuals. And that they have individual preferences, likes and dislikes—that they feel and experience emotions that are not dissimilar to our own." Weil also contends that we must consider individual animals when making decisions, such as about invasive species, recognizing that they are worthy of the same protection we are.

In support of compassionate conservation, Marino agrees that poisoning or killing nonnative animals should be "taken off the table as an option" and recommends that we follow the golden rule: "'Ok, don't do anything to these animals that you wouldn't want done to you. Now try to find a solution.' And that's harder, but that is what compassionate conservation is about. It's about finding a solution where you respect the other." Marino goes on to suggest that we acknowledge how humans are often to blame for introducing the nonnative species in the first place: "Humans have to take much more responsibility for what they've produced—the problems that they've produced." Because other animals "have just as much at stake," then "sometimes the humans have to be the ones to make the sacrifice."

Wildlife protection groups can adopt policies that are against wildlife captivity, as Sutherlin explains that RAN does, so that they also support animal rights interests by not working with zoos and aquarium organizations on conservation efforts. Newkirk recommends environmental organizations stop asking for toxicity tests on animals (as they have in the United States) and instead push for non-animal-based safety tests in their attempts to reduce pollutants as another way to protect individuals.

Human individuals can also be harmed by otherwise ecofriendly products. For example, Khalfan mentions environmental activists promoting hybrid cars without taking into account that child labor is used to mine the cobalt in those car batteries: "This is the direction we need to go in [for preventing climate change], but let's be responsible about how we source our materials." With a similar humanitarian concern, Lappé suggests anti-population-growth campaigns are counterproductive and, instead, we should focus on supporting women's rights and promoting plant-based foods and equitably distributing vegan foods to more efficiently feed the world's human population.

Lloyd finds it counterproductive when "eco-modernists" promote biotech or nuclear solutions or monetize nature via assigning monetary values to "forest delivery services" instead of acknowledging the forest's inherent value. Regarding money, Sutherlin cautions environmentalists to avoid falling prey to the "divide and conquer tactic" that some industries will take toward environmental NGOs by funding the NGO's projects and then agreeing to make some sustainability improvements at their company; those corporate concessions then make it hard for other environmentalists to hold that company accountable for making the larger systemic changes that are really necessary. Sutherlin uses the Roundtable on Sustainable Palm Oil as an example.

For Animal Protection Groups. Marino expresses similar concerns to Sutherlin's, lamenting when welfare organizations cut deals with animal exploitation industries that preclude the opportunity to achieve a rights-based solution: "Every inch that [egg-laying] chickens get in battery cages makes it less likely that we will get the chickens out of the cages altogether." Núñez believes campaigns are most productive when they focus on how citizens can make changes in their lives to reduce animal suffering rather than proposing analogies with terminology (e.g., rape, holocaust, slavery, etc.) that is potentially offensive or distracting from that core anticruelty goal. Tercek recommends a "kinder approach" to animal rights advocacy: "If their motive is to be kind to these other species, then be kind to all species, including folks who don't understand the folly of their habits. In a kind way, help them see the light."

Sometimes be willing to sidestep smaller, culturally entrenched issues in favor of solving larger problems to gain more consensus, says Weil, a vegan advocate who lives in Maine where many generations of families have relied on fishing for their livelihood. She shares a pragmatic suggestion that in food campaigns, it may make sense to leave aside small-scale farming and fishing, and focus instead on larger systemic problems with commercial fishing and animal agribusiness, which most people can agree on. This avoids what Lloyd describes as "not always a very constructive dynamic about" the "'how good is good enough'" debate between vegans and environmentalists, which fits with Pica's recommendation that the animal rights and environmental movements should work together to fight "mechanized meat animal operations." As part of this critique of factory farming and fishing, another area of opportunity would be to also highlight the abuses of human workers in those industries, as suggested by human rights activists Rohani and Daly.

For Human Rights Groups. Moncrief explains how NGO programs gifting farmed animals to poor people is ultimately not helpful to the human families (e.g., the animal can become a burden, and/or girls may be prevented from going to school to serve as animal caretaker, such as fetching water), and the practice if scaled up can be environmentally harmful, and it is obviously harmful to the animal who is being used as an economic resource (he or she may be mistreated, lack access to any veterinary care when suffering, and ultimately be killed). Rather than telling a poor community without alternative nutrient options to stop eating animals or dairy, Moncrief suggests enhancing their plant-based food options. She recommends alternative gifting of plant-based foods and farming capabilities, done in a culturally appropriate way. In that vein, her group, A Well Fed World, prefers to support local people who are already championing their own vegan projects rather than coming into a community and imposing a new program.

Moncrief's approach complements Rohani's general suggestion that any NGO should aid and support local communities in their own efforts, rather than the NGO coming into town and "bulldozing" or "co-opting" the local agenda. Rohani explains, "If we're actually serious about empowerment, we need to be thinking about the places where she's exercising her power" and find ways to assist: "Oh, we give a woman a dozen chickens or we give her access to a well, but we don't think about the types of empowerment that she's getting on her own, which is political or community organizing." Listen and work to earn trust with people on the ground: "Solidarity works at the speed of trust."

Daly brings up the paradox of single-issue campaigns that attempt to advance the rights of one human group while suppressing the rights of another. For example, some Islamic groups may have campaigns that are homophobic and, conversely, an LGBTQ group may then have a countercampaign that comes across as Islamophobic.

For All Activist Causes. Ali points out that younger generations of activists expect a "twenty-first-century intersectional approach" that embraces diversity and addresses problems in a holistic manner, recognizing that all issues are connected. Several animal activists I interviewed mention race and gender representation issues. For example, Moncrief and Núñez emphasize the need to avoid racist and sexist images. Núñez explains, "Of course, our primary goal is animal protection, but we don't need to be hurting other movements with our messages," in particular, not using women's bodies to attract attention for animal causes. Newkirk acknowledges that PETA is called offensive for "using nudity" in their campaigns (such as in their well-known "I'd rather go naked than wear fur" campaigns). While Newkirk was unapologetic about nudity, she did concede that in response to criticism, PETA does sometimes change campaigns, such as altering their "fat ads" to be less upsetting (in terms of ads highlighting obesity issues with standard animal-based diets).

Related to race, Newkirk feels PETA is "falsely attacked" as racist for certain animal rights campaigns, such as those that expose the suffering involved in kosher slaughtering of farmed animals. Indeed, Khalfan brings up kosher slaughter as an example when he says animal protection campaigns can seem racially prejudiced, or even racially motivated, when they criticize a minority group's cultural practices. But Newkirk insists PETA's kosher slaughter campaigns are not meant to be anti-Semitic, just as her choosing to speak in Israel isn't meant to be anti-Arab (as some people claim). When it comes to campaigns that are critical of certain indigenous groups, Watson explains that Sea Shepherd will only target a community if he sees them as "selling out" and siding with industries that harm wildlife (as his clients are marine wildlife); but he cites many instances when Sea Shepherd works with indigenous communities on protecting marine wildlife and ecosystems. Watson admits Sea Shepherd's communication approach is unique in that it is less 'strategic,' as they do not necessarily court public opinion but are instead motivated to take stands "because it's the right thing to do": "We are not here to satisfy everybody. We are not all things to all people. We defend our clients and their interests, which is the marine wildlife—the species that live in the ocean. That's who we defend. So we're not really interested in people's opinions on whether they [wildlife] should be exploited or not. They shouldn't be." In concluding the larger point of these paragraphs on race and gender, I think self-reflection, cultural awareness, and cultural sensitivity are warranted before any organization singles out particular ethnic practices for critique or rhetorically uses human bodies in ways that seem objectifying.

Expressing concern for respectful representation of humans, Rohani asks activists not to stereotype and assume some people are "inherently oppressive or oppressed," instead realizing "it's not about saving the voiceless. They have a voice; they're just not being heard," so SMOs can offer opportunities to amplify their voices. In Ali's experience in the environmental justice movement, he has learned it is best if "the community speaks for themselves." To have messages resonate within certain cultures, Ali encourages activists to listen to what concerns that community raises and what they care about, honor their culture, and employ cultural influencers to reach them.

In addition to listening to communities they seek to work with, activists should also listen to one another. To work together, Watson requests that NGOs communicate with one another before jumping on the bandwagon of a certain campaign issue, as their approach may jeopardize the efforts of people from other NGOs working on the front lines. Watson is speaking from a specific experience when other advocacy groups also wanted to save endangered vaquita porpoises in Mexico, so these groups, working remotely, called for a boycott of Mexican shrimp. But that tactic caused the local Sea Shepherd ship's activists to face harassment from shrimp fishers working in the same waters off of Mexico, who lumped all the vaquita activists together as if they were a unified movement. That foreign boycott made it harder for Sea Shepherd activists in Mexico to try to collaborate with the shrimping industry on reforming practices that threaten vaquitas.

When there are conflicts between causes, Weil suggests enacting a "solutionary" problem-solving perspective and asking, "What would do the most good and least harm to people, animals, and the environment?" This means also considering non-human animals as being individuals "worthy of the same protection." Along those lines, Núñez says SMOs must not use another entity as a means to an end to save 'their' entity (environment, wildlife, or humans). To do so, she says we can frame our messages in ways that are supportive and thoughtful of other movements.

COMMON TERMINOLOGY: ARE HUMANS ANIMALS TOO?

I asked interviewees about the use of the word "animal" to describe humans and to remind us that we are part of the animal kingdom. Everyone interviewed understood that humans are part of the animal kingdom in terms of a scientific classification, but it is not something that is acknowledged or celebrated in the campaign discourses of most of their advocacy organizations, even by some animal protection organizations. Even though all interviewees care about nonhuman animals to some degree, most do not see the strategic benefit or purpose of challenging social norms and cultural identities by using a triggering or potentially offensive label for humans like 'animal' that risks causing audiences to dismiss their entire message or become distracted or confused. Most interviewees mention the strategic choice, in general, to adjust their language to resonate with their intended audience (most of whom presumably do not identify with being an animal). But several animal activists mention the benefits of using animating pronouns "he," "she," or "they" and not "it" to accurately describe fellow animals. Soderbergh thinks the conversation about animals will change in twenty or thirty years "because of all the fascinating research going on to do with animal behavior and intelligence. The dividing lines between humans and nonhumans, to me as a human rights activist, are starting to feel more and more untenable."

No, We Do Not Tend to Refer to Humans as Animals. Environmental organizations are more likely than human rights organizations to talk about animals in their campaigns, but even then, most eco organizations still do not use language that describes humans as 'animals,' instead often sticking with broader or vaguer categorical terms like *species* or *life*. Tercek says the Nature Conservancy prefers the unifying term 'all life' to collectively describe humans, animals, and plants; he explains that to be called an 'animal' might offend some religious audiences, and it is not worth alienating those folks when they care about animals and nature. He prefers to use phrases like "I care about future generations and all species." In a similar vein, Hemley explains, WWF is a conservation organization that is science-based, so they often refer to humans broadly as part of "life on earth," saying, "Humans are a species and there are millions of other species out there that share the planet. . . . We say humans are connected." The term *wildlife* is more commonly used than *animal* at WWF, and from a legal standpoint, wildlife can include plants.

Most interviewees at human rights organizations admit they do not think about or discuss the possibility of referring to humans as 'animals,' as it does not fit their discourse, which is centered primarily (if not solely) on human concerns. Daly explains that human rights organizations find it useful to stick within international legal discourse, which uses the term *human* (and not *animal*). She says that the human rights movement is primarily working to build a shared humanity and admits they have not yet extended that notion to animals. Khalfan at Amnesty thinks it would not be productive to call people animals when trying to build solidarity between human rights and animal rights movements, as many people might not like to have their "elevated human self-image" challenged or "taken down a notch." And Soderbergh explains the Minority Rights Group would not call people 'animals,' as it might seem like othering those particular minority groups. But he notes his organization tries to use the terminology preferred by the minority communities they work with, and it is important to let cultures self-identify. So if a particular indigenous culture viewed themselves as part of the animal world, then that would be a time when the term *animal* could be appropriate in the context of that community's cultural language. Also taking a cultural perspective in working with communities of color, Ali notes humans can technically be described as 'animals' in a scientific sense, but in a cultural sense, he does not use 'human animal' and instead expresses species solidarity by talking about everyone as "God's creatures" or through a family metaphor of us all living on "Mother Earth."

We Might in Certain Circumstances Refer to Humans as Animals. Even as animal rights advocates, Núñez and Moncrief consider terms like *nonhuman* somewhat cumbersome and confusing to most audiences (outside of the animal rights community) and therefore privilege the clarity and simplicity of phrases such as *people and animals*. Additionally, Moncrief's hunger-relief charity works in communities of color and is sensitive to use terminology they would consider respectful. Similarly, Sutherlin says that RAN does not tend to refer to humans as animals. Taking cultural context into consideration, he does not think it would work well to refer to other societies as animals, but he can see how it might be acceptable to call *your own* society animals sometimes. Sutherlin's personal belief is that it would be valuable from a humility and ecological standpoint to remind us that we are part of the animal kingdom: "Because it helps put us back in our place; we are a dazzling, amazing superlative animal, but we are an animal, and I think that by centering that as a definition the awareness really helps put us back in the order of things rather than somehow lording from above, outside of it." Lloyd notes that Greenpeace, as an ecological organization, might sometimes remind humans they are animals, but they primarily refer to humans more broadly as part of the biosphere or larger ecosystem. Lappé says she might occasionally say "human animal" but would more likely emphasize the connection by expressing human's nature as social beings or "social animals."

Yes, We Often Refer to Humans as Animals. In their organizations, Newkirk, Marino, and Weil primarily use the terms *human and nonhuman animal* or *other animals* to strategically challenge speciesist social norms and remind us that we humans are animals too. Newkirk says PETA tries to include their motto in all correspondence: "Animals are not ours to eat, wear, experiment on, to use in entertainment or abuse for any purpose." While that may not convey that humans are also animals, it does challenge human supremacy and entitlement to view animals as tools for human endeavors. Travers thinks it is useful to express that we humans are animals, who, while quite adaptable, are equally as evolved as every other animal species, not more so. And with a similar nod to humility for humanity, Watson says he sees nothing wrong with referring to humans as animals: "I find it offensive when people say we're *not* animals. I say, what the hell are we, then? . . . We're animals. We're not gods."

Summary

Activists agree that the causes of animal protection, human rights, and environmentalism have much that unifies them (standing up to the powerful in protection of the vulnerable), and, thus, collaboration in many cases would be advantageous. To facilitate this, they suggest that coalitions focus on a shared goal and agreed-upon tactics rather than inevitable differences. To be allies, each cause should make accommodations for the others. For example, environmentalists protecting wilderness can practice compassionate conservation toward animal individuals and be inclusive of the needs and interests of indigenous human populations. Animal protection groups can focus on ending industrialized fishing and farming (rather than vegan-only campaigns) while also protecting the human rights of workers in those industries. Human rights groups can gift poor communities with plant farming resources instead of individual farmed animals. And all activist groups should ensure that their campaign messages and terminology amplify the voices of minority communities and be respectful to race and ethnicity, gender, sexual orientation, class, religion, body types, and species.

The opposing forces all three causes commonly combat are exploitative corporations, corrupt governments, our economic system, and discriminatory views. The social attitudes or behaviors that fundamentally cause problems and impede positive social change include discrimination and superiority, fear, selfishness, divisive misunderstandings and ignorance, unaccountability (naming and blaming), mass killing of animals, and authoritarianism and civic disengagement.

To tackle these problems, activists across all causes appeal to the public's sense of fairness, first and foremost, but also personal agency and empowerment, compassion, and care/protection. Activists wish that society would prioritize compassion, equality, fairness, respect (for all beings), and a sense of community/interconnectedness. In essence, to facilitate social change, activists from all causes hope people will feel compassion and empathy for other beings, show them respect, and feel a sense of connection that promotes sharing, fair and equitable treatment, and harmonious coexistence.

CHAPTER NINE

Recommendations to Cultivate a Human Animal Earthling Identity

In the introduction, I proclaimed the goal of this book project is "to identify and promote the values that are foundational to fostering and framing a more inclusive, biocentric worldview and human identity as 'human animal earthlings' in the hope that this expanded sense of self on an individual level will foster human cultures on the societal level that are inherently more sustainable and just toward all living beings." Toward that goal, this final chapter will build on all previous chapters to answer the last two prescriptive research questions:

RQ1: **Which values are most applicable to a human animal earthling's identity?** This will comprise part 1 of this chapter, including a comprehensive list of values for activists to promote and virtues for humans to embody.

RQ2: **In what ways do these universal values need reframing to be less anthropocentric (or more biocentric or sentience focused) in their application and scope?** This will comprise part 2 of this chapter, including examples of missed opportunities by advocacy organizations in my study to be mutually supportive of each other's efforts in their campaign messages (for protection of humans, all animals, and the environment), and illustrative examples of when they were more inclusive of other beings, expanding the notion of who matters. Part 2 also provides a list of thirteen promising project areas for building alliances against common opponents and problematic systems, sharing some examples.

In answering these two research questions, I consider insights gained from:

- The sixteen advocacy organizations I studied (chapter 7 on common ground)
- The nineteen activists I interviewed (chapter 8)
- My pilot study on six rights charters/declarations (chapter 3)
- Scholars I cited (in the review of scholarly studies in chapter 1)
- My own assessment as a scholar and activist (chapter 2, in part)

Part 1: Values Most Applicable to
Foster a Human Animal Earthling Identity

In this first part, I describe my recommendations for the values and the virtues that social movement organizations (SMOs) can embed and promote in campaigns, which ultimately helps foster a human animal earthling identity across societies. They center on supporting life, fairness, social and ecological responsibility, and unification across cultures and species.

VALUES

To create the synthesized list of values most befitting a human animal earthling identity (table 18), I began with the common values identified in chapter 7 (table 14) that encompass the most popular values highlighted by all three, or at least two, of the social movement causes. I then synthesized and streamlined some of those values to make the list (table 18) more manageable and targeted, expressing values as nouns and verbs (i.e., we value these things and these actions) and continuing to organize them within the four core categories of *life, fairness, responsibility,* and *unification* that I have used throughout this book. I also ensured that the values in table 18 included the universal values identified in my pilot study of rights charters: life and health; nonviolence, peace and coexistence; protection; justice; respect; liberty (freedom); equality; recognition of rights; dignity; education; sentience/capacity for feelings. For the latter, I brought in sentience not as a distinct value, per se, but as context for identifying to whom some other values applied: rights *for sentient individuals,* freedom *for sentient beings,* compassion and empathy *for sentient beings,* and respect *for humans and other animals.*

In the following cases, I explain where I added values to table 18. For example, because food is so critical to life, and because I thought that the current value of "livelihood (ensuring access to resources)" did not quite encapsulate the emphasis that all three causes put on food, I moved "sustainable farming" from the responsibility category to the life category, expressing it as "agroecology and sustainable crop farming." The word *crop* indicates my aspiration for human animal earthlings to privilege plant-based agriculture rather than farming anyone, as it feeds people in ways that are the most efficient and least destructive of other life-forms. I also added "naturalness" to the life category as a way to indicate the healthy attributes of nonpolluted, nontoxic, non-GMO, nonartificial products (including foods); naturalness, a value identified in the pilot study, is more specific than just what was indicated by the existing value of "safe, secure, and clean living spaces." Related to the notion of naturalness, I also synthesized two items from the animal protection organization and environmental organization values' lists to add "wildness and nature" as a fairness value. The Rainforest Action Network contends that wildness has intrinsic value. And wildness relates to the value of freedom but is more specific to the more-than-human world being free from human domestication—allowing animals

TABLE 18 Values That Foster a 'Human Animal Earthling' Identity (Expressed as Nouns and Verbs, Listed in Alphabetical Order)

VALUES RELATING TO LIFE	• Agroecology and sustainable crop farming • Biological diversity • Caretaking (aiding and helping others in need, especially dependents) • Health and well-being (physical and mental) • Life-saving • Livelihood (ensuring access to needed resources) • Naturalness • Peace and nonviolence • Protection (of living beings and ecosystems, especially vulnerable beings, from threats) • Restoration and healing (including endangered species) • Safe, secure, and clean habitats / living spaces • Sanctuaries and reserves • Stable climate
VALUES RELATING TO FAIRNESS	• Coexistence • Cultural diversity and inclusivity • Democratic decision-making and people power • Equality and equity • Fairness and justice • Freedom (over a sentient being's own body, speech, mobility, labor, and life choices) • Legal protection and enforcement by government • Reparation for harms • Respect (for humans, other animals, and nature) • Rights (for sentient individuals and ecosystems) • Sharing (with fellow beings) • Territory / land rights (access to meaningful, traditional, or vital spaces) • Wildness and nature (freedom from unwanted domestication)
VALUES RELATING TO RESPONSIBILITY	• Accountability (especially for harmful actions of persons or organizations) • Being responsible; taking responsibility (to do what is right and needed) • Careful and wise actions (following the precautionary principle and avoiding unnecessary risks) • Collective action for problem-solving • Conscientious consumption (e.g., fair trade, vegan, cruelty-free, sweatshop-free, living wage, biodegradable, organic, green, etc.) • Education (for children and adults: developing skills, sharing knowledge, and raising awareness) • Empowerment (especially providing agency and voice for marginalized groups) • Engaged political citizenship; commitment to causes • Integrity (moral integrity and authenticity of research and information) • Investment in a sustainable future (long-term ecologically responsible organizational policies and practices) • Productivity (efficacy of solutions enacted) • Speaking out and challenging abuses of power (peaceful protest) • Sustainable and wise use of natural resources • Truth-telling and transparency (investigating and exposing issues, operating openly, and being factually accurate)

VALUES RELATING TO UNIFICATION	• Biocentrism
	• Community
	• Compassion and empathy (for sentient beings)
	• Dignity (sentient beings' need to maintain self-respect)
	• Family
	• Harmony and cooperation
	• Humility
	• Love and friendship (social bonds); biophilia
	• Inclusivity and openness
	• Interdependence (social, economic, and ecological)
	• Joining together in solidarity
	• Understanding

and natural areas to remain wild or be rewilded instead of 'developed,' tamed, or manipulated (Donaldson and Kymlicka 2016). Sometimes in animal rights vernacular, we use the term "free" or "free-roaming animals" instead of "wild animals" because the latter can have a negative (and unfair) connotation marking nondomesticated animals as being irrational, violent, and in need of control. Lastly, I also added "biocentrism" as a value to the unity category to represent the life-centered approach that many animal and environmental groups like to promote instead of just considering a human-centered approach.

I also looked at input from my activist interviews (chapter 8) to incorporate their values into the human animal earthling table. The majority of my interviewees said their campaigns currently appealed to values already represented in table 18 (as it was based on values I found in their campaigns). The top values interviewees noted were fairness, compassion, care/protection, and empowerment. Other popular values included respect, rights and freedoms, democracy, dignity, solidarity, equality, sharing, and taking action, such as challenging corporate power. I made sure table 18 also comprised values my interviewees most wanted society to prioritize (from chapter 8), which included fairness, compassion, respect (for all beings), equality, and a sense of community and interconnectedness. Even less commonly mentioned values (in terms of values they wanted society to prioritize) were already present in table 18: empowerment, harmony, sharing, biodiversity, human diversity and inclusiveness, accountability, responsibility, and human dignity.

I added two values to table 18, both in the category of unification, based on singular mentions from two interviewees: (1) Captain Paul Watson's desire for humans to have more *humility* in respect to other species, and (2) Mark Tercek's desire for humans to be more *understanding* and tolerant in seeing past the differences that keep us divided. I see the practice of seeking understanding as a path to more fully perceiving the truth. In fact, five of the interviewees mentioned misunderstandings as a root cause of many problems and divisions. This leads to table 19, where I outline how the values of a human animal earthling (from table 18) will help address the seven major root causes of global problems that were identified by activists in chapter 8.

TABLE 19 Values of the Human Animal Earthling Identity
That Address Root Causes of Problems

ROOT CAUSES OF PROBLEMS	VALUES THAT ADDRESS THEM FOR THE HUMAN ANIMAL EARTHLING
Discrimination and domination	respect, diversity, biocentrism, humility, rights, speaking out against abuses of power, legal protection and enforcement, fairness and justice, equality, inclusivity and openness, harmony and cooperation
Fear and inertia that hold back change	courage, commitment to causes, engaged citizenship, integrity, transparency and truth-telling, understanding, collective action for problem-solving, productivity, joining together in solidarity, careful and wise actions (precautionary principle)
Selfishness and greed; short-term thinking	compassion and empathy, caretaking, life-saving, protection, legal protection and enforcement, democratic decision-making and people power, investment in a sustainable future, conscientious consumption, sustainable and wise use of natural resources, sharing
Misunderstandings that divide us	understanding, education, inclusivity and openness, love and friendship, community, transparency and truth-telling, empowerment (providing voice to marginalized groups), collective action for problem-solving, joining together in solidarity
Passing the buck; failure to take responsibility; blaming and shaming others	accountability, taking responsibility, restoration and healing, inclusivity and openness, investment in a sustainable future, people power, collective action for problem-solving, empowerment, integrity, courage, interdependence
Systemically violent and ecologically irresponsible treatment of animals	respect, peace and nonviolence, life-saving, protection, caretaking, sanctuary and reserves, wildness and nature, biocentrism, compassion and empathy, biophilia, coexistence, conscientious consumption, organic crop agriculture, transparency and truth-telling, speaking out to challenge abuses
Lack of democracy and public engagement	democratic decision-making and people power, engaged citizenship, commitment to causes, empowerment, fairness and justice, community

The four organizational categories in table 18 (life, fairness, responsibility, and unity) are also foundational to the emphasis that my interviewees put on how values should function. I summarized interviewee responses in chapter 8 by saying activists hope that we:

- Feel compassion and empathy for others;
- Show respect for them (respect for human dignity, animal sentience, and the inherent value of nature); and
- Feel a sense of community that promotes sharing, fair and equitable treatment, and harmonious coexistence.

So, while I listed the unity category last on table 18, if I was listing values in order of importance, perhaps unifying values should come first because experiencing a sense of kinship and community is fundamental to adopting and sustaining the other values. For example, related to the above bullet points: a feeling of empathy enables us to identify with other living beings (especially sentient beings) as individuals and potentially feel a kinship, and that creates a respect for their lives, interests, and basic rights, which then compels us to treat these fellow beings fairly and act responsibly toward them and the habitats we share, which further unifies us as an interdependent community that appreciates diversity. In this view, unifying values come full circle.

In a collective sense, the human animal earthling values in table 18 also align with Crompton and Kasser's (2009) strategic communication recommendations that SMOs should promote and appeal to intrinsic values (such as community, relationships, and self-development) and self-transcendent values, such as benevolence (compassion, caring, and honesty) and universalism (justice, protection, responsibility, and inclusivity), instead of extrinsic, self-enhancing, or materialistic values. In opposition to the negativity and conflict caused by authoritarianism, secrecy, and impunity from wrongdoing, Frances Moore Lappé (2011) clarified the values (or sociopolitical conditions) that bring out the best in humanity, and those values are found in table 18 in the responsibility and fairness categories: (1) inclusive, democratic decision-making and people power; (2) transparent organizations; and (3) mutual accountability. Table 18 also includes values that are part of Steven Best's (2014) vision for the total liberation of species—freedom, community, and harmony.

VIRTUES

In creating a human animal earthling identity based on shared values, I assume people should be inspired by these values to put them into action in daily life—in large part to act ethically as a virtuous person. Here I draw on virtue ethics, an ethical system initially attributed to Plato and Aristotle, which believes if you are a virtuous person—a person of character—you will naturally exhibit virtuous actions beneficial to human well-being and flourishing (but I broaden its scope to include the well-being of the more-than-human world) (Alvaro 2019; Sandler 2007). Virtues can be taught by role models (through mentoring) and in schools (through character-building and humane education), and by extension I view activists' discourse as educational and activists themselves (or the heroic citizens they highlight) serving as role models for the human animal earthling identity.

To determine the following list of virtues (table 20) that a human animal earthling should embody, I started with the virtues promoted in the campaign messages of the sixteen SMOs from my study (see chapter 7). The only changes I made were to replace *generous and altruistic* more succinctly with *giving* and to take out *competent and reliable*, as that was already inherent to the existing virtues of *trustworthy, committed,* and *responsible.*

I then added *cooperative and understanding.* I determined these *virtues* encapsulated the universal *values* of *unity* and *tolerance* from Kidder's (1994) list. In looking at Kidder's list of eight universal values across cultures, the ones that could be expressed as virtues (which excludes freedom) are all included in my list of virtues: love (expressed as compassion and caring), truthfulness (expressed as honest and trustworthy), fairness (expressed as fair), unity (expressed as cooperative), tolerance (expressed as open-minded and understanding), responsibility (expressed as responsible), and respect for life (expressed as respectful and peaceful). Christians's (2008) list of universal values across cultures includes sacredness of human life, human dignity, nonviolence, and truthfulness. The first two are exclusive to privileging the human species and also do not represent virtues per se, but the virtue of *respectful* comes closest to encapsulating them in a broader sense for the human animal earthling identity. The remaining values on Christians's list are expressed in table 20 by the virtues of being *peaceful, honest,* and *trustworthy.*

I also added *humble* because it is a necessary trait for a human animal earthling to be less anthropocentric and able to see themselves as one small part of a larger community of living beings. Humility was mentioned explicitly in the Earth Charter (2000) and by Captain Watson during the interview, and it was implied by some other animal rights and environmental activists who lamented that humans are too anthropocentric in our outlook. Additionally, Marino and Mountain (2015) propose humility as a way for humans to reduce our existential angst and exceptionalist view of ourselves by accepting our mortality as yet another animal who is part of the natural world, not above it. In other words, let's not be too proud to embrace our animality. Nocella (2014) reminds us that to be an ally for other oppressed groups, we must be humble as well as authentic and accountable for the part we also play in oppressive systems (all these virtues are part of the human animal earthling identity, table 20).

I also added in the virtue *humorous.* While this was not specifically mentioned by interviewees or typically found in most campaigns, humor and wit, when deployed with compassion and humility (laughing *with,* not at), helps act as a social lubri-

TABLE 20 Twenty Virtues to Be Embodied by Human Animal Earthlings

These positive characteristics are expressed as adjectives; a human animal earthling is . . .
(listed in alphabetical order)

• Accountable	• Giving	• Prudent
• Caring	• Honest and authentic	• Respectful
• Compassionate and kind	• Humble	• Responsible
• Committed	• Humorous	• Trustworthy
• Cooperative	• A person of integrity	• Understanding
• Courageous	• Open-minded	• Wise
• Fair	• Peaceful	

cant for problem-solving and cooperation, bringing together disparate groups and breaking down defensive barriers when serious issues are at stake. Humor and wit can also be deployed to laugh at an oppressive regime, illuminate moral incongruities, and take on new perspectives (Lippit 2005), and this form of satirical "corrective humor" provokes improvement and aligns with the virtues of justice, courage, and wisdom (Ruch and Heintz 2016, 35). I'm exercising my artistic license in adding it because humor and wit are my favorite characteristics of human beings. Our species has caused massive problems worldwide, but I find our penchant for satire and levity (as well as our ability to be extremely altruistic) to be the saving grace of humanity.

In thinking about Frances Moore Lappé's (2011) list of positive traits of human nature that lead humanity toward ecological problem-solving, many of them are found among the virtues in table 20, namely, cooperation, empathy (compassion), and fairness. The other four human traits she listed—efficacy (problem-solving), meaning, imagination, and creativity—are supported by the related virtues in table 20 of wisdom, commitment, open-mindedness, and humor. I hope these latter virtues, with the addition of responsibility, also enable humanity to be flexible enough to productively weather the challenges and uncertainty caused by the climate crisis, as suggested by Ronald Sandler (2012). In general, activists, especially Lappé, express an optimism or hopefulness about the future and our ability to solve problems and avoid apathy in the face of seemingly overwhelming odds. But rather than adding in *optimistic*, I feel this hopefulness is encompassed in the virtues of being *committed* and *open-minded*.

The next part focuses on how to frame the values in table 18 to best foster a *just and sustainable humanimality*; this builds on environmental justice scholar Julian Agyeman's (2007) notion of cultivating biophilia for nature along with altruism for humans—an altruism I suggest we extend out to all sentient beings based on expressing love and care for animality.

Part 2: Reframing Values in Campaigning to Foster Biocentrism and Solidarity

Crompton and Kasser (2009) suggest social justice activist campaigns can reduce discrimination against animals by reminding humans they are part of the animal kingdom and the natural world, while engaging people's identities by valuing empathy and equality (values that should be applied to nonhuman animals too). A notion of interdependence with all living beings is key to developing an environmental identity (Clayton 2012) that increases people's pro-environmental behaviors and their belief that nonhuman animals have rights and that other species' interests should be included in decision-making (Clayton 2008).

To increase connection and reduce species and race-based bias that can lead to dehumanization of any one deemed 'different,' studies have shown a benefit to eliminating the human/animal hierarchy by likening animals to us humans (Costello and Hodson 2010); ideologically, I also see the benefits of making the comparison in the other direction and likening humans to fellow animals, implying we should be flattered to have things in common with these amazing beings (Freeman 2010b). Advocacy in favor of a human animal earthling identity should blend continuity and diversity rhetorics, creating connections based on our kinship with animals while still appreciating diversity among species. In terms of connecting all human cultures, Castells (2010, 185) recommends blending "biological commonality" and "historical diversity" to foster a green culture—one that transcends nation-based identities toward a global identity necessary to solve global environmental issues; thus, green culture addresses both the 'human' and the 'earthling' aspect of the human animal earthling identity.

Some of the human animal earthling values in table 18 overtly apply to caring about multiple species and the natural world (e.g., biocentrism, nature, sustainable and wise use of natural resources, stable climate), but many others are general concepts that humans tend to apply mainly to fellow humans (e.g., health, caretaking, lifesaving, justice, community, family, freedom) and think of anthropocentrically. Therefore, it is important to clarify that the human animal earthling applies these values more widely and biocentrically, and does not solely care about the lives, unity, and fair and responsible treatment of humans in their group (especially not just humans who look like them) but expands their 'in-group' to include all other human cultures, other animal cultures, and the natural world. In some places in the table, I specifically included a reference to various beings (e.g., respect for humans, other animals, and nature; rights for sentient individuals and ecosystems; sharing with fellow beings). But in other places, the value is open to be applied to whichever species needs it:

- Lifesaving can be saving the lives of old-growth trees or salmon.
- Health and well-being can be ensuring the emotional well-being of injured hawks at a sanctuary as well as taking a companion animal to the vet for vaccinations.

- *Family* can be keeping asylum-seeking human families together, keeping families of elephants together in reserves, or not separating families of cats or cows in human care.
- *Love and friendship* can be respecting interspecies friendships and the social bonds that form and make life worth living for social animals.
- *Reparation for harms* can be given to indigenous peoples in the form of land rights and to humans who were enslaved but also to forests that need rewilding, the regeneration of rivers that need to have dams removed, toxic mining sites that need cleanup, or an atmosphere that needs cleansing of pollutants.
- *Freedom* can be freedom of mobility for bears to migrate between parks and for goats not to be kept, bred, milked, or killed for food.
- *Livelihood* can be enabling human and nonhuman animals to have access to resources they need to survive and thrive (e.g., shelter, water, food, habitat, etc.).
- *Equality* can be treating others the way you would want to be treated and applying similar standards of care and fairness to nonhumans as you would to fellow humans.
- *Dignity* in the traditional usage is something that is probably most applicable to humans, but other social animals have some similar sense of self-respect and want to be powerful and free to act in ways that come naturally to them and display their strongest attributes (Gruen 2014). And this cannot be fully accomplished by a lion held captive in a zoo, a chicken caged in a coop, a donkey hauling a cart, or anyone stuck in a tank, whether they be a killer whale, goldfish, or king cobra. Kymlicka (2018) cautions that dignity should not be used as the rationale to secure human rights if conceived in a way that promotes "species entitlement" (781) of humans over (undignified) animals; additionally, he notes dignity-based rationales often also lead to dehumanization rhetoric than can disadvantage vulnerable beings in general.

I like Donaldson and Kymlicka's (2016) suggestion that we consider our broader relations with nonhuman animals within an "interspecies justice" (226) framework (rather than one based on 'humaneness'). The notion of *justice* forces us to assess whether we even have the authority to make claims on fellow animals (self-determining agents) and what our legally legitimate responsibility to them is. To make these determinations, Donaldson and Kymlicka (2016, 227) state: "We need to start asking what kinds of lives they [nonhuman animals] want to lead and whether our interactions with them bolster or inhibit their ability to lead such lives." Part of bolstering interspecies justice is prioritizing a path to achieve the Half-Earth Project's goal of protecting half the planet's land and sea habitats for millions of other species to thrive alongside humans (Wilson 2016).

As a clarification, the values in table 18 (like conscientious consumption, legislation, and engaged citizenship) are generally actions that *humans alone* are supposed to take (the list is not directed at what ecosystems or nonhuman animals should do, even though there is some agency exhibited by all living beings). The point is for human animal earthlings to direct altruistic actions outward, acting both as engaged *citizens* who work on behalf of all beings when advocating for political change and conscientious *consumers* who avoid harming the planet or fellow animals.

In this last half of the chapter, I outline a prescription for an inclusive list of beings that all three causes should advocate for and then provide examples of where the sixteen SMOs in my study *missed* opportunities to serve as allies in their campaigns versus productive examples when they *were* serving as allies in supporting total liberation of species. I end with suggestions for thirteen project areas ripe for collaboration between the three causes.

WHO MATTERS

Table 21 is a listing of entities that should matter to human animal earthlings, across a variety of life categories comprising nature, animals, and the human species. This is an expansion of the "who matters" list (table 13) in chapter 7 to remove the anthropocentric limitations. These are the primary groups and individuals whose interests get (and need) the consideration of human animal earthlings in all social movement advocacy campaigns.

TABLE 21 Who Matters to the Human Animal Earthling

LIFE CATEGORIES	WHO MATTERS TO THE HUMAN ANIMAL EARTHLING (WHOSE INTERESTS WE CHAMPION) (IN NO PARTICULAR ORDER)
General category	Individuals, all life, living beings, earth, the planet, future generations, species, endangered species, vulnerable beings, innocent beings
Nature-specific category	Nature, wildlife habitats, biodiverse ecosystems (land-based and aquatic), nature parks and reserves, wildlife migration corridors, trees, reefs, endangered plants, phytoplankton, the biosphere, the atmosphere, oceans, freshwater rivers, lakes, and streams
Animal category	Animals, wildlife, farmed animals, companion animals, captive animals, sentient beings, mammals, reptiles, fishes, birds, amphibians, insects, pollinators, crustaceans, invertebrates, vertebrates, animals who are injured, suffering, or orphaned and in need of help
Human-only category	Humans, people living in poverty, people without secure housing, women and girls, minority groups, children, indigenous and Native peoples, marginalized groups, exploited people, enslaved people, laborers, the LGBTQ community, refugees, individuals with (dis) abilities and special needs, local communities, local farmers, victims and survivors, those falsely imprisoned or silenced, activists, journalists, scientists, public servants, those injured or suffering and in need of help

To review respectful and inclusive terminology that I suggest activists use to describe all these types of living beings, see table 4 in chapter 3.

Rhetorical Suggestions for Including Humans as Animals. While not all SMOs are currently amenable to nor see the benefit of directly calling humans *animals* or using the term *nonhuman animals* as I do in my writing, there are other ways for activists to remind us we too are animals; this reminder could be achieved using rhetoric that fits the organization's values and style. Activists could simply provide a disclaimer at some point in the campaign materials that acknowledges humans are part of the animal kingdom, even if they do not plan to allude to that status frequently or change their terminology throughout. Laurel Sutherlin suggests that we avoid referring to other human societies as animals, as that may be perceived as condescending or culturally inappropriate, but we may potentially be more welcome to call our *own* society animals. Sometimes, slightly different terms can express a similar sentiment; Frances Moore Lappé uses the term "social animals" to describe humans, and Mustafa Ali uses broader kinship terms to connect us with fellow animals by saying "all God's creatures" or fellow beings on "Mother Earth," and I frequently describe us as "sentient beings."

When talking about all of us animals (including humans), I find the phrases "humans and animals" or "people and animals" problematic and believe it would be better expressed in less binary ways as "humans and fellow animals" or "people and other animals" or "all animals, humans included." At the very least, it is respectful to give animals the courtesy of accurately referring to their sex when known (e.g., he or she), as we do for humans. You should acknowledge the fact that they are gendered—even when the sex isn't known or you are speaking about a nonspecific individual (e.g., she/he or they)—and avoid referring to someone as something with the inanimate pronoun "it."

ALLY OPPORTUNITIES MISSED FOR INCREASED INCLUSIVITY BY SOCIAL MOVEMENTS IN THIS STUDY

An important purpose of this book is to encourage the three causes—for animal protection, human rights, and environmentalism—to work in groundless solidarity (Colling, Parson, and Arrigoni 2014) as *allies* supporting one another for interspecies justice (Donaldson and Kymlicka 2016) and total liberation of species (Best 2014). This does not necessarily mean that they are always unified in all the same projects or messages, as they are still diverse. To be an ally is to be mutually supportive every day, which is not quite the same as collaborating to form coalitions, which should be done when it makes sense to join forces to leverage resources toward a shared campaign goal. To be allies every day, the interviewees suggest that activists must avoid myopic thinking and perspectives; show respect to a wide variety of beings in campaign terminology, images, and tactics (see table 21); and not use or objectify someone as a means to an end for your cause.

In my discourse analysis of sixteen global SMO websites, I looked for missed opportunities where I thought these advocacy organizations (at least in the campaign sections of their websites that I studied in 2017) could have been more inclusive of the interests of humans, nonhuman animals, nature, and/or ecosystems (the entities in table 21). In this section I categorize those opportunities grouped by social movement cause—human rights, animal protection, and environmentalism.

Human Rights Organizations. The human rights groups do an excellent job of advocating for a variety of human groups, particularly those who are the most disadvantaged, marginalized, or exploited; therefore, the main opportunities for inclusivity center on showing some concern for other animals and the natural world, which are affected by some of the same things threatening human well-being. For example, when Amnesty International critiques the palm oil industry for worker abuses, they could also show the parallel abuses of wildlife and forest ecosystems as an example of the industry's callous disrespect for life; or in Amnesty's campaigns against nuclear weapons and war, they could also explain warfare's destructive effects on wildlife and nature. Human Rights Watch and Minority Rights Group do mention environmental issues (mostly their impacts on humans), but they could emphasize the ecological interdependence of all species to show that deleterious effects on wildlife and ecosystems also threaten humans and vice versa.

Because the concept of human rights is predicated on the belief that human lives and freedom matter because we are each sentient individuals who deserve protection from injustice and harm, there is an opportunity for human rights organizations to acknowledge the animal rights view that nonhuman animal individuals, as fellow sentient beings, also deserve protection from suffering injustice and harm at the hands of humans. For example, when Amnesty International speaks out against the unfair imprisonment of people worldwide, they could acknowledge that humans are not the only innocent individuals unfairly imprisoned, as nonhuman animals are suffering massive and unwarranted confinement against their will (even though it is natural that Amnesty's campaigns still want to focus on their mission of rescuing humans). And Anti-Slavery International's charter specifies slavery as something that happens illegally to humans, but they could recognize that nonhuman animals are also enslaved (albeit often legally) with billions held against their will in various industries and on farms (even small farms still count, just like a single family enslaving an immigrant girl as their housekeeper counts as enslavement). For example, Anti-Slavery International's "What We Do" section discusses purchasing farmed animals as a financial resource for humans, but it fails to acknowledge that this is sanctioning a form of enslavement by an antislavery organization, which could be seen as illogical and unjust if one takes a nonanthropocentric view of the situation.

The farmed-animal enslavement issue becomes more acute in CARE's charitable giving program advocating that their supporters gift a farmed animal (all kinds of species) to a struggling human family in a developing country. CARE's catalog of giving options uses whimsical language and puns to cheerfully describe the animals as gifts, which trivializes the serious issue that the animal him/herself is not given a choice and will be used (or perhaps killed) as a food or income source for someone else. Many of these farmed animals are females, and CARE is a female advocacy organization, so there could be some acknowledgment that breeding and using female animals (of any species, human or nonhuman) for their milk, eggs, or babies is a morally problematic form of female exploitation. Instead of gifting live animals, CARE could help needy human families by empowering them to grow plant-based crops for sustenance or for income, or otherwise find income opportunities that do not cause harm to another individual.

While I have been advocating opportunities for CARE to champion the *rights* of animals, CARE could also, at the very least, advocate for the *welfare* of these animals if they are still going to give them to impoverished humans, as they currently offer no guarantee that the family can afford to support the needs of the animal or provide long-term veterinary care. There is no indication that anyone follows up to see if the farmed animal him/herself is neglected or suffering or even if there are some unintended consequences the farmed animal is causing the human family, such as the need for a child to stay home from school to care for the goat or cow.

There are times when mistreatment of humans is described as being 'treated like an animal,' without any acknowledgment from the human rights organizations that perhaps, in some cases, *nonhuman animals* do not deserve to be treated that way either (such as living in filth or being chained, beaten, forced into manual labor, or exploited as a resource). I offer this suggestion because if the only thing wrong with treating a human 'like an animal' is the mistreatment of the *human*, then it may imply that mistreating *nonhuman animals* is fine or at least much less important than ensuring human well-being. However, I do understand that some ways that we treat nonhuman animals (or ways they treat one another) are not necessarily mistreatment but just a way that is culturally appropriate for their species but not appropriate for most members of the human species (such as animals eating off or sleeping on the ground, not burying their dead, living outside in certain natural shelters and not in buildings, not showering, not wearing clothes, etc.). In the case where Amnesty International has a campaign to help Malawi people with albinism who face being killed to have their body parts sold for ritual ceremonies, one girl declares, "We are not animals to be hunted or sold," which implies it may be fine for *nonhuman animals* to be hunted and killed for their body parts (horns, fur, organs, flesh, etc.) to be sold in the marketplace. There's an opportunity for Amnesty to speak out against commodification of *anyone's* body parts.

There are chances for wildlife to also be included more in human rights organizations' campaigns that involve them, such as how Minority Rights Group could consider wildlife as stakeholders in decisions about how to resolve issues where human communities native to an area may be displaced by conservation efforts to create wildlife migration corridors or parks. Currently, their campaigns seem to imply that the interests of native nonhuman animals in maintaining their home territory may not be as legitimate as a native human's right to a home territory. As a positive example from another social movement cause, the wildlife animal protection groups IFAW and WWF both discuss resolution of human-wildlife conflicts in ways that are mutually beneficial to human and nonhuman stakeholders who may need to coexist in the same space. Another example to include wildlife is when Minority Rights Group laments the extinction of human cultures and language; an opportunity exists to connect the need to protect human cultural diversity with the need to protect biodiversity—to keep animal species (and their cultures) from going extinct. In general, protecting the cultural diversity of marginalized groups can present challenges, as human rights groups must seek productive ways to engage with a human minority culture that is intolerant or discriminatory toward other human or nonhuman beings and hurts them. How to 'tolerate the intolerant' is one of many great debates over how to protect the rights of the group/society (including nonhuman life too) while not trampling too heavily on individuals' personal freedoms.

Animal Protection Organizations. With animal protection organizations, there are opportunities to diversify the type of animals they protect, to link more with environmental protection, and to show parallels with human rights abuses. In terms of animals, the vegan campaigns of PETA and Animal Equality obviously champion the rights of domesticated animals (and wild fishes), and they do mention the environmental benefits of veganism, but they could further emphasize the various benefits to *wild/free* animals of humans ending animal agriculture and commercial fishing; this goes along with opportunities for these groups to demonstrate that, due to ecological interdependence of species, animal rights (especially for free-living animals) require that we be environmentalists and support broader efforts to curb pollution, greenhouse gas emissions, GMOs, habitat destruction, and freshwater overconsumption.

On the other hand, wildlife organizations could do more to champion the rights of all individual animals (not just endangered species or charismatic wildlife). For example, when talking about fish species, Sea Shepherd could use the same strident rights language that they do when talking about marine mammals—focusing on individuals, not just species or groups—so mammals do not seem more worthy of protection as inherently valuable beings than other sea animals. While they do use the word "wildlife," the WWF could incorporate the word "animal" more into their discourse to emphasize *individuals* (instead of primarily talking more broadly about "species" and "nature"). They can maintain their emphasis on ecological concerns but also incorporate welfare and rights concerns for individual free-living animals, thereby more overtly supporting principles of compassionate conservation in their campaigns, just as human rights are overtly supported.

The WWF should discuss the benefits to all animals and the environment of humans shifting to a largely plant-based diet. When discussing human diets at all, their focus is currently on improving the efficiency of fishing and animal agriculture, but this "supply-side" focus would be better served with campaigns to increase the supply of affordable organic crops and produce, as the most resource-efficient and animal-friendly human food option. IFAW protects both wild animals and domesticated animals (namely companion animals), but they largely overlook the most abused and prolific domesticated animals—farmed animals. Opportunities abound for discussions of improvements to farmed animal welfare while also touting the benefits to all animals of humans switching away from farming and hunting/fishing animals to eating plant-based foods.

Animal rights groups like PETA and Animal Equality mention the value of human rights when discussing how a similar ethical logic justifies animal rights, but more could be done to show concern for how the human animal is adversely affected by the same industries that exploit nonhuman animals (they demonstrate this best with farming). And if any animal rights group wants to draw comparisons between current mass exploitation of animals and historical atrocities perpetrated on marginalized human groups (namely, comparisons with the Jewish concentration camps during the Holocaust and enslavement of African people in the eighteenth and nineteenth centuries), knowing that these human groups were 'animalized' as 'subhuman' by the perpetrators, greater care should be taken to have those campaigns overtly designed and publicly led by members of those affected human demographic groups. Better yet, partnering in a coalition with a civil rights group that is interested in a campaign against human and nonhuman animal discrimination (drawing parallels between speciesism and racism, sexism, homophobia, or ableism) would allow the animal rights group to serve as an ally to a marginalized human group (and vice versa) rather than being seen as speaking about or for them (or using their cause to promote one's own). Additionally, care should be taken to show the same respect for historically marginalized humans, such as women, as animal rights groups want for marginalized nonhumans, by avoiding objectification of anyone's bodies as a means to an end.

Environmental Organizations. I was impressed with the way that environmental organizations show concern for human rights and respect for the interests of marginalized human groups. The main opportunities for improvements in inclusivity I see are in adequately addressing issues impacting (nonendangered) animals, such as offering a more strident critique of animal agribusiness and fishing. In a broad sense, one place to start is for environmental organizations' verbal and visual discourse to include nonhuman animals more frequently as affected parties, which would impart to them some status and importance rather than merely being lumped in with nature. For example, FOE's mission and vision statements should mention (nonhuman) animals, instead of only using the vague terms *species* and *diversity*. A phrase mentioned once on FOE's site, "demanding rights for people and rules for business," could be expanded to "demanding rights for living beings and rules for business." 350.org and RAN do not feature or mention nonhuman animals very often. They promote cultural diversity but could further promote the benefits of biodiversity (especially important for a rainforest organization) by including a wider variety of animals as stakeholders (including insects, amphibians, reptiles, fishes, etc.), showing and discussing how these beings are affected by climate change and deforestation, along with affected humans. For example, since 350.org rightly asks for justice and restitution for the innocent people (largely in the Global South) affected by the climate impacts caused largely by industrialized societies in the Global North, then wildlife too, as innocent affected parties, deserve to be considered climate refugees and victims who warrant resources and aid.

In fact, all environmental justice campaigns, which are big with FOE and RAN especially, could be more inclusive if they also considered the injustices perpetrated on wildlife as a marginalized group or culture. Nonhuman animal cultures require rights to their native territories or places that can serve as sources of livelihood (not to be displaced by land-grabbing) and to have these home spaces free of pollution. And just as indigenous or local human cultures are to be respected by environmental organizations, so should the nonhuman animal cultures that are threatened with extinction.

One of the most glaring issues to rectify is the need for environmental organizations to more overtly speak out against the practice of farming and fishing animals for profit, instead of characterizing these businesses as capable of reform and potentially sustainable food production systems to feed a growing human population (in a nonindustrial fashion). Showing support for vegan foods and the wide-scale production of organic plant-based agriculture deserves to be a priority. For example, the Nature Conservancy does not ask for the level of reduction in meat and dairy that is ecologically necessary but, instead, settles for merely suggesting consumers eat one meatless meal a week, rather than suggesting plants be the primary food source (a reduction in eating fish was also overlooked). Like many environmental organizations, rather than working on reforming the consumer demand side, the Nature Conservancy focuses more on supply-side reforms—helping producers of animal-based foods to be 'more sustainable' (when 'somewhat less harmful' would be a more honest framing of animal agribusiness). Animal farming consumes an absurd level of resources (the Nature Conservancy notes that growing farmed animals and their feed takes up land approximately the size of the continent of South America plus the continent of Africa), yet there is a logical disconnect between this unsustainable reality and the Nature Conservancy's approach of working with farmers and ranchers to be stewards who produce animal products in a less destructive way. While making animal farming 'greener' is less controversial and less upsetting to consumers and business interests than is vegan advocacy, the former does not seem a feasible way to create the kind of vast environmental improvements needed to protect wildlife, preserve land and sea habitats, conserve precious freshwater, and reduce pollution like greenhouse gas emissions, especially if environmental organizations are not actively campaigning to decrease the growing demand for animal products as human populations rise (Freeman 2010a).

Oceana and 350.org also both overlook the need to suggest that societies transition to eating a plant-based diet. As a climate organization, 350.org seems remiss in failing to educate the public on the major role animal agribusiness and animal-based diets play in greenhouse gas emissions; even if 350.org still prefers to focus on reducing dependence on fossil fuels, given the massive climate impacts of meat and dairy, 350.org should also at least suggest that societies divest in animal agribusiness and move toward a vegan diet. Despite all the problems with commercial fishing that Oceana documents (including extinction of species), they actively promote billions of people eating fish daily, as they say it is a necessary food source. For reasons of ecology, animal rights, and animal welfare, Oceana should instead suggest the vast majority of humans be fed on nutritious produce, nuts, beans, and grains (all of which contain protein and likely are not contaminated with mercury) and then only mention the need for low levels of subsistence fishing as part of feeding coastal human communities for whom a plant-based diet is not a viable/accessible option geographically.

Instead of primarily being discussed as a food source, fish, like any other conscious being, could be portrayed as inherently valuable individuals by environmental organizations. Greenpeace's campaign rhetoric around fish promotes their utility as both a food source and an ecologically beneficial species but not as sentient individuals whose lives and communities are important to them, which is different from how Greenpeace portrays the value of other animal species (especially wild mammals). While Greenpeace advocates for a reduction in meat eating, they do not ask for similar reductions in the consumption of sea animals and, instead, support people eating "sustainable seafood" (which, for the sake of comparison, does not include "sustainably raised" marine mammals, as those individuals are someone not to be commodified). Another example of the bias in overlooking fishes' inherent value as individuals is Oceana's campaign to fight rampant mislabeling of "sustainable seafood," partially because it threatens human health. But Oceana could point out the obvious fact that fishing of any type is threatening to the health (and lives) of *individual fish*, whose dead bodies are pictured in the campaign that emphasizes defrauding human consumers as the major problem (which belittles the inherent value of sea animals). Environmental organizations should not succumb to the status quo bias of lumping fishes in with domesticated animals as both being inherently 'food' species—a utility—rather than seeing them as individual wild/free animals who deserve to be respected and protected just as much as land-based wild/ free animals, even ones whom humans tend to eat, such as deer or fowl.

In conclusion, I have pointed out specific ways that the campaigns of the sixteen environmentalist, human rights, and animal protection groups could better support one another and advocate for a wider variety of vulnerable beings. Next, I want to give credit to the times when these SMOs were doing just that so they can serve as positive examples to emulate.

ALLY EXAMPLES: INCLUSIVITY SHOWN BY
SOCIAL MOVEMENTS IN THIS STUDY

In this book's previous discourse analysis of sixteen global SMO websites, I looked for areas where these organizations were serving as allies for one another—being inclusive, not just of their 'primary' constituent group (either humans, nonhuman animals, or ecosystems/nature), but also expressing concern for *another one or more* of these entities (such as in table 21)—as this facilitates the human animal earthling identity. Below I have categorized some inclusive trends seen among the three social movement causes, which can serve as models for human animal earthling campaigns.

Human Rights Organizations. The main area of inclusivity for the human rights organizations in my study was with the environmental movement in terms of achieving environmental justice for humans. Amnesty International and Human Rights Watch both mention concern about dirty and extractive industries polluting local communities, with Amnesty emphasizing threats to indigenous peoples as well as noting the ability of Native peoples to serve as good environmental stewards of their traditional lands. Climate change was mentioned by CARE and by Human Rights Watch as an example of an environmental issue that will have repercussions for humanity. Considering the severity of these impacts, I would expect to see more of an emphasis on the climate crisis by all human rights organizations. CARE also includes ecological farming as an issue, mentioning the benefits of planting trees and organic crops.

Animal Protection Organizations. Certain campaigns of animal protection organizations overlap with a concern for human rights as well as some ecological issues that connect with domesticated animals or wildlife issues. In addition to discussing saving lives and sparing the suffering of farmed animals and fishes, vegan campaigns by the animal rights organizations (PETA and Animal Equality) mention the environmental benefits of eschewing animal products. And PETA includes the benefits of a plant-based diet to improve human health, relieve human hunger, and spare workers from frequent labor rights violations at slaughterhouses.

The language used by IFAW and WWF is especially inclusive of many types of living beings, including humans along with nonhuman animals and nature, such as saying that certain reforms will benefit "people and wildlife." IFAW also frequently says we should make improvements "for animals and people," and WWF says to do it "for life on our planet, including our own" and "for every living thing, including ourselves." These wildlife-oriented groups also show concern for the interests of the local people who live near or with wildlife. For example, IFAW seeks mutually beneficial solutions to wildlife-human conflicts, and WWF also wants to include local communities in wildlife decisions affecting them. Sea Shepherd Conservation Society has a campaign working with First Nations peoples in Canada who want to stop salmon farms from damaging their coastal territory; through this coalition, Sea Shepherd amplifies the voices of indigenous leaders and also speaks out against the Canadian government for not respecting indigenous territorial rights. And during the hurricanes that devastated communities in the Caribbean, Sea Shepherd used their ships to provide aid to human victims and their companion animals; this humanitarian outreach in a crisis is useful for the animal protection movement to demonstrate that it cares about humans too.

The animal rights groups PETA and Animal Equality both discuss a belief in human rights and avoiding discriminatory practices or human enslavement in favor of freedom and respect—fighting hierarchical thinking and the belief that some are 'more important' and have the right to use others who are 'less important'; this comparison is done in the service of exposing what is wrong when researchers, agribusiness, or zoos perpetrate a similar discrimination and enslavement against nonhuman animals. This alignment between human and animal rights in the animal advocacy discourse can be seen as a celebration of human rights and mutual respect for sentient beings, but it could also be perceived as offensive if someone finds it belittling to humans to compare them and their injustices to other animal species.

I noticed that animal protection groups have more diverse visual representations of humans in terms of race but also gender identity and body types at times, in particular Animal Equality and PETA. Since the animal protection movement tends to be associated with white people primarily marketing to white audiences, more racial inclusivity is an improvement.

Environmental Organizations. Since 'the environment' is such a broad category, perhaps it is not surprising that environmental organizations do a good job of including the interests of many species—nature, ecosystems, humans, and wildlife. The language is often inclusive, such as Greenpeace including "all of us" and "everyone," and saying the rainforest is home to many "animals, plants, and people," and Oceana showing concern for "marine wildlife, habitat, and human health," which are all being threatened by pollution. Similarly, the Nature Conservancy says we should do things for "people and nature" or "people and wildlife." And RAN says we should make improvements "for people and planet," where the term *planet* represents such a broad category that it is not clear if it is meant to imply an environmental rationale (such as ecosystem health) or to subsume all species in the more-than-human world into one planetary community. And climate change impacts are not just a concern for "the environment" but also humans, as emphasized by Greenpeace, 350.org, and the Nature Conservancy, with the latter also including climate impacts on wildlife.

In their environmental campaigns, RAN and FOE emphasize environmental justice issues to provide protection for humans, especially marginalized communities such as the poor, or indigenous peoples, who endure land-grabbing, pollution or environmental degradation, or worker exploitation at the hands of industry. And Oceana's marine protection campaigns express frequent concern for coastal communities, starving humans, poor people, and women. The Nature Conservancy says it is devoted to human diversity as well as biodiversity.

While human rights and the intrinsic value of humans is a given, environmental organizations sometimes portray the more-than-human world as inherently valuable, regardless of its utility to humanity. The Nature Conservancy's mission says that nature should be conserved for "its own sake" in addition to its ability to "fulfill our needs and enrich our lives"; RAN states that wildlife and biodiversity have "intrinsic value"; and Greenpeace frequently marvels at how wondrous and amazing animal species are.

In support (albeit indirectly) for domesticated farmed animals, several of the environmental organizations' statements on agricultural issues critique meat eating, "livestock production," or factory farming as problematic for the environment (and sometimes inhumane to the animals), with RAN, FOE, and Greenpeace suggesting that people should eat less meat. Some of these campaigns also include concern for human health or forest-dwelling human communities being displaced by agribusiness, as RAN holistically declares that we need to "create a more equitable, compassionate and responsible food system" in which healthy, plant-based foods are accessible and affordable to all. While Oceana thinks billions of humans worldwide must eat fish as a protein source, they do criticize the suffering of marine animals caused by fish farming and common industrial fishing tactics that discard dying or bleeding 'nontarget' animals like certain fish species and sharks. And they advocate for an end to seismic air blasting by the oil and gas industry, as it harms marine animals, including fish.

WORKING THROUGH DIFFERENCES TO COLLABORATE ON PROJECTS

The previous sections focused on examples of how an SMO can construct its own campaign messages in ways that are also supportive of other causes, even tangentially, to be an ally. This section discusses the times when it makes sense for SMOs, especially from different causes, to join forces and actively collaborate with one another on projects, perhaps forming coalitions. I discuss ways to overcome some ideological divides as well as offer thirteen potential project areas for cross-cause collaboration in promoting a human animal earthling identity. It is useful here to review the following tips that interviewees in this study suggested for working effectively in collaborative campaigns with other advocacy groups:

- Have a shared vision for success—a common goal with agreed-upon objectives and tactics.

- Build on one another's strengths rather than focusing on differences. Don't be too ideologically principled that you can't find bridges to join with groups who have some similar interests (or similar opponents).
- Lead by example rather than trying to convert other activists to your cause. Get to know each other as you are—seek understanding to build relationships and networks.
- Work with groups who have similar activism styles as you (in terms of matching radical to moderate approaches).
- Be bottom-up not top-down when working in and with local human communities, especially marginalized folks (practice inclusive decision-making), making sure they too benefit from the teamwork.

ADDRESSING IDEOLOGICAL DIFFERENCES AND TENSIONS BETWEEN CAUSES

The following subsections review some issues that present moral dilemmas for bridging the ideological divides between social causes, as introduced in chapter 1. The tensions mainly center on whether and when humans should kill nonhuman animals and how to balance interests in perceived conflicts between human and nonhuman animals. All three causes support the continuing struggle for human and civil rights, and to a large extent they all support some level of environmental responsibility and animal welfare. It is *animal rights* that are lacking widespread support. Therefore, campaigns that foster a human animal earthling identity need to make the life and liberty rights of individual sentient beings a central ethical concern, including civil rights and equity issues facing injustice in human society, and then put that in the context of fulfilling strong human obligations to be ecologically responsible and care for living systems. This fits with Jamieson's (2002) recommendation that we value sentient individuals inherently and value nature more holistically as providing homes and livelihoods for sentient beings. The human animal earthling advocates for justice for living beings, as expressed by green postcolonial scholars Huggan and Tiffan (2007; 2010): "No social justice without environmental justice; and without social justice—for all ecological beings—no justice at all" (2007, 11).

Here I summarize some ideas from the interviews and from scholars, including myself, for applying human animal earthling identity values (table 18) toward resolving issues that are contentious between the three social movement causes, such as animal-based diets, nonnative/introduced species, wildlife management, parks and reserves, and human cultural practices that harm animals.

Animal Meat and Milk. Given the right access and circumstances, humans can thrive as herbivores, and this diet can save billions of animal lives, increase human longevity, and decrease our environmental footprint in significant ways; therefore, a plant-based diet makes sense as an ideal goal for sustainably and fairly feeding bil-lions of humans. As interviewee Dawn Moncrief explains, if being a reducitarian is good, then veganism must be even better since "vegans are reducitarians too, but they've just gone all the way." On an individual level, she suggests speaking in terms of each of us "minimizing, ideally *eliminating*" meat and dairy, in commu-nities who have the ability. And if people don't have nutritional access to enough plant-based foods, programs should be created to provide those nutrients or to sus-tain communities through crop agriculture programs. On a global level, Moncrief talks more pragmatically about needing to *reduce* meat consumption trends. The in-vestment in developing affordable clean/cultured meat and in improving the plant-based meats and milks is one way to reverse these global trends. Another idea is scaling up veganic farming practices (organic crop farming fertilizing with com-post and thus no domesticated animal inputs).

From an ethics standpoint, related to rights for fellow sentient beings, it is not fair to farm anyone and raise and breed them for one's own purposes, with agri-business essentially functioning as a form of enslavement that we would not le-gally tolerate if done to our own species (Freeman 2014). However, if certain hu-mans must be more omnivorous at times, given someone's geographic area and lack of access to plant-based nutrition there, then hunting and fishing for animals becomes morally tenable in that case, as other omnivorous animals do (and ob-viously carnivorous species must). Sustenance hunting and fishing by humans in need (and without other nutritional choices) do not have the same ethical problems as do commercialized hunting and fishing to kill, accumulate, and sell bodies for profit (Freeman 2014). Zoe Weil pragmatically suggests that food campaigns could focus on critiquing larger commercial fishing and animal agribusiness operations, rather than targeting small-scale enterprises, for more widespread support.

Nonnative/Introduced Animal Species. We might rightly first try to clarify what param-eters constitute a native species. From a long-term anthropological perspective, outside of Africa, humans could be considered nonnative to many continents and islands, especially colonists (in terms of years that count toward native status), and throughout history *Homo sapiens* have caused extinctions of species (Harari 2015). Species do travel around the world of their own volition and also as introduced by humans through our travels and trade (Huggan and Tiffan 2007). So, achieving some kind of ecological purity for each region may not be a feasible solution.

That said, the main ethical issues revolve around killing nonnative *animal* spe-cies (rather than plants), as the former are sentient beings. Before any corrective measures are undertaken, authorities need to determine beyond a doubt if any par-ticular introduced animal species is *significantly* contributing to the decline of an en-dangered or threatened native species. If so proven, then compassionate conserva-tion principles can be used in problem-solving. Interviewee Lori Marino explains that compassionate conservation is based on the golden rule of not doing to some animal what you would not find tenable to do to the human animal (or yourself) in times we are found to be ecologically harmful. Rights of individual sentient beings should be respected when problem-solving. Marino contends that, to be fair and effective, we should examine the extent to which our own species is to blame for the existence of the introduced species or the bulk of the threats facing the endangered species. Thus, we would need to transform our own practices accordingly by taking responsibility for harms caused and some sacrifices that we humans might need to make, such as reducing human population growth and our consumption of animal products and fossil fuels (Almiron and Tafalla 2019). This echoes Donaldson and Kymlicka's (2011) critique of extermination solutions, as they see culling as "an animal equivalent to ethnic cleansing" (211) and suggest that any accommodations made should be mutual, including humans too.

Wildlife Management. Similar to the solutions described above, compassionate conservation can be a guiding principle in decision-making on how or if humans should get involved with managing any 'problematic' native wildlife species in a specific area. If it is determined that a population is suffering or causing significant ecological damage because there are too many of them for an area to sustain, rather than culling, it would be better to provide these individuals with more space, including migration corridors to reach other populations, or reintroduce native predators to the area (Bekoff 2013; Ramp and Bekoff 2015). These are ecologically sustainable solutions over time that are better than encouraging humans to shoot individuals to reduce their numbers, as human hunters often seem to need to repeat that lethal and artificial solution year after year. This ritual then fosters a sport hunting culture that begins to recreationally and financially rely on having 'excess' nonhuman animals to view as 'game,' diminishing our respectful relationship with fellow animals (Luke 2007). Additionally, relocating animals as a solution should be a last resort, and then if so, family units must be kept together, and we must scientifically understand how their social order contributes to their well-being and the ecological well-being of the ecosystem (Kemmerer 2015a).

Parks and Reserves. When there is a need to designate an area as a park or reserve to protect the habitat and the animal species who rely on that area for their livelihood, environmental and animal protection groups must also consider and involve the local human communities who already live near or in the park area. Those communities should not automatically be sacrificed or have their interests completely dismissed in favor of an endangered species or wilderness area, especially if the people in question do not have many resources, are otherwise marginalized and dependent on the land or coastal area for their livelihood, or are historically indigenous to the area (Huggan and Tiffan 2007). Many of the interviewees expressed their beliefs that wildlife reserves must be workable with and allow some access to these local human groups, viewing their subsistence needs as separate from the park being off-limits to business development, sport hunting/fishing, and commercial extraction of resources. Interviewee Carl Soderbergh contends that many indigenous people are the best custodians of the area and should be entrusted with leadership in environmental stewardship. Thus, in making decisions about any park policies, these local communities should be involved throughout as a primary stakeholder and allowed to speak for themselves (not subsumed within the eco-advocacy organization).

What didn't get mentioned in the interviews was that problems may arise in isolated cases where local or indigenous communities fail to act as good stewards or are doing things that can objectively be determined as harmful to certain individuals or the greater good of the wilderness area. It is important to also count the wild animal residents as having an interest in this shared habitat, and their needs should not automatically be trumped by any human's interests. A fair process for balancing human and nonhuman needs should be enacted, and if certain human activities need to be curtailed, then governments or NGOs should provide resources and retraining so that local people can fulfill their needs in ways that are more just and ecologically beneficial.

Human Cultural Practices That Harm Nonhuman Animals. Conflicts between social movements can arise when certain human cultures' traditional (or sometimes modern) practices cause nonhuman animals harm and do not meet the standards for animal care and protection as judged by other human cultures. This is especially ethically fraught when the group in question is an ethnic minority community being critiqued by members of a dominant ethnic group. In *Dangerous Crossings*, Kim (2015) outlines several examples of this (e.g., dog fighting, indigenous killing of whales, and Asian street meat markets), and provides guidance on how to resolve disagreements in ways that don't resort to accusations of animal cruelty versus racism. Kim suggests that white animal activists must be cognizant of the cultural imperialism, hypocrisy, and resentment that can result from criticizing people of color and telling them how to live. Conversely, she notes that people of color should not necessarily assess any interest whites have in animal protection as an indication of racism, as that dismisses the animals' interests. Kim (2015, 20) recommends that advocates from both groups look at the situation empathetically through a multioptic lens and with "mutual avowal" to acknowledge how race and species put racial minorities and nonhuman animals at a disadvantage.

Because racism and speciesism are historically intertwined within white human supremacy, they must be dismantled simultaneously. Kim explains, "Race has been articulated in part as a metric of animality" (18), and Ko (2016) explains that the oppression black people experience is yet another *layer* of animal oppression. Thus, she suggests, animal rights activism may function best from within an antiracism movement (Ko and Ko 2017). Kim and Ko both recommend coalition building between oppressed groups (human minority groups and nonhuman animals) to "dismantle the systems that oppress us all very differently" (Ko 2015). Practicing "revolutionary decolonization" (Colling, Parson, and Arrigoni 2014, 58) is another way to marry human and nonhuman movements for total liberation by drawing on precolonial indigenous viewpoints that celebrate kinship with the more-than-human world, trying to decolonize our own mind-sets, and allying with current indigenous rights struggles against colonial systems that unjustly exterminated and exploited indigenous living beings (nonhuman animals, humans, and nature).

Pellow (2014) and Best (2014) both remind animal activists who want to engage in supporting total liberation of species not to insinuate that nonhuman animals have it the worst now; there is a need to acknowledge that human rights struggles against enslavement and injustice continue and are not resolved, and the animal rights movement is now joining in that ongoing abolitionist movement. This fits with Colling et al.'s (2014) recommendation that a total liberation effort must support "groundless solidarity" (64) that does not privilege one resistance movement as more important than others. Additionally, Kymlicka (2013) suggests that if animal protection campaigns focused more on animal *rights* (liberation) rather than animal cruelty (welfare) issues, it might get closer to providing a larger and more constructive critique of institutional oppression in an attempt to be both posthumanist and postcolonial.

PROJECT AREAS AROUND WHICH WE CAN
BUILD SOLIDARITY BETWEEN CAUSES

In offering my suggestions of projects around which various SMOs can team up, one place to begin is to revisit the common opponents identified by activists I interviewed: exploitative corporations (especially extractive industries and agribusiness), the global economic system, corrupt or weak governments, societal discrimination, and selfish people. To address the latter two, the human animal earthling identity components (discussed at the beginning of this chapter), if adopted over time, would promote an individual and societal outlook that is altruistic rather than selfish and encourages inclusiveness, diversity, equality, fairness, and compassion for all sentient beings.

The bigger and more entrenched problem is the selfishness and discrimination fundamentally built into existing systems and institutions—poorly designed systems that concentrate power in the hands of a few and tie business and/or government incentives to 'growth' and exploitation more so than health, equity, productive cycles of life, regeneration, and conservation of shared resources. This implies that SMOs should work collectively to transform our economic, business, and governance systems so they are designed to function productively for the benefit of all species (not just privileged human groups) and have built-in accountability mechanisms to respond fairly to the demands of citizens. These projects work toward the seven outcomes of a "new human ecology" championed by Green Vegans activist Will Anderson (2012), as discussed in chapter 1.

The idea of systemic transformation has influenced the first two common causes below, namely democratic and economic reform. Then I go on to detail eleven other specific topics worthy of collaboration by SMOs working toward animal rights, human rights, and environmentalism, namely: biocultural diversity, climate justice, sustainable food, clean environments, economic equality, green and animal-friendly urban design, female and minority empowerment, transformation away from violent masculinity, indigenous land rights, abolition of slavery, and freedom from unfair imprisonment.

Democratic Reforms. Empower the people to lead governments; in essence, reduce the ability for money to influence politics so elected officials are not beholden to special-interest donors and the financial ties involved with getting reelected. Reinvigorate engaged citizenship and ensure that everyone has the right and ability to conveniently vote. Call for transparency, accountability, and productivity from government agencies (Lappé and Eichen 2017). Strengthen the influence of international governing bodies in an ecologically interdependent world. This includes the need to defend the rights of activists and journalists worldwide who experience violence and harassment at the hands of corrupt governments and industry (Glazebrook and Opoku 2018).

Economic Systemic Reforms. Reform the neoliberal global economic system as well as corporate culture and policies to create a system that is incentivized to support life and share more profits with all stakeholders rather than to maximize profits for shareholders and grow at any cost. It must account for unpaid labor (like work women have traditionally performed, such as childcare, eldercare, meal preparation, vegetable gardening, water procurement, and household cleaning and management) as well as wildlife conservation efforts and investment in clean and healthy environments (Waring 1999). It should interrogate the healthy limits that must be put on capitalism to ensure corporate activities do not continue to overconsume, overpollute, and overexploit our planet, putting all of us at risk for the benefits of a few (Foster, York, and Clark 2011).

Besides GDP, consider other ways to measure a country's productivity, such as the Good Country Index that ranks countries according to how much they give to all other species: "Today, leaders must realise that they're responsible not only for their own people, but for every man, woman, child and animal on the planet; not just responsible for their own slice of territory, but for every square inch of the earth's surface and the atmosphere above it" (thegoodcountry.org).

Biocultural Diversity Protection. Stem the tide of mass extinction of species. Save endangered species and support rewilding projects, protection of whole land and marine habitats, and migration corridors in collaboration with local, indigenous community leadership. Lead efforts for coexistence between human and nonhuman animal cultures. Protect Native peoples and their languages from going extinct.

As an example, biologist E. O. Wilson's Half-Earth Project (half-earthproject
.org) advocates for vast preservation of the earth's land and sea surfaces to adequately enable restoration of lifesaving biodiversity, so humanity more equitably
shares space with the millions of other species on the planet. The Half-Earth Project supports conservation initiatives that are led by indigenous groups. There is
also a consortium of environmental groups that started the Conservation Initiative
on Human Rights (thecihr.org) to integrate human rights into conservation policies. Their scoping paper (Springer and Campese 2011, 27) provides great details
on how to involve and support rural and indigenous communities; it utilizes the
concept of "biocultural diversity" to advance the idea that cultural groups can be
excellent stewards of local biodiversity projects in their home area. An example of
a biocultural diversity group is Canada's Terralingua (terralingua.org), which supports the preservation of Native cultures and languages as part of a vital store of
knowledge about the human connection to the natural world necessary to maintain
our planet's ecocultural health (Maffi and Woodley 2010).

Climate Justice. Naomi Klein (2014) advocates for the climate change movement to be
a rallying movement to create global solidarity for progressive change. SMOs can engage citizens to drastically reduce greenhouse gas emissions across all sources, including animal agribusiness and deforestation, while nations transition to a clean
and renewable energy future. Klein is on the advisory council for the Women's Earth
and Climate Action Network (wecaninternational.org), which engages women, especially indigenous women, as leaders in the movement for global climate justice. To
further support climate justice, we must fight for equitable adaptation to climate crisis across nations and consider how the international community can accommodate
the needs of climate refugees (human and nonhuman). To be egalitarian and avoid
an anthropocentric bias, climate advocacy should emphasize the immense negative
impacts on free-living animals and, thus, what ethical obligations climate-polluting
nations have to repair and restore wildlife livelihoods (Almiron and Faria 2019).

Shift to Sustainable and Fair Food Systems. Phase out the cruel and environmentally
destructive industrial animal farming and fishing practices on (see photos 2–4, 8,
9, and 13). Given the recent corona virus pandemic, there is clearly a need to reduce
humanity's risk of zoonotic diseases from crowding and selling animals. Shift toward systems (including government subsidies and policies) supporting organic,
plant-based foods and "clean meats" (cultured flesh not grown on an individual),
making animal-based food systems less economically viable to match their ecological unviability (Poore and Nemecek 2018; Simon 2013). Help existing animal
agriculture and commercial fishing owners and employees transition to sustainable agricultural jobs or alternative career paths, such as protecting marine reserves
(Kemmerer 2015a; see thetransfarmationproject.org by Mercy for Animals). Interviewee Erich Pica says he could envision fellow environmentalists working in coalition with animal advocates on meat-reduction campaigns. Similarly, interviewee

Sharon Núñez, an animal rights advocate, suggests a coordinated campaign to encourage governments to reduce national meat consumption on the grounds of public health, ecological responsibility, and animal rights. Provide communities equal access to healthy plant-based foods (in schools, markets, and restaurants), and offer agricultural land and veganic farming techniques to communities worldwide to support sustainable and healthy food supplies, supported with fair trade policies.

As examples, the Food Empowerment Project (foodispower.org), run by vegan social justice advocate [L]auren Ornelas, not only promotes plant-based agriculture but also economic policies and conscientious consumerism that protects the rights and well-being of farmworkers. Another innovative nonprofit, Encompass (encompassmovement.org), advocates for a more racially inclusive farmed-animal protection movement. And interviewee Frances Moore Lappé is on the advisory board for Brighter Green, an organization seeking to influence policies worldwide, mainly on food issues, linking sustainability, social equity, and animal welfare. Their programs include combating the growth of factory farms in the Global South and supporting veganism and sustainable food systems in an era of climate crisis.

Restoration of Clean, Healthy Habitats within a Justice Context. Prevent, reduce, and clean up pollution to restore and maintain healthy living spaces/ecosystems, concentrating on protecting poor communities worldwide. Make polluting industries pay for the restoration and health-care costs to affected communities. An example of a coalition approaching human health holistically (in terms of environmental health as well) is the Bridge Collaborative (bridgecollaborativeglobal.org), which works across the health, development, and environmental sectors to share resources to make communities across developing nations healthier and more ecologically sustainable.

Demand natural and organic products free of chemicals. Promote the phase-out of all plastics in support of a biodegradable replacement material. Celebrated artist Pam Longobardi's Drifters Project (driftersproject.net) is an example of plastic ocean cleanup across the world that helps educate and provide some income opportunities for people in affected area (transforming plastic trash into educational art and also into products for sale). Any nonbiodegradable products should be designed with fully recyclable materials along with proactive, convenient recycling programs where the manufacturers lead the efforts rather than consumers bearing all the burdens. To promote natural products and reuse, make landfills and any toxic waste disposal cost-prohibitive while supporting widespread composting of yard and food waste. And for equity in burden sharing, start making wealthier nations and neighborhoods responsible for housing the trash/toxins they produce, thereby incentivizing waste reduction.

Economic Justice and Elimination of Poverty. Make it a goal to eliminate global poverty, including human malnutrition and massive income inequality to better share resources and support people's right to a healthy life and basic necessities (which, in the digital age, includes internet access). Out of a sense of altruism and fairness, provide equitable access to resources and rights to healthy living environments, addressing environmental justice concerns for humans while also respecting the interests of wild animals as ecological citizens who share the earth. Invest in vitalization of poor neighborhoods in each nation to support holistic well-being, equitable education for boys and girls, livelihood opportunities, food security, housing, and sustainable development. For those nonhuman animals who are unable to live on their own and are thus in sanctuaries or otherwise within the care of humans, their fundamental physical and mental health needs should be provided for to avoid an impoverished existence. These campaigns could utilize Pellow's (2014) notion of socio-ecological inequality that recognizes how inequalities, domination, and violence intertwine to negatively affect all species. For example, Moncrief's nonprofit, A Well-Fed World (awfw.org), is a vegan food-relief organization that fights world hunger in ways that also help animals and the environment, such as supporting groups like the Fruit Tree Planting Foundation in Central America (see photo 10). And the anarchist nonprofit Food Not Bombs (foodnotbombs.net) uses vegan food to feed the homeless, reclaiming food that would go to waste. And the U.S. nonprofit My Dog Is My Home (mydogismyhome.org) respects interspecies social bonds by sponsoring a Co-Sheltering Collaborative that helps people who are experiencing homelessness find shelter that also accommodates their nonhuman companion animals.

Sustainable, Equitable, and Animal-Inclusive Urban Design. Advocate for cities to be designed for green living, centered around micro/compact, pleasant, natural light–filled, ecofriendly living spaces in mixed-income neighborhoods, dense enough to reduce urban sprawl and the need for commuting. Focus on accommodating pedestrians and those using bikes and wheelchairs first, mass transit second, and privately owned motor vehicles last (prioritize renewable-energy vehicle-charging stations over gas stations). Incorporate green infrastructure to capture rainwater and reduce flooding, and include shared green spaces and plentiful, native vegetation and tree canopies for wildlife livelihood, beauty, recreation, permaculture, farmers markets, cooling, air quality, and community. Be a 'zoopolis' where culturally diverse human urban-dwellers coexist with diverse urban wildlife, and where nonhuman animal companions are welcome in mass transit and public and commercial buildings.

Empowerment for Women and Minority Groups to Combat Discrimination. Institute antidiscrimination and restitution programs to empower females and historically marginalized ethnic or minority groups and enable them to get a chance to be the majority of leaders in the world's institutions this century. Acknowledge and compensate for unfair privileges based on sex and gender identity, sexual orientation, ethnicity, race, class, and physical ability. Strive for equality in graduation rates, pay, career advancement, and health outcomes for all ethnicities, socioeconomic classes, and gender identities, requiring all organizations to be transparent about any disparities that remain and facilitate a path to improvement. For women and girls, increasing education, career opportunities, leadership roles, and reproductive health care worldwide will provide myriad benefits, including potentially reducing human population growth over time, reducing some of the pressure humanity puts on the environment. The International Union of Conservation of Nature (iucn.org) includes a Global Gender Office because not only is gender equity a human right, it's also a requirement for sustainable development.

It's also important that the environmental movement reflect the gender and racial/ethnic makeup of the human population globally. Organizations like Green 2.0 and WECAN (Women's Earth and Climate Action Network) work for a more inclusive environmental movement where the voices and leadership of women and people of color are recognized. As another example, the Black Mambas Anti-Poaching Unit near Kruger National Park in South Africa is led by a predominantly female local staff of rangers: "It is our belief that the 'war' on poaching will not be won with guns and bullets, but through social up-liftment and the education of local communities surrounding the reserves. The Black Mambas are not only Anti-Poaching Rangers, they are role models who cherish life and do not want to live in a village of orphans and widows" (blackmambas.org). (See photos 11 and 12.)

And to foster new generations of open-minded, caring, and inclusive leaders, support a movement called Humane Education, such as that championed by Zoe Weil and the Institute for Humane Education (humaneeducation.org). It helps develop 'solutionary' thinking in the classroom by addressing social justice, animal protection, and environmental ethics as interrelated issues to get students to recognize multiple inequities and propose humane, just, and sustainable solutions.

Transformation of Masculinity away from Violence. Because much of the world's violence against humans, other animals, and nature is perpetuated by human men (more often than women), social movements should interrogate patriarchy and the various cultural constructions of masculinity, especially hypermasculinity and its association with violence, toughness, control, independence, and rationality at the expense of emotionality and interconnectedness (Adams 1990; Gaard 2014; Katz 2019; Kheel 2008; Luke 2007). In addition to portraying virtuous humans in gender-neutral or queer ways, showcase more compassionate and diverse models of masculinity so those who identify as men see caring/caretaking, compassion, kindness, cooperation, and responsibility as an integral part of their identity (see tables 18 and 20). Consider Facebook groups like "Real Men Are Kind to Animals" that feature daily examples of men displaying kindness to nonhuman animals, and activists (of all genders) within the Save Movement (thesavemovement.org) who provide comfort to animals headed to slaughter (see photos 13 and 14). Vegan Athlete groups for men and women help demonstrate that building muscle and physical prowess is not predicated on killing and eating fellow animals. Strength, for any gender identity, can be expressed in terms of courage to stand up for and support the protection of vulnerable beings of any species.

Create support groups for men to address violence in their own ranks and also to access affordable mental health counseling to receive the emotional support all humans need to flourish (Katz 2019). Provide refuge and rehabilitation for those who have been the victims of violence, such as Ahimsa House (ahimsahouse.org) here in my city of Atlanta, which provides temporary shelter for the companion animals of women who are in domestic violence shelters, enabling both humans and nonhumans to escape an abusive household. Hope Ferdowsian's (2018) book on sanctuaries that rehabilitate traumatized human and nonhuman animals provides many inspiring models of caretaking and peaceful, therapeutic coexistence between species.

A Green Postcolonial and Posthumanist Approach to Indigenous Land Rights. Follow the lead of indigenous and green postcolonial scholars to institute programs to acknowledge injustices and restore certain land rights and sovereignty to Native peoples worldwide, with expectations of environmental stewardship (Huggan and Tiffan 2010). Include posthumanist and animal scholars' insights to ensure that the territorial rights of native and migrating wildlife are also considered (Donaldson and Kymlicka 2013). Marino, a compassionate conservation advocate, notes that nonhuman animal cultures can be indigenous too. One challenge I see to imbuing certain wild animal species and their cultures with the respected status of 'indigenous' is that *nonnative* species, by comparison, are more likely to be discriminated against or killed (as is the case now). To entirely privilege who was here first over who is also here now can create more injustice (and even lead to extermination) if we demonize 'nonnative' sentient beings as 'invasives' who don't belong (for sociopolitical or ecological reasons). Thus, it is necessary to make some accommodation to the needs of all sentient beings (human and nonhuman) who are stakeholders in a geographic region—even considering immigrants and climate refugees—to avoid disrespecting individual liberties when attempting to compensate for past wrongs and create revitalized, diverse, and healthy communities and ecosystems.

The Tiny House Warriors (tinyhousewarriors.com) are leaders from the Secwepemc First Nations tribe in British Columbia whose strategy to defend their unceded territorial land rights is to build tiny homes along a proposed route of an oil pipeline to block access. This project combines sustainable living and needed affordable housing with climate activism and indigenous land rights activism.

Abolition of Enslavement of Sentient Beings. Coordinated campaigns could champion the liberation of human and nonhuman animals held captive or financially entrapped as tools for someone else's gain, emphasizing their status as individual subjects of a life, not objects. All sentient beings have the rights to be self-determining of how their body and labor are used and should have reproductive and sexual freedom to voluntarily mate with consenting adults of their own species and not be bred (or domesticated) by anyone, with reproduction being voluntary for all females. An example of a grassroots organization that aims to overcome inequality and oppression for all beings is the Peace Advocacy Network (peaceadvocacynetwork .org)—a social-justice-oriented grassroots nonprofit in the United States that supports peaceful coexistence for all the earth's inhabitants, including educating people about ethical veganism and solutions to end human trafficking.

Freedom from Unfair Imprisonment for Sentient Beings. While some individuals may merit imprisonment if they have proven to be dangerous or lawbreaking, it is unfair to imprison others because of a *perception* that they are less inherently valuable, more 'criminalistic' or 'wild'—a discriminatory bias perpetuated on many nonhuman animal species and disproportionately on human men of color, both rendered vulnerable to state violence through othering as 'subhuman' (Deckha 2010; Stanescu 2012). All innocent sentient beings deserve freedom of mobility and the right to choose their own companions (and, conversely, not to be kept in solitary confinement) (see photo 5). For guidance, the connection between criminal justice reform and animal liberation is examined in the "Prison and Animals" issue of the *Journal of Critical Animal Studies* (2012), with editors noting the similarities between the prison-industrial complex and the animal-industrial complex and forms of neo-slavery. In that issue, Anthony Nocella (2012) acknowledges: "Just as nonhuman animals are cheap labor and are often property of the State, so too are human prisoners" (124). Liberation campaigns could be combined for getting individuals out of farms, zoos, aquariums, circuses, entertainment facilities, and laboratories, and freeing human political prisoners and the unfairly incarcerated, while also enacting criminal justice and prison reforms that abolish unpaid labor and eliminate race and class prejudices, similar to speciesist prejudices. Support productive rehabilitation of imprisoned people back into society, providing economic and social supports, and return captive wildlife to home habitats or provide them a lifelong home in a nonprofit sanctuary.

Admittedly, this animal-inclusive take on the last three subject issues (indigenous rights, antislavery, anti-imprisonment) all would take courage and finesse for human rights groups to tackle in coalitions with animal protection organizations; it requires open acknowledgment that 'animal' rights issues are related to human rights issues, without belittling the human victims for whom they are advocating. Activists must denote how respecting humans (or some notion of human dignity) does require some different treatment unique to the human species (e.g., clothing, privacy, food, bathroom facilities, religious observances, and cultural etiquette), but that doesn't mean that there aren't similarities in terms of how all sentient beings deserve to have their life, liberty, and primary interests respected. There are plenty of conceptions for why human rights are important that do not rely on notions of human supremacism over other animals or a definition of dignity that is exclusionary to nonhumans (Kymlicka 2018). If being treated 'like an animal' means being abused, chained, left exposed to harsh elements, forced to labor, violated sexually or bred, tamed, or held captive and unfairly imprisoned, then no animal deserves that. In support of human rights coalitions with animal rights groups, Kim (2015, 21) explains that a transformation away from oppressive relationships among all species is necessary: "The answer to neoliberalism's destructive practices and values is not to marginally broaden the category of beneficiaries of this destructiveness but rather, through a critical and transformational politics, to radically restructure our relationship with each other, animals, and the earth outside of domination."

FINAL RECOMMENDATIONS FROM ACTIVISTS INTERVIEWED

To conclude, I summarize some broader recommendations from the activists I interviewed, which seem apropos to my book's overall goals for building solidarity among these lifesaving movements in fostering a human animal earthling identity through values-based campaigns. These activists suggest a focus on (1) supporting individuals (human and nonhuman animals), (2) appealing to altruism (while showing how it benefits all of us), and (3) reframing campaign messages to support your allies in other causes.

Focus on Individuals. To cut through partisan divides, Laurel Sutherlin suggests we "show the bold actions of individuals from the heart," such as a mother bravely sitting in front of a pipeline bulldozer to stop an oil project. If SMOs show ordinary people making themselves vulnerable in defiance of something destructive, that can serve as a motivating image to which everyone can relate. SMOs should give these people, in particular minority communities, a platform to tell their own stories, Carl Soderbergh suggests. To describe the wide applicability to all causes of focusing on individuals, Will Travers explains, "That can be the individual animal, the individual human being, and you know we can scale up individuality to individual species and individual ecosystems or environments." Lori Marino agrees that conservation is about individuals, as every animal population is comprised of individuals, "and they have lives and they have mothers and fathers and children."

Appeal to Altruistic Values. An appeal that is widely relatable and adaptable is MOGO (do the most good and least harm); Zoe Weil contends that everyone can strive for MOGO in their own way. Marino champions the golden rule to do unto others as we would have done to us. In favor of marrying an altruistic and self-interested appeal, Emma Daly contends, "Really, I think the sweet spot is where you can bring together somebody's altruistic feelings toward others and then understanding that treating others well will ultimately benefit you and yours." Ashfaq Khalfan agrees that altruistic appeals to help others also appeal to self-interest, by implicitly asking, "Is this the type of society you want to be? Do you want our society to be an open society? A welcoming society?" Similarly, Maria Rohani says effective campaigns are not just about "helping folks in other parts of the world; it's about creating a society and a world that we all want to live in and that upholds the values that we all believe in."

Create Inclusive Messages to Support Allies across Causes. Regarding strategic communication, Moncrief suggests SMOs become allies or at least not undercut one another's efforts, "not necessarily that you are going to stop your work and work on their issues, but at least not stepping on their toes and undermining their work if you can just do some shifts to your own work in use of language or tactics." Showing similar flexibility and courtesy to other causes, Travers recommends, you must be willing to "reframe your messages in more agreeable ways." And Mustafa Ali encourages activists across causes to have "much more inclusive messages . . . helping people to understand that it's all connected." Ingrid Newkirk proposes a strategic communication suggestion that I think summarizes the solidarity goal of my book: "Each movement's arguments should bolster the other as we move toward a mutual goal."

Research Method

Discourse Analysis Methodology

To help identify overlapping values between the three causes I'm examining (human rights, animal protection, and environmentalism), I wanted to study the campaigns of prominent international social movement organizations (SMOs). So I started by including the ones that are quite well known and fairly large (Amnesty International, PETA, Greenpeace, WWF, the Nature Conservancy, etc.) and then used my knowledge as a longtime activist to identify others that I knew about. I also looked up various lists of SMOs and checked out their websites to see how active and productive they were. I ruled out organizations that were not international in their scope (so the Sierra Club, the Center for Biological Diversity, and the Humane Society of the USA didn't make the cut, for example, since they are primarily United States focused). I also wanted to ensure that, with just five or six SMOs per cause, I was getting enough variety in types of issues being addressed. For example, within the human rights cause, CARE focuses a lot on women's issues and poverty, and Human Rights Watch on LGBTQ issues, and Anti-Slavery International on human enslavement, and Amnesty International on peace and free speech, and Minority Rights Group on indigenous peoples (not that the other groups don't also cover some of these same topics). Within the environmental cause, Oceana and Greenpeace specialize in marine life, and Rainforest Action Network on rainforests, and 350.org on climate change, and the Nature Conservancy on wilderness protection, and Friends of the Earth on environmental justice. And within the animal protection cause, I had animal *rights* groups (Sea Shepherd Conservation Society, PETA, and Animal Equality) that all supported veganism but also worked on various issues and species (wild and domestic); and I also included an animal *welfare* group, IFAW, and a wildlife group, WWF (and Sea Shepherd qualifies here too). The latter two consider themselves 'conservation' organizations, so they could have been counted in the environmental category too. That does skew my overall sample more heavily toward environmental and wildlife issues (rather than a focus on domesticated animals, for example).

To make my critical discourse analysis consistent across all sixteen SMOs' websites, and somewhat manageable in size for a qualitative study, my sample included all the written and visual content on the following parts of each organization's website: the home page, the "about us" mission and values page, the main pages associated with each of the primary issues/campaigns they address, and the most recent news/announcement items for each campaign. Thus, my analysis of their websites does not include everything on all pages of their website and is also limited to a snapshot in time when I gathered this data (usually a particular week or two in 2017 for each SMO, sometime between the months of January and September). The bulk of the values and entities I identified in chapters 4, 5, and 6, and other examples I include in the book, are quite representative of each SMO's main mission and campaigns at that time in 2017. But, as a disclaimer, there would likely be a few additional or different values, and especially different examples, if I had looked at their websites during a different month or year, or if I examined every single page, blog entry, video, and report on their vast websites.

My method of critical discourse analysis is influenced by Stuart Hall (1997) and Teun Van Dijk (2009). Upon reviewing each SMO's campaign pages and reading their messages (including images and videos),* I typed up notes on each SMO's web content (in answering my first few research questions) related to whom they were featuring and how they represented them, and what they were promoting as good versus bad (right versus wrong), noting language choices. These notes averaged between 4,000–6,000 words per SMO. I printed out all the notes and organized them in a three-ring binder in order by human rights groups, animal protection groups, and environmental groups. This allowed me to read through all the notes various times and highlight the best quotes, circle words, make handwritten notations of implicit and explicit values, and designate common trends with colored sticky notes. I also typed up tables categorizing each SMO's virtues and values (these were too specific and numerous to include in the book, but they fed into the book's tables that categorized and synthesized popular values for each cause). That was all very useful in the summer of 2018 when I wrote up each discourse analysis chapter (4, 5, and 6) and listed the main concepts, traits, entities, and behaviors that many of the SMOs valued as good or ideal. To clarify how I broadly constituted a value, it includes:

* Going through the web pages of these sixteen organizations was emotionally draining work to become so educated about all ways that humans, other animals, and nature are being exploited and abused across the planet. I would get sidetracked by doing some of the action items that the SMOs recommended, such as signing climate change petitions, taking a veg pledge, or sending letters to get political prisoners out of jail. It was encouraging to see how the organizations were trying to improve the situations.

- Concepts you might hold dear (e.g., honesty, freedom, friendship, justice)
- Virtues/character traits you could embody (e.g., compassion, integrity, fairness, wisdom)
- Things or entities/beings/organizations that you might value (e.g., family, effective activism, food, health, stable climate, a fair legal system, clean environment)
- Behaviors you could value or appreciate (e.g., protecting the vulnerable, punishing criminals, saving lives, making a difference)

The values categories (life supporting, fair, responsible, and unifying) evolved from my earlier pilot study on global rights declarations (chapter 3), and I determined they were also applicable to the values promoted in the SMO campaign discourses.

Interview Methodology

To have more background on the producers of the campaigns I studied in the discourse analysis, I tried to interview the president of each of the sixteen SMOs in my study, and in five cases that worked. In cases where the president could not be interviewed, I asked to interview a head communications professional at each SMO, as that job fits with the type of strategic communication and language questions I was asking. To round out the insights gained, I also added six prominent activist leaders (from outside the sixteen SMOs in my study) that represented 'intersectional' activist efforts on behalf of human and nonhuman beings. I went through the IRB (Institutional Review Board) process at Georgia State University to gain approval to interview all nineteen activists in ways that are in accordance with respecting their rights as human subjects, having them give informed consent (see the results in chapter 8 and interviewee profiles in appendix B).

I was pleased that each person allowed me to use their real name and to record the interview so I could transcribe it for more accuracy in quoting them. I conducted hour-long interviews by phone in 2018, as it fit people's schedules, asking the same types of questions to each person (Ingrid Newkirk of PETA requested to answer the questions via email, so that was the exception). Like my notes for the discourse analysis, I printed out the interview transcripts and put them in a three-ring binder so I could make notations in writing and with colored stickers.

As a small token of appreciation for the contribution these activists made to my book project, I am giving each interviewee a book, and, unbeknownst to them, I donated twenty dollars to each of the sixteen nonprofits in my sample and to the nonprofits of the six additional activists I interviewed. These SMOs deserve as much support as they can get.

Activist Profiles

This book benefited from the wisdom offered by the following nineteen activists who allowed me to interview them and use their names. I profile them here in alphabetical order with the titles and experience they had when interviewed in late 2017 or early 2018.

Mustafa Ali is the Senior VP of Climate, Environmental Justice, and Community Revitalization at the Hip Hop Caucus in Washington, D.C. Prior to this, Ali worked for twenty-four years at the U.S. Environmental Protection Agency (EPA), quitting in protest during the Trump administration. He joined as a student and became a founding member of the EPA's Office of Environmental Justice, pioneering new educational programs and going on to serve as their Senior Adviser for Environmental Justice and Community Revitalization. In 2010 he served as the Environmental Justice Lead for the BP *Deepwater Horizon* oil spill. Ali has also been an instructor and guest lecturer at many universities, cohosted a social justice radio program, and served several years as a Brookings Institution Congressional Fellow.

Emma Daly is the Communications Director at Human Rights Watch in New York. She received a bachelor of arts in philosophy and literature from the University of East Anglia. She has held the position of Communications Director since 2007, overseeing the organization's media communication output. Daly previously worked as a foreign correspondent for news outlets such as the *New York Times*, the *Independent*, and Reuters, covering Spain, the Balkans, and Costa Rica. Based on her field expertise, she contributed to books such as *Secrets of the Press: The Penguin Book of Journalism* and *Crimes of War: What the Public Should Know*.

Devadass Gnanapragasam is the Deputy Director of Campaigns at Amnesty International in London. He earned his law degree from the University of Madras in Chennai, India. As Deputy Director of Campaigns since September 2009, Gnanapragasam leads global projects related to effective organizing and mobilizing for change and managing a global team of experts in youth empowerment and engagement, active participation, and activism. Before joining Amnesty International in 1985, he worked as the Executive Director at Legal Resources for Social Action in Chennai.

Ginette Hemley is Senior Vice President of Wildlife Conservation at the World Wildlife Fund (WWF) in Washington, D.C. She has a bachelor of science from the College of William & Mary and was an ELIAS Fellow at MIT. At WWF, she oversees programs to secure a future for endangered and iconic species, including the elimination of urgent threats in the wildlife trade; species protection and recovery; and mobilization of public, political, and financial support for conservation. An authority on endangered species and conservation policy over the course of thirty years, Hemley has developed global species-recovery strategies and built solution-focused projects, with partners such as local women's groups and multinational corporations.

Martin Lloyd is the Senior Mobilisation Strategist for Greenpeace Netherlands. He has a master of business administration and a bachelor's in history from Oxford University. At Greenpeace, he works on projects related to corporate accountability and developing binding regulations on transnational corporations. In prior roles at Greenpeace, Lloyd has run global information and communication technology projects and worked as the Global Communications Manager for climate as well as developing Greenpeace's corporate communication strategies.

Ashfaq Khalfan, PhD, is the Director of Law and Policy for Amnesty International in London. He has a doctor of philosophy in law from Exeter College at Oxford University. In his position, he focuses on issues of access to clean water and sanitation while advancing social justice issues. Before assuming his current role, Khalfan worked as a policy coordinator on legal enforcement of economic, social, and cultural rights with Amnesty International. Using his expertise, he has contributed to approximately twenty books, articles, and reports, including *From Promises to Delivery: Putting Human Rights at the Heart of the Millennium Development Goals* and *Global Justice, State Duties: The Extraterritorial Scope of Economic, Social, and Cultural Rights in International Law*.

Frances Moore Lappé is the Co-founder and Co-president at Small Planet Institute, which she runs with her daughter Anna in Massachusetts. The author of nineteen books on environmentalism, world hunger, and democracy, she first became well known in 1971 for her best-selling book *Diet for a Small Planet*, which the Smithsonian's National History Museum described as "one of the most influential political tracts of the time." Lappé has earned many awards for her food advocacy, including a Right Livelihood Award in 1987 and the James Beard Foundation Humanitarian of the Year Award in 2008. Lappé has served as a visiting scholar at universities world-wide and has earned honorary doctorates from eighteen universities.

Lori Marino, PhD, is Co-founder and President of the Whale Sanctuary Project and Founder and Executive Director of the Kimmela Center for Animal Advocacy in Utah. She earned a doctorate in biopsychology from SUNY Albany in 1995. Formerly a faculty member at Emory University in Atlanta, Marino is a neuroscientist and expert in animal behavior and intelligence. Internationally known for her work on the evolution of the brain and intelligence in dolphins and whales, she has more than 130 peer-reviewed publications. Marino coauthored a groundbreaking study in 2001 offering the first conclusive evidence for mirror self-recognition in bottlenose dolphins, after which she decided against further research with captive animals for ethical reasons and has become an outspoken critic of the captivity industry (including being featured in the documentary *Blackfish*).

Dawn Moncrief is Founder and President of A Well Fed World in Washington, D.C. She has two master's degrees, in international relations and women's studies, from George Washington University. After working in vegan advocacy at the Farm Animal Rights Movement, Moncrief founded A Well Fed World as a hunger relief and farmed animal advocacy organization that provides grants globally to vegan feeding/farming programs in low-income communities as part of broader efforts worldwide to empower food justice and mitigate climate change through plant-based foods. Moncrief also serves as Board Advisor for partnering organizations such as International Fund for Africa, Grow Where You Are, Help Animals India, Brighter Green, Beyond Carnism, and Food for Life Global.

Ingrid Newkirk is President of People for the Ethical Treatment of Animals in Virginia, a nonprofit she co-founded in 1980 and has developed into the largest and most well-known animal rights group in the world, with offices in many nations. For decades, Newkirk has spoken internationally on animal rights issues, from the steps of the Canadian Parliament to the streets of New Delhi, India, where she spent her childhood. Early in her career, she worked in law enforcement as an anticruelty officer. Newkirk has authored more than ten books, including *Free the Animals*, *Making Kind Choices* and *Fifty Awesome Ways Kids Can Help Animals*. A provocative media figure, Newkirk was the subject of the HBO documentary *I Am an Animal*. She has been honored with many awards, including being an inaugural inductee into the Animal Rights Hall of Fame in 2000.

Sharon Núñez is President of Animal Equality International, based in Los Angeles. As a vegan advocate, Núñez and her two co-founders started Animal Equality to protect animals, with an emphasis on ending cruelty to farmed animals; founded in Spain as Igualdad Animal in 2006, it now has offices in eight countries and is recognized as a top-rated advocacy organization by Animal Charity Evaluators. On behalf of Animal Equality's investigations, open rescues, and provocative street demonstrations, Núñez speaks internationally at conferences and in mainstream media platforms, including CNN, BBC, the Guardian, and El País. She is also the coeditor of "LiberAnima," a book collection that promotes animal rights in Spanish-speaking countries.

Erich Pica is President and CEO for Friends of the Earth (FOE) USA, in Washington, D.C. He has a bachelor's from Western Michigan University, studying political science, environmental studies, and economics, and has expertise in clean energy policies and energy subsidies. Under his tenure, FOE membership grew to a million supporters across all fifty states. Prior to becoming President in 2009, Pica served as FOE's Director of Domestic Programs. He works to build coalitions for climate justice and believes that the solution to climate change involves racial justice, focusing on indigenous and grassroots advocacy. Active both in protests and in many environmental organization boards and committees, Pica was named by the Washingtonian as one of Washington's "40 under 40: New Generation of Lobbyists."

Maria Rohani is the Social Movements Advisor for CARE USA in Brooklyn, New York. She has a master's in human rights studies from Columbia University and a bachelor's in peace and conflict studies and political science from University of California, Berkeley. Her master's thesis examined the relationship between the international human rights system and the Black Lives Matter movement. At CARE, she works on the Policy and Advocacy team, where she leads CARE's strategy for engaging with social movement actors and grassroots leaders in the United States and internationally. In 2017 Rohani also co-founded the photography campaign #BanThis in response to Trump's executive order limiting travel into the United States by nationals from seven Muslim-majority countries. This campaign showcases the diverse stories of the immigrant experience inherent to many in the United States.

Carl Soderbergh is the Director of Policy and Communications for Minority Rights Group International in London. Working in this position since 2009, he often speaks on behalf of minority issues at United Nations forums and to the media in response to MRG's State of the World's Minorities and Indigenous Peoples reports. A professional advocate for human rights, Soderbergh previously worked for Amnesty International in Sweden and assisted in opening Amnesty's office in Afghanistan. He also worked for the UNHCR (the United Nations High Commissioner for Refugees) in Pakistan and Sudan.

Laurel Sutherlin is the Senior Communication Strategist for the Rainforest Action Network (RAN) in California. He has a bachelor's in history and environmental education from Prescott College. Sutherlin works on all of RAN's campaigns in message development, communication strategy, content writing, and media relations. He is a naturalist, environmental educator, and lifelong activist for environmentalism and human rights, with decades of experience using bold and creative tactics to nonviolently stand up to some of the most powerful forces on the planet that are destroying nature and oppressing people.

Mark Tercek is the President and CEO of the Nature Conservancy in Virginia, the world's largest conservation NGO. He received an MBA from Harvard University in 1984. Tercek became the head of the Nature Conservancy in 2008, inspired by the opportunity to help businesses, governments, and environmental organizations work together in innovative ways. He previously worked for twenty-four years in finance as a managing director and partner at Goldman Sachs. Tercek is the author of the best-selling book *Nature's Fortune: How Business and Society Thrive by Investing in Nature*. He is active on many boards and councils. In 2016 President Barack Obama appointed Tercek to the President's Advisory Committee for Trade Policy and Negotiations.

Will Travers, OBE, is Co-Founder and President of the Born Free Foundation, Born Free USA. In 1984 he founded the Born Free Foundation with his parents, who starred in the 1966 film *Born Free* (about the rehabilitation of an orphaned lioness, Elsa, back into the wild). Travers is also President of the Species Survival Network, an international coalition of more than one hundred organizations committed to the promotion and strict enforcement of CITES (Convention on the International Trade in Endangered Species of Wild Fauna and Flora) and has participated in every CITES meeting since 1989. He conducts wild animal rescues and advises the UK government on matters relating to captive wildlife and the wildlife trade. In 2012 Queen Elizabeth honored Travers for his animal protection work with an OBE designation (Officer of the Most Excellent Order of the British Empire).

Captain Paul Watson is the Founder and President of the Sea Shepherd Conservation Society in Canada. After having left Greenpeace as one of their original members working on anti-sealing and whaling campaigns, Watson founded Sea Shepherd in 1977 as a direct action conservation movement to protect sea animals. He has served as master and commander of seven different Sea Shepherd ships and is recognizable from his appearances on seven seasons of the Animal Planet television documentary series *Whale Wars*, profiling Sea Shepherd's actions against the Japanese whaling fleet on the high seas. Some of Watson's many honors include being inducted into the Animal Rights Hall of Fame (2002), being chosen as a twentieth-century environmental hero by *Time* magazine (2000), and receiving President George H. W. Bush's Daily Points of Light Award (1999).

Zoe Weil is Co-founder and President for the Institute for Humane Education in Maine. She has a master's in theological studies from Harvard Divinity School (1988), a master's and bachelor's in English literature from the University of Pennsylvania, and is a certified psychosynthesis counselor. Weil created the first humane education certificate program and master of education in humane education in the United States. She is the author of multiple TEDx talks and seven books, including *Most Good Least Harm*, the Nautilus Book Award Silver Winner for 2010. As a pioneer in humane education, Weil was inducted into the Animal Rights Hall of Fame in 2010, and, in 2012, she was honored with the Women in Environmental Leadership award at Unity College.

NOTES

Introduction

1. Environmentalist Derrick Jensen (2016) argues that calling this era the Anthropocene ("the age of man"), while meant to be pejorative, sounds benign or even narcissistic, when the name should more adequately reflect our destructiveness. He prefers the term Sociopocene to represent the sociopathic genocides and ecocides perpetrated by certain human cultures in this era (270–272).

2. One exception can be "invasive species" that begin to obliterate competitive species, coming to dominate an ecosystem, threatening its diversity.

3. In his book *Sapiens: A Brief History of Humankind*, Yuval Noah Harari (2015) argues that *Homo sapiens'* unique ability to tell fictional stories created humanity's belief in god(s) and over the years culminated in our belief that we *are* god. He thinks this master narrative is what will end our species as we know it because we will genetically reengineer *Homo sapiens* into something unnatural (or a different species), as we do to other species.

4. Weil (2014) sees values-based education as a foundational part of other systemic changes: "As we infuse humane education into all levels of society, and focus on true campaign finance reform so that legislators are not beholden to their corporate funders, it will become easier to change corporate charters, to reform capitalism, and to put the true costs of products, foods, and clothing (among other things) where they belong—with the producer" (300).

5. I do acknowledge the downside of depending on SMOs to enact change, based in part on sociologists' resource mobilization theory and its critiques of how fractured and self-serving SMOs can be as they grow in size and often become more moderate; competition for funding may limit their willingness in some cases to collectively work in solidarity with other organizations to create a mass movement (Pendergrast 2014).

6. I recognize that wildlife conservation is perhaps most essential, even though most of my own activism and scholarship is spent advocating for animal liberation from agribusiness. But I do believe vegan advocacy is a necessary component of conservation, as animal agribusiness does disproportionately contribute to most forms of environmental degradation (Poore and Nemecek 2018), which ultimately affects all humans and nonhumans (Freeman 2014).

7. I do want to acknowledge the posthumanist scholars' concerns that humanism is antithetical to animal rights in many ways, posing a legitimate philosophical tension (see Calarco 2008; Derrida and Roudinesco 2004). I address this in chapters 1 and 2.

8. The next chapter will cover *how* various social movement groups can work together and overcome their differences while capitalizing on similarities.

Chapter 1. Literature and Thoughts on Identifying Common Values between Different Social Movements

1. Robert Brulle (2010) argues against framing strategies as a top-down, one-way approach to environmental communication and instead promotes dialogic approaches that motivate civic engagement. However, I believe that campaigns framed to promote certain values that invoke the best of human character can inspire the widespread democratic participation Brulle advocates.

2. The exception was that cultures where very large families were common ranked conformity first.

3. An oversight is that their self-transcendent values typology leaves out sentientism (inherent value for nonhuman animal individuals). In fact, an exploratory study by Dietz, Allen, and McCright (2017, 120) indicates that in relation to values-orientations for environmental decision-making, "concern for animals" is a separate value that should be added, as animal-focused values are complementary to yet distinct from biospheric altruism.

4. Note that when I use the term *altruism* in this book (outside of this Steg and DeGroot study), I am not limiting it to concern only for humans. I mean to imply that altruistic people care about helping others (which can include nonhuman animals) in contrast to being primarily self-centered.

5. This may be more anxiety-producing for people who live in degraded or unhealthy environments (Clayton 2012).

6. I don't know the exact origin of the term *humanimal*, but William Mitchell used it in the introduction to Cary Wolfe's (2003) book, and there is also a posthumanist journal named *Humanimalia*. Chapter 2 on deconstructing the human/animal dualism also expands on the usefulness of *humanimality*.

7. For example, for information on leftist political movement alliances of the 1960s, 1970s, and 1980s in North and Central America that formed across racial justice, feminist, indigenous, antinuclear, animal protection, and environmental fronts, see Colling, Parson, and Arrigoni (2014) and Epstein (1993), such as the origin story of the multifaceted anarchist service group Food Not Bombs. Also see Van Dyke and McCammon's 2010 anthology on SMO strategic alliances.

8. I am tempted to say 'pro-life' or 'pro-choice' for animals, as those are fitting terms for what animal rights affirms, but these terms are too closely associated with the U.S. debates over women's reproductive rights.

9. Consider this quote from scholar Steve Best (2014) in his book on total liberation: "Earthworms, dung beetles, butterflies, and bees are far more important to the integrity and diversity of nature than humans are—the latter being the only species one could remove from earth ecosystems with positive effect. From an ecological perspective, humans are an overpopulated, parasitic swarm, living in total ignorance of natural 'laws' they foolishly think they can master, but in truth must conform to and harmonize with if they intend to survive." (120).

10. Mainstream environmental philosophies and discourses tend to be anthropocentric, but some, such as deep ecology and species egalitarianism, explicitly question human exceptionalism (see Devall and Sessions 1985; Dryzek 2013; Taylor 1993).

11. Faria and Paez (2019) argue that animal ethics and mainstream environmental ethics are logically incompatible, and environmental viewpoints that inconsistently privilege human sentient individuals but negatively intervene in the lives of nonhuman sentient individuals should be rejected in favor of antispeciesist viewpoints that show concern for well-being. The authors also favor positive interventions to reduce wild animal suffering (a moral consideration we offer to humans suffering from natural disasters). Because I agree that some fundamental moral inconsistencies between the animal and eco philosophies exist, in my book I am calling for a transformation in environmental viewpoints to incorporate moral consideration

for sentient individuals (i.e., animal rights and compassionate conservation principles), similar to how human rights have been incorporated in environmentalism. To increase compatibility, Kemmerer (2019) suggests both animal and earth activists draw upon ecofeminism and indigenous principles emphasizing species equality and interconnection of humans and the natural world.

12. This does not mean humans should interfere with natural processes of predation from carnivorous or omnivorous wild animals trying to survive.

13. In his contention that our legal treatment of nonhuman animals constitutes a war on animals, Dinesh Wadiwel (2009, 291) describes animal welfare as "a way to blunt the full force of violence (to remove apparent pain and distress, to enable continuing nutrition, to enable a degree of physical movement) even if a right to a domination until death remains a continuing prerogative."

14. Pellow (2014) advocates for anarchism because he describes how the state has managed humans in a way that causes inequalities and only benefits elites.

15. I have not seen animal rights stickers that convey this broader "live and let live" message, but I believe part of merging animal rights with environmentalism is to embrace animal rights' core emphasis on animal liberation—freeing animals from negative human interference and domestication (see L. Hall 2010; Kheel 2008; Nibert 2013; Regan 1983). Ecofeminist Marti Kheel (2008) claims, "Often the most caring thing we can do for other-than-human animals is to leave them alone" (226). Similarly, Tom Regan (1983) states: "With regard to wild animals, the general policy recommended by the rights view is: let them be!" (361). This principle of respecting animal agency and independence was inspirational to the title of Lee Hall's (2010) animal rights book *On Their Own Terms*. However, Donaldson and Kymlicka (2011) contend that we cannot just leave all nonhuman animals alone; we also must coexist, as some free-living animals will always be denizens/residents in urban culture with a closer relationship to, and in some cases dependence upon, humans. They say the key to animal rights is not to eliminate all kinds of human-animal interactions but to focus on "prohibiting exploitative relationships" (10), ensuring that relations are "respectful and mutually enriching" (10). This is reminiscent of principles of social justice and environmental ethics.

Chapter 2. Posthumanist Philosophies Challenging the Human/Animal Dualism

An earlier version of this chapter was published as a book chapter in Goodale and Black's *Arguments about Animal Ethics* (Freeman 2010b). Reproduced with permission of the licensor through PLSclear.

1. I define *posthuman* as a new ideology that envisions the human as an animal in a larger ecological community where humans no longer privilege their own species and society as a wholly separate and superior category and begin to include themselves as one among other animated subjects (as opposed to envisioning other living beings as objects devoid of perspective). I believe posthumanism incorporates the human rights goals of humanism and struggles to blend them with concerns for animal rights and environmentalism.

2. The term *infrahuman* is used by Derrida and by Wolfe, and William J. T. Mitchell uses the term *humanimal* in the foreword to Wolfe's book. See Wolfe, *Animal Rites* (2003), xiii; and Derrida, "Eating Well," (1995), 255–287.

3. See the style guidelines and thesaurus in Dunayer (2001) and the terminology guide for journalists at www.animalsandmedia.org.

4. Consider how the feminist dictionary functions for the women's movement to combat the patriarchy inherent in terms like *mankind* or *chairman* (Kramarae and Treichler 1985).

5. American attorney Steven Wise and the Nonhuman Rights Project use a similar rationale for seeking legal personhood status for a nonhuman being, focusing on beloved mammals

like chimpanzees and elephants. This is considered a logical first step for other species to attain similar legal status as persons not objects.

6. For instruction, see an article I coauthored with biologists instructing journalists how to incorporate the animal voice (Freeman, Bekoff, and Bexell 2011).

7. See Balcombe, *Pleasurable Kingdom* (2006); Fouts, *Next of Kin* (1997); Friend, *Animal Talk* (2004); Masson and McCarthy, *When Elephants Weep* (1995); Page, *Inside the Animal Mind* (1999); and Bekoff and Pierce, *Wild Justice* (2009).

Chapter 3. Pilot Study

1. A version of this pilot study is also published as "Perceiving Ecocultural Identities as Human Animal Earthlings," chapter 26 in the anthology *Routledge Handbook of Ecocultural Identity*, edited by Tema Milstein and José Castro-Sotomayor (New York: Routledge, 2020), 431–444.

2. I am not conducting a full critical discourse analysis that seeks to interrogate the distinctions, goals, and claims of these documents in sociohistorical context. I am being more utilitarian in mining them for indications of whom and what we value.

3. For this question, I was less interested in parsing out differences between the *declarations* but rather in parsing out different values emphasized between *causes* (environmental versus nonhuman animal versus human causes). So I used the human rights declaration as representing human rights causes, the two animal rights declarations as representing animal rights causes, and the remaining three environmental declarations as representing environmental causes. This is, of course, imperfect in the sense that these three types of causes are interrelated, not mutually exclusive, and thus all declarations incorporated human rights with the rights of nonhuman life, especially the Principles for Environmental Justice (with the exception of the UN Human Rights Declaration, which was exclusive in its focus on humans).

4. In these sections where I answer research questions on values, I often put the values in italics.

5. *Education* is mainly a global human rights value meant to provide equal opportunity, but the 1989 Animal Rights Declaration encouraged the education of children as a way to create citizens who are understanding and respectful toward animals.

6. I did not indicate that "killing" per se was a universally condemned action by all three causes, although it was mentioned by some declarations and it could be implied by all the declarations' emphasis on nonviolence, well-being, and life. But the wrongness of killing is likely muddled by its necessity in some cases (in human and nonhuman culture), such as for self-defense (including nourishment for carnivores) or as deserved punishment. So the general notion of condemning harm is mitigated by that harm being considered excessive or unnecessary.

7. Here I draw on scholarship defining and comparing these movements' philosophies, such as Adams 1990; Jamieson 2002; Kemmerer 2015a; Kheel 2008; Regan 2002; Sagoff 1993; Sandler and Pezzullo 2007; Taylor 1993; Varner 1998.

8. The values of *courage* and *imagination* were inspired by Lappé's (2011) book *EcoMind* and Moore and Nelson's (2010, 192) list of virtues needed for sustainable flourishing.

9. Some of the primary philosophy to overtly blend environmentalism with civil rights and animal rights is the pioneering work of ecofeminist animal rights scholars like Adams (1990) and Kheel (2008).

10. This could also be framed in a postcolonial sense for more industrialized human cultures to gain more respect for the sustainability and wisdom of so-called primitive human cultures that live a more natural existence. And for a discussion of nonhuman animals as ethical beings, see Bekoff and Pierce (2009).

REFERENCES

Abram, David. 1997. *The Spell of the Sensuous: Perception and Language in a More-Than-Human World*. New York: Vintage Books.

Adams, Carol J. 1990. *The Sexual Politics of Meat: A Feminist-Vegetarian Critical Theory*. New York: Continuum.

Adams, Carol J. 2014. "Foreword: Connecting the Dots." In *Circles of Compassion: Essays Connecting Issues of Justice*, edited by Will Tuttle, 10–18. Danvers, Mass.: Vegan.

Adams, Carol J., and Josephine Donovan. 1995. *Animals and Women: Feminist Theoretical Explanations*. Durham, N.C.: Duke University Press.

Agamben, Giorgio. 2004. *The Open: Man and Animal*. Trans. Kevin Attell. Stanford, Calif.: Stanford University Press.

Agyeman, Julian. 2007. "Communicating 'Just Sustainability.'" *Environmental Communication* 1(2): 119–122.

Agyeman, Julian. 2013. *Introducing Just Sustainabilities*. London: Zed Books.

Almiron, Núria, and Catia Faria. 2019. "Climate Change Impacts on Free-Living Nonhuman Animals: Challenges for Media and Communication Ethics." *Studies in Media and Communication* 7(1): 37–48.

Almiron, Núria, and Marta Tafalla. 2019. "Rethinking the Ethical Challenge in the Climate Deadlock: Anthropocentrism, Ideological Denial and Animal Liberation." *Journal of Agricultural and Environmental Ethics*. https://doi.org/10.1007/s10806-019-09772-5.

Alvaro, Carlo. 2019. *Ethical Veganism, Virtue Ethics, and the Great Soul*. Lanham, Md.: Lexington Books.

Andersen, Kip, and Keegan Kuhn. 2014. *Cowspiracy: The Sustainability Secret*. Documentary. www.cowspiracy.com.

Anderson, Will. 2012. *This Is Hope: Green Vegans and the New Human Ecology*. Winchester, UK: Earth Books.

Armstrong, Philip. 2002. "The Postcolonial Animal." *Society and Animals* 10(4): 413–419.

Atapattu, Sumudu. 2018. "Extractive Industries and Inequality: Intersections of Environmental Law, Human Rights, and Environmental Justice." *Arizona State Law Journal* 50(2): 431–454.

Balcombe, Jonathan. 2006. *Pleasurable Kingdom: Animals and the Nature of Feeling Good*. New York: Palgrave.

Bardi, Anat, and Shalom Schwartz. 2003. "Values and Behavior: Strength and Structure of Relations." *Personality and Social Psychology Bulletin* 29(10): 1207–1220.

Becker, Ernest. 1973. *The Denial of Death*. New York: Free Press.

Beers, Diane. 2006. *For the Prevention of Cruelty: The History and Legacy of Animal Rights Activism in the United States*. Athens: Ohio University Press.

Beierlein, Constanze, Anabel Kuntz, and Eldad Davidov. 2016. "Universalism, Conservation and Attitudes toward Minority Groups." *Social Science Research* 58 (July): 68–79.

Bekoff, Marc. 2013. *Ignoring Nature No More: The Case for Compassionate Conservation*. Chicago: University of Chicago Press.

Bekoff, Marc, and Jessica Pierce. 2009. *Wild Justice: The Moral Lives of Animals*. Chicago: University of Chicago Press.

Belcourt, Billy-Ray. 2015. "Animal Bodies, Colonial Subjects: (Re)Locating Animality in Decolonial Thought." *Societies* 5: 1–11.

Best, Steven. 2014. *The Politics of Total Liberation: Revolution for the 21st Century*. Gordonsville, Va.: Palgrave Macmillan.

Birke, Lynda, and Luciana Parisi. 1999. "Animals Becoming." In *Animal Others: On Ethics, Ontology, and Animal Life*, edited by H. Peter Steeves. Albany: State University of New York Press.

Bormann, Ernest G. 1971. *Forerunners of Black Power: The Rhetoric of Abolition*. Englewood Cliffs, N.J.: Prentice-Hall.

Brockhoff, Gene. 2010. *Shop 'Til You Drop: The Crisis of Consumerism*. Documentary. Northampton, Mass.: Media Education Foundation.

Brulle, Robert J. 2010. "From Environmental Campaigns to Advancing the Public Dialog: Environmental Communication for Civic Engagement." *Environmental Communication* (4)1: 82–98.

Bullard, Robert D. 2005. *The Quest for Environmental Justice: Human Rights and the Politics of Pollution*. San Francisco: Sierra Club Books.

Burke, Peter J., and Jan E. Stets. 2009. *Identity Theory*. Oxford: Oxford University Press.

Calarco, Matthew. 2008. *Zoographies: The Question of the Animal from Heidegger to Derrida*. New York: Columbia University Press.

Callicott, J. Baird. 1993. "The Conceptual Foundations of the Land Ethic." In *Environmental Philosophy: From Animal Rights to Radical Ecology*, edited by Michael E. Zimmerman, 110–134. Englewood Cliffs, N.J.: Prentice-Hall.

Campbell, Karlyn Kohrs. 1989. *Man Cannot Speak for Her*. New York: Greenwood Press.

Cantor, David. 2014. "Beyond Humanism, toward a New Animalism." In *Circles of Compassion: Essays Connecting Issues of Justice*, edited by Will Tuttle, 22–36. Danvers, Mass.: Vegan.

Carson, Rachel. 1962. *Silent Spring*. Boston: Houghton Mifflin.

Castells, Manuel. 2010. *The Power of Identity*. 2nd ed. Malden, Mass.: Blackwell.

Cavalieri, Paola, and Peter Singer. 1993. "Preface and a Declaration on Great Apes." In *The Great Ape Project: Equality beyond Humanity*, edited by Paola Cavalieri and Peter Singer, 1–7. New York: St. Martin's Press.

Chagani, Fayaz. 2016. "Can the Postcolonial Animal Speak?" *Society and Animals* 24: 619–637.

Chilton, Paul, Tom Crompton, Tim Kasser, Greg Maio, and Alex Nolan. 2012. "Communicating Bigger-Than-Self Problems to Extrinsically-Oriented Audiences." Common Cause Interdisciplinary Research Report. Retrieved from www.valuesandframes.org/downloads.

Christians, Clifford. 2008. "Universals and the Human." In *Communication Ethics: Between Cosmopolitanism and Provinciality*, edited by Kathleen G. Roberts and Roger C. Arnett, 5–21. New York: Peter Lang.

Clark, Stephen R. L. 1988. "Is Humanity A Natural Kind?" In *What Is an Animal?*, edited by Tim Ingold, 17–34. London: Unwin Hyman.

Clark, Stephen R. L. 1993. "Apes and the Idea of Kindred." In *The Great Ape Project: Equality Be-*

yond Humanity, edited by Paola Cavalieri and Peter Singer, 113–125. New York: St. Martin's Press.

Clayton, Susan D. 2008. "Attending to Identity: Ideology, Group Membership, and Perceptions of Justice." In Justice, edited by Karen A. Hegtvedt and Jody Clay-Warner, 25:241–266. Bingley, West Yorkshire: JAI Press.

Clayton, Susan D. 2012. "Environment and Identity." In The Oxford Handbook of Environmental and Conservation Psychology, edited by Susan D. Clayton, 164–180. New York: Oxford University Press.

Colling, Sarat, Sean Parson, and Alessandro Arrigoni. 2014. "Until All Are Free: Total Liberation through Revolutionary Decolonization, Groundless Solidarity, and a Relationship Framework." Counterpoints 448: 51–73.

Collins, Patricia Hill. 2000. Black Feminist Thought. New York: Routledge.

Connell, Raewyn. 2007. Southern Theory. Cambridge: Polity Press.

Corbett, Julia. 2006. Communicating Nature: How We Create and Understand Environmental Messages. Washington, D.C.: Island Press.

Costello, Kimberly, and Gordon Hodson. 2010. "Exploring the Roots of Dehumanization: The Role of Animal-Human Similarity in Promoting Immigrant Humanization." Group Processes and Intergroup Relations 13: 3–22.

Costello, Kimberly, and Gordon Hodson. 2014. "Explaining Dehumanization among Children: The Interspecies Model of Prejudice." British Journal of Social Psychology 53(1): 175–197.

Cox, Robert. 2006. Environmental Communication and the Public Sphere. Thousand Oaks, Calif.: Sage.

Crompton, Tom. 2008. Weathercocks and Signposts: The Environmental Movement at a Crossroads. World Wildlife Fund-UK, Strategies for Change Project. Retrieved from wwf.org.uk/strategiesforchange.

Crompton, Tom, and Tim Kasser. 2009. Meeting Environmental Challenges: The Role of Human Identity. Surrey, UK: WWF-UK.

Davies, Kate. 2015. The Rise of the U.S. Environmental Health Movement. New York: Rowman & Littlefield.

Day, Richard. 2005. Gramsci Is Dead: Anarchist Currents in the Newest Social Movements. London: Pluto.

Deckha, Maneesha. 2010. "The Subhuman as a Cultural Agent of Violence." Journal for Critical Animal Studies 3(3): 28–51.

Deckha, Maneesha. 2012. "Towards a Postcolonial, Posthumanist Feminist Theory: Centralizing Race and Culture in Feminist Work on Nonhuman Animals." Hypatia 27(3): 527–545.

Deemer, Danielle, and Linda Lobao. 2011. "Public Concern for Farm Animal Welfare: Religion, Politics, and Human Disadvantage in the Food Sector." Rural Sociology 76(2): 167–196.

Deleuze, Gilles, and Félix Guattari. 2004. "Becoming Animal." In Animal Philosophy: Ethics and Identity, edited by Matthew Calarco and Peter Atterton, 87–100. New York: Continuum.

Derrida, Jacques. 1995. "Eating Well, or the Calculation of the Subject." In Points . . . Interviews, 1974–1994, edited by Elisabeth Weber, trans. Peter Conner and Avital Ronell, 255–287. Stanford, Calif.: Stanford University Press.

Derrida, Jacques. 2002. "The Animal That Therefore I Am (More to Follow)," trans. David Willis. Critical Inquiry 28(2): 369–418.

Derrida, Jacques, and Elisabeth Roudinesco. 2004. For What Tomorrow: A Dialogue, trans. Jeff Fort. Stanford, Calif.: Stanford University Press.

Devall, Bill, and George Sessions. 1985. *Deep Ecology: Living as if Nature Mattered.* Salt Lake City, Utah: Peregrine Smith Books.

Diamond, Jared M. 1992. *The Third Chimpanzee: The Evolution and Future of the Human Animal.* New York: HarperCollins.

Diamond, Jared M. 2005. *Collapse: How Societies Choose to Fail or Succeed.* New York: Viking.

Dietz, Thomas, Summer Allen, and Aaron McCright. 2017. "Integrating Concern for Animals into Personal Values." *Anthrozoos* 30(1): 109–122.

Dodson, Michael. 1997. "Land Rights and Social Justice." In *Our Land Is Our Life,* edited by Galarrwuy Yunupingu, 39–51. Brisbane: University of Queensland Press.

Donaldson, Sue, and Will Kymlicka. 2011. *Zoopolis: A Political Theory of Animal Rights.* Oxford: Oxford University Press.

Donaldson, Sue, and Will Kymlicka. 2016. "Comment: Between Wild and Domesticated: Rethinking Categories and Boundaries in Response to Animal Agency." In *Animal Ethics in the Age of Humans,* edited by Bernice Bovenkerk and Jozef Keulartz, 225–239. New York: Springer International.

Donovan, Josephine, and Carol Adams. 2007. *The Feminist Care Tradition in Animal Ethics.* New York: Columbia University Press.

Dryzek, John. 2013. *The Politics of the Earth: Environmental Discourses.* Oxford: Oxford University Press.

Dunayer, Joan. 2001. *Animal Equality: Language and Liberation.* Derwood, Md.: Ryce.

The Earth Charter Initiative. 2000. The Earth Charter. Retrieved from www.earthcharterin action.org/content/pages/Read-the-Charter.html.

EAT-Lancet. 2019. "Food in the Anthropocene: The EAT-Lancet Commission on Healthy Diets from Sustainable Food Systems." *The Lancet* 393(10170): 447–492. https://eatforum .org/eat-lancet-commission.

Elstein, Daniel. 2003. "Species as a Social Construction: Is Species Morally Relevant?" *Animal Liberation Philosophy and Policy Journal* 1(1): 1–19.

Epstein, Barbara. 1993. *Political Protest and Cultural Revolution: Nonviolent Direct Action in the 1970s and 1980s.* Los Angeles: University of California Press.

Erenberg, Debra. 2015. "Enforcing Human Rights for People, Animals, and the Planet." In *Animals and the Environment: Advocacy, Activism, and the Quest for Common Ground,* edited by Lisa Kemmerer, 239–248. New York: Earthscan.

Essemlali, Lamya, with Paul Watson. 2013. *Captain Paul Watson: Interview with a Pirate.* Richmond Hill, Ont.: Firefly Books.

FAO. 2006. "Livestock a Major Threat to Environment." Report of the Food and Agriculture Organization of the United Nations (November 29). www.fao.org/newsroom/en/ news/2006/1000448/index.html.

Faria, Catia, and Eze Paez. 2019. "It's Splitsville: Why Animal Ethics and Environmental Ethics Are Incompatible." *American Behavioral Scientist* 63(8): 1047–1060.

Ferdowsian, Hope. 2018. *Phoenix Zones: Where Strength Is Born and Resilience Lives.* Chicago: University of Chicago Press.

Fisher, Linda. 2011. "Freeing Feathered Spirits." In *Sister Species: Women, Animals and Social Justice,* edited by Lisa Kemmerer, 110–116. Champaign: University of Illinois Press.

Fitzgerald, Amy. 2018. *Animal Advocacy and Environmentalism: Understanding and Bridging the Divide.* Cambridge: Polity Press.

Foss, Sonja K., Karen A. Foss, and Robert Trapp. 1991. *Contemporary Perspectives on Rhetoric.* 2nd ed. Prospect Heights, Ill.: Waveland Press.

Foster, John Bellamy, Brett Clark, and Richard York. 2011. *The Ecological Rift: Capitalism's War on the Earth.* New York: Monthly Review Press.

Foucault, Michel. 1980. *Power/Knowledge*. Brighton, Sussex: Harvester Press.

Foucault, Michel. 1990. "From *The Order of Discourse*." In *The Rhetorical Tradition: Readings from Classical Times to the Present*, edited by Patricia Bizzell and Bruce Herzberg, 1154–1164. Boston: Bedford Books.

Francione, Gary L. 1996. *Rain without Thunder: The Ideology of the Animal Rights Movement*. Philadelphia: Temple University Press.

Freeman, Carrie P. 2007. "Who's Harming Whom? A Public Relations Ethical Case Study of PETA's Holocaust on Your Plate Campaign." Public Relations Division. International Communication Association annual conference, San Francisco (May). https://works.bepress.com/carrie_freeman/21.

Freeman, Carrie P. 2010a. "Meat's Place on the Campaign Menu: How U.S. Environmental Discourse Negotiates Vegetarianism." *Environmental Communication* 4(3): 255–276.

Freeman, Carrie P. 2010b. "Embracing Humanimality: Deconstructing the Human/Animal Dichotomy." In *Arguments about Animal Ethics*, edited by Greg Goodale and Jason Edward Black, 11–30. Lanham, Md.: Lexington Books.

Freeman, Carrie P. 2014. *Framing Farming: Communication Strategies for Animal Rights*. Amsterdam: Rodopi Press.

Freeman, Carrie P. 2015. "Earthlings Seeking Justice: Integrity, Consistency, and Collaboration." In *Animals and the Environment: Advocacy, Activism, and the Quest for Common Ground*, edited by Lisa Kemmerer, 50–58. New York: Earthscan.

Freeman, Carrie P., Marc Bekoff, and Sarah M. Bexell. 2011. "Giving Voice to the 'Voiceless': Incorporating Nonhuman Animal Perspectives as Journalistic Sources." *Journalism Studies* 12(5): 590–607.

Friend, Tim. 2004. *Animal Talk: Breaking the Codes of Animal Language*. New York: Free Press.

Fouts, Roger. 1997. *Next of Kin: My Conversations with Chimpanzees*. New York: Avon Books.

Gaard, Greta. 2014. "Toward New Ecomasculinities, Ecogenders, and Ecosexualities." In *Ecofeminism: Feminist Intersections with Other Animals and the Earth*, edited by Carol Adams and Lori Gruen, 225–239. New York: Bloomsbury.

Gaarder, Emily. 2011. *Women and the Animal Rights Movement*. New Brunswick, N.J.: Rutgers University Press.

Gallo, Travis, and Liba Pejchar. 2016. "Improving Habitat for Game Animals Has Mixed Consequences for Biodiversity Conservation." *Biological Conservation* 197(May): 47–52.

George, Kelly, Kristina Slagle, Robyn Wilson, Steven Moeller, and Jeremy Bruskotter. 2016. "Changes in Attitudes toward Animals in the United States from 1978 to 2014." *Biological Conservation* 201: 237–242.

Giddens, Anthony. 1991. *Modernity and Self-Identity: Self and Society in the Late Modern Age*. Stanford, Calif.: Stanford University Press.

Giddens, Justine L., Julie A. Schermer, and Philip A. Vernon. 2009. "Material Values Are Largely in the Family: A Twin Study of Genetic and Environmental Contributions to Materialism." *Personality and Individual Differences* 46: 428–431.

Glasser, Carol. 2015. "Beyond Intersectionality to Total Liberation." In *Animals and the Environment: Advocacy, Activism, and the Quest for Common Ground*, edited by Lisa Kemmerer, 41–49. New York: Earthscan.

Glazebrook, Trish, and Emmanuela Opoku. 2018. "Defending the Defenders: Environmental Protectors, Climate Change and Human Rights." *Ethics and the Environment* 23(2): 83–109.

Global Witness. 2017. "Defenders of the Earth: Global Killing of Land and Environmental Defenders in 2016." Accessed July 21, 2018, at www.globalwitness.org/en/campaigns/environmental-activists/defenders-earth.

Goldenberg, Jamie, Tom Pyszczynski, Jeff Greenberg, Sheldon Solomon, Benjamin Kluck, and Robin Cornwell. 2001. "I Am Not an Animal: Mortality Salience, Disgust and the Denial of Human Creatureliness." *Journal of Experimental Psychology: General* 130(3): 427–435.

Gruen, Lori. 2014. "Dignity, Captivity, and an Ethics of Sight." In *The Ethics of Captivity*, ed. Lori Gruen, 231–247. Oxford: Oxford University Press.

Hale, Stephen. 2010. "The New Politics of Climate Change: Why We Are Failing and How We Will Succeed." *Environmental Politics* 19(2): 255–275.

Hall, Lee. 2010. *On Their Own Terms: Bringing Animal Rights Philosophy down to Earth*. Darien, Conn.: Nectar Bat Press.

Hall, Stuart. 1997. *Representation: Cultural Representations and Signifying Practices*. Thousand Oaks, Calif.: Sage.

Harari, Yuval N. 2015. *Sapiens: A Brief History of Humankind*. New York: Harper.

Haraway, Donna J. 2008. *When Species Meet*. Minneapolis: University of Minnesota Press.

Harper, A. Breeze. 2010. *Sistah Vegan: Black Female Vegans Speak on Food, Identity, Health, and Society*. New York: Lantern Books.

Haslam, Nick. 2006. "Dehumanization: An Integrative Review." *Personality and Social Psychology Review* 10: 252–264.

Herman, Edward S., and Noam Chomsky. 1988. *Manufacturing Consent: The Political Economy of the Mass Media*. New York: Pantheon Books.

Hitlin, Steven, and Jane A. Piliavin. 2004. "Values: Reviving a Dormant Concept." *Annual Review of Sociology* 30: 359–393.

Huggan, Graham, and Helen Tiffin. 2007. "Green Postcolonialism." *Interventions* 9(1): 1–11.

Huggan, Graham, and Helen Tiffin. 2010. *Postcolonial Ecocriticism: Literature, Animals, Environment*. New York: Routledge.

Hunt, Alex, and Bonnie Roos. 2010. *Postcolonial Green : Environmental Politics and World Narratives*. Charlottesville: University of Virginia Press.

Imhoff, Daniel. 2010. *The CAFO Reader: The Tragedy of Industrial Animal Factories*. Foundation for Deep Ecology.

Ingold, Tim. 1988. "Introduction." In *What Is an Animal?*, edited by Tim Ingold, 1–16. London: Unwin Hyman.

Jamieson, Dale. 2002. *Morality's Progress: Essays on Humans, Other Animals, and the Rest of Nature*. New York: Oxford University Press.

Jamieson, Dale. 2007. "The Moral and Political Challenges of Climate Change." In *Creating a Climate for Change: Communicating Climate Change and Facilitating Social Change*, edited by Lisa Dilling and Susan Moser, 475–482. New York: Cambridge University Press.

Jenkins, Richard. 2004. *Social Identity*. 2nd ed. London: Routledge.

Jensen, Derrick. 2016. *The Myth of Human Supremacy*. New York: Seven Stories Press.

Joy, Melanie. 2010. *Why We Love Dogs, Eat Pigs, and Wear Cows: An Introduction to Carnism*. San Francisco: Conari Press.

Joy, Melanie. 2014. "Carnism: Why Eating Animals is a Social Justice Issue." In *Circles of Compassion: Essays Connecting Issues of Justice*, edited by Will Tuttle, 80–89. Danvers, Mass.: Vegan.

Kasser, Tim, Richard Ryan, Charles Couchman, and Kennon Sheldon. 2004. "Materialistic Values: Their Causes and Consequences." In *Psychology and Consumer Culture: The Struggle for a Good Life in a Materialistic World*, edited by Tim Kasser and Allen D. Kanner, 11–28. Washington, D.C.: American Psychological Association.

Katz, Jackson. 2019. *The Macho Paradox: Why Some Men Hurt Women and How All Men Can Help*. Naperville, Ill.: Sourcebooks.

Kellert, Stephen. 1983. "Affective, Cognitive, and Evaluative Perceptions of Animals." In *Behavior and the Natural Environment*, edited by Irwin Alman and Joachim Wohlwill, 241–267. New York: Plenum Press.

Kellert, Stephen. 1989. "Perceptions of Animals in America." In *Perceptions of Animals in American Culture*, ed. R. Hoage, 5–24. Smithsonian Institution Press.

Kellert, Stephen. 1995. "Attitudes toward Animals: Age-Related Development among Children." *Journal of Environmental Education* 16(3): 29–39.

Kelly, Petra. 1994. *Thinking Green: Essays on Environmentalism, Feminism, and Nonviolence.* Berkeley, Calif.: Parallax Press.

Kemmerer, Lisa. 2015a. *Animals and the Environment: Advocacy, Activism, and the Quest for Common Ground.* New York: Earthscan.

Kemmerer, Lisa. 2015b. *Eating Earth: Environmental Ethics and Dietary Choice.* Oxford: Oxford University Press.

Kemmerer, Lisa. 2019. "The Interconnected Nature of Anymal and Earth Activism." *American Behavioral Scientist* 63(8): 1061–1079.

Kheel, Marti. 2008. *Nature Ethics: An Ecofeminist Perspective.* Lanham, Md.: Rowman & Littlefield.

Kidder, Rushworth M. 1994. *Shared Values for a Troubled World: Conversations with Men and Women of Conscience.* San Francisco: Jossey-Bass.

Kim, Claire Jean. 2015. *Dangerous Crossings: Race, Species, and Nature in a Multicultural Age.* New York: Columbia University Press.

Klein, Naomi. 2014. *This Changes Everything: Capitalism vs. the Climate.* New York: Simon & Schuster.

Knox, John H. 2018. "The Past, Present, and Future of Human Rights and the Environment." *Wake Forest Law Review* 53(4): 649–665.

Ko, Aph. 2015. "What Does Animal Oppression Have to Do with Our Anti-Racist Movements?" (December 22). Accessed on November 5, 2016, at https://aphro-ism.com.

Ko, Aph. 2016. "Why Animal Liberation Requires an Epistemological Revolution." (February 24). Accessed on November 5, 2016, at https://aphro-ism.com.

Ko, Aph, and Syl Ko. 2017. *Aphro-ism: Essays on Pop Culture, Feminism, and Black Veganism from Two Sisters.* New York: Lantern Press.

Kolbert, Elizabeth. 2014. *The Sixth Extinction: An Unnatural History.* New York: Henry Holt.

Kopnina, Helen, and Brett Cherniak. 2015. "Cultivating a Value for Non-Human Interests through the Convergence of Animal Welfare, Animal Rights, and Deep Ecology in Environmental Education." *Education Sciences* (5): 363–379.

Kramarae, Cheris, and Paula A. Treichler. 1985. *A Feminist Dictionary.* Boston: Pandora Press.

Kropotkin, Peter. 2004. "Nature Teaches Mutual Aid." In *Animal Rights: A Historical Anthology* (1939), edited by Andrew Linzey and Paul Barry Clarke, 88–90. New York: Columbia University Press.

Kymlicka, Will. 2013. "Animal Rights, Multiculturalism, and the Left." Lecture at the 2012–2013 Mellon Sawyer Seminar Series "Democratic Citizenship and the Recognition of Cultural Differences," Graduate Center, CUNY (April 25). www.youtube.com/watch?v=GsIf6xJoVuw.

Kymlicka, Will. 2018. "Human Rights without Human Supremacism." *Canadian Journal of Philosophy* 48(6): 763–792.

Laestadius, Linnea, Roni Neff, Colleen Barry, and Shannon Frattaroli. 2013. "Meat Consumption and Climate Change: The Role of Non-Governmental Organizations." *Climatic Change* 120(1–2): 25–38.

Laestadius, Linnea, Roni Neff, Colleen Barry, and Shannon Frattaroli. 2016. "No Meat, Less Meat, or Better Meat: Understanding NGO Messaging Choices Intended to Alter Meat Consumption in Light of Climate Change." *Environmental Communication* 10(1): 84–103.

Lakoff, George. 2004. *Don't Think of an Elephant! Know Your Values and Frame the Debate.* White River Junction, Vt.: Chelsea Green.

Lappé, Frances Moore. 2011. *EcoMind: Changing the Way We Think, to Create the World We Want.* New York: Nation Books.

Lappé, Frances Moore, and Adam Eichen. 2017. *Daring Democracy: Igniting Power, Meaning, and Connection for the America We Want.* Boston: Beacon Press.

Lawrence, Elizabeth A. 1995. "Cultural Perceptions of Differences between People and Animals: A Key to Understanding Human-Animal Relationships." *Journal of American Culture* 18(3): 75–82.

Laws, Rita. 2014. "Mother Corn, Father Pumpkin, Sister Bean." In *Circles of Compassion*, edited by Will Tuttle, 96–107. Danvers, Mass.: Vegan.

Leopold, Aldo. 2003. "The Land Ethic." In *The Environmental Ethics and Policy Book: Philosophy, Ecology, Economics* (3rd ed.), edited by Donald VandeVeer and Christine Pierce, 215–223. Belmont, Calif.: Wadsworth.

Linzey, Andrew, and Paul B. Clarke. 2004. *Animal Rights: A Historical Anthology.* New York: Columbia University Press.

Lippit, John. 2005. "Is a Sense of Humor a Virtue?" *The Monist* 88(1): 72–92.

Lis, Kamila. 2012. "Coalitions in the Jungle: Advancing Animal Welfare through Challenges to Concentration in the Meat Industry." *Animal Law* 19: 63–89.

Luke, Brian. 2007. *Brutal: Manhood and the Exploitation of Animals.* Urbana: University of Illinois Press.

MacFarland, Sam. 2010. "Authoritarianism, Social Dominance, and Other Roots of Generalized Prejudice." *Political Psychology* 31(3): 454–477.

Macy, Joanna. 1991. *World as Lover, World as Self.* Berkeley, Calif.: Parallax Press.

Maffi, Luisa, and Ellen Woodley. 2010. *Biocultural Diversity Conservation: A Global Sourcebook.* London: Earthscan.

Maio, Gregory, James M. Olson, Lindsay Allen, and Mark Bernard. 2001. "Addressing Discrepancies between Values and Behavior: The Motivating Effect of Reasons." *Journal of Experimental Social Psychology* 37(2): 104–117.

Maio, Gregory, James M. Olson, Mark Bernard, and Michelle Luke. 2003. "Ideologies, Values, Attitudes, and Behavior." In *Handbook of Social Psychology*, edited by John DeLamater, 283–308. New York: Plenum.

Manfredo, Michael J., Tara L. Teel, and Kimberly L. Henry. 2009. "Linking Society and Environment: A Multilevel Model of Shifting Wildlife Value Orientations in the Western United States." *Social Science Quarterly* 90(2): 407–427.

Marino, Lori, and Michael Mountain. 2015. "Denial of Death and the Relationship between Humans and Other Animals." *Anthrozoos* 28(1): 5–21.

Martinelli, Dario. 2008. "Anthropocentrism as a Social Phenomenon: Semiotic and Ethical Implications." *Social Semiotics* 18(1): 79–99.

Mason, James. 1997. *An Unnatural Order: Why We Are Destroying the Planet and Each Other.* New York: Continuum.

Masson, Jeffrey M., and Susan McCarthy. 1995. *When Elephants Weep: The Emotional Lives of Animals.* New York: Dell.

McAdam, Doug, John D. McCarthy, and Mayer Zald. 1996. *Comparative Perspectives on Social Movements: Political Opportunities, Mobilizing Structures, and Cultural Framings.* Cambridge, Mass.: Cambridge University Press.

McJetters, Christopher-Sebastian. 2014. "Slavery. It's Still a Thing." In *Circles of Compassion: Essays Connecting Issues of Justice*, edited by Will Tuttle, 127–132. Danvers, Mass.: Vegan.

Merskin, Debra. 2018. *Seeing Species: Re-Presentations of Animals in Media and Popular Culture.* New York: Peter Lang.

Midgley, Mary. 1988. "Beasts, Brutes and Monsters." In *What Is an Animal?*, edited by Tim Ingold. London: Unwin Hyman.

Midgley, Mary. 2004 "The Lure of the Simple Distinction." In *Animal Rights: A Historical Anthol-*

ogy, edited by Andrew Linzey and Paul Barry Clarke, 48–50. New York: Columbia University Press.

Moore, Kathleen Dean, and Michael P. Nelson. 2010. *Moral Ground: Ethical Action for a Planet in Peril*. San Antonio: Trinity University Press.

Neumann, Jean-Marc. 2012. "The Universal Declaration of Animal Rights or the Creation of a New Equilibrium between Species." *Animal Law* 19(91): 91–109.

Nibert, David A. 2013. *Animal Oppression and Human Violence: Domesecration, Capitalism, and Global Conflict*. New York: Columbia University Press.

Nibert, David A. 2014. "Animal Rights Equal Human Rights: Domesecration and Entangled Oppression." In *Circles of Compassion: Essays Connecting Issues of Justice*, edited by Will Tuttle, 149–158. Danvers, Mass.: Vegan.

Nocella, Anthony J. 2012. "Animal Advocates for Prison and Slave Abolition." *Journal of Critical Animal Studies* 10(2): 119–126.

Nocella, Anthony J. 2014. "Building an Animal Advocacy Movement for Racial and Disability Justice." In *Circles of Compassion: Essays Connecting Issues of Justice*, edited by Will Tuttle, 159–170. Danvers, Mass.: Vegan.

Nussbaum, Martha. 2006. *Frontiers of Justice: Disability, Nationality, Species Membership*. Cambridge: Belknap Press.

Ornelas, [L]auren. 2014. "A Hunger for Justice." In *Circles of Compassion: Essays Connecting Issues of Justice*, edited by Will Tuttle, 182–197. Danvers, Mass.: Vegan.

Pachirat, Timothy. 2011. *Every Twelve Seconds: Industrialized Slaughter and the Politics of Sight*. New Haven, Conn.: Yale University Press.

Page, George. 1999. *Inside the Animal Mind: A Groundbreaking Exploration of Animal Intelligence*. New York: Doubleday.

Pearson, Susan J. 2011. *The Rights of the Defenseless: Protecting Animals and Children in Gilded Age America*. Chicago: University of Chicago Press.

Pellow, David Naguib. 2014. *Total Liberation: The Power and Promise of Animal Rights and the Radical Earth Movement*. Minneapolis: University of Minnesota Press.

Pendergrast, Nick. 2014. "A Sociological Examination of the Contemporary Animal Advocacy Movement: Organisations, Rationality and Veganism." PhD diss., Curtin University, Perth, Australia.

People of Color Environmental Leadership Summit. 1991. Principles of Environmental Justice (October). www.ejrc.cau.edu/princej.html.

Pew Environmental Group. 2007. "Protecting Life in the Sea." Philadelphia: Pew Charitable Trust. www.pewtrusts.org/uploadedFiles/wwwpewtrustsorg/TaxonomyCopy/Enviroment/oceans_final_web.pdf.

Plante, Courtney, Stephen Reysen, Sharon Roberts, and Kathleen Gerbasi. 2018. "'Animals Like Us': Identifying with Nonhuman Animals and Support for Nonhuman Animal Rights." *Anthrozoos* 31(2): 165–177.

Plec, Emily. 2015. "(Black) 'Man v. Cheetah': Perpetuations and Transformations of the Rhetoric of Racism." In *Critical Animal and Media Studies: Communication for Nonhuman Animal Advocacy*, edited by Núria Almiron, Matthew Cole, and Carrie P. Freeman, 138–153. New York: Routledge.

Pollan, Michael. 2006. *The Omnivore's Dilemma: A Natural History of Four Meals*. New York: Penguin Press.

Poore, Joseph, and Tomas Nemecek. 2018. "Reducing Food's Environmental Impacts through Producers and Consumers." *Science* 360: 987–992.

Ramp, Daniel, and Marc Bekoff. 2015. "Compassion as a Practical and Evolved Ethic for Conservation." *BioScience* 65(3): 323. doi:10.1093/biosci/biu223.

Regan, Tom. 1983. *The Case for Animal Rights*. Berkeley: University of California Press.

Regan, Tom. 2002. "How to Worry about Endangered Species." In *Environmental Ethics: What*

Really Matters, What Really Works, edited by David Schmidtz and Elizabeth Willott, 105–108. New York: Oxford University Press.

Ridley, Matt. 1996. *The Origins of Virtue*. London: Viking.

Rokeach, Milton. 1973. *The Nature of Human Values*. New York: Free Press.

Rolston, Holmes. 1993. "Challenges in Environmental Ethics." In *Environmental Philosophy: From Animal Rights to Radical Ecology*, edited by Michael E. Zimmerman, 135–157. Englewood Cliffs, N.J.: Prentice-Hall.

Ruch, Willibald, and Sonja Heintz. 2016. "The Virtue Gap in Humor: Exploring Benevolent and Corrective Humor." *Translational Issues in Psychological Science* 2(1): 35–45.

Sagoff, Mark. 1993. "Animal Liberation and Environmental Ethics: Bad Marriage, Quick Divorce." In *Environmental Philosophy: From Animal Rights to Radical Ecology*, edited by Michael E. Zimmerman, 84–94. Englewood Cliffs, N.J.: Prentice-Hall.

Sandler, Ronald L. 2007. *Character and Environment: A Virtue-Oriented Approach to Environmental Ethics*. New York: Columbia University Press.

Sandler, Ronald L. 2012. *The Ethics of Species: An Introduction*. New York: Cambridge University Press.

Sandler, Ronald L., and Phaedra C. Pezzullo. 2007. *Environmental Justice and Environmentalism: The Social Justice Challenge to the Environmental Movement*. Cambridge, Mass.: MIT Press.

Saul, Graham. 2018. "Environmentalists: What Are We Fighting For?" Metcalf Foundation's Innovation Fellowship Paper. https://metcalffoundation.com.

Schultz, P. Wesley. 2001. "The Structure of Environmental Concern: Concern for Self, Other People, and the Biosphere." *Journal of Environmental Psychology* 21: 327–339.

Schwartz, Shalom H. 1994. "Are There Universal Aspects in the Structure and Contents of Human Values?" *Journal of Social Issues* 50(4): 19–45.

Schwartz, Shalom H. 2010. "Basic Values: How They Motivate and Inhibit Prosocial Behavior." In *Prosocial Motives, Emotions, and Behavior: The Better Angels of Our Nature*, edited by Mario Mikulincer and Phillip Shaver, 221–241. American Psychological Association Press.

Schwartz, Shalom H., and Anat Bardi. 2001. "Value Hierarchies across Cultures: Taking a Similarities Perspective." *Journal of Cross-Cultural Psychology* 32(3): 268–290.

Schwartz, Shalom H., J. Cieciuch, M. Vecchione, E. Davidov, R. Fischer, C. Beierlein, A. Ramos, M. Verkasalo, J. Lönnqvist, K. Demirutku, O. Dirilen-Gumus, and M. Konty. 2012. "Refining the Theory of Basic Individual Values." *Journal of Personality and Social Psychology* 103(4): 663–688.

Shanahan, James, and Katherine McComas. 1999. *Nature Stories: Depictions of the Environment and Their Effects*. Cresskill, N.J.: Hampton Press.

Signal, Tania, and Nicola Taylor. 2007. "Attitude to Animals and Empathy: Comparing Animal Protection and General Community Samples." *Anthrozoos* 20(2): 125–130.

Simon, David R. 2013. *Meatonomics*. San Francisco: Conari Press.

Sinclair, Upton. 2005. *The Jungle* (1906). New York: St. Martin's Press.

Singer, Peter. 1990. *Animal Liberation* (2nd ed.). New York: Random House.

Singer, Peter, and Jim Mason. 2006. *The Ethics of What We Eat: Why Our Food Choices Matter*. New York: Rodale.

Smith, Andrea. 2010. "Indigeneity, Settler Colonialism, White Supremacy." *Global Dialog* 12: 1–13.

Souder, William. 2013. "How Two Women Ended the Deadly Feather Trade." *Smithsonian Magazine* (March). www.smithsonianmag.com/science-nature/how-two-women-ended-the-deadly-feather-trade-23187277.

Spiegel, Marjorie. 1996. *The Dreaded Comparison: Human and Animal Slavery*. New York: Mirror Books.

Springer, Jenny, and Jessica Campese. 2011. "Conservation and Human Rights: Key Issues and Contexts." *Conservation Initiative on Human Rights*. www.thecihr.org/publications.

Stanescu, Vasile. 2012. "'Man's' Best Friend: Why Human Rights Needs Animal Rights." *Journal for Critical Animal Studies* 10(2): 69–100.

Steffen, Will, Paul Crutzen, and John R. McNeill. 2007. "The Anthropocene: Are Humans Now Overwhelming the Great Forces of Nature?" *Ambio* 36(8): 614–621.

Steg, Linda, and Judith I. M. De Groot, 2012. "Environmental Values." In *The Oxford Handbook of Environmental and Conservation Psychology*, edited by Susan D. Clayton, 81–92. New York: Oxford University Press.

Steiner, Gary. 2008. *Animals and the Moral Community: Mental Life, Moral Status, and Kinship.* New York: Columbia University Press.

Stewart, Tracie, Ioana Latu, Nyla Branscombe, Nia Phillips, and Ted Denney. 2012. "White Privilege Awareness and Efficacy to Reduce Racial Inequality Improve White Americans' Attitudes toward African Americans." *Journal of Social Issues* 68(1): 11–27.

Su, Bingtao, and Pim Martens. 2018. "How Ethical Ideologies Relate to Public Attitudes toward Animals: The Dutch Case." *Anthrozoos* 31(2): 179–194.

Taylor, Paul. 1993. "The Ethics of Respect for Nature." In *Environmental Philosophy: From Animal Rights to Radical Ecology*, edited by Michael E. Zimmerman, 67–81. Englewood Cliffs, N.J.: Prentice-Hall.

Todd, Nathan, Elizabeth McConnell, and Rachael Suffrin. 2014. "The Role of Attitudes toward White Privilege and Religious Beliefs in Predicting Social Justice Interest and Commitment." *American Journal of Community Psychology* 53: 109–121.

Tuttle, Will. 2014. *Circles of Compassion: Essays Connecting Issues of Justice.* Danvers, Mass.: Vegan.

Ucko, Peter J. 1988. "Foreword." In *What Is an Animal?*, edited by Tim Ingold, ix–xvi. London: Unwin Hyman.

Uncaged. 2001. Universal Declaration of Animal Rights (December). www.uncaged.co.uk/declarat.htm.

United Nations General Assembly. 1948. Universal Declaration of Human Rights (December). www.un.org/en/documents/udhr/index.shtml.

United Nations General Assembly. 1982. World Charter for Nature. www.earthcharterin action.org/content/pages/Read-the-Charter.html.

Van Dijk, Teun. 2009. "Critical Discourse Studies: A Sociocognitive Approach." In *Methods of Critical Discourse Analysis*, edited by Ruth Wodack and Michael Meyer, 62–86. Washington, D.C.: Sage.

Van Dyke, Nella, and Holly J. McCammon. 2010. *Strategic Alliances: Coalition Building and Social Movements, Protest, and Contention.* Minneapolis: University of Minnesota Press.

Varner, Gary E. 1998. *In Nature's Interests? Interests, Animal Rights, and Environmental Ethics.* New York: Oxford University Press.

Verplanken, Bas, and Rob W. Holland. 2002. "Motivated Decision Making: Effects of Activation and Self-Centrality of Values on Choices and Behavior." *Journal of Personality and Social Psychology* 82(3): 434–447.

Wadiwel, Dinesh Joseph. 2009. "The War against Animals: Domination, Law and Sovereignty." *Griffith Law Review* 18(2): 283–297.

Wadiwel, Dinesh Joseph. 2015. *The War against Animals.* Amsterdam: Rodopi Press.

Walters, Kerry S., and Lisa Portmess. 1999. *Ethical Vegetarianism: From Pythagoras to Peter Singer.* New York: SUNY Press.

Waring, Marilyn. 1999. *Counting for Nothing: What Men Value and What Women Are Worth.* Toronto: University of Toronto Press.

Weil, Zoe. 2004. *The Power and the Promise of Humane Education.* New Society.

Weil, Zoe. 2014. "The MOGO Principle for a Peaceful, Sustainable, and Humane World." In *Circles of Compassion: Essays Connecting Issues of Justice*, edited by Will Tuttle, 291–304. Danvers, Mass.: Vegan.

Wilson, Edward O. 2016. *Half-Earth: Our Planet's Fight for Life*. New York: Live Right.

Wise, Steven M. 2000. *Rattling the Cage: Toward Legal Rights for Animals*. Cambridge, Mass.: Perseus.

Wise, Steven M. 2005. *Though the Heavens May Fall: The Landmark Trial That Led to the End of Human Slavery*. Cambridge, Mass.: Da Capo Press.

Wolfe, Cary. 2003. *Animal Rites: American Culture, the Discourse of Species, and Posthumanist Theory*. Chicago: University of Chicago Press.

Wrenn, Corey L. 2014. "Abolition Then and Now: Tactical Comparisons between the Human Rights Movement and the Modern Nonhuman Animal Rights Movement in the United States." *Journal of Agricultural and Environmental Ethics* 27(2): 177–200.

Wrenn, Corey L. 2015. "The Role of Professionalization Regarding Female Exploitation in the Nonhuman Animal Rights Movement." *Journal of Gender Studies* 24(2): 131–146.

Zelko, Frank. 2013. *Make It a Green Peace! The Rise of Countercultural Environmentalism*. New York: Oxford University Press.

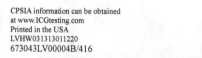